Hangups From Way Back

Historical Myths and Canons

Hangups From Way Back

Historical Myths and Canons
Volume II

Frederick Gentles

Melvin Steinfield

San Diego Mesa College

 Canfield Press

San Francisco

A Department of Harper & Row, Publishers, Inc.

New York • Evanston • London

PROMETHEUS

An end to words. Deeds now.
The world is shaken.
The deep and secret way of thunder
is rent apart.
Fiery wreaths of lightning flash.
Whirlwinds toss the swirling dust.
The blasts of all the winds are battling in the air,
and sky and sea are one.
On me the tempest falls.
It does not make me tremble.
O holy Mother Earth, O air and sun,
behold me. I am wronged.

—AESCHYLUS

HANGUPS FROM WAY BACK: Historical Myths and Canons, Vol. II.
  Copyright © 1970 by Frederick Gentles and Melvin Steinfield

LIBRARY OF CONGRESS CATALOG CARD NUMBER: 78-119012

Design by Michael Rogondino
Illustrations by Robert Bausch
Copyediting by Gracia A. Alkema

Contents

v

Contents

Contents

Contents

Preface

The blame for student criticism of the lack of relevance in their education—for their feeling that what they are studying somehow does not relate to the world they live in—must be shared by teachers and the books they use. Although teachers of world and Western civilization defend their courses—justifiably—as being necessary to an understanding of today's world, it is clear many have failed to communicate history's relevance. Obviously, more effective teaching tools are needed.

This book attempts to demonstrate this relevance. And what is more relevant today than the way man handles myth, an idea that seems eternal but is actually only transient? "A myth," as Ashley Montagu observes, "is something which is in fact not true, but in which we believe and act upon as if it were true." Myths later become canons—that is, rules, regulations, and laws, the correct and accepted ways of doing things. We build our cultures on myths; indeed, myths are necessary for the stability of a culture. All of us live by myths and canons, taking them for reality. And for certain myths that man has held dear, he has become involved, frustrated, paranoid, and even vicious.

Here we are concerned with some ideas that have caused endless controversy and bloodshed throughout history. The intoxicating, man-made idea is the myth, the canon, the hangup. By seeing how myths have determined man's behavior in the past and how some of them are still with us, perhaps we can better resist their influence. It is, of course, not enough to simply *say* that history is relevant; it must be shown. The selections in each chapter, therefore, focus on those basic patterns of intellectual, social, political, military, and economic history—the myths—that especially pertain to today's problems.

It is impossible to acknowledge every individual who assisted in the development of this book, but a few names do stand out for the magnitude of their contribution. Among the reviewers, Melvin Lesser of Los Angeles City College read the manuscript twice and offered many valuable suggestions. The entire Canfield Press staff—especially Joseph Dana, Brian Williams, Gracia Alkema, and Wendy Cunkle—offered expert assistance in many ways. Thanks are also due our wives, Marian and Dorothy, for their patience. Of course, the authors assume responsibility for all interpretations in their essays and any errors that might appear in the book.

Frederick Gentles
Melvin Steinfield

Hangups
From
Way
Back

Historical Myths and Canons

1

The Violent World of Juveniles

Just after one of our recent wars, the psychologist Harry A. Overstreet published "The Mature Mind" in which he proposed that very few of the world's leaders have had mature minds. By a mature mind he meant a person who is dedicated to the great insight of Jesus Christ: "A new commandment I have unto you that ye love one another." As examples of men possessing maturity of mind in the ancient world, he suggested Christ and Socrates. Overstreet quoted G. B. Chisholm as saying that the only real threat to man is man himself. " . . . The difficulty man has with himself is that he cannot use his highly developed intellect effectively because of his neurotic fears, his prejudices, his fanaticism, his unreasoning hates, and equally unreasoning devotions; in fact, his failure to reach emotional maturity, or mental health."[1] Would you say that both past and current history show the immaturity of many of the world's famous men?

A Century for Juveniles

Frederick Gentles

History, as Eric Hoffer states, is made by juveniles. The fact is a testament to the immaturity of the human mind. Man's hangups, the intoxicating ideas he has—his fears, prejudices, fanaticism, hates, and devotions—have caused him to act in juvenile ways toward his fellow man. Neither physical maturity nor chronological age are immunization against childishness; adults who have deplored juvenile delinquency through the ages have often overlooked their own immaturity and delinquent behavior.

The history of seventeenth century Europe was no different. It was a time marked by expanded exploration and competition for foreign markets and by the colliding interests of vigorous peoples intent on fulfilling themselves in the bodily comforts of food, booze, sex, and excitement. As in previous centuries, human beings continued to exhibit their immaturity in relation to other human beings. In "civilized" London, wife-beating was declared illegal after 9 P.M. because too many neighbors complained about the noise, and the Murgatroyds were taken to court for knocking down and kicking another family when its members entered church ahead of them. There were complaints about student morals and riotous conduct; one college in southern England was considered to be a hotbed of dissent. Everyday language was spiced with "the most filthye termes."

Nor was sunny Italy exempt from delinquent actions on the part of her people. Religious orders competed to exalt their separate patrons on festival days, and there was dueling and thieving by the classes, both high and low. Although Spain and Russia were Christian lands, the love that Christ taught had not permeated very far into the medieval structure of these countries. Monarchs compelled obedience of provinces struggling to remain free of the centralized tyranny, and both central and local authorities had great tolerance of the grinding poverty and abysmal ignorance of the masses. The Holy Roman Empire was rocked by religious strife between Protestants and Catholics, and Frenchmen spent the greater part of the century spilling the blood of fellow Frenchmen as well as alien enemies. Europeans were even beginning to export their brand of immaturity and hate and violence to America. Violence in Europe. Violence in America.

Christ—as a man possessing maturity of mind—is not associated with hate and violence. He did not fear, though he knew of man's ways with fellow man. He saw man not as bad, just immature: "Father, forgive them, for they know not what they do." Overstreet states, "It is this insight—that the evil men do is the evil of their immaturity—that may yet save the world." There is hope. Hope that man can recognize his juvenility and learn to act with wisdom and love toward his fellow man. Hope that man can overcome his paranoia and his hangups.

Both hope and despair for mankind can be seen in some of the great delinquents of the seventeenth century. In particular, three famous Christians—Protestant Oliver Cromwell, Roman Catholic Cardinal Richelieu, and Russian Orthodox Peter the Great (whose reign lapped over into the eighteenth century)—personify much of the temper of this tumultuous time. All of them failed to one degree or another in exemplifying Christ's maxim of love, and yet all believed fervently in the "justness" of the causes they propounded. All acted maturely at times; all acted like juveniles at other times. Was the history of the seventeenth century influenced to a greater degree by their maturity or by their immaturity?

Oliver Cromwell

The British got hung up on several different ideas during the seventeenth century; indeed, many became fanatically devoted to such things as their own particular "brand" of Christianity, the necessity for revenge, and the traditional ignominious way of killing a man condemned to death. The hates and devotions of Britishers during this time—like so many other nationalities in so many different centuries —resulted in the Civil Wars, which saw families divided on religious and political issues with father fighting son, brother fighting brother, and even mother taking one side or another. The immaturity that seems to possess man when he himself embraces fanaticism was evident in one hundred Irish women being put to the sword, run through, or slaughtered (however one puts such things in so many words) by Cromwell's troops at Naseby in 1645. And four thousand defenders of the "faith" (they were all Christians) were killed at Marston Moor a few days before Naseby.

There were other atrocities. The House of Commons agreed, in a divided vote, that Archbishop Laud of the Anglican Church—who had supported an unpopular king and a traditional church that refused to bow to Puritan demands—should be hanged, drawn, and quartered in that order because it was not traditional to do the deed in any other way. However, the sick old man who had languished in the Tower of London pleaded to have his head cut off instead, and the authorities, acting now in a more mature fashion, agreed. "The old man's head was chopped off in a dignified manner," says Winston Churchill in his *History of the English Speaking People.*

The Civil Wars also saw King Charles I get his head chopped off in 1649, and Parliament and Oliver Cromwell took charge of England's destiny for the next decade. Oliver, Puritan divines, and the victorious Ironside army embarked on a holy crusade against Catholics in Ireland and, with "God on their side," put about two thousand Irishmen to death at Drogheda. Of course, this massacre was excused because it was partly in revenge for the Irish rebellion of a few years before which saw the Irish slaughter thousands of English partisans, many of them unarmed and defenseless.

As Lord Protector, the puritanical Cromwell dictated over an England that was restricted in many of its historic freedoms. Puritans had instituted fines for profanity such as "Mercy me," and "Oh, Heavens," and "othere blasphemous termes." Blue laws established a commission which had the authority to expel ministers and schoolmasters "scandalous in their lives and conversations" such as swearers, papists, adulterers, gamblers, drunkards, users of the Anglican prayer book, scoffers at the godly, defenders of maypoles and stage plays, etc., etc. Card playing, dancing, and Sabbath-breaking were not only frowned upon, they were forbidden in this puritanical concern for morals. Holy crusades against those who did not possess the "truth" were frequent.

Cromwell is a riddle to historians of this period. He was a brilliant man, but he was also a mystic who often surrendered his intellect to religious vision and prophecy. C. V. Wedgwood says his speech was impulsive and confused and that he prevailed in arguments not by logic but by the force of his own convictions. According to one of his biographers, Maurice Ashley:

> His worst fault—he admitted it to himself—was his temper, which he lost rather easily when he was young, though later he had it under better control. His finest virtues were his humaneness and his tolerance. The man who ordered the slaughter of the garrison at Drogheda, or the dismissal of two parliaments by the sword, was infinitely tender towards those who suffered. Many of his letters that have come down to us are concerned with helping his old soldiers and assisting their widows. Again, the same man who was brutal in condemning the public celebration of Mass in Ireland, loathed any kind of religious intolerance in England, and in the end, at the height of his supremacy as Protector, permitted the holding of Communion according to the rites of the Church of England, or even of the Mass in many private houses in London.*

Cromwell had doubts about his dictatorship, and though he treated the Irish as savages—more or less as the Americans were beginning to treat the Indians as savages—he was sincere in wanting to save their souls from Papal authority. He had his own brand of truth, and he often used rather extreme means of imposing it on others. He wasn't all bad, though more than a few Irishmen would not be convinced of this. Neither was he all good, even though the scholar Maurice Ashley wrote an adulatory biography. Despite the admirable qualities to be found in his character, the immaturity of Cromwell's mind is suggested by his temper tantrums, his hatreds, his fanaticism, his unreasoning devotions, and his acceptance of killing in order to compel others to his will.

Cardinal Richelieu

Cardinal Richelieu, chief minister under Louis XIII, was quite a different person from England's Cromwell. Though a bishop and cardinal in the Roman Catholic Church, he didn't exhibit nearly as much sympathy for the welfare of the people as did his contemporary St. Vincent de Paul, who founded hospitals for incurables, looked after orphans, and helped the poor in countless ways. Vincent's concern was with mankind. Richelieu's concern was with himself, his

*From *Oliver Cromwell and the Puritan Revolution* by Maurice Ashley (London: University of London Press, 1958), p. 111. By permission of the University of London Press, Macmillan & Company and Lawrence Verry Inc.

Church, his King, and France. Though brilliant, his narrow outlook suggests he was not fully mature. St. Vincent de Paul, on the other hand, might not have been so brilliant—especially in political and military matters—but it can be suggested that, with his broader and more humanitarian views, he possessed a greater maturity of mind.

The old hangup that appeared in ancient Egypt of states' rights versus centralized government is again apparent in seventeenth century France with Richelieu taking the side of national law and order under Louis XIII against the traditional-minded feudal lords who favored local law and order. In the process of unifying France more solidly, he destroyed the power of the nobility and made it subservient to the crown. As a result, he opened the way for another seventeenth century man of some immaturity of mind, Louis XIV, to bring France to great power and glory. Richelieu made France powerful in the affairs of man by making alliances with Protestant kings during the Thirty Years' War and by sending French troops to battle fellow Catholics of Spain and of the Holy Roman Empire. Indeed, Richelieu was instrumental in turning that war from a religious struggle between Protestants and Catholics into a dynastic struggle that saw Protestant killing Protestant and Catholic killing Catholic on battlefields all over Europe.

His system of alliances was questioned by the "devout" party in France, one of whose members was the King's confessor and whom Richelieu found cause to replace with someone more trustworthy. He appointed well-born clergy with administrative ability to positions of importance, preferring them to scholars and devout ones who would not be as dependable in carrying out his policies.

The dilemma of whom to kill or not to kill was one for both Catholics and Protestants. Usually, even at this early time when modern romantic nationalism was just getting underway, the national idea won out over God's commandments of "thou shalt not kill," and "to love thy neighbor as thyself." An exception is when the Dutch Prince of Orange ordered his navy to help Richelieu regain power over Huguenot rebels on France's Atlantic Coast. The sailors rioted and refused to go; they would not kill fellow Protestants to help a Catholic Cardinal even if that same Cardinal was supplying them with money to fight Spanish Catholics. In this compassion for the Huguenots, the sailors were demonstrating maturity of mind. In being willing to fight Catholics, however, they demonstrated immaturity —that is, if we define maturity as the Christian concept of love for all mankind.

Richelieu's reply to Louis XIII and others who had doubts about his policy of making treaties of alliance with heretic Protestant princes was not to meddle in affairs of state. State and Church were separate in matters of national interest, as far as Richelieu was concerned. Morality was not the same for the individual Catholic and the Catholic state; hence, treaties could be made and broken according to the first principle of foreign policy for any nation—self-interest. Cardinal Richelieu admired Machiavelli's doctrine that the state is the supreme good and that any means may be used to enhance its interests. My country, right or wrong. But Richelieu was not the only one to act on Machiavelli's principles; history records a long list of shattered promises in the form of treaties from these earlier states down to the U.S.A. and the U.S.S.R.

Such are the games people play in the name of national interest. In many ways they are childish games and quite unreasonable. Had Richelieu been born an Italian or a Swede or a German he would have been playing on the other side as a true believer in a particular holy cause against France or Catholics or something. The games of the seventeenth century certainly did the millions of maimed, mutilated, and muted forever little good. Richelieu played the game, and people are playing it today for all they are worth. Juveniles? Delinquents?

Peter the Great

It would be incorrect to label Peter the Great solely as an aging child. Like many other aging children down through history, he was childish only at times—but at important times in the history of his people. Like Richelieu, he was a brilliant man and accomplished many things we would call deeds of a mature mind. He built a great city and called it Saint Petersburg (now Leningrad), he freed women from their servile position, he endeavored to rid the ignorant and superstitious of their hatred of foreigners, he organized an Academy of Science, and he counselled religious toleration in an age of intolerance. He established hospitals, almshouses, and sponsored Russia's first textbook on social behavior which advised people not to talk with their mouths full, not to pick their noses in public, and not to spit on the floor. He wasn't all bad.

Peter could easily have gone the way of most of his contemporaries in Russia, a country still very much in the Middle Ages. There were the Old Believers who so hated new ideas that thousands of them set fire to themselves when Church ritual was changed from Greek to Russian form. Now they had to cross themselves with three fingers instead of two. Two fingers represented the dual nature of the Person on the Cross. Three fingers represented the Trinity, of which only one Person was on the cross. At any rate, these traditionalists were willing to die for the old ways; but Peter was equally willing to have them die for the new ritual, especially when they refused to obey the rules and tried to undermine his authority. He forced the conservatives to shave their traditional beards, he took the veil from women, he changed established Russian dress to western style, and he flouted other established ceremonies and practices in pointing out hangups that had kept the Russians mired in medieval ways.

But even while Peter strove to modernize his country, he was also part of this turbulent, infantile Russian world. His lack of maturity was apparent in his wild and destructive drinking parties and in his participation in various forms of torture, such as tying people to a wheel and breaking their bones, whipping others with great savagery, and burying a woman up to her neck and hanging her friends over her head. She managed to live for five days in the cold, cold ground; her friends didn't have so long to suffer. In a milder mood he simply had the tongues of some adversaries burned out. But, again in an ugly mood, he put 799 palace police to death by hanging, beheading, or breaking them on the wheel because they conspired against his authority.

Peter was a devout Christian. People in the West were constantly impressed with his knowledge of the Scriptures, and he never failed to call upon God for help before a battle or to thank him after a victory. Although he often made fun of the conservatism and bigotry of the old Orthodox faith, he sincerely wanted to liberalize it and have it accept other forms of Christianity as possessing at least a glimmer of the truth. Of course, he hated the Turks and at one time initiated an alliance for a holy crusade to kill the Muslim infidels. But, just as readily, he was willing to turn his troops on fellow Christians when it meant defending Russia or extending her territory. Defensive wars have always had a way of turning into offensive wars for the conquest of territory, and Russia expanded at a great cost of Christian lives on various sides of national borders.

From an early age, Peter was fascinated with the mechanics of war, and as a youngster in the Kremlin he directed his playmates in the use of live ammo with real guns and cannon in this fortress overlooking the River Moscow. These play soldiers became the nucleus for officers and technicians in real war later on. He liked to play boats, and as Tsar he created Russia's navy to defend and enlarge the frontiers. As he carried these childish interests into manhood and nearly constant warfare, he apparently did not consider national warfare contrary in any way to the principles of the Christ he loved. As with Cromwell and Richelieu, God was on his side to justify the killings as well as an occasional atrocity, should one occur.

But why in our haste to point out and condemn the immaturity of historical leaders pick on poor old Cromwell, Richelieu, and Peter the Great? Why not criticize James and Charles I and II in England, Louis XIII and XIV in France, the Frederick Williams of Prussia, and Charles XII of Sweden whose reign, like Peter's, lapped over into the eighteenth century? Why not take a roll call of twentieth century juveniles including, unfortunately, the greater majority of all of us, because is not this juvenilization the fate of man? Wealth and power only make the degree of our actions, whether responsible or irresponsible, the greater. With few exceptions, possibly a Vincent de Paul among others, juvenile acts characterize us all. We cannot escape however hard we may try.

Wherefore, carry on, fools, said Erasmus in his *In Praise of Folly* a century before the seventeenth. We must carry on with our neurotic fears, our prejudices, our fanaticism, our unreasoning hates and equally unreasoning devotions to one cause or another. We must get hung up on something. *N'est-ce pas? Nicht wahr? No es verdad?*

Note

1 H. A. Overstreet, *The Mature Mind* (New York: W. W. Norton, 1949), p. 102. Quoted from G. B. Chisholm, *Survey Graphic,* October, 1947.

C. V. Wedgwood, in her vividly-written histories of the English civil wars, speaks of King Charles I as "The Grand Delinquent" because of his foolish acts as king. He was beheaded on January 30, 1649, an act which his followers considered as the most monstrous crime since the Crucifixion. His enemies, on the other hand, considered his execution a blow against tyranny that would live forevermore to the honor of the English state. Miss Wedgwood describes the rugged, immensely-alive people of this time. Were they more a mature or more a juvenile people?

The City of London and Country Pleasures

C. V. Wedgwood

In the recently opened Hyde Park, on London's western perimeter, rich citizens strolled with courtiers and visiting gentry. The occupants of smart coaches showed themselves off in the Ring; there was horse racing and foot racing, two bowling greens, a gaming house and an eating house, and dairymaids walked round with milk for the thirsty. For the humbler citizens of London, Finsbury fields were a favourite walking place although of late years much spoiled by the brick-works which supplied London's builders. Within the city itself Moorfields was set aside for citizens' wives and maids; here they could hang out their laundry or spread it on the grass; shady trees, specially planted, bore the names of those who had placed them there, and wooden shelters had been put up against sudden rain. It was pleasant by daylight but with nightfall it grew disreputable, even dangerous.

London was first and foremost a seaport. The tidal river lapped at the streets' end; high masts and furled sails closed the narrow vistas of its ancient alleys. Greater than all the other seaports of the realm together, London was the mart of the known world. The Venetian envoy, who had experience in ships and shipping, reckoned that twenty thousand craft, small and great, were to be seen from London in a day. Rowing-boats and ferry-boats carried the citizens upstream and down, or from bank to bank; heavy barges distributed goods from London up river and brought back to London the produce of the Thames valley. Merchantmen from Antwerp and Amsterdam, Calais and Bordeaux, Lisbon, Leghorn and Cadiz, Bergen, Hamburg and Archangel, Constantinople, the East and West Indies, rode at anchor in the Pool or unloaded at the wharves. Some were

Reprinted with permission of The Macmillan Company from *The King's Peace, 1637-1641* by C. V. Wedgwood. © C. V. Wedgwood, 1959. Also by permission of Joyce Weiner Associates, London.

privately owned, others belonged to trading companies—the Muscovy Company, the Levant Company, the West India Company and the Merchant Adventurers. Greatest of all towered the huge ships of the East India Company, "mobile, maritime fortresses" embattled against piracy and storm.

London was a huge port and a huge town and, at its worst, as dark and wicked as such towns are. In the porch of St. Paul's, in the arcaded shopping centre of the New Exchange, the "coney catcher" loitered to ensnare some wide-eyed country rabbit with a little money in his foolish paws. The "jeering, cunning courtesan, the rooking, roaring boy" conspired to wheedle and bully unsuspecting fools. All day the shouts of oyster and tripe women, the swearing of draymen, the creak and clatter of hackney coaches dazed and deafened the newcomer, and after sunset

> "riotous sinful plush and tell-tale spurs
> Walk Fleet Street and the Strand, when the soft stirs
> Of bawdy ruffled silks turn night to day."

London was not a safe place for the innocent, although those accustomed to it, born in "the scent of Newcastle coal and the hearing of Bow bells," knew how to avoid the dangers, and the more experienced revellers who came in for a spree, like Sir Humphrey Mildmay who got home "mad, merry and late" after "playing the fool with two punks in a barge on the Thames," were very well able to take care of themselves. But country boys and girls, driven to the capital by bad times or tempted by tales of easy money, drifted through disappointment and disaster into the criminal depths of the city, to die in the common gaol or of the "Tyburn ague" on the gallows.

As the town grew, and it was growing fast, its gaieties increased. Beer gardens and pleasure gardens spread along Bankside, puppet-theatres showed *Bel and the Dragon* and other apocryphal matter; peep-shows advertised *The Creation of the World* represented to the life in pasteboard. The two principal theatres, now both covered in and lit by wax candles, attracted the rich and fashionable. Blackfriars on Bankside carried on the Shakespeare-Burbage tradition, with Taylor, thought to be the greatest Hamlet yet seen, and Swanston's much praised Othello; the portly comedian Lowin played Falstaff and the whole Jonsonian gallery of grotesques, and the fair youth Stephen Hammerton drew tears with his Juliet and Desdemona. Christopher Beeston's company at the Cockpit in Drury Lane concentrated on more modern topical works. These two had the highest reputation though half a dozen lesser theatres, more old-fashioned, open-roofed and playing by daylight, still drew large audiences. A French company brought over the neo-classical drama from Paris but the Londoners, taking it into their heads to be scandalised at seeing women on the stage, pelted them with rotten apples. The Queen, who patronised the company, was indignant, and after a little the Londoners forgot their moral views and accepted the novelty.

The tidal Thames, creeping into the heart of the city up many an open inlet, ditch and hithe [small port], did something to purify the town. Fresh water had been brought within reach by the New River Company which had diverted the river Lea to Islington. But rosemary and jasmine were in constant demand to disguise the putrid smells of streets and houses. London children already suffered badly from rickets, and the various epidemic diseases vaguely defined as plague caused ten thousand deaths in the bad year 1636. In the following year, still bad, there were something over three thousand victims.

The respectable citizens of London drew together against the underworld of the criminal, the drunken, the defeated. Their city might be one of the wickedest in Europe; it was also, as a natural consequence, one of the most austerely pious. The virtues of plain living and hard work were extolled and practised; the Bible and the hundred churches stood firm against the ballads and the playhouses. Religion was a fighting force in the city because it could never cease from fighting, "the miles between Hell and any place on earth being shorter than those between London and St. Albans." . . .

The countryside offered many simple delights. Izaak Walton and his companions could pass a summer's day in happy argument on the relative merits of their favourite sports, catch trout and chub in the clear streams, listen to the milkmaids singing and watch with tranquil interest the striped caterpillars on the leafy trees and the painted butterflies in the meadows. John Milton in one of his rare idle hours may have seen such dancing in the chequered shade as he attributed to "the upland hamlets." Girls as pretty if not as eloquent as Perdita gave out posies at the sheepshearing. On winter evenings the young jigged and danced by firelight at Leap Candle or the Cushion Dance; all the year long they had their singing rounds and games, Sellenger's Round, John Come Kiss Me, and Barley Break. Rush-bearing ceremonies, blessing of cornfields and of springs, crowning the May Queen, roasting geese at Michaelmas and sucking pig at Lammas, varied the laborious year. Free beer flowed merrily at Whitsun-ales and harvest festivals, and boys in wigs and petticoats bounced about on hobby-horses to the uproarious delight of all. In strongly Protestant districts traditional Hallowe'en jollities were being ingeniously transferred to Gunpowder Treason Day on November 5th. But religious disapproval so far had had little effect on the celebrations which marked the end of August when London's Bartholomew Fair lasted close on a fortnight, and all over Lancashire and Somerset the wakes were held, usually in the churches, with dancing, drinking, pipe, tabor and fiddle. During the time of general holiday between Christmas and Twelfth Night a Lord of Misrule was still sometimes elected to preside over the festivities, and the old mockery of church ceremonies, permitted in medieval times, was occasionally indulged, but at greater peril. The King, when he came to hear of it, viewed with grave disapproval a swineherd's impersonation of an Anglican priest at a mock marriage. At all times of year, bridals and christenings were an excuse for merry-making and the distribution of gifts, garters, posies, ribbons and—if they could be afforded—gloves. In the lowlands of Scotland the poor people had thriftily invented the "penny bridal," an occasion when each guest paid his penny towards the day's revelling. As anyone could become a guest at such feasts, they were the occasion of noisy mirth, on which the respectable frowned and the Kirk [national church of Scotland] made determined but unsuccessful war.

In the summer months picnic parties from the towns rode out into the country with baskets full of pasties, and London apprentices carried their girls to Islington, Tottenham and Hogsden for cheese cakes and cream. The rich and fashionable favoured the Three Pigeons at Brentford for week-end parties. The sports and pleasures of the gentlefolk were hawking and hunting, and bowls as they grew older; they matched their hawks and greyhounds against each other, and their horses at the local race meetings which were becoming regular events. Sometimes, as at Kiplingcotes in Yorkshire, a piece of plate [silver] was the reward of the winner. Newmarket and Epsom Downs were already famous, and horses, like Bay Tarrell, a Newmarket winner, and Toby, whose owner, a London merchant, had gilded his hoofs, were popular favourites. With racing went the bagpipes, and the winner was escorted through the crowds to their shrill music.

Travelling pedlars and mountebanks entertained the villages with their wares and their news; they performed simple operations, drew teeth, cut corns, lanced boils and successfully straightened wry-necked children by cutting the tendons. The crowder, or fiddler, ready to play for any festivity, the rope-dancer, the juggler, and the showman with a bear, or perhaps a monster, were popular figures in the villages and country towns. In Scotland a solitary camel, the King's property, was leased out to a warden who was permitted to show him off, by tuck of drum, at all times of day except during divine service.

In their leisure time students and apprentices competed with the bow; village boys played ninepins, cudgels [stick fighting], or a rough kind of football. In some places local sports were annually held. The famous Cotswold Games, sponsored by jolly Captain Dover, took place every year on a broad-topped down that still bears his name. From miles around came men and boys to compete in running, wrestling, quarter staff and shooting, for a great distribution of prizes and favours. The enterprise enjoyed royal favour and aimed at creating a new Olympia. The King's Court had graced it once with their presence and several poets had celebrated it in rhyme.

The people had the free and spontaneous gaiety of those who live in the moment because the next may bring disaster. The happy lovers who in the summer embraced "between the acres of the rye," would in a famine-stricken winter cling together for warmth before a cold hearthstone. They enjoyed the good times, they endured the bad. Drought, frost, fire, flood were the enemies of all who lived by the land.

With the easy laughter and song went also a primitive delight in violence. Cock-fighting and bull- and bear-baiting were the sports of all classes when they could get to them, and a light-hearted squire like Sir Humphrey Mildmay in Essex would from time to time let out his bull to be baited by the village dogs. Cock-throwing, which meant pelting the poor birds with sticks or stones, was a traditional annual sport among village boys. The ducking of scolds, or leading them through the village bitted and bridled, and compelling their husbands to ride the pole were occasional village amusements. Domestic quarrels were violent in all classes of society; a London regulation forbade wife-beating after nine in the evening because of the noise. Gentlemen who were known to "fling cushions at one another's heads only in sport and for exercise" descended with ease from horseplay to fisticuffs; blows were exchanged on very small provocation and in the most unseemly places. The Murgatroyds, for instance, annoyed because another family walked into church ahead of them, knocked down and trampled on their rivals, causing a disturbance the echoes of which were several years dying away in the ecclesiastical courts.

In "The Age of the Baroque, 1610–1660," Carl J. Friedrich weighs the reasons for the diversity of man's behavior on the European continent at this time in history. He speaks of man's restless search for power over fellow men. What are the modern relationships? How is art tied to man's behavior—myths, canons, and hangups?

The Restless Search for Power

Carl J. Friedrich

These general remarks about baroque would not be complete without some explicit comment on "national" aspects of this style. It would really be more appropriate to speak of "regional" variations; for while some regional peculiarities were national, as in England, France and Spain, others like Roman as contrasted with Venetian, Hapsburg as contrasted with Saxon or Rhineland baroque, were not fully integrated into a national style. Baroque in the Austrian lands of the Hapsburgs bore a greater kinship to Spanish baroque than to North German forms. An attempt adequately to characterize the several national and regional variations would be difficult; indeed to this day historians of art are seriously at odds concerning important features of these contrasts. The situation is complicated by the fanning out of Italian, Flemish and other artists and musicians all over Europe; it often becomes very difficult to decide whether they were influencing or being assimilated. Nor was this cosmopolitan wandering entirely one-sided: Poussin spent most of his life in Rome, the German poet Opitz went to Poland, Descartes to the Netherlands, Grotius to France. Baroque was a European way of feeling and thinking, of experiencing the world and man and creating works of art and letters in the image of these *Erlebnisse*. Yet, regional variations there were, and they were strongest where the national life was most nearly integrated. Thus the baroque of Spain was the most extreme in its contrasts and tensions, so that some have felt it to be the *most* baroque. In France, greater restraint and an emphasis on classical themes obscured for a long time the essentially baroque quality of Corneille, Pascal and Descartes, if not of Poussin and Claude Lorrain. In England, the revolutionary implications of Protestantism, so long held in check by the skill and power of the Tudors, and the long-range effects which link the Puritans with modern liberalism, hid from many the

From pp. 42–47 in *The Age Of The Baroque, 1610–1660*, by Carl J. Friedrich. Copyright, 1952 by Harper & Row, Publishers, Inc. Reprinted by permission of the publishers.

sway of baroque feeling in letters and art in the England of the Stuarts and their court. The extraordinary flowering of German litera- ture in the "classic" age of Kant, Goethe, and Schiller who, inspired by Lessing, fought the baroque heritage in letters, art and life with a neohumanist enthusiasm for classical antiquity, prevented appreciation of the extraordinary achievements of that preceding age; in any case much of the finest baroque in these regions was created in the genera- tions following our period. Typically, Heinrich Schutz' memory was virtually blotted out by the towering achievements of Handel and Bach. Yet his musical creations were superb in their depth and novelty. The same may be said even more emphatically of the Slavic world; the Czechs, the Poles and the Russians responded with truly baroque violence to the artistic possibilities of this style, especially in architecture. Indeed, it may be said that baroque is *the* European art form most nearly commensurate with the depth of feeling and the extravagance of conduct expressive of the Slavic spirit. But most of the Slavic baroque belongs to the generations after 1660.

The Common Ground

Perhaps all styles are less unified than is usually assumed by those who write and talk about them. Regional and period styles on closer inspection seem often to contain mutually exclusive aspects and traits. . . .

At the height of the baroque, architects, sculptors, painters, poets and musicians strove to accomplish the impossible in *all* directions. Hence materialism vied with spiritualism, radical naturalism with extreme formalism, the most terrifying realism with the most precious illusionism. Metaphysical poetry sought to probe into ultimate mys- teries, while voluptuous and lascivious erotic poetry violated all canons of good taste. Here are some typical, concrete *"sujets"* of baroque artistic endeavor: monarchs, cardinals and princesses, devout nuns and praying saints competed with beggars, miscreants and cripples in the canvases of Velasquez, Rubens, Rembrandt and his fellow Dutchmen; highly ornamented altars decorated in gold contrast with severe church exteriors, colorful and dramatic murals with geometri- cally rigid gardens. Such an age, excited beyond measure by the po- tentialities of man, might well through some of its representatives establish the foundations of modern science, while through others it would persecute superstitious old women as witches; for both pre- sume an exaggerated belief in the power of man to think and to do as with heightened powers he confronts a mysterious, exciting world.

God by his limitless will orders the universe; Satan by a comparable effort seeks to disturb this order. The fascination which Satan seems to have had for Milton has often been remarked upon; it was born of the admiration for the kind of strength that will challenge rather than be subordinated. The statesmen of this age made a cult of power and of its adornments: the vast spectacle, the impenetrable intrigue, the gruesome murder. Power has always been *one* of man's dominant ends, and the search for it one of his great passions. But probably no age allowed this passion to become so all-engulfing, unless it be our own, in many ways so strangely akin to the baroque. Hence Thomas Hobbes, self-styled "child of fear," in his uncompromising adulation of power, coined perhaps the age's most revealing phrase: "So that in the first place, I put for a generall inclination of all mankind, a perpetuall and restlesse desire of Power, after Power, that ceaseth only in Death." To him, all passions were in the last analysis reducible to that dominant passion for power, "for Riches, Knowledge and Honour are but severall sorts of Power."[1]

The same sense of power inspired Milton as he faced the cosmic struggle of good and evil, of God and Satan. In confronting the Son of Man with Satan the Tempter, Milton created a scene which "is one of the high moments of Milton's art, an English masterpiece of the baroque, analogous to great Italian painting."[2] There was in Milton, more perhaps than in any other poet of his time, a deep sense of the dynamic spiritual potential of language; he "did not merely use language: he carved it, shaped it with the vigor of a baroque architect, and piled it up until it became a monument of words in marble." A sense of power calls in the artist for the capacity to portray, to dramatize tension; that is the quintessence of baroque.

Personal Behavior

Of all those peculiarities of personal behavior by which an age or nation is seen as it were "naked to the watchful eye," the wig is probably the most revealing symbol of the baroque. Its origin is by legend attributed to Louis XIII who, it is said, wished to hide his baldness. It was in fact a vivid expression of that desire to push things to the extreme and to cultivate the theatrical exaggeration of reality. In the first generation of the seventeenth century hair became longer, beards more flowing and dramatic. As the century progressed, beards and mustaches became smaller, eventually vanished; for they hide the face, instead of setting it off as does a wig.

Costumes were very stately and elaborate, except where strong moral convictions led to startling simplifications; the Puritans and the fellowship of Port Royal achieved a highly dramatic effect by their monklike uniformity, as did individuals like Father Joseph. Ladies' fashions were similarly elaborate and often bordered on the disguise. The passion of the age for "dressing up" in weird attire made even the exalted, such as the king of Spain, indulge in occasional "masques."

The sense of "face" was as highly developed as ever in the Orient, and men went to great lengths to avenge any infringement of their honor. Honor became the most sought-after sign of power, and the endless quarreling and dueling took such a toll of the aristocracy in countries like France that the government felt compelled to take vigorous measures to combat it. Corneille's drama was preoccupied with the portrayal of clashes of honor, and the same theme dominated the stage of Spain, England and Germany.

At the same time, gross sensuality engulfed both high and low. The excesses in eating and drinking, while probably most extreme at the courts of Germany, were a universal habit, taking the subtler forms of elaborate gourmanderie in Italy and France. Associated with these lusts of the palate were violent sexual debauchery, both male and female. Again, there was a contrasting fanatical enthusiasm for chastity which may be considered a perverted form of sexuality. The cloisters of Spain and France, circles like the Port Royal, and the notorious Puritanical extremities were as characteristic of the age as the libidinous and licentious court circles of Britain, France and Spain, Italy and Germany. Figures like Simplicius Simplicissimus show that the common folk were as prepared to glory in the exhibitionism of sexual swagger as the aristocracy. Yet, in contrast to the renaissance and to later periods, there was a displayful enthusiasm for the passions as such, and an unprecedented sense for the drama of the struggle between these passions and the rational mind, heightening their role by ordained efforts to control them.

If one asks oneself, what was the baroque's view of man, he finds a view closely linked to these aspects of personal behavior. The stress was on action, personal success, constant combat and the resulting heightening of the sense of self. The ceremonial of social contact was related to dignity and gravity; it has been argued that even the Cartesian formula, *"Cogito, ergo sum,"* expressed this self-centered activism; for through the process of thought the ego is here held to be manifest.[3] Therefore, baroque man emphasized having rather than being something, and the passions were believed central to man's essence: Descartes, Hobbes, Pascal, Spinoza all philosophized in terms of the passions and their great power over human destiny; these baroque philosophers sought to explore and understand them; hence the beginning of psychology in this generation. At the same time, man struggling passionately and willfully to master his fate was yet seen as fate's helpless victim. The meteoric rise and the cataclysmic fall of favorites, conquering heroes, royal concubines, were highly symbolic of the baroque. Buckingham and Olivárez, Gustavus Adolphus and Wallenstein, Father Joseph and Sor Maria, the duchess of Chevreuse and the dowager queen, these and ever so many others crowded the baroque period as so many tragic characters, storming heaven, plunging into damnation, crying out: "I shall yet force my fate." It is almost as if baroque man had insisted that the final consummation of man's striking exhibition of the never-ending quest for power was a violent death, or at least banishment, exile, oblivion.

Notes

1 *Leviathan*, Chs. VIII, X, XI.

2 James H. Hanford, *John Milton, Englishman* (1949), 211. The subsequent quotation is from Louis Untermeyer's comment in *A Treasury of Great Poems* (1942), 460.

3 Willi Flemming, "Die Auffassung des Menschen im 17. Jahrhundert," *Deutsche Vierteljahrschrift für Literatur und Geistesgeschichte* (1928), VI, 403 ff.

Peter's son, Alexei, was a great disappointment to the Russian Tsar. He was
a weakling and a drunkard who planned to undo his father's reforms and
return Russia to its old and traditional ways after he inherited the crown.
But the immaturity the father deplores in his son is also apparent in
Peter's letters—for they reveal the Tsar's character as tyrant, lover of war,
and brute insensible to the feelings of others. He finally turned his son
over to a "neutral" tribunal which condemned the young man to death.
And yet, ironically, in these same letters, Peter pays homage to God and
quotes from Saint Paul.

The Duties of a Russian Tsar

Peter the Great

Peter's Declaration to Alexei, October 11, 1715

Declaration to My Son,

You cannot be ignorant of what is known to all the world, to what
degree our people groaned under the oppression of the Swedes before the beginning of the present war.

By the usurpation of so many maritime places so necessary to our
state, they had cut us off from all commerce with the rest of the
world, and we saw with regret that besides they had cast a thick
veil before the eyes of the clear-sighted. You know what it has cost us
in the beginning of this war (in which God alone has led us, as it
were, by the hand, and still guides us) to make ourselves experienced
in the art of war, and to put a stop to those advantages which our
implacable enemies obtained over us.

We submitted to this with a resignation to the will of God, making no doubt but it was he who put us to that trial, till he might lead
us into the right way, and we might render ourselves worthy to experience, that the same enemy who at first made others tremble, now
in his turn trembles before us, perhaps in a much greater degree.
These are the fruits which, next to the assistance of God, we owe to
our own toil and to the labour of our faithful and affectionate children, our Russian subjects.

But at the time that I am viewing the prosperity which God has
heaped on our native country, if I cast an eye upon the posterity that
is to succeed me, my heart is much more penetrated with grief on
account of what is to happen, than I rejoice at those blessings that
are past, seeing that you, my son, reject all means of making yourself

From *The Development of Civilization* by Harry J. Carroll *et al.*(Scott, Foresman, 1969), pp. 35–37.

capable of well-governing after me. I say your incapacity is voluntary, because you cannot excuse yourself with want of natural parts and strength of body, as if God had not given you a sufficient share of either; and though your constitution is none of the strongest, yet it cannot be said that it is altogether weak.

But you even will not so much as hear warlike exercises mentioned; though it is by them that we broke through that obscurity in which we were involved, and that we made ourselves known to nations, whose esteem we share at present.

I do not exhort you to make war without lawful reasons; I only desire you to apply yourself to learn the art of it; for it is impossible well to govern without knowing the rules and discipline of it, was it for no other end than for the defense of the country.

I could place before your eyes many instances of what I am proposing to you. I will only mention to you the Greeks, with whom we are united by the same profession of faith. What occasioned their decay but that they neglected arms? Idleness and repose weakened them, made them submit to tyrants, and brought them to that slavery to which they are now so long since reduced. You mistake, if you think it is enough for a prince to have good generals to act under his orders. Everyone looks upon the head; they study his inclinations and conform themselves to them: all the world owns this. My brother during his reign loved magnificence in dress, and great equipages of horses. The nation was not much inclined that way, but the prince's delight soon became that of his subjects, for they are inclined to imitate him in liking a thing as well as disliking it.

If the people so easily break themselves of things which only regard pleasure, will they not forget in time; or will they not more easily give over the practice of arms, the exercise of which is the more painful to them, the less they are kept to it?

You have no inclination to learn the war, you do not apply yourself to it, and consequently you will never learn it: And how then can you command others, and judge of the reward which those deserve who do their duty, or punish others who fail of it? You will do nothing, nor judge of anything but by the eyes and help of others, like a young bird that holds up his bill to be fed.

You say that the weak state of your health will not permit you to undergo the fatigues of war: This is an excuse which is no better than the rest. I desire no fatigues, but only inclination, which even sickness itself cannot hinder. Ask those who remember the time of my brother. He was of a constitution weaker by far than yours. He was not able to manage a horse of the least mettle, nor could he hardly mount it:

Yet he loved horses, hence it came, that there never was, nor perhaps is there actually now in the nation a finer stable than his was.

By this you see that good success does not always depend on pains, but on the will.

If you think there are some, whose affairs do not fail of success, though they do not go to war themselves; it is true: But if they do not go themselves, yet they have an inclination for it, and understand it.

For instance, the late King of France did not always take the field in person; but it is known to what degree he loved war, and what glorious exploits he performed in it, which made his campaigns to be called the theatre and school of the world. His inclinations were not confined solely to military affairs, he also loved mechanics, manufactures and other establishments, which rendered his kingdom more flourishing than any other whatsoever.

After having made to you all those remonstrances, I return to my former subject which regards you.

I am a man and consequently I must die. To whom shall I leave after me to finish what by the grace of God I have begun, and to preserve what I have partly recovered? To a man, who like the slothful servant hides his talent in the earth, that is to say, who neglects making the best of what God has entrusted to him?

Remember your obstinacy and ill-nature, how often I reproached you with it, and even chastised you for it, and for how many years I almost have not spoke to you; but all this has availed nothing, has effected nothing. It was but losing my time; it was striking the air. You do not make the least endeavors, and all your pleasure seems to consist in staying idle and lazy at home: Things of which you ought to be ashamed (forasmuch as they make you miserable) seem to make up your dearest delight, nor do you foresee the dangerous consequences of it for yourself and for the whole state. St. Paul has left us a great truth when he wrote: If a man know not how to rule his own house, how shall he take care of the church of God?

After having considered all those great inconveniences and reflected upon them, and seeing I cannot bring you to good by any inducement, I have thought fit to give you in writing this act of my last will, with this resolution however to wait still a little longer before I put it in execution, to see if you will mend. If not, I will have you to know that I will deprive you of the succession, as one may cut off a useless member.

Do not fancy, that, because I have no other child but you, I only write this to terrify you. I will certainly put it in execution, if it please

God; for whereas I do not spare my own life for my country and the welfare of my people, why should I spare you who do not render yourself worthy of either? I would rather choose to transmit them to a worthy stranger than to my own unworthy son.

Peter

Alexei's Reply

Most Clement Lord and Father,

I have read the paper your Majesty gave me on the 27th of October, 1715, after the funeral of my late consort.

I have nothing to reply to it, but, that if your Majesty will deprive me of the succession to the Crown of Russia by reason of my incapacity, your will be done; I even most instantly beg it of you, because I do not think myself fit for the government. My memory is very much weakened, and yet it is necessary in affairs. The strength of my mind and of my body is much decayed by the sickness which I have undergone, and which have rendered me incapable of governing so many nations; this requires a more vigorous man than I am.

Therefore I do not aspire after you (whom God preserve many years) to the succession of the Russian Crown, even if I had no brother as I have one at present, whom I pray God preserve. Neither will I pretend for the future to that succession, of which I take God to witness, and swear it upon my soul, in testimony whereof I write and sign this present with my own hand.

I put my children into your hands, and as for myself, I desire nothing of you but a bare maintenance during my life, leaving the whole to your consideration and to your will.

Your most humble servant and son,
Alexei

Peter's Letter to Alexei, January 19, 1716

My last sickness having hindered me till now from explaining myself to you about the resolution I have taken upon your letter which you wrote to me in answer to my first; at present I answer that I observe you talk of nothing in it but of the succession, just as if I needed your consent to do in that affair what otherwise depends on my will. But whence comes it that in your letter you say nothing of that incapacity wherein you voluntarily put yourself, and of that aversion you have for affairs, which I touched in mine more particularly than the ill state of your health, and which you barely mention. I also remonstrated to you the dissatisfaction your conduct has given me for so many years, and you pass all that over in silence, though I strongly insisted upon it. Thence I judge that those paternal exhortations have no weight with you. I have therefore taken a resolution to write to you once more by this present which shall be the last. If you slight the advices I give you in my lifetime, how will you value them after my death?

Can one rely on your oaths, when one sees you have a hardened heart? David said: All men are liars. But supposing you have at present the will of being true to your promises, those great beards [men of corrupted morals] may turn you as they please, and make you break them.

Instead that at present their debauches and sloth keep them out of posts of honour, they are in hopes that one day or other their condition will mend by you who already show much inclination for them.

I do not see that you are sensible of the obligations you have to your father, to whom you owe your very being. Do you assist him in his cares and pains since you have attained the years of maturity? Certainly in nothing; all the world knows it; quite contrary you blame and abhor all the good I do, at the hazard and expense of my own health for the sake of my people and for their welfare, and I have all the reasons in the world to believe you will be the destroyer of it, if you out-live me. And so I cannot resolve to let you live on according to your own will, like an amphibious Creature, neither fish nor flesh. Change therefore your conduct, and either strive to render yourself worthy of the succession, or turn monk. I cannot be easy on your account, especially now that my health begins to decay. On sight therefore of this letter, answer me upon it either in writing, or by word of mouth. If you fail to do it, I will use you as a malefactor.

Peter

In this thoughtful and provocative article, Eric Hoffer, author of
"The True Believer" and "The Ordeal of Change," defines the juvenilization
of history, especially with reference to the twentieth century. Rapid change,
the Industrial Revolution, and leisure time have helped to shape the
modern primitive and plastic mind. What hope is there that man will
mature? Can maturity come before the end of this century?

A Time of Juveniles

Eric Hoffer

There was a week several years ago during which the newspapers
reported an epidemic of student riots spreading from Istanbul to Te-
heran, Bombay, Saigon, Seoul, Tokyo, and Mexico City. Most of the
riots had an anti-American flavor. And I remember how, early one
morning, while waiting for the bus that would take me to the waterfront, I saw the headline of still another riot, and heard myself
snorting with disgust: "History made by juvenile delinquents!"

The sound of my words had a peculiar effect on me. Inside the
bus I did not look at the newspaper but sat staring in front of me.
Who makes history? Is it the old? How much of a role did the young
play in shaping events? Things were coming together in my mind; I
remembered that years ago I had inserted in *The Passionate State of
Mind* an aphorism which read: "History is made by men who have
the restlessness, impressionability, credulity, capacity for make-be-
lieve, ruthlessness, and self-righteousness of children. It is made by
men who set their hearts on toys. All leaders strive to turn their followers into children." This insight which came to me from observing
two willful godchildren in action had been filed away in my mind
and did not affect my thinking. Now I concluded that we can hardly
know how things happened in history unless we keep in mind that
much of the time it was juveniles who made them happen.

Until relatively recent times man's span of life was short. Throughout most of history the truly old were a rarity. In an excavation of
one of the world's oldest cemeteries, the skeletons showed that the
average age of the population at death was less than twenty-five, and
there is no reason to suppose that the place was unusually unhealthy.
Thus it seems plausible that the momentous discoveries and inventions of the Neolithic Age—such as the wheel, calendar, and brick-

making—were the work of an almost childlike population and were probably made in the course of play. Nor is it likely that the ancient myths and legends, with their fairytale pattern and erotic symbolism, were elaborated by burnt-out old men.

The history of less ancient periods, too, reveals the juvenile character of their chief actors. Many observers have remarked on the smallness of the armor which has come down to us from the Middle Ages. Actually, the men who wore this armor were not grown-ups. They were married at thirteen, were warriors and leaders in their late teens, and senile at thirty-five or forty. Without some familiarity with the juvenile mentality and the aberrations of juvenile delinquency it would be difficult to make sense of the romanticism, trickery, and savagery which characterized the Middle Ages. Nor did things change markedly in the sixteenth century. Montaigne tells us that he hardly ever met a man as old as fifty. In the first half of the sixteenth century, Charles V became Holy Roman Emperor at the age of twenty, Francis I became King of France at twenty-one, and Henry VIII King of England at eighteen.

They Never Grew Up

But is juvenile mentality confined to adolescents? Do people automatically grow up as they grow older? Are there not teen-agers of every age? In 1502 Cardinal Giuliano della Rovere was elected Pope at the age of fifty-nine. He took the name of Julius II in honor of Julius Caesar, whom he esteemed the greatest man who ever lived, and whose career he determined to emulate. So on the threshold of old age he put on helmet and cuirass, mounted a horse and set out to become a conqueror. Clearly, the juvenile mentality may persist or reemerge later, even in old age.

In all times there are people who cannot grow up, and there are times when whole societies begin to think and act like juveniles. The twentieth century in particular has seen juvenilization on an almost global scale. No one can fail to discern the juvenile character of communism, fascism, racism (Ku Klux Klan), and the mass movements erupting at present in the underdeveloped parts of the world. Almost all the leaders of the new or renovated countries—de Gaulle, Castro, Sukarno, Nkruma, and the rest—have a pronounced juvenile element in their make-up.

Arthur Koestler suggests that there is in the revolutionary "some defective quality" which keeps him from growing up. The indications are, however, that the present trend toward juvenile behavior has been gathering force for over a century and has affected people who cannot be classed as revolutionaries. Such behavior was rampant on the frontier and in gold-rush camps, and the American go-getter, though he has no quarrel with the status quo, is as much a perpetual juvenile as any revolutionary. Militant nationalism, too, though not primarily revolutionary in character, fosters juvenile manifestations in all sorts of people. Laurens Van der Post calls nationalism "the juvenile delinquency of the contemporary world." Clearly, the childish pattern is not confined to people with "some defective quality" which keeps them from growing up, but may arise or be induced in all types.

To understand the process we must know something about the genesis of the juvenile mentality in the adolescent. We shall not get anywhere by looking for differences in brain structure or the nervous system between adolescent and adult. I know of no demonstrable differences. The reasonable approach is to assume that the adolescent's behavior is induced largely by his mode of existence, by the situation in which he finds himself. This would imply that adults, too, when placed in a similar situation, would behave more or less like juveniles.

Now, the chief peculiarity of the adolescent's existence is its in-betweenness: It is a phase of transition from childhood to manhood, a phase of uprootedness and drastic change. If our assumption is correct, other types of drastic change should evoke a somewhat similar psychological pattern. There should be a family likeness between the adolescents and people who migrate from one country to another, or are converted from one faith to another, or pass from one way of life to another—as when peasants are turned into industrial workers, serfs into free men, civilians into soldiers, and people in undeveloped countries are subjected to rapid modernization.

Staging a Madhouse

Let us have a close look at the experience of change. After the second world war, backward countries in Asia and Africa began to modernize themselves in an atmosphere charged with passion and a deafening clamor. As a naïve American I asked myself why the sober, practical task of modernization—of building factories, roads, dams, schools, and so forth—should require the staging of a madhouse. In *The Ordeal of Change* I tried to find answers to this question. My central idea was that drastic change is a profoundly upsetting experience, that when we face the new and unprecedented, our past experience and accomplishments become obsolete and are a hindrance rather than an aid. What Montaigne said of death is also true of the wholly new: "We are all apprentices when we come to it." We are all misfits when we have to fit ourselves to a new situation. And misfits live and breathe in an atmosphere of passion. We used to think that revolutions are the cause of change. Actually it is the other way around: change prepares the ground for a revolution. The difficulties and irritations inherent in the experience of change render people receptive to the appeal of a revolution. Change comes first. Where things have not changed at all there is the least likelihood of revolution.

However, the staging of a madhouse in the process of modernization is not peculiar to backward countries in Asia and Africa. We have been living in an apocalyptic madhouse staged on a global scale by Germany, Russia, and Japan, which set out to industrialize themselves at breakneck speed. There is also more to the experience of drastic change than a state of unfitness—the mass movements, upheavals, and wars which are a by-product of change indicate that the process involves the deeper layers of man's soul. After all, change such as the world has seen during the last hundred years is something wholly unprecedented in human experience. It would be legitimate, therefore, to assume that there is in man's nature a built-in resistance to change. We are not only afraid of the new, but convinced that we cannot really change, that we can adapt ourselves to the new only by getting out of our skin and assuming a new identity. In other words, drastic change generates a need for a new birth and a new identity. And it perhaps depends on the way this need is satisfied whether the process of change runs smoothly or is attended with convulsions and explosions.

It is of interest to have a quick look at the means employed by some ossified primitive societies to tackle the passage from childhood to manhood. In the Congo, boys at the age of fifteen are declared dead, taken into the forest and there subjected to purification, flagellation, and intoxication with palm wine, resulting in anesthesia. The priest-magician (*ngànga*) who is in charge teaches them a special language and gives them special food. Finally come the rites of reintegration in which the novices "pretend not to know how to walk or eat and, in general, act as if they were newly born and must relearn all the gestures of ordinary life."[1] In several Australian tribes the boy is taken violently from his mother who weeps for him. He is subjected to physical and mental weakening to simulate death, and is finally resurrected and taught to live as a man.

The interest of their rites is in their motif of rebirth rather than in any bearing they may have on change in a civilized society. In the modern world change overtakes a whole population, and the denouement is not a return to an immemorial way of life. Here the sense of rebirth and a new identity are created by mass movements or mass migrations. One becomes a member of a glorious Germany, a glorious Japan, a master race, a nation of heroic warriors destined to conquer the world; or one joins a revolutionary or religious movement which envisages a new life; or one actually emigrates to a new country and becomes a new man.

The tale of Moses and the exodus is a luminous example of the difficulties encountered, and the outlandish means that have to be employed, in the realization of drastic change.

Moses wanted to accomplish a relatively simple thing: he wanted to transform the enslaved Hebrews into free men. But being a genuine leader, Moses knew that the task of endowing the liberated slaves with a new identity and immersing them in a new life was not at all simple and required the employment of extravagant means. The exodus from Egypt was the first step. But more vital was the fiction of a chosen people led by a mighty Jehovah to a promised land—the kind of milieu essential for a drastic human transformation.

Now the human transformation which took place during the last hundred years was not the turning of slaves into free men but drastic changes brought about by the Industrial Revolution. Here too the sense of rebirth was generated by exoduses (mass migrations), the fiction of a chosen people, and the vision of a promised land. In Europe, during the second half of the nineteenth century, the wholesale transformation of peasants into industrial workers gave rise not only to nationalist and revolutionary movements but also to mass rushes to the New World, particularly the United States, where the European peasant was literally processed into a new man—made to learn a new language, adopt a new mode of dress, a new diet, and often a new name.

Primitive and Plastic

The juvenile, then, is the archetypal man in transition. Juvenile impulses manifest themselves in people of all ages—even the change of retirement may evoke a juvenile pattern in the old. Retired shopkeepers and farmers have made southern California a breeding ground of juvenile cults, utopias, and wild schemes. The Birch movement with its unmistakable flavor of juvenile delinquency was initiated by a retired candy maker and is sustained largely by retired business executives, generals, and admirals.

The significant point is that juvenilization inevitably results in some degree of primitive social behavior. We are up against the great paradox of the twentieth century; namely, that a breakneck technological advance has gone hand in hand with a return to tribalism, charismatic leaders, medicine men, credulity, and tribal wars. The tendency has been to blame the machine. There is a considerable literature on the barbarizing and dehumanizing effects of the machine: how it turns us into robots and slaves, stifles our individuality, and dwarfs our lives. Most of the indictments of the machine come of course from writers, poets, philosophers, and scholars—men of words—who have no firsthand experience of working and living with machines. It should also be noted that long before the advent of the machine age the same types of men of words looked upon common people who did the world's work as soulless robots and automated ghouls. They have always viewed as materialistic the effort to turn matter to the service of man. Anyone who has worked with machines knows that they can be as temperamental and willful as any living thing, and that communion with machines does not blunt our sensibilities. The proficient mechanic is an alert and intuitive human being. On the waterfront one can see how the ability to make a forklift or a winch do one's bidding with precision and finesse generates a peculiar exhilaration, so that the skilled lift-driver and winch-driver are as a rule of good cheer, and work as if at play. Even if it were proven beyond a doubt that the assembly line makes robots of workers, it still affects only a small fraction of the population, and cannot be held responsible for the nature of a whole society.

No, it is not the machine as such but drastic change which produces this social primitivism. Where a new identity is found by embracing a mass movement, for example, the reason is obvious: a mass movement absorbs and assimilates the individual into its corporate body, and does so by stripping the individual of his own opinions, tastes, and values. He is thereby reduced to an infantile state, for this is what a new birth really means: to become like a child. And children are primitive beings—they are credulous, follow a leader, and readily become members of a pack. Immigration produces a similar reaction. Like a child, the immigrant has to learn to speak, and how to act and assert himself. Finally primitivism also follows when people seek a new identity by plunging into ceaseless action and hustling. It takes leisure to mature. People in a hurry can neither grow nor decay; they are preserved in a state of perpetual puerility.

The question is whether this social primitivism is merely an unfortunate by-product or whether it is a vital factor in the process of change. What a society needs above all when it has to adjust itself to wholly new conditions is a high degree of human plasticity. Now, a population rendered juvenile and primitive tends to become a homogeneous, plastic mass. We who have lived through the Stalin-Hitler era know that one of the most striking functions of a mass movement is the inducement of plasticity—the creation of a population that will go through breathtaking somersaults at a word of command, and can be made, in the words of Boris Pasternak, "to hate what it loves and love what it hates."

The True Believer is, then, a plastic human type thrown up by a century of ceaseless change. The adaptation to change has also produced the American hustler, a type as juvenile, primitive, and plastic as the True Believer, but functioning without ideology and the magic of communion. The immigrant, too, having been stripped of his traditions and habits, is easily molded. Finally, there is the plastic type of the warrior. All through history conquerors have learned more willingly and readily from the conquered than the other way around. The conqueror does not see imitation as an act of submission and proof of his inadequacy. It is a fact that nations with a warrior tradition, such as the Japanese and the inheritors of Genghis Khan in Outer Mongolia, find the transition of modernization less difficult than nations of subjected peasants such as Russia and China. There is thus a kernel of practicalness in the preposterous tendency of an Indonesia or an Egypt to cast its people in the role of warriors. It is also plausible that the defeat of forty million Arabs by tiny Israel is rendering the modernization of the Arab world difficult and painful.

The Uneasy and Uprooted

To sum up: The throes of the machine age stem not from the machine as such but from the social dislocation caused by the rapid transformation of millions of peasants into urban industrial workers. It was this abrupt change in the life of the European masses in the second half of the nineteenth century which released the nationalist, revolutionary, and racialist movements that are still with us. A similar change in the backward countries of Asia, Africa, and Latin America is now setting off the social tremors that keep our world in a state of perpetual shock.

In instances where large-scale movement of peasants into the cities has taken place without industrialization, the social consequences have been equally explosive, as we have seen in recent decades in Latin America. In largely nonindustrial Argentina, Chile, Cuba, Uruguay, and Venezuela, restless, unemployed townsmen already outnumber countrymen. Here rapid industrialization when it comes will find masses of urbanized peasants ready to be processed into factory workers, and the result is likely to be a considerable easing of social unrest rather than revolution.

The curious thing is that with the coming of automation we may see something like the present Latin American pattern emerging in the advanced industrialized countries. The banishing of workers by automation from factories, warehouses, etc. will fill the cities with millions of unemployed workers waiting for something to happen. Condemned to inaction, and deprived of a sense of usefulness and worth, they will become receptive to extremism, and to political and racial intolerance. Thus it seems that in our present world problems come and go but the by-products remain the same, and the end of The Time of Juveniles is nowhere in sight.

Note

1 Arnold van Gennep, *The Rites of Passage* (University of Chicago Press, 1960).

Questions

1 How have certain devotions—devotions to a cause or a faith—brought on great crimes against humankind?

2 Are brilliant men any more or less subject to childish behavior than ordinary men? Why?

3 What are factors conditioning immature behavior in adults?

4 What have been some of the great crimes committed against mankind in the twentieth century? Were they caused by men with immature minds? In what ways were the men of the seventeenth and earlier centuries responsible for these crimes?

5 Although he was about seven feet tall, Peter the Great liked to travel incognito. What do you think of his maturity?

6 Are patriots of whatever country the potential enemies of mankind? Explain.

7 Is it fair to compare Vincent de Paul with Richelieu since their roles in life were so different? Suppose Monsieur Vincent had been the chief minister of France between 1624 and 1642.

8 Is immaturity due to a narrow mind? Would people gain a greater perspective if they were exposed to world civilization and anthropology courses so they could see themselves in other places and other times? Would not a world view of ourselves help? For the more broadminded, why not a galactic view of our hangups from way back?

2

Enlightenment Thought and Democratic Revolutions

The ideas of the Enlightenment "philosophes" helped inspire two
revolutions which historians have not yet stopped writing about: the
American Revolution in 1776, and the French Revolution in 1789. While
both events resulted in part from the revolutionary implications of
Enlightenment political theory, thus sharing some resemblances, there
were striking differences between the two. How did the two revolutions
differ? Which one had a greater impact on the Western world? Which one
accomplished more? These are some of the questions discussed briefly in
the introductory essay which follows.

French Visions and American Practices

Melvin Steinfield

One of the most sacred myths of the seventeenth century was the
theory of the divine right of kings, from which absolute monarchies
throughout Europe drew justification and support. At the beginning
of this period King James I of England described kings as "God's
lieutenants upon earth," and toward the end, King Louis XIV's influential crony Bishop Bossuet wrote that "Royal authority is sacred.
. . . Royal authority is absolute. . . . The prince need render account
of his orders to no one." But even without these religious arguments,
supporters of the status quo found a convincing case for absolutism
based on secular grounds in Thomas Hobbes' *Leviathan,* written in
1651.

With all the arguments, both religious and secular, presented in
favor of absolutism in the seventeenth century, it certainly looked
as if kings and their absolute monarchies were indestructible. They
weren't. These theories, and the absolutism they upheld, were first
challenged and overthrown in the English Revolution of 1688. During the American Revolution George III was made the symbol of
tyranny as the colonists tried to gain their rights as Englishmen in
the 1760s, and then their independence after 1775. Those two
political revolutions in America and England were, of course, important historical events. But it was in neither England nor America
that the most important revolution of the Enlightenment period took
place.

It was in France. The revolutionary implications of Enlightenment thought came to have their widest application and most significant test in that country. It was in France that the tide of revolution,
swollen by the writings of the *philosophes,* reached beyond the narrow limits of mere political revolution and crashed against the desic-
cated bulwarks of the Frenchman's oldest hangup: *l'ancien regime.*

It was in France that the entire society was confronted with the tidal wave of reform.

In England and America, as well as in France, the intellectual basis of absolutism had been weakened by Enlightenment theorists who sought to create rational institutions within the framework of natural law. However, in two of those countries, the theorists tended to translate Enlightenment ideas almost exclusively into political reform. It was in France, and in France alone, that the full sweep of the Enlightenment vision—as it affected not only politics and economics, but also as it affected society, religion, and people—became the official goal as well as the guiding spirit. The British and the Americans were more pragmatic than the French in their goals. After all, many of the injustices still found in the French system had already been eliminated in Britain and America.

This is not to say that similarities did not exist between the French Revolution and the American Revolution. Every age has its own catchwords, phrases, and slogans, and the eighteenth century was no different in this respect. Some of the ideas of French revolutionaries in 1789 were quite similar to those espoused by American revolutionaries in 1776. And both Thomas Jefferson, in writing the Declaration of Independence, and those who justified the French Revolution borrowed heavily from the Enlightenment concepts of political theory. It would be surprising not to find such similarities in the two revolutions. Both occurred during the same historical period; both drew from the same body of prevailing thoughts, trends, and expressions; both were manifestations of the middle-class militancy of the time; both were led by groups seeking to wrest power from the established, older orders of society; both revolutions went through a moderate phase (although in France this was followed by a radical takeover, the moderate phase in America became the permanent mode); and both were divided by contending factions.

But for all the similarities between the two revolutions, there was a vital difference—that of scope. The Americans had more limited, pragmatic goals: independence from Great Britain and the establishment of a stable government, with moderate political reform. On the whole, they succeeded. The French, on the other hand, had lofty visions: overthrow of *l'ancien regime,* a total restructuring of the entire society, and creation of a Utopian state. They fell short of achieving everything they had hoped for.

It may be disturbing to Americans for their revolution to be categorized merely as a political revolution. It was not, of course, as simplistic as that. While it was primarily a movement for political independence led by the bourgeoisie, there were also elements of reform embodied in it. Few American leaders of the revolution advocated wholesale upheaval of their society, but some tried to expand the role of the revolution. For example, individual state constitutions contained features beyond mere political reform, as Burns points out:

> A few states attacked the foundations of aristocracy—primogeniture, tithes, quit-rents, and entail. Others abolished their state churches or wiped out religious qualifications for holding office. Radical economic legislation was also enacted. Several of the states confiscated crown lands and the princely estates of wealthy loyalists and divided them up among small farmers and war veterans. After the war the radicals in some states gained enough power to pass laws for the benefit of the debtor classes.[1]

For the Americans in general, however, social reform was never a major objective. For John Adams, Alexander Hamilton, James Madison, Benjamin Franklin, George Washington, and most of the others who plotted, fought, convened, debated, and ruled, the primary goals were achieved with the surrender at Yorktown and with the ratification of the Constitution. The Constitutional Convention itself was a gathering of the moderates in an effort to preserve their newly-won power and they employed ingenious devices to prevent the dilution of this power by radical experiments with democratic aspirations. The Constitution consolidated the conservatives' canons.

With the moderates in power, it is not surprising that the system which emerged at Philadelphia in 1787 was consistent with their conservative outlook. Slavery was sanctioned in several clauses of the Constitution; an elaborate check and balance system was devised; election of the president, vice president, and senators was by indirect method; the power of potential mass movements with democratic aspirations was effectively checked. If it had not been for the persistent efforts of the Jeffersonian faction after 1788, the Bill of Rights would not have been appended to the Constitution in 1791. During the struggle for ratification of the Constitution, it was only the promise of such a Bill of Rights that swung the vote in some closely contested elections.

The disgust for the masses which some of the revolutionary leaders such as John Adams and Alexander Hamilton displayed is fairly common knowledge. The people, said Hamilton, is "a beast!" And the second President of the United States concluded that Government should be by "the rich, the well-born, and the able." It should not be forgotten that John Adams' term as Chief Executive was sandwiched between the presidencies of two Virginia slaveholding planta-tion-owners. Thomas Jefferson may have written that all men are created equal, but that didn't stop him from owning an average of two hundred slaves throughout his adult life.

Reforms ultimately were realized in America, but it was a slow evolutionary process. The Bill of Rights in 1791, the Jeffersonian Revolution in 1800, the Jacksonian Revolution in 1828, the Civil War in 1861, and the various reform movements of the latter nine-teenth and the twentieth century attempted to reach the social and economic goals most revolutionaries had not dreamed of pursuing.

In France the historical situation, like the revolution itself, was quite different. Grievances were more widespread, covering a host of social and economic and religious, as well as political arenas. Those grievances were nursed longer, the discontent simmered with a greater intensity, and the explosive atmosphere was more highly charged than in America. The bitterness that was engendered by centuries of gov-ernmental mismanagement created a volatile situation that made a revolution practically inevitable. One has only to consider the long reigns of Louis XIV, Louis XV, and Louis XVI—and the way these absolute monarchs exhausted the coffers of France, as well as the patience of the population, by war and by their extravagant tastes in personal luxury—to gain an understanding of the causes which pro-pelled Frenchmen to attack *l'ancien regime.* Man's propensity for re-venge, especially if he has suffered such injustices as those inherent in the French system, is almost limitless. Or so it would seem in view-ing the course of the revolution in France. Was it surprising, there-fore, that a few heads—including those of Louis XVI and Marie Antoinette—were to meet the fate of the guillotine?

In 1789–1791 the leaders of the French Revolution were mod-erates very much like the American conservative revolutionaries, and the reforms enacted by the National Assembly reflect the limited aspirations of these men. Similar to the efforts of the conservatives of the Constitutional Convention in the United States, the moderates in France tried to consolidate their power. In fact, the last act of the National Assembly was to declare that the revolution was officially over and to forbid any changes in the constitution for at least ten years. But importantly for the outcomes of the revolutions, striking differences were apparent in the radical elements of the two countries. Radicals in France were able to exert their influence to a greater de-gree and pursued their goals more flamboyantly than the radicals in America. After the failure of the National Assembly to solidify the moderate phase into a stable government, they came to dominate the course of the French Revolution.

That never happened in America, for the radical group was smaller in number and more limited in their aspirations. They did not have the general French radical vision of the many specific types of sweeping democratic reforms that were contemplated. Indeed, although Tom Paine was considered extremely radical in America, he almost lost his head for not being radical enough in France. Furthermore, at the Constitutional Convention, the American radicals were virtually powerless. Jefferson, Paine, and Sam Adams were absent and could exert only a little influence—and then it was indirect—upon it. The most that the American radicals at first salvaged in the way of permanent reform was the Bill of Rights. And that hardly qualified as social upheaval.

Why were French aspirations higher? Why did the radicals become dominant in France and submerged in America? The answer lies primarily in the nature of the grievances confronting the French and the Americans. American grievances were comparatively mild. No one would claim that conditions were Utopian, of course, but they were certainly a lot better than in France. Despite the well-documented record of mistreatment of minority groups that is too well-known to require restatement here, Americans enjoyed, on the whole, advantages which no other people possessed. They were not burdened with a hereditary nobility, entrenched privileged groups, or any of the other components of the typical closed society. In America there were great possibilities of upward social mobility for most people, by and large the Church was separate from the State by the time of the revolutionary period, and there was a wider measure of freedom to worship, speak, write, publish, meet, and participate in the political life of the nation. As the Frenchman J. Hector St. John de Crevecoeur noted in 1782:

> The American ought therefore to love this country much better than that wherein either he or his forefathers were born. Here the rewards of his industry follow with equal steps the progress of his labour; his labour is founded on the basis of nature, self-interest; can it want a stronger allurement? Wives and children, who before in vain demanded of him a morsel of bread, now, fat and frolicsome, gladly help their father to clear those fields whence exuberant crops are to arise to feed and to clothe them all; without any part being claimed, either by a despotic prince, a rich abbot, or a mighty lord.[2]

But that was not the case in France. As Thomas Jefferson noted in 1785: "Of twenty millions of people supposed to be in France, I am of opinion there are nineteen millions more wretched, more accursed in every circumstance of human existence than the most conspicuously wretched individual of the whole United States."[3] Jefferson had little good to say about France: "I find the general fate of humanity here most deplorable. The truth of Voltaire's observation, offers itself perpetually, that every man here must be either the hammer or the anvil."[4]

Crevecoeur the Frenchman toured America before its revolution and found conditions praiseworthy. Jefferson the American toured France just before its Revolution and found the situation bad. No wonder the aspirations of the French radicals were not confined to political reforms. The whole *ancien regime* was examined and found wanting. The Americans enjoyed far better conditions at the outset, they didn't have as far to go, and thus they could be satisfied with more limited results.

How bad was it in France? Was Jefferson exaggerating? To an extent, he was; he compared conditions with those in America and came to the conclusion that Frenchmen lived a bleak existence. But the Third Estate, which comprised ninety-eight percent of the population (the remaining two percent was split between the first two estates of the clergy and the nobility), was composed not only of the laboring poor of Jefferson's description but also of the middle-class bourgeoisie. The bourgeoisie element was quite diversified in itself and included not only the wealthy burghers of the cities but also a host of minor officials, lawyers, and tradesmen who had established themselves in the countryside and who lived quite comfortably; some were even landowners in their own right.

It was the generally well-educated bourgeoisie and not the peasants who were influenced to the greatest extent by the Enlightenment ideals of liberty, equality, and fraternity, and who became the leaders of the revolution. The wealth they had gained from trade and business pursuits was often greater than that of the entrenched, class-conscious nobility and clergy; yet because birth and legal status—and not education, talent or wealth—were awarded prestige and privilege in eighteenth century France, the bourgeoisie were denied the social and political mobility that seemed to them the logical result of their economic mobility. They were unable to break through the class lines of the Third Estate and move upward, and thus they came to reject the system that rested on hierarchical privileges. Although the bourgeoisie in 1789 had more opportunities than ever before to advance themselves via education and business, the most flagrant aspects of the feudal structure remained as an insult to their enlightened sense of justice.

The peasants and the workers, on the other hand, ultimately became involved in the revolution for much more basic reasons. They, too, were incensed at the feudal system, but their dissatisfaction was based primarily on economic considerations. Since the wealth of the nobility and the clergy was exempt as a result of feudal privileges, the monarchy continued to levy unreasonable taxes on the peasantry even after their taxable resources had been exhausted. The three Louises who ruled France for the 150 years prior to the revolution sank the country into deeper and deeper financial straits. The monarchy under Louis XIV ("I am the State") had a powerlock on the status quo for 72 years—from 1643 to 1715. During that time Frenchmen survived under the despotic regime of this arrogant monarch who squandered the resources of the State to further his own greed for power. The press was censored, men were imprisoned for the slightest pretext, and the Palace at Versailles was built for the personal enjoyment of the King. Yet Louis XIV's own extravagant private Disneyland at Versailles was far less costly than the wars in which he involved France throughout his reign.

Louis relished power: "I was King, and born to be one. I experienced next a delicious feeling, hard to express, and which you will not know yourself except by tasting it as I have done." France did not relish Louis XIV, however. Nor did they enjoy Louis XV or Louis XVI, both of whom continued the absolute monarchy of their Sun-King predecessor. Both continued to preside over a society that was strangling in its own infamous restrictions, while boasting about its "enlightenment."

No wonder Voltaire kept repeating his battle cry against the French Establishment: "Crush the infamy!" The infamy to eighteenth century enlightened Frenchmen was the absolute monarchy, the whole structure of outmoded privileges, feudal customs, religious bigotry, economic injustice, and inhumane lack of concern. The impediments to enlightenment for the revolution-minded Frenchmen were the Church, the monarchy, and the medieval carry-overs of a feudal system. Frenchmen, on the whole, were seeking total liberation from the injustices inherent in these institutions.

"Man is born free; but everywhere he is in chains," wrote Rousseau in *The Social Contract*. "Man will never be free until the last king is strangled with the entrails of the last priest," wrote Diderot. Those direct calls to violent destruction of ancient regimes, those indictments of the entire Establishment, those vitriolic anti clerical outpourings were not characteristic of American revolutionary rhetoric. The Americans already enjoyed many of the liberties that Rousseau could only envision. Furthermore, if one didn't like conditions

in Virginia for example, he could always move to another colony
(unless he was a slave, or an Indian, or one of the other oppressed
peoples within America). Or, he could move West. Roger Williams,
who was evicted from early Massachusetts for his religious beliefs,
was able to establish a new order in Rhode Island. America was, for
most Americans, a land with many safety valves, a land of unlimited
new beginnings.

But not France. There was no haven in France for the thousands
of French Protestants (Huguenots) who were no longer tolerated
after Louis XIV revoked the Edict of Nantes in 1685. They had to
flee the country. And with social mobility denied to the ninety-eight
percent of the population that comprised the Third Estate, there
were no new beginnings in France; there were only visions of what
the revolution could accomplish when it came.

When the Revolution came, many of those visions were fulfilled,
but not all. During the first stage from 1789 to 1792, many changes
were enacted: feudal privileges that had been traditional since medieval times were abolished by the August 4th decrees in 1789. No
longer could nobles hunt on peasants' lands, or claim special tax
privileges, or demand excessive fees from peasants. The Declaration
of the Rights of Man in the same year combined many of the sentiments that had been expressed in the English Bill of Rights and in
the American Declaration of Independence, and that were soon to
be expressed in the Bill of Rights appended to the United States Constitution. Also, the power of the Church was shaken by the confisca-
tion of much of its lands and by the secularization of the clergy.

But these changes were not radical enough for the group of revolutionaries who came to dominate the revolution after 1792. The
second stage, led by the French radicals, executed Louis XVI, inaugurated a Reign of Terror with mass executions of political suspects, abolished slavery in the colonies, ended prison for debtors,
repealed primogeniture and broke up the large estates, instituted the
metric system of weights and measures, divided France into more
logical subentities for local government purposes, and created a new
calendar. In the eyes of the radicals, the complete revolutionary vision
had arrived in all its glory. It was the Year I.

This infant state was in trouble, however. The revolutionary
zeal subsided, internal wrangling and interminable factional violence
sapped the energies of the remakers of society. By 1795 a reactionary
third stage, again conservative, began. The Revolution struggled for
a few more years, but little else was accomplished. It was 1799,
France was exhausted, and Napoleon—with more wars aiming at

the domination of Europe by France—was just around the corner.

Were those two revolutions worth the political, social, and economic upheaval they generated? What had been accomplished by all that violence in America and France? Both revolutions inspired other peoples to strive for a better society and to try to convert Enlightenment ideals into enlightened practices. Prodded by more acute conditions, the French articulated the ideals more thoroughly than the Americans. While the American Revolution helped inspire the French Revolution, the French Revolution exerted a greater influence overall. It imparted a broader meaning to the concept of revolution; it institutionalized violence as a necessary feature of total revolution; it influenced nationalistic uprisings in other European countries; it struck a decisive blow against absolute monarchy and feudal relics in Europe as well as against *l'ancien regime* in France; it prepared the way for Napoleon's educational and legal reforms; it retarded the growth of conservatism and was truly the revolutionary spectre that haunted Europe during the nineteenth century; it brought to light the potential power of the urban masses and rural poor; it gave birth to Utopian socialism.

Just as the Civil Rights movement in America ultimately came to influence the goals and tactics of student power groups, women's liberation campaigns, and the struggles of the minorities for justice, the French Revolution expanded the vision of social reformers everywhere, and became a catalyst for future revolutions. Nevertheless, it must not be forgotten that while the French fashioned the vision of what widespread reform could accomplish, the Americans supplied the proof of that reform. For, despite its many shortcomings, America, more than any other country in the late eighteenth century, had come the closest to realizing the goals which the French envisioned. Throughout the nineteenth century and into the twentieth, America remained "the last, best hope on earth."

Notes

1 Edward McNall Burns, *Western Civilizations* (New York: W. W. Norton, 1968), pp. 765–766.

2 J. Hector St. John de Crevecoeur, *Letters From an American Farmer,* 1782 in Marvin Meyers, John G. Cawelti, Alexander Kern, *Sources of the American Republic, Vol. I,* (Glenview, Ill.: Scott, Foresman, 1967), pp. 282–283.

3 Thomas Jefferson, letter to Mrs. Trist, 1785, in Saul K. Padover, ed., *Thomas Jefferson on Democracy* (New York: New American Library, 1953), p. 140.

4 Thomas Jefferson, letter to Bellini, 1785, in Padover, *ibid.,* p. 138.

The Declaration of Independence, wrote Thomas Jefferson during his later years, "was intended to be an expression of the American mind." Subsequent generations have been inclined to canonize Jefferson's classic document as if it were a unique expression of revolutionary ideas. Yet historians have long since exploded the twin myths of Jefferson as an original thinker on the subject of revolution and of his ideas as peculiarly American. The Declaration of Independence was a typical eighteenth century document, rooted in the ideas of John Locke and other political philosophers of the European Enlightenment. In reading the Declaration below, note the use of such typical Enlightenment concepts as natural law, popular sovereignty, social contract, natural rights, and the right to resist tyranny. Note also that the emphasis is on political revolution, not fundamental social reform.

The Declaration of Independence

Thomas Jefferson

In Congress, July 4, 1776
The Unanimous Declaration of the Thirteen
United States of America

When, in the course of human events, it becomes necessary for one people to dissolve the political bands which have connected them with another, and to assume among the powers of the earth the separate and equal station to which the laws of nature and of nature's God entitle them, a decent respect to the opinions of mankind requires that they should declare the causes which impel them to the separation.

We hold these truths to be self-evident: That all men are created equal; that they are endowed by their Creator with certain unalienable rights; that among these are life, liberty, and the pursuit of happiness; that, to secure these rights, governments are instituted among men, deriving their just powers from the consent of the governed; that whenever any form of government becomes destructive of these ends, it is the right of the people to alter or to abolish it and to institute a new government, laying its foundation on such principles, and organizing its powers in such form, as to them shall seem most likely to effect their safety and happiness. Prudence, indeed, will dictate that governments long established should not be changed for light and transient causes; and, accordingly, all experience hath shown that mankind are more disposed to suffer while evils are sufferable, than to right themselves by abolishing the forms to which

From *Readings in Western Civilization*, George H. Knoles and Rixford K. Snyder, eds. (Philadelphia: Lippincott, 1960), Vol. II, pp. 521–523.

they are accustomed. But when a long train of abuses and usurpations, pursuing invariably the same object, evinces a design to reduce them under absolute despotism, it is their right, it is their duty, to throw off such government and to provide new guards for their future security. Such has been the patient sufferance of these colonies; and such is now the necessity which constrains them to alter their former systems of government.

The history of the present King of Great Britain is a history of repeated injuries and usurpations, all having in direct object the establishment of an absolute tyranny over these States. To prove this, let facts be submitted to a candid world:

He has refused his assent to laws, the most wholesome and necessary for the public good.

He has forbidden his Governors to pass laws of immediate and pressing importance, unless suspended in their operation till his assent should be obtained; and, when so suspended, he has utterly neglected to attend to them.

He has refused to pass other laws for the accommodation of large districts of people, unless those people would relinquish the right of representation in the Legislature, a right inestimable to them and formidable to tyrants only.

He has called together legislative bodies at places unusual, uncomfortable, and distant from the depository of their public records, for the sole purpose of fatiguing them into compliance with his measures.

He has dissolved representative Houses repeatedly for opposing with manly firmness his invasions on the rights of the people.

He has refused for a long time after such dissolutions to cause others to be elected; whereby the legislative powers, incapable of annihilation, have returned to the people at large for their exercise; the State remaining, in the meantime, exposed to all the dangers of invasions from without and convulsions within.

He has endeavored to prevent the population of these States; for that purpose obstructing the laws for naturalization of foreigners, refusing to pass others to encourage their migration hither, and raising the conditions of new appropriations of lands.

He has obstructed the administration of justice by refusing his assent to laws for establishing judiciary powers.

He has made judges dependent on his will alone for the tenure of their offices and the amount and payment of their salaries.

He has erected a multitude of new offices, and sent hither swarms of officers to harass our people and eat out their substance.

He has kept among us, in times of peace, standing armies, without the consent of our Legislatures.

He has affected to render the military independent of, and superior to, the civil power.

He has combined with others to subject us to a jurisdiction foreign to our Constitution and unacknowledged by our laws, giving his assent to their acts of pretended legislation:

For quartering large bodies of armed troops among us;

For protecting them, by a mock trial, from punishment for any murders which they should commit on the inhabitants of these States;

For cutting off our trade with all parts of the world;

For imposing taxes on us without our consent;

For depriving us, in many cases, of the benefits of trial by jury;

For transporting us beyond seas to be tried for pretended offenses;

For abolishing the free system of English laws in a neighboring province, establishing therein an arbitrary government, and enlarging its boundaries so as to render it at once an example and fit instrument for introducing the same absolute rule into these colonies;

For taking away our charters, abolishing our most valuable laws, and altering fundamentally the forms of our governments;

For suspending our own Legislatures, and declaring themselves invested with power to legislate for us in all cases whatsoever.

He has abdicated government here by declaring us out of his protection and waging war against us.

He has plundered our seas, ravaged our coasts, burnt our towns, and destroyed the lives of our people.

He is at this time transporting large armies of foreign mercenaries to complete the works of death, desolation, and tyranny, already begun with circumstances of cruelty and perfidy scarcely paralleled in the most barbarous ages, and totally unworthy the head of a civilized nation.

He has constrained our fellow citizens, taken captive on the high seas, to bear arms against their country, to become the executioners of their friends and brethren, or to fall themselves by their hands.

He has excited domestic insurrections amongst us, and has endeavored to bring on the inhabitants of our frontiers the merciless

Indian savages, whose known rule of warfare is an undistinguished destruction of all ages, sexes, and conditions.

In every stage of these oppressions we have petitioned for redress in the most humble terms: our repeated petitions have been answered only by repeated injury. A prince, whose character is thus marked by every act which may define a tyrant, is unfit to be the ruler of a free people.

Nor have we been wanting in attentions to our British brethren. We have warned them from time to time of attempts by their Legislature to extend an unwarrantable jurisdiction over us. We have reminded them of the circumstances of our emigration and settlement here. We have appealed to their native justice and magnanimity, and we have conjured them by the ties of our common kindred to disavow these usurpations which would inevitably interrupt our connections and correspondence. They, too, have been deaf to the voice of justice and of consanguinity. We must, therefore, acquiesce in the necessity which denounces our separation, and hold them, as we hold the rest of mankind, enemies in war; in peace, friends.

WE, THEREFORE, THE REPRESENTATIVES OF THE UNITED STATES OF AMERICA, in General Congress assembled, appealing to the Supreme Judge of the world for the rectitude of our intentions, do, in the name and by the authority of the good people of these colonies, solemnly publish and declare that these United Colonies are, and of right ought to be, FREE AND INDEPENDENT STATES; that they are absolved from all allegiance to the British Crown, and that all political connection between them and the State of Great Britain is, and ought to be, totally dissolved; and that as free and independent states they have full power to levy war, conclude peace, contract alliances, establish commerce, and to do all other acts and things which independent States may of right do. And for the support of this declaration, with a firm reliance on the protection of Divine Providence, we mutually pledge to each other our lives, our fortunes, and our sacred honor.

Adopted by the National Assembly on August 26, 1789, the French
Declaration of the Rights of Man and Citizen is a compact document
containing ideas that appeared in both the American Declaration of
Independence and the English Bill of Rights. Some of the ideas also
parallel the American Bill of Rights, ratified in 1791.

The French Declaration
of the Rights of Man and of the Citizen

National Assembly

The representatives of the French people, organized in National
Assembly, considering that ignorance, forgetfulness or contempt of
the rights of man are the sole causes of the public miseries and of
the corruption of governments, have resolved to set forth in a solemn
declaration the natural, inalienable, and sacred rights of man, in
order that this declaration, being ever present to all the members of
the social body, may unceasingly remind them of their rights and
their duties: in order that the acts of the legislative power and those
of the executive power may be each moment compared with the aim
of every political institution and thereby may be more respected; and
in order that the demands of the citizens, grounded henceforth upon
simple and incontestable principles, may always take the direction
of maintaining the constitution and the welfare of all.

In consequence, the National Assembly recognizes and declares,
in the presence and under the auspices of the Supreme Being, the
following rights of man and citizen.

1. Men are born and remain free and equal in rights. Social distinctions can be based only upon public utility.

2. The aim of every political association is the preservation of the
natural and imprescriptible rights of man. These rights are liberty,
property, security, and resistance to oppression.

3. The source of all sovereignty is essentially in the nation; no
body, no individual can exercise authority that does not proceed
from it in plain terms.

4. Liberty consists in the power to do anything that does not in-
jure others; accordingly, the exercise of the natural rights of each
man has for its only limits those that secure to the other members of

From *Readings in Western Civilization*, George H. Knoles and Rixford K.
Snyder, eds. (Philadelphia: Lippincott, 1960), Vol. II, pp. 528–529.

society the enjoyment of these same rights. These limits can be determined only by law.

5. The law has the right to forbid only such actions as are injurious to society. Nothing can be forbidden that is not interdicted by the law and no one can be constrained to do that which it does not order.

6. Law is the expression of the general will. All citizens have the right to take part personally or by their representatives in its formation. It must be the same for all, whether it protects or punishes. All citizens being equal in its eyes, are equally eligible to all public dignities, places, and employments, according to their capacities, and without other distinction than that of their virtues and their talents.

7. No man can be accused, arrested, or detained except in the cases determined by the law and according to the forms that it has prescribed. Those who procure, expedite, execute, or cause to be executed arbitrary orders ought to be punished: but every citizen summoned or seized in virtue of the law ought to render instant obedience; he makes himself guilty by resistance.

8. The law ought to establish only penalties that are strictly and obviously necessary and no one can be punished except in virtue of a law established and promulgated prior to the offense and legally applied.

9. Every man being presumed innocent until he has been pronounced guilty, if it is thought indispensable to arrest him, all severity that may not be necessary to secure his person ought to be strictly suppressed by law.

10. No one ought to be disturbed on account of his opinions, even religious, provided their manifestation does not derange the public order established by law.

11. The free communication of ideas and opinions is one of the most precious of the rights of man; every citizen then can freely speak, write, and print, subject to responsibility for the abuse of this freedom in the cases determined by law.

12. The guarantee of the rights of man and citizen requires a public force; this force then is instituted for the advantage of all and not for the personal benefit of those to whom it is entrusted.

13. For the maintenance of the public force and for the expenses of administration a general tax is indispensable; it ought to be equally apportioned among all the citizens according to their means.

14. All the citizens have the right to ascertain, by themselves or by their representatives, the necessity of the public tax, to consent

to it freely, to follow the employment of it, and to determine the quota, the assessment, the collection, and the duration of it.

15. Society has the right to call for an account from every public agent of its administration.

16. Any society in which the guarantee of the rights is not secured or the separation of powers not determined has no constitution at all.

17. Property being a sacred and inviolable right, no one can be deprived of it unless a legally established public necessity evidently demands it, under the condition of a just and prior indemnity.

In 1792 the French Revolution entered a new stage as power shifted from the moderates, who had written the Declaration of the Rights of Man and Citizen, to the radicals. One of the leaders of the radical phase was Maximilien Robespierre who drew up the following Declaration of Rights for the republican constitution. Though it also contains many Enlightenment thoughts, the tone is markedly different from the preceding documents. This declaration was not adopted, but Robespierre's proposal shows the passionate fervor of the radicals as they extended the zeal of revolutionary reform to social and economic realms.

Proposed Declaration of Rights

Maximilien Robespierre

The representatives of the French people, met in National Convention, recognizing that human laws which do not flow from the eternal laws of justice and reason are only the outrages of ignorance and despotism upon humanity; convinced that neglect and contempt of the natural rights of man are the sole causes of the crimes and misfortunes of the world; have resolved to set forth in a solemn declaration these sacred and inalienable rights, in order that all citizens, being enabled to compare constantly the acts of the government with the purpose of every social institution, may never permit themselves to be oppressed and disgraced by tyranny; and in order that the people may always have before their eyes the foundations of their liberty and their welfare; the magistrate, the rule of his duties; the legislator, the purpose of his mission.

In consequence, the National Convention proclaims in the face of the world and under the eyes of the Immortal Legislator the following declaration of the rights of man and citizen.

1. The purpose of every political association is the maintenance of the natural and imprescriptible rights of man and the development of all his faculties.

2. The principal rights of man are those of providing for the preservation of his existence and his liberty.

3. These rights belong equally to all men, whatever may be the difference of their physical and mental powers.

4. Equality of rights is established by nature: society, far from impairing it, exists only to guarantee it against the abuse of power which renders it illusory.

From *Readings in Western Civilization,* George H. Knoles and Rixford K. Snyder, eds. (Philadelphia: Lippincott, 1960), Vol. II, pp. 530–532.

5. Liberty is the power which belongs to man to exercise at his will all his faculties; it has justice for rule, the rights of others for limits, nature for principle, and the law for safeguard.

6. The right to assemble peaceably, the right to express one's opinions, either by means of the press or in any other manner, are such necessary consequences of the principle of the liberty of man, that the necessity to enunciate them supposes either the presence or the fresh recollection of despotism.

7. The law can forbid only that which is injurious to society; it can order only that which is useful.

8. Every law which violates the imprescriptible rights of man is essentially unjust and tyrannical; it is not a law.

9. Property is the right which each citizen has, to enjoy and dispose of the portion of goods which the law guarantees to him.

10. The right of property is restricted, as are all the others, by the obligation to respect the possessions of others.

11. It cannot prejudice the security, nor the liberty, nor the existence, nor the property of our fellow creatures.

12. All traffic which violates this principle is essentially illicit and immoral.

13. Society is under obligation to provide for the support of all its members either by procuring work for them or by assuring the means of existence to those who are not in condition to work.

14. The relief indispensable for those who lack the necessities of life is a debt of those who possess a superfluity; it belongs to the law to determine the manner in which this debt must be discharged.

15. The citizens whose incomes do not exceed what is necessary for their subsistence are exempted from contributing to the public expenses; the others shall support them progressively, according to the extent of their fortunes.

16. Society ought to favor with all its power the progress of public reason and to put instruction at the door of all the citizens.

17. Law is the free and solemn expression of the will of the people.

18. The people are the sovereign, the government is their creation, the public functionaries are their agents; the people can, when they please, change their government and recall their mandatories.

19. No portion of the people can exercise the power of the entire people; but the opinion which it expresses shall be respected as the opinion of a portion of the people who ought to participate in the formation of the general will. Each section of the assembled sovereign ought to enjoy the right to express its will with entire liberty; it is

essentially independent of all the constituted authorities and is capable of regulating its police and its deliberations.

20. The law ought to be equal for all.

21. All citizens are admissible to all public offices, without any other distinctions than those of their virtues and talents and without any other title than the confidence of the people.

22. All citizens have an equal right to participate in the selection of the mandatories of the people and in the formation of the law.

23. In order that these rights may not be illusory and the equality chimerical, society ought to give salaries to the public functionaries and to provide so that all the citizens who live by their labor can be present in the public assemblies to which the law calls them, without compromising their existence or that of their families.

24. Every citizen ought to obey religiously the magistrates and the agents of the government, when they are the organs or the executors of the law.

25. But every act against the liberty, security, or property of a man, committed by anyone whomsoever, even in the name of the law outside of the cases determined by it and the forms which it prescribes, is arbitrary and void; respect for the law even forbids submission to it; and if an attempt is made to execute it by violence, it is permissible to repel it by force.

26. The right to present petitions to the depositories of the public authority belongs to every person. Those to whom they are addressed ought to pass upon the points which are the object thereof; but they can never interdict, nor restrain, nor condemn their use.

27. Resistance to oppression is a consequence of the other rights of man and citizen.

28. There is oppression against the social body when one of its members is oppressed. There is oppression against each member of the social body when the social body shall be oppressed.

29. When the government violates the rights of the people, insurrection is for the people and for each portion of the people the most sacred of rights and the most indispensable of duties.

30. When the social guarantee is lacking to a citizen he re-enters into the natural right to defend all his rights himself.

31. In either case, to tie down to legal forms resistance to oppression is the last refinement of tyranny. In every free State the law ought especially to defend public and personal liberty against the abuse of the authority of those who govern: every institution which is not based upon the assumption that the people are good and the magistrate is corruptible is vicious.

32. The public offices cannot be considered as distinctions, nor as rewards, but only as duties.

33. The offences of the mandatories of the people ought to be severely and quickly punished. No one has the right to claim for himself more inviolability than other citizens. The people have the right to know all the transactions of their mandatories: these ought to render to them a faithful account of their own administration and to submit to their judgment with respect.

34. Men of all countries are brothers and the different peoples ought to aid one another, according to their power, as if citizens of the same State.

35. The one who oppresses a single nation declares himself the enemy of all.

36. Those who make war on a people in order to arrest the progress of liberty and to destroy the rights of man ought to be pursued by all, not as ordinary enemies, but as assassins and rebellious brigands.

37. Kings, aristocrats, and tyrants, whoever they may be, are slaves in rebellion against the sovereign of the earth, which is mankind, and against the legislator of the universe, which is nature.

One of the individuals who feared the excesses of radical change was Edmund Burke, one of the most articulate conservative spokesmen in modern European history. Though Burke was known as a champion of the Irish Catholics and American revolutionaries, he was not anxious to be identified as a radical. He felt he was emphasizing the "traditional rights of Englishmen," rather than proposing radical new courses of Parliamentary action when he urged more lenient policies toward the colonials. The French Revolution was a completely different situation, according to Burke. Before the French Revolution had entered its radical phase, he wrote a scathing indictment of it in "Reflections on the Revolution in France," published in 1790. Imagine the vehemence Burke would have shown if the book were written after the Reign of Terror! Just as John Locke's writings in 1690 heralded the dominant views of the eighteenth century, Burke's ideas as expressed in his 1790 work foreshadowed many elements of nineteenth century romantic nationalism.

Reflections on the Revolution in France

Edmund Burke

A state without the means of some change is without the means of its conservation. Without such means it might even risk the loss of that part of the constitution which it wished the most religiously to preserve. The two principles of conservation and correction operated strongly at the two critical periods of the Restoration and Revolution, when England found itself without a king. At both those periods the nation had lost the bond of union in their ancient edifice; they did not, however, dissolve the whole fabric. On the contrary, in both cases they regenerated the deficient part of the old constitution through the parts which were not impaired. They kept these old parts exactly as they were, that the part recovered might be suited to them. They acted by the ancient organized states in the shape of their old organization, and not by the organic *moleculae* of a disbanded people. . . .

You will observe, that from Magna Charta to the Declaration of Right, it has been the uniform policy of our constitution to claim and assert our liberties, as an *entailed inheritance* derived to us from our forefathers, and to be transmitted to our posterity; as an estate specially belonging to the people of this kingdom, without any reference whatever to any other more general or prior right. By this means our constitution preserves a unity in so great a diversity of its parts.

From *Reflections on the Revolution in France* by Edmund Burke (Chicago: Regnery, 1955), pp. 53–61.

We have an inheritable crown; an inheritable peerage; and a House of Commons and a people inheriting privileges, franchises, and liberties, from a long line of ancestors.

This policy appears to me to be the result of profound reflection; or rather the happy effect of following nature, which is wisdom without reflection, and above it. A spirit of innovation is generally the result of a selfish temper, and confined views. People will not look forward to posterity, who never look backward to their ancestors. Besides, the people of England well know, that the idea of inheritance furnishes a sure principle of conservation, and a sure principle of transmission; without at all excluding a principle of improvement. It leaves acquisition free; but it secures what it acquires. Whatever advantages are obtained by a state proceeding on these maxims, are locked fast as in a sort of family settlement; grasped as in a kind of mortmain for ever. By a constitutional policy, working after the pattern of nature, we receive, we hold, we transmit our government and our privileges, in the same manner in which we enjoy and transmit our property and our lives. The institutions of policy, the goods of fortune, the gifts of providence, are handed down to us, and from us, in the same course and order. Our political system is placed in a just correspondence and symmetry with the order of the world, and with the mode of existence decreed to a permanent body composed of transitory parts; wherein, by the disposition of a stupendous wisdom, moulding together the great mysterious incorporation of the human race, the whole, at one time, is never old, or middle-aged, or young, but, in a condition of unchangeable constancy, moves on through the varied tenor of perpetual decay, fall, renovation, and progression. Thus, by preserving the method of nature in the conduct of the state, in what we improve, we are never wholly new; in what we retain, we are never wholly obsolete. By adhering in this manner and on those principles to our forefathers, we are guided not by the superstition of antiquarians, but by the spirit of philosophic analogy. In this choice of inheritance we have given to our frame of polity the image of a relation in blood; binding up the constitution of our country with our dearest domestic ties; adopting our fundamental laws into the bosom of our family affections; keeping inseparable, and cherishing with the warmth of all their combined and mutually reflected charities, our state, our hearths, our sepulchres, and our altars.

Through the same plan of a conformity to nature in our artificial institutions, and by calling in the aid of her unerring and powerful instincts, to fortify the fallible and feeble contrivances of our reason, we have derived several other, and those no small benefits, from considering our liberties in the light of an inheritance. Always acting as if in the presence of cannonized forefathers, the spirit of freedom, leading in itself to misrule and excess, is tempered with an awful gravity. This idea of a liberal descent inspires us with a sense of habitual native dignity, which prevents that upstart insolence almost inevitably adhering to and disgracing those who are the first acquirers of any distinction. By this means our liberty becomes a noble freedom. It carries an imposing and majestic aspect. It has a pedigree and illustrating ancestors. It has its bearings and its ensigns armorial. It has its gallery of portraits; its monumental inscriptions; its records, evidences, and titles. We procure reverence to our civil institutions on the principle upon which nature teaches us to revere individual men; on account of their age, and on account of those from whom they are descended. All your sophisters cannot produce anything better adapted to preserve a rational and manly freedom than the course that we have pursued, who have chosen our nature rather than our speculations, our breasts rather than our inventions, for the great conservatories and magazines of our rights and privileges.

You might, if you pleased, have profited of our example, and have given to your recovered freedom a correspondent dignity. Your privileges, though discontinued, were not lost to memory. Your constitution, it is true, whilst you were out of possession, suffered waste and dilapidation; but you possessed in some parts the walls, and, in all, the foundations, of a noble and venerable castle. You might have repaired those walls; you might have built on those old foundations. Your constitution was suspended before it was perfected; but you had the elements of a constitution very nearly as good as could be wished. In your old states you possessed that variety of parts corresponding with the various descriptions of which your community was happily composed; you had all that combination, and all that opposition of interests, you had that action and counteraction, which, in the natural and in the political world, from the reciprocal struggle of discordant powers, draws out the harmony of the universe. These opposed and conflicting interests, which you considered as so great a blemish in your old and in our present constitution, interpose a salutary check to all precipitate resolutions. They render deliberation a matter not of choice, but of necessity; they make all change a subject of *compromise,* which naturally begets moderation; they produce *temperaments* preventing the sore evil of harsh, crude, unqualified reformations; and rendering all the headlong exertions of arbitrary power, in the few or in the many, for ever impracticable. Through that diversity of members and interests, general liberty had as many securities as there were separate views in the several orders; whilst by pressing down the whole by the weight of a real monarchy, the separate parts would have been prevented from warping, and starting from their allotted places.

You had all these advantages in your ancient states; but you chose to act as if you had never been moulded into civil society, and had everything to begin anew. You began ill, because you began by despising everything that belonged to you. . . .

Compute your gains: see what is got by those extravagant and presumptuous speculations which have taught your leaders to despise all their predecessors, and all their contemporaries, and even to despise themselves, until the moment in which they became truly despicable. By following those false lights, France has bought undisguised calamities at a higher price than any nation has purchased the most unequivocal blessings! France has bought poverty by crime! France has not sacrificed her virtue to her interest, but she has abandoned her interest, that she might prostitute her virtue. All other nations have begun the fabric of a new government, or the reformation of an old, by establishing originally, or by enforcing with greater exactness, some rites or other of religion. All other people have laid the foundations of civil freedom in severer manners, and a system of a more austere and masculine morality. France, when she let loose the reins of regal authority, doubled the licence of a ferocious dissoluteness in manners, and of an insolent irreligion in opinions and practices; and has extended through all ranks of life, as if she were communicating some privilege, or laying open some secluded benefit, all the unhappy corruptions that usually were the disease of wealth and power. This is one of the new principles of equality in France. . . .

This was unnatural. The rest is in order. They have found their punishment in their success. Laws overturned; tribunals subverted; industry without vigour; commerce expiring; the revenue unpaid, yet the people impoverished; a church pillaged, and a state not relieved; civil and military anarchy made the constitution of the kingdom; everything human and divine sacrificed to the idol of public credit, and national bankruptcy the consequence; and, to crown all, the paper securities of new, precarious, tottering power, the discredited paper securities of impoverished fraud and beggared rapine, held out as a currency for the support of an empire, in lieu of the two great recognised species that represent the lasting, conventional credit of mankind, which disappeared and hid themselves in the earth from whence they came, when the principle of property, whose creatures and representatives they are, was systematically subverted.

Were all these dreadful things necessary? Were they the inevitable results of the desperate struggle of determined patriots, compelled to wade through blood and tumult, to the quiet shore of a tranquil and prosperous liberty? No! nothing like it. The fresh ruins of France, which shock our feelings wherever we can turn our eyes, are not the devastation of civil war; they are the sad but instructive monuments of rash and ignorant counsel in time of profound peace.

John Ellison wrote this take-home essay, while a sophomore student at San Diego Mesa College, in response to the quotation below from Condorcet's "Sketch for a Historical Picture of the Progress of the Human Mind." The Enlightenment faith in progress and in the perfectibility of man was never more enthusiastically articulated than in Condorcet's celebrated work. The following essay questions the basis of this Enlightenment optimism as it cites some imperfections in France and America which Condorcet conveniently overlooked.

What's With Condorcet?

John Ellison

"Will not every nation one day arrive at the state of civilization attained by those people who are most enlightened, most free, most exempt from prejudices as the French, for instance, and the Anglo Americans?"

—CONDORCET

Condorcet's idealism was out of touch with the reality of France and the United States in the eighteenth century. He must have been looking at the two peoples with eyes squinted to have made such a blanket statement. Furthermore, that statement is no more accurate in relation to France or America in the nineteenth and twentieth centuries. For example, if one took his thought and viewed it in light of contemporary times, such a person might very well ask, "Is there anything more American than prejudice?" or, "Is there anything more French than unenlightenment?"

Of course, all countries share traits such as prejudice and unenlightenment. No country on the globe could rightfully stand back and be so smug and hypocritical as to attack the United States and France for being societies riddled with imperfection. In the United States, however, a negative trait such as prejudice is all the more obvious since there is more freedom of expression here than in a country like the U.S.S.R. (nonetheless recent reports which have leaked out of Russia do show a rather large degree of prejudice directed toward blacks and Jews living there).

In analyzing Condorcet's statement, I'll look separately at each of the three characteristics he so definitely ascribed to the people of the United States and France of his time: " . . . most enlightened, most free, most exempt from prejudices." My view will be attuned to the eighteenth and twentieth centuries.

From "What's With Condorcet?" by John Ellison. By permission of John Ellison.

It should be noted first that in both France and the United States of the eighteenth century only a small group of brilliant men could be called truly "men of the Enlightenment." They were doing most of the reading, important writing and leading in this period. Jefferson, Hamilton, and Washington of this country, and Voltaire, Montesquieu, and Rousseau of France are excellent examples of the small, educated group of enlightened men whose public voices were loud and who figured prominently either directly or indirectly in the affairs of their respective countries.

The Enlightenment is looked upon as a period when science became firmly established, when science was recognized as the only valid means of describing national phenomena. This was a time when man recognized a new mechanical vision of the universe through science. Taking a hint from what seemed to be its almost omnipotent nature, science was also used in an attempt to construct a new philosophy and society. But, again, one must remember the large majority of people in the United States, in France, and in the rest of "enlightened" Europe were uneducated or had only meager educational backgrounds. These people knew little, if anything, about science, the new philosophy, or the prominent political theories of the period.

The minority group of intellectuals and scientists did put forth many thought-provoking, important ideas. For instance, the Marquis de Condorcet in the eighteenth century stated population growth would eventually have to be checked by a system of birth control. Voltaire in his satires attacked such conditions as the inhumanity of man to his fellow man, the absurdity of war, and the hypocritical nature of organized religion. Thomas Jefferson, truly a man of the Enlightenment, stated, "That government is best which governs least." And, the Declaration of Independence in which Jefferson borrowed some of John Locke's ideas, is a masterful piece of writing slanted toward the cause of the eighteenth century American revolutionists. It contains many ideas which have supported twentieth century liberal and progressive advocates of social change and revolution.

In roughly the same historical period, the intellectuals of the Western countries, including the United States and France, put forth such questionable ideas as: the belief in the possibility of human perfectibility, a belief in the complete wisdom of nature, the idea of an almost limitless capability of human reason to acquire knowledge, and the belief that physical laws could be used to study and amend human relations to create valid moral principles. Yes, there was much new knowledge and important theory, but it is important to put Enlightenment thinking of Europe and America as a whole into proper perspective, for many of the basic tenets of this thinking would be denied today. All one has to do is look through a science book of the eighteenth century and compare it with the knowledge we possess today.

Getting specifically back to the United States and France, I now actually question the use of the term "enlightenment" at all, even in a comparative sense, when applied to an entire national group. "Enlightenment" would indicate to me to be (and I'll use this personal definition in my judgment) a mass ingestion of real knowledge in a country or in Western Civilization as a whole. It is certainly true that there was questioning of traditional doctrine and values, but a widespread absorption of new scientific knowledge did not occur anywhere, and, as has been stated, much of the knowledge and theory is invalid by today's standards.

I acknowledge that France and the United States were the most vigorous of eighteenth century countries in trying to apply and correlate the speculations or attitudes of Enlightenment thinking to their institutions, and indeed, to everyday life. They weren't "the most enlightened" per se.

How would we judge any two countries as the most enlightened of the twentieth century? If we continue to speak of enlightenment as the widespread attainment of real knowledge, not using it in any ethical or moral sense, we might now be able to apply the term "enlightened" and the adjective "most" to the United States. We have a vast educational system which allows a far larger number of people in this country than ever before to be called "educated." Science rules in twentieth century American society, and the whole of everyday life seems to be saturated with its presence. As a result, the uneducated man, the man not knowing what is going on in the scientific revolution around him, carries an unmistakable burden in coping with the new complexity of existence.

France probably compares quite well to the United States in its people's pursuit of knowledge. She also has a well-developed educational system and boasts of a knowing citizenry. Still, the whole question of the extent of a people's knowledge or enlightenment depends on the observer's personal point of view as to what constitutes real knowledge; the relativity of the situation can be seen with its warning lights of more philosophical openmindedness toward such questions.

I feel it is important to stress that it is more difficult to compare today the amount of so called knowledge which individual peoples possess; the level of education from country to country tends to be more equal since much knowledge is shared across national boundaries. I am not about to fall into the semantic trap of making "enlightenment" synonymous with "technological advancement" (an easy way for the United States to be "the most"). As with the eighteenth century, the term "enlightened" or "most enlightened" is a loaded term today. This is why the largest part of this essay concentrates on the first of the three of Condorcet's attributed national characteristics.

Should the Americans and French be characterized as the freest of peoples throughout their histories, ". . . the most free"? Eighteenth century America was the first large nation of the modern era to give its citizens a large share of freedom, but there are qualifications to this concept of freedom. For instance, in that century there still existed the requirement a person hold property to be able to vote; that only a citizen with a clump of land to call his own should have the privilege. And, of course, women did not get the vote until 1920. The far from free, non-citizen Negroes were, as everyone knows, far worse off. Besides being unable to vote, they were exempt from other rights of American citizens; this was much like the case of the early Greek "democracy" of Athens, but their slaves fared better.

The French citizens did get a measure of freedom through their Revolution, though, initially most of it was granted to the middle class. Later on, when feudalism was abolished by the National Assembly of 1789–1791, the peasants gained a larger share of freedom, but certainly not a great deal. Now, the freedom of the French citizenry compared more equally with that of the American.

I would say the *real* citizens of the two countries were the most free of those of any other large nation at that time. Here, I would reservedly agree with Condorcet's quote. But I cannot see how he could overlook or choose not to see the scores of non-citizens leading a second rate existence, especially the blacks in the United States when he spoke of freedom. How could he not consider the slaves? His was really a narrow view of freedom. Condorcet should have taken a slave count here in America. He might then have had reservations about his statement.

Twentieth century citizens of the two countries have suddenly found their individual freedoms dwindling through much stronger, very restrictive central governments purportedly operating under the authority (maybe I should say guise) of majority rule. The United States is one of the freest nations among a small group of Western Countries which would probably include France. Sad to say, Britain in many respects has more of a claim than the United States to being " . . . the most free." Also, Communists are able to operate in the political systems of many Western countries.

What about being " . . . most exempt from prejudices"? It is true that back in the 1700s our country had attempted to start with a denial that we would view any men as different from ourselves; as it turned out, this was only in principle. The Declaration of Independence said, " . . . all men are created equal . . . they are endowed by their Creator with certain unalienable rights; that among these are Life, Liberty, and the Pursuit of Happiness." Admirable ideas, but they were never fully put into effect in the eighteenth century and have not been done so today. Prejudice has always been too much an integral part of this country to allow all people to share a like amount of freedom.

Prejudicial thinking rationalized black slavery in the minds of many eighteenth century Americans. Even George Washington had slaves. I guess Condorcet allowed for this. Then there was (and is) the case of our atrocious treatment of the American Indian. Would Condorcet have made such a glowing report on the lack of American prejudice if he had spent a night under one of those smallpox-infected blankets Anglo-Americans gave the Indians?

The French showed class prejudice when the peasants were denied freedom for a length of time even after the revolutionary middle class had taken the rule from the crown; they didn't have Indians.

The contemporary United States has shown a more indirect form of black slavery which is probably no less degrading. Blacks being made to work for less than whites, job discrimination, and forced segregation are but a few manifestations of this prejudice.

Many people who have settled here retain their own ethnocentric ideas and are unwilling to accept other nationalities or races as equal to their own. Scores of Americans must believe blacks, or maybe Jews, are a real threat; why else would they hate them? This might appear to some to be too simplistic a conclusion; I believe it is a valid one.

France has had its share of anti-Semitism. One could surely say that the prejudicial feelings of the French run the racial spectrum, too.

It is a fact that prejudice is not as easily separated by geographical boundaries as some would like to think. I am not just speaking of racial and ethnic prejudice; almost everywhere one could expect to find social prejudice ("You surely can't marry a peasant!"), and religious prejudice ("You want to marry a Catholic?"), economic prejudice ("My daughter will never marry a pauper!"), and on, and on. No people really has a monopoly on prejudice. It is a widespread, common human phenomenon—a failing unmistakably human.

No people could ever be judged " . . . most exempt from prejudices" or, for that matter, most prejudiced. I could not believe this any-more than I could judge, for instance, that the Polish are most exempt from falling in love. All through the history of man, prejudicial thinking has been as common as measles and mumps in the population.

When he made his famous statement, Condorcet was obviously fired up by the Enlightenment spirit. He could in no way see the Americans and French of the twentieth century, and his view of the two peoples in the eighteenth was certainly myopic.

Questions

1 Under what conditions would you justify revolution?

2 Do you favor Burke's or Robespierre's views? Is there a middle ground?

3 Is it disturbing to think about the extent to which Jeffer-son borrowed from Locke and other Enlightenment theorists?

4 How relevant today are the Enlightenment documents included in this chapter?

5 Were the colonists treated more unjustly than some minorities in America in the late twentieth century?

6 Without the revolutionary documents, could there have been an American or a French Revolution? Can an idea change history?

7 Did the American South have reasons to rebel in 1861 against the tyranny of the North? Was Jefferson Davis as correct in his cause as Thomas Jefferson had been in his?

8 Why do the leaders of egalitarian movements usually come from affluent professional backgrounds?

3

Romanticism and Reality

Essay

Escape to the Other Side of Reality
Melvin Steinfield

Readings

Romantic Repercussions
William L. Langer

An Incurable Romantic Makes a Pathetic Confession
Jean Jacques Rousseau

Dissecting Romantic Melancholy
Irving Babbitt

Many factors contribute to the way people behave. One of the most significant of these is the "image" people have of appropriate behavior patterns. In turn, that image tends to reflect the prevailing spirit of the age. Rationalists of the Enlightenment period (such as Thomas Jefferson) deliberately sought to demonstrate their self-disciplined emotions, their control of the irrational, and their neoclassical restraint. As long as people believed in the essential logic of the well-ordered Newtonian universe, this image of rational moderation served as an effective guide for individual behavior. When that image changed with the advent of Romanticism, the behavior patterns also began to change.

Escape to the Other Side of Reality

Melvin Steinfield

Escapism is one of the oldest tricks of man's innate survival kit. When the world gets too complex to comprehend, when pressures grow too painful to put up with, and when the cold hard facts of everyday reality become intolerably repressive, man must somehow find escape routes to sanity. He must hide from harsh reality. Unable to face the outside world, men often seek refuge in the inside world of their own minds.

Thus men fabricate myths and launch flights of fantasy in desperate attempts to make the baffling exterior world less formidable. Like Wheaties for the athlete in the morning, or martinis for the executive at night, those imaginative contortions of reality give men the extra lift they think they need to face the rest of each day. Mythology is their crutch which makes life more bearable.

One of the most important functions of myth is to supply man with a purpose in life and an acceptance of his place in society. Armed with such a purpose, men will suffer stoically, resting content in the faith that there is a deeper meaning to their lives, that they are fulfilling their role in society, and that they are earning the esteem of their fellow man as well as the blessing of the higher powers. But stripped of purpose, men tend to wander aimlessly, bemoaning the lack of meaning to their existence.

Viewed from this perspective, it now appears that Western civilization's medieval man lived in the best of times, at least as far as the effectiveness of his myth-system is concerned. His life was fraught with purpose: he lived for the greater glory of God, the world was part of a static system, purpose was clearly explained to his satisfaction in the Scriptures and other sacred writings, he knew his place in the God-oriented scheme of the universe, *and* with passionate faith he accepted that place. He was able to purposefully shun "success" in this life while waiting patiently for his allotted span of thirty or forty years to pass. What he looked forward to was the reward of eternity.

The spiritually-oriented medieval world is a classic example of harsh conditions of existence bearing no significant correlation to the inner contentment of man. In sharp contrast to the effectiveness of the medieval mythology which endowed man with an ego-satisfying purpose in life, with a satisfactory position in society, and with a peaceful place in the universe, the nineteenth and twentieth centuries cannot claim a monolithic mythological grip. By the early nineteenth century there were multiple myth-systems competing with each other for acceptance by the majority of men. Just a casual glance at the spectrum of nineteenth century "isms" is enough to sense the proliferation. There was liberalism, nationalism, Marxism, socialism, conservatism, Romanticism, and many others.

Enlightenment mythology broke down the traditional tranquility of the medieval world, of the God-oriented scheme of the universe, and the "isms" of the nineteenth century suggest that it was necessary to respond to this dissolution. To a great extent the Romantic Period was a reaction against Enlightenment rationalism or, as some historians have put it, a protest against the Age of Reason. In contrast to the medieval world, where man believed in a one-to-one relationship with his God, and unlike the Renaissance which placed the highest value on the individual man and his accomplishments, the Age of Reason emphasized the mechanical aspects of a perfectly-functioning universe. Medieval mythology had placed the earth in the center of the universe, with the sun and other heavenly bodies revolving around it, and thus it was concluded that man held a lofty place in creation. But the objective scientific reasoning of the seventeenth and eighteenth centuries showed that the sun did not revolve around the earth, that all the planets (earth included) orbited in orderly succession around the sun; also, our solar system was but one such system in an entire galaxy, with an infinite number of galaxies beyond. In the scheme of this scientific reasoning, man could no longer claim to be the center of the universe; he was demoted to an infinitesimal cog in a vast impersonal system. Where could man find meaning, or the purpose of his existence, in such an impersonal world?

But there is another important element in Romanticism that perhaps has been overlooked. Among other things, the Romantic movement was a desperate effort to reassert the Renaissance meaning of individualism in an age of the emerging mass man. It was a reaction against the new industrial order that was threatening to destroy the purpose of individual lives. The factory system took the joy out of work. The machine took the poetry out of labor. What sense of pride could a creative individual take in a mass-production assembly line of precision specialization and standardized parts? What sort of identity could the individual retain in the world of the nineteenth century with its urban bustle and mechanized muscle? Having sacrificed beauty in order to gain efficiency, the new industrial order was crowding the older humanistic values of the Renaissance into a lonely corner. People were looking for some means of escape from this impersonal pressure; they sought a restoration of purpose, of meaning, and of the personal dimension in life. They found it in Romanticism.

Romanticism, with its emphasis on imagination, knew no limits to individual creativity. Romanticists soared to heights of ecstasy never before attained, but they also sank into the despair of melancholy. They reveled in the delightful folk tales of the common people in the countryside, and they scared the wits out of the most urbane with their grotesque horror stories. No matter which direction the Romanticist's pendulum was swinging, it was never toward the industrial society. It was away from the machines and toward favored places of refuge. "Back to nature" was Rousseau's cry, which was re-echoed in the pastoral serenity of Romantic artists and poets. Some sought refuge in a return to the past:

> Children of a highly refined intellectual age, suffering under the complexity of modern life, thrown into the maelstrom of dissolving empires and a dissolving pattern of society, the romanticists were yearning for the simplicity, spontaneity of experience, and innocence of man's lost childhood, for the great unity where man was still an integral part of an encompassing organism. All this the romanticists thought to find in the political, social, and religious order of the Middle Ages.[1]

Others found the greatest expression of their Romantic nature by turning to the fertile fields of their imaginations. There are many vivid examples of escapist flights into the realm of imagination. It was more than coincidence that *Frankenstein, The Pit and the Pendulum,* and *The Hunchback of Notre Dame* were all written during the Romantic period by Mary Shelley, E. A. Poe, and Victor Hugo. The well-known acting performances by Boris Karloff, Vincent Price, and Charles Laughton, respectively, were possible only because three Romantic writers produced those gothic, horror-filled works. They are typical samples of a new genre which emerged when the neo-classical restraints were thrust aside by the highly-imaginative Romantic writers. Less frightening, but still romantic, were such works as *The Legend of Sleepy Hollow* and *Ivanhoe.* Sometimes, to stimulate their imaginations to the farthest limits possible, and as Thomas DeQuincy wrote in *Confessions of an English Opium Eater,* Romantic writers tried to induce hallucinations and traumas through the use of opium and other drugs. Often their writings seemed to indicate that they had succeeded in creating those hallucinations.

Freed from the conventional confines of religious and background music, composers such as Chopin, Beethoven, and Wagner reflected the influence of Romanticism by experimenting with a variety of musical forms as well as by innovating new concepts in melody and harmony. Painters such as Delacroix and Constable exuded Romanticism with every stroke of the brush; they sought to convey the spirit and the variety of moods inherent in nature. Delacroix summed up the Romantic attitude when he stated a painting should be "a feast to the eye."

But it is probably with poetry that Romanticism reached its greatest expression of creativity; some of the sharpest images of Romanticism come from the poets. In "The Tables Turned" Wordsworth wrote:

> One impulse from a vernal wood,
> May teach you more of man,
> Of moral evil and of good,
> Than all the sages can.

Those lines stand in sharp contrast to the words penned by the Enlightenment poet, Alexander Pope:

> Nature and Nature's laws lay hid in night,
> God said, Let Newton be! and all was light.

What a difference in attitude between Wordsworth and Pope! Pope praised Newton for having revealed the natural laws of the universe. He held the typical Enlightenment attitude which valued the mathematical, structured framework of the universe in all its rational manifestations. Wordsworth, on the other hand, glorified the dimension of feeling, of emotion, of the irrational. For Wordsworth and the other Romanticists, formal learning and rational pursuits did not merit the same prestige as impulsive, personal passions. Therein lay the contrast between the two successive ages. The Enlightenment emphasized rational thought, balance, restraint, moderation, cosmopolitanism, and the image of the general. In many respects, it stressed the basic values of classical Greece. Romanticism valued just the opposite: feeling, spontaneity, subjectivity, and the image of the particular.

As a consequence of these contrasting views, the purpose of art differed in the two historical periods. The Enlightenment artist or writer tried to teach, spread knowledge, imitate the classics, and add to human progress. But the Romantic artist or writer was trying to achieve the highest form of self-fulfillment, namely creative expression via art. "Art for art's sake" was never more fully supported than in the philosophy of Romanticism. Wordsworth's emotional outbursts were not the only vibrations from the other side of reality. Shelly's poem, "Music, When Soft Voices Die," illustrates the heights of expression sought by Romanticists even in relation to the simplest of subjects:

> Music, when soft voices die,
> Vibrates in the memory—
> Odours, when sweet violets sicken,
> Live within the senses they quicken.
> Rose leaves, when the rose is dead,
> Are heap'd for the beloved's bed;
> And so thy thoughts, when thou art gone,
> Love itself shall slumber on.

The noises of the city were shut out; the music of the heavens chimed in their place. In poetry the Romanticists successfully escaped the harsh reality of everyday life. They, like the person "who kisses the joy" in William Blake's "Eternity," grabbed their pleasures where they could:

> He who bends to himself a joy
> Does the winged life destroy;
> But he who kisses the joy as it flies
> Lives in eternity's sunrise.

The nineteenth century Romanticists reacted to the cold, calculating mathematical systems of the Enlightenment by unleashing their fiery irrational passions. Emotional realms that were shunned with scorn in the eighteenth century were enshrined in the nineteenth. Jean Jacques Rousseau, a spiritual father of Romanticism, wrote in his *Confessions*: " . . . objects generally make less impression on me than does the memory of them. . . . " The Romanticist dwelled in the spheres of his imagination.

Sometimes, however, the Romanticist did not find the inner world of his mind a satisfactory escape; the feeling of community was absent. Alienation from society could not always be remedied by retreat into isolation and fantasyland. Sometimes, the only satisfactory escape was to join with those who shared a common cause, a common history, and common values. Romantic nationalism was born because the cosmopolitanism of the Enlightenment had failed to satisfy man's peculiar hangup of needing to belong to a special in-group. The concept of "humanity" espoused during the eighteenth century was so broad as to be unworkable and meaningless. In the days of Thomas Jefferson, "mankind" was a reasonable idea to work with. But with the advent of the Romantic attitudes, man's differences rather than his "equalities" were stressed. With each individual seeking to develop his particular feelings and emotions in a highly individualistic way, differences were highlighted and the doctrine of equality was dissipated.

Early stirrings of romantic nationalism could be sensed in the writings of Edmund Burke and Johann Gottfried von Herder, who tended to stress the uniqueness of each society. They regarded the history of a people as a special private possession of that people alone. They looked to the past, as the Romanticists often did, for the inherent greatness they expected to emerge. Each society for the nationalists, just as each individual for the Romanticists, was a worthy thing in and of itself. There were many nationalistic configurations, no one being better than any other.

If the symbol for the Enlightenment was the machine, the corresponding symbol for Romanticism was the plant. To Jefferson and other eighteenth century thinkers, all men and all societies were basically equal. What could justify a revolution in one society under certain circumstances could justify revolution in any other society under similar circumstances. Society was like a mechanized system. But to the Romantic nationalists, each society was like a unique and precious plant. One could not tamper with the organism by making wholesale substitution of its parts. What was suitable for one society as a result of its evolution might not be a healthy goal for another society. That, of course, is basically how Burke explained his opposition to the French Revolution. It is how Herder called for the Germans to try to develop their own latent uniqueness and free themselves from a slavish imitation of the French model.

The Romantic individual, seeking to escape from the impersonal world of the new industrial order, could find no comfort in the cosmopolitanism of the Enlightenment. But he could find considerable comfort in joining with those of his countrymen who shared a fervent passion for their native land with its unique cultural heritage. Nationalism was not solely the result of Romanticism, but Romanticism definitely contributed much to its development. It was another form of Romantic escapism, for the individual could find community in his identification with a national group.

Although people have always engaged in self-delusion of one kind or another, usually it has been on an individual basis rather than the entire society acting collectively. With the Romantic Period, something new was added: every man was encouraged *by the society itself* to be his own myth-maker. Individual imagination was unleashed *en masse,* and the irrational side of life was given official sanction. Why did this happen when it did? Perhaps because the Enlightenment dream of Utopia, based as it was on the myth of the perfectibility of society and the goodness of man was not realized as the eighteenth century drew to its revolutionary close. If there could not be a societal Utopia, at least each individual could hope to create his own glorious world from the workings of his own imagination.

Because we live in an "age of science" where the irrational is simply not respectable, we may be tempted to frown condescendingly at the escapist tendencies of the Romantic movement. As the inheritors of the great rational traditions of the Enlightenment Age, we summarily dismiss anything that even resembles the irrational. We do not live the way the nineteenth century Romanticists did. Or do we? How many of us stumble through life leaning heavily on the escapist crutches of our individual mythologies, desperately deluding ourselves that our lives do have real meaning after all, and that we are indeed experiencing high levels of individual self-fulfillment?

Note

1 Werner Friederich, *An Outline History of German Literature* (New York: Barnes & Noble, 1948), p. 116.

Was Romanticism a fleeting phase of Western civilization? Hardly.
The following concise statement of its influence takes us up to the
twentieth century. With its continuing application in art and literature,
as well as with its emphasis on individual expression and creativity,
Romanticism is still very much a part of our culture today.

Romantic Repercussions

William L. Langer

The general principles of Romanticism—the assertion of the autonomy of European culture, the stress on individual self-fulfillment and complete creative freedom, the escapism from the industrial and urban toward the exotic and rural—had implications beyond literature and art. The Romantics, in the early phases of their movement, supported liberal causes all over Europe and were in the forefront of revolutionary upheavals directed against the conservative establishment. Romanticism had profound repercussions in philosophy and historical writing, in religious thought, in social theory, and even in science.

Romanticism at its height influenced all the countries within the orbit of Western civilization, from Russia in the East to Latin America in the West. But it was peculiarly a movement of northern Europe. Its home was Germany and England, and its impact was most felt in Teutonic countries. This is not surprising, in view of the fact that classicism, against which the Romantics rebelled, had its roots in Latin culture. Romanticism had difficulty penetrating France, Italy, or Spain; it did so belatedly, and never with the same force as in the north.

Chronologically, the Romantic movement may be divided into three periods: proto-Romanticism of the eighteenth century; Romanticism proper (approximately 1790–1830), with a high point in the 1820s; and decline, which set in during the 1830s, when it weakened and began to lose ground to realism and materialism. . . .

Romanticism in the narrow sense of the word was a new literary and artistic style that rejected formalized classicism in favor of spontaneous forms and themes. But in a broader sense it was the beginning of a cultural revolution, the first assertion of an autonomous

Abridged from pp. 344 and 359 in *Western Civilization: The Struggle for Empire to Europe in The Modern World*, edited by William L. Langer. Text copyright © 1968 by William L. Langer, Paul MacKendrick, Deno J. Geanakoplos, J. H. Hexter, Richard Pipes. Reprinted by permission of Harper & Row, Publishers, Inc.

Western civilization. As the Renaissance had freed Western culture from its subservience to religion and facilitated the emergence of secularism, so Romanticism reduced the authority of classicism and inaugurated an era of artistic and literary freedom, which is the essence of modernity.

The full implications of this revolution were not then seen, because the Romantics still adhered to many classical values—more so than they realized, or than one could infer from their anti-classical zeal. But the principle of creativeness as an end in itself and subject only to its own criteria, once launched, has been subsequently pushed to ever greater extremes. Our own culture is a linear descendant of Romantic culture in the sense that it is uncompromisingly individualistic and rejects all restraints on creative freedom.

Romanticism enormously enriched Western art and thought, if only because it enlarged the variety of means available to creative talent. It permitted the use of a vocabulary and a meter, of color combinations, and of harmonies that the preceding age rejected as barbarous. It also opened up to serious inquiry subjects (e.g., folklore or the history of smaller nations) that had previously been deemed unworthy of attention.

But everything has its price. Until the advent of Romanticism, Western culture had rested on a consensus of values and tastes, whether Christian or classical. Romanticism began to destroy that consensus. By rejecting absolute criteria and making self-realization the aim as well as the standard of all creativity, it not only undermined the cultural unity of Western civilization, but contributed heavily to the eventual breakdown of understanding between the creator and his audience. The aesthetic theories of Romanticism, when revived on the eve of the twentieth century, caused a growing estrangement between art and literature on the one hand and the public on the other. For better or worse, twentieth-century modernism derives from the aesthetic of Romanticism pushed to its logical conclusion.

Rousseau's "Confessions" ranks with the most celebrated
autobiographical outpourings of Western man. Only St. Augustine's
"Confessions" and Goethe's "Poetry and Truth" are mentioned in the
same breath by those who revere such creations. In the following
selection, dealing with his childhood, we see the author reveal his most
intimate feelings about intimate subjects. In only a few pages Rousseau
gives us considerable insight into his Romantic nature.

An Incurable Romantic Makes a Pathetic Confession

Jean Jacques Rousseau

Since Mlle Lambercier treated us with a mother's love, she had
also a mother's authority, which she exercised sometimes by inflicting
on us such childish chastisements as we had earned. For a long while
she confined herself to threats, and the threat of a punishment entirely unknown to me frightened me sufficiently. But when in the
end I was beaten I found the experience less dreadful in fact than
in anticipation; and the very strange thing was that this punishment
increased my affection for the inflicter. It required all the strength
of my devotion and all my natural gentleness to prevent my deliberately earning another beating; I had discovered in the shame and
pain of the punishment an admixture of sensuality which had left
me rather eager than otherwise for a repetition by the same hand.
No doubt, there being some degree of precocious sexuality in all this,
the same punishment at the hands of her brother would not have
seemed pleasant at all. But he was of too kindly a disposition to be
likely to take over this duty; and so, if I refrained from earning a
fresh punishment, it was only out of fear of annoying Mlle Lambercier; so much am I swayed by kindness, even by kindness that is
based on sensuality, that it has always prevailed with me over sensuality itself.

The next occasion, which I postponed, although not through fear,
occurred through no fault of mine—that is to say I did not act deliberately. But I may say that I took advantage of it with an easy
conscience. This second occasion, however, was also the last. For
Mlle Lambercier had no doubt detected signs that this punishment
was not having the desired effect. She announced, therefore, that
she would abandon it, since she found it too exhausting. Hitherto

From *The Confessions* by Rousseau, translated by J. M. Cohen (London:
Penguin, 1954), pp. 25–30. Reprinted by permission.

we had always slept in her room, and sometimes, in winter, in her bed. Two days afterwards we were made to sleep in another room, and henceforward I had the honour, willingly though I would have dispensed with it, of being treated as a big boy.

Who could have supposed that this childish punishment, received at the age of eight at the hands of a woman of thirty, would determine my tastes and desires, my passions, my very self for the rest of my life, and that in a sense diametrically opposed to the one in which they should normally have developed. At the moment when my senses were aroused my desires took a false turn and, confining themselves to this early experience, never set about seeking a different one. With sensuality burning in my blood almost from my birth, I kept myself pure and unsullied up to an age when even the coldest and most backward natures have developed. Tormented for a long while by I knew not what, I feasted feverish eyes on lovely women, recalling them ceaselessly to my imagination, but only to make use of them in my own fashion as so many Mlle Lamberciers.

My morals might well have been impaired by these strange tastes, which persisted with a depraved and insane intensity. But in fact they kept me pure even after the age of puberty. If ever education was chaste and decent, mine was. My three aunts were not only women of remarkable virtue, but examples of a modesty that has long since disappeared from womankind. My father was a pleasure lover, but a gallant of the old school, and never made a remark in the hearing of those women he loved most that would have brought a blush to a virgin's cheek; and never was the respect due to children more scrupulously observed than in my family and in my case. I did not find the slightest difference in this respect at M. Lambercier's; a very good servant maid was dismissed for a dubious word pronounced in our hearing. Not only had I not till adolescence any clear ideas concerning sexual intercourse, but my muddled thoughts on the subject always assumed odious and disgusting shapes. I had a horror of prostitutes which has never left me, and I could not look on a debauchee without contempt and even fear. Such had been my horror of immorality, even since the day when, on my way to Petit Saconex along the sunken road, I saw the holes in the earth on either side where I was told such people performed their fornications. When I thought of this I was always reminded of the coupling of dogs, and my stomach turned over at the very thought.

These adolescent prejudices would themselves have been sufficient to retard the first explosions of an inflammable temperament. But they were reinforced, as I have said, by the effect upon me of the promptings of sensuality. Imagining no pleasures other than those I had known, I could not, for all the restless tinglings in my veins, direct my desires towards any other form of gratification. Always I stopped short of imagining those satisfactions which I had been taught to loathe, and which, little though I suspected it, were in fact not so far divorced from those I envisaged. In my crazy fantasies, my wild fits of eroticism, and in the strange behaviour which they sometimes drove me to, I always invoked, imaginatively, the aid of the opposite sex, without so much as dreaming that a woman could serve any other purpose than the one I lusted for.

Not only, therefore, did I, though ardent, lascivious, and precocious by nature, pass the age of puberty without desiring or knowing any other sensual pleasures than those which Mlle Lambercier had, in all innocence, acquainted me with; but when finally, in the course of years, I became a man I was preserved by that very perversity which might have been my undoing. My old childish tastes did not vanish, but became so intimately associated with those of maturity that I could never, when sensually aroused, keep the two apart. This peculiarity, together with my natural timidity, has always made me very backward with women, since I have never had the courage to be frank or the power to get what I wanted, it being impossible for the kind of pleasure I desired—to which the other kind is no more than a consummation—to be taken by him who wants it, or to be guessed at by the woman who could grant it. So I have spent my days in silent longing in the presence of those I most loved. I never dared to reveal my strange taste, but at least I got some pleasure from situations which pandered to the thought of it. To fall on my knees before a masterful mistress, to obey her commands, to have to beg for her forgiveness, have been to me the most delicate of pleasures; and the more my vivid imagination heated my blood the more like a spellbound lover I looked. As can be imagined, this way of making love does not lead to rapid progress, and is not very dangerous to the virtue of the desired object. Consequently I have possessed few women, but I have not failed to get a great deal of satisfaction in my own way, that is to say imaginatively. So it is that my sensibility, combined with my timidity and my romantic nature, have preserved the purity of my feelings and my morals, by the aid of those same tastes which might, with a little more boldness, have plunged me into the most brutal sensuality.

Now I have made the first and most painful step in the dark and miry maze of my confessions. It is the ridiculous and the shameful, not one's criminal actions, that it is hardest to confess. But henceforth I am certain of myself; after what I have just had the courage to say, nothing else will defeat me. How much it has cost me to make such revelations can be judged when I say that though sometimes labouring under passions that have robbed me of sight, of hearing, and of my senses, though sometimes trembling convulsively in my whole body in the presence of the woman I loved, I have never, during the whole course of my life, been able to force myself, even in moments of extreme intimacy, to confess my peculiarities and implore her to grant the one favour which was lacking. That confession I was only able to make once, when I was a child to a child of my own age, and then it was she who made the first overtures.

When I trace my nature back in this way to its earliest manifestations, I find features which may appear incompatible, but which have nevertheless combined to form a strong, simple, and uniform whole. I find other features, however, which, though similar in appearance, have formed by a concatenation of circumstances combinations so different that one could never suppose them to be in any way related to one another. Who would imagine, for instance, that I owe one of the most vigorous elements in my character to the same origins as the weakness and sensuality that flows in my veins? Before we leave the subject I have been dwelling on, I will show it under a very different light.

One day I was learning my lessons alone in the room next to the kitchen, where the servant had left Mlle Lambercier's combs to dry on the stove top. Now when she came to take them off, she discovered that the teeth of one were broken off, all down one side. Who was to be blamed for this? I was the only person who had been in the room; but I said I had not touched it. M. and Mlle Lambercier jointly lectured, pressed, and threatened me; but I stubbornly maintained my denial. Appearances were too strong for me, however, and all my protests were overruled, although this was the first time that I had been convicted of a downright lie. They took the matter seriously, as it deserved. The mischief, the untruth, and my persistent denials, all seemed to deserve a punishment; but this time it was not Mlle Lambercier who inflicted it. They wrote to my Uncle Bernard, and he came. My cousin was accused of another crime no less grave; we were awarded the same chastisement, which was a severe one. If they had intended to allay my depraved tastes for ever by using the evil as its own remedy, they could not have gone about it in a better way. For a long time my desires left me in peace.

They were unable to force from me the confession they required. Though the punishment was several times repeated and I was reduced to the most deplorable condition, I remained inflexible. I would have died rather than give in, and I was resolved to. So force had to yield before the diabolical obstinacy of a child. For that is what they called my persistence. But finally I emerged from that cruel ordeal shattered but triumphant.

It is now nearly fifty years since this occurrence, and I have no fear of a fresh punishment for the offense. But I declare before Heaven that I was not guilty. I had not broken, nor so much as touched, the comb. I had not gone near the stove, nor so much as thought of doing so. But do not ask me how the mischief occurred. I have no idea, and I cannot understand it. But I do most positively know that I was innocent.

Imagine a person timid and docile in ordinary life, but proud, fiery, and inflexible when roused, a child who has always been controlled by the voice of reason, always treated with kindness, fairness, and indulgence, a creature without a thought of injustice, now for the first time suffering a most grave one at the hands of the people he loves best and mostly deeply respects. Imagine the revolution in his ideas, the violent change of his feelings, the confusion in his heart and brain, in his small intellectual and moral being! I say, imagine all this if you can. For myself I do not feel capable of unravelling the strands or even remotely following all that happened at that time within me.

I had not yet sufficient reasoning power to realize the extent to which appearances were against me, to put myself in my elders' position. I clung to my own, and all I felt was the cruelty of an appalling punishment for a crime I had not committed. The physical pain was bad enough, but I hardly noticed it; what I felt was indignation, rage, and despair. My cousin was in a more or less similar case; he had been punished for what had only been a mistake but was taken for a premeditated crime, and he, following my example, got into a rage, and so to speak, worked himself up to the same pitch as myself. Lying together in the same bed, we embraced wildly, almost stifling one another; and when our young hearts were somewhat assuaged and we could give voice to our anger, we sat up and shouted a hundred times in unison at the tops of our voices: 'Carnifex!* carnifex! carnifex!'

I feel my pulse beat faster once more as I write. I shall always remember that time if I live to be a thousand. That first meeting with violence and injustice has remained so deeply engraved on my heart that any thought which recalls it summons back this first emotion. The feeling was only a personal one in its origins, but it has since

*Executioner.

assumed such a consistency and has become so divorced from personal interests that my blood boils at the sight or the tale of any injustice, whoever may be the sufferer and wherever it may have taken place, in just the same way as if I were myself its victim. When I read of the cruelties of a fierce tyrant, of the subtle machinations of a rascally priest, I would gladly go and stab the wretch myself, even if it were to cost me my life a hundred times over. I have often run till I dropped, flinging stones at some cock or cow or dog, or any animal that I saw tormenting another because it felt itself the stronger. This is perhaps an innate characteristic in me. Indeed I think it is. But the memory of the first injustice I suffered was so painful, so persistent, and so intricately bound up with it that, however strong my initial bent in that direction, this youthful experience must certainly have powerfully reinforced it.

There ended the serenity of my childish life. From that moment I never again enjoyed pure happiness, and even to-day I am conscious that memory of childhood's delights stops short at that point.

Though the following excerpt is from a book published in 1919,
the brilliant insights into Romanticism which it provides are still valid
today. Professor Babbitt spells out the connection between the Romantic
notion of happiness and its paradoxical opposite, Romantic melancholy.

Dissecting Romantic Melancholy

Irving Babbitt

Rousseau and his early followers—especially perhaps his early
French followers—were very much preoccupied with the problem
of happiness. Now in a sense all men—even those who renounce the
world and mortify the flesh—aim at happiness. The important point
to determine is what any particular person means by happiness and
how he hopes to attain it. It should be plain . . . that the Rousseauist
seeks happiness in the free play of the emotions. The "Influence of
the Passions on Happiness" is the significant title of one of Madame
de Staël's early treatises. The happiness that the Rousseauist seeks
involves not merely a free play of feeling but—what is even more
important—a free play of the imagination. Feeling acquires a sort
of infinitude as a result of this coöperation of the imagination, and
so the romanticist goes . . . in quest of the thrill superlative, as appears so clearly in his nympholepsy, his pursuit of the "impossible
she." But the more imaginative this quest for emotional happiness
grows the more it tends to become a mere nostalgia. Happiness is
achieved so far as it is achieved at all in dreamland. Rousseau says
of himself: *Mon plus constant bonheur fut en songe.** Every finite
satisfaction by the very fact that it is finite leaves him unsatisfied.
René says that he had exhausted solitude as he had exhausted society:
they had both failed to satisfy his insatiable desires. René plainly
takes his insatiableness to be the badge of his spiritual distinction. To
submit to any circumscribing of one's desires is to show that one has
no sense of infinitude and so to sink to the level of the philistine.

But does one become happy by being nostalgic and hyperaesthetic,
by burning with infiite indeterminate desire? We have here perhaps
the chief irony and contradiction in the whole movement. The Rousseauist seeks happiness and yet on his own showing, his mode of
seeking it results, not in happiness but in wretchedness. One finds
indeed figures in the nineteenth century, a Browning, for example,

*My most durable love was in a dream.—*Publisher's translation.*

who see in life first of all an emotional adventure and then carry this adventure through to the end with an apparently unflagging gusto. One may affirm nevertheless that a movement which began by asserting the goodness of man and the loveliness of nature ended by producing the greatest literature of despair the world has ever seen. No movement has perhaps been so prolific of melancholy as emotional romanticism. To follow it from Rousseau down to the present day is to run through the whole gamut of gloom.[1]

> Infections of unutterable sadness,
> Infections of incalculable madness,
> Infections of incurable despair.

According to a somewhat doubtful authority, Ninon de Lenclos, "the joy of the spirit measures its force." When the romanticist on the other hand discovers that his ideal of happiness works out into actual unhappiness he does not blame his ideal. He simply assumes that the world is unworthy of a being so exquisitely organized as himself, and so shrinks back from it and enfolds himself in his sorrow as he would in a mantle. Since the superlative bliss that he craves eludes him, he will at least be superlative in woe. So far from being a mark of failure this woe measures his spiritual grandeur. "A great soul," as René says, "must contain more grief than a small one." The romantic poets enter into a veritable competition with one another as to who shall be accounted the most forlorn. The victor in this competition is awarded the palm not merely for poetry but for wisdom. In the words of Arnold:

> Amongst us one
> Who most has suffered, takes dejectedly
> His seat upon the intellectual throne;
> And all his store of sad experience he
> Lays bare of wretched days.
> Tells us his misery's birth and growth and signs,
> And how the dying spark of hope was fed,
> And how the breast was soothed, and how the head,
> And all his hourly varied anodynes.
>
> This for our wisest! and we others pine,
> And wish the long unhappy dream would end,
> And waive all claim to bliss, and try to bear;
> With close-lipped patience for our only friend,
> Sad patience, too near neighbor to despair.

Though Arnold may in this poem, as some one has complained, reduce the muse to the rôle of hospital nurse, he is, like his master

Senancour, free from the taint of theatricality. He does not, as he said of Byron, make "a pageant of his bleeding heart"; and the Byronic pose has a close parallel in the pose of Chateaubriand. An Irish girl at London once told Chateaubriand that "he carried his heart in a sling." He himself said that he had a soul of the kind "the ancients called a sacred malady."

Chateaubriand, to be sure, had his cheerful moments and many of them. His sorrows he bestowed upon the public. Herein he was a true child of Jean-Jacques. We are told by eye-witnesses how heartily Rousseau enjoyed many aspects of his life at Motiers-Travers. On his own showing, he was plunged during this period in almost unalloyed misery. Froude writes of Carlyle: "It was his peculiarity that if matters were well with himself, it never occurred to him that they could be going ill with any one else; and, on the other hand, if he was uncomfortable, he required everybody to be uncomfortable along with him." We can follow clear down to Gissing the assumption in some form or other that "art must be the mouthpiece of misery." This whole question as to the proper function of art goes to the root of the debate between the classicist and the Rousseauist. "All these poets," Goethe complains to Eckermann of the romanticists of 1830, "write as though they were ill, and as though the whole world were a hospital. . . . Every one of them in writing tries to be more desolate than all the others. This is really an abuse of poetry which has been given to make man satisfied with the world and with his lot. But the present generation is afraid of all solid energy; its mind is at ease and sees poetry only in weakness. I have found a good expression to vex these gentlemen. I am going to call their poetry hospital poetry."[2]

Now Goethe is here, like Chateaubriand, mocking to some degree his own followers. When he suffered from a spiritual ailment of any kind he got rid of it by inoculating others with it; and it was in this way, as we learn from his Autobiography, that he got relief from the *Weltschmerz* of "Werther." But later in life Goethe was classical not merely in precept like Chateaubriand, but to some extent in practice. The best of the poetry of his maturity tends like that of the ancients to elevate and console.

The contrast between classic and romantic poetry in this matter of melancholy is closely bound up with the larger contrast between imitation and spontaneity. Homer is the greatest of poets, according to Aristotle, because he does not entertain us with his own person but is more than any other poet an imitator. The romantic poet writes, on the other hand, as Lamartine says he wrote, solely for the "relief of his heart." He pours forth himself—his most intimate and private self; above all, his anguish and his tears. In his relation to his reader, as Musset tells us in a celebrated image,[3] he is like the pelican who rends and lacerates his own flesh to provide nourishment for his young (*Pour toute nourriture il apporte son coeur**):

> Les plus désespérés sont les chants les plus beaux,
>
> Et j'en sais d'immortels qui sont de purs sanglots.†[4]

To make of poetry a spontaneous overflow of powerful emotion, usually of sorrowful emotion, is what the French understand by lyricism (*le lyrisme*); and it may be objected that it is not fair to compare an epic poet like Homer with a lyricist like Musset. Let us then take for our comparison the poet whom the ancients themselves looked upon as the supreme type of the lyricist—Pindar. He is superbly imaginative, "sailing," as Gray tells us, "with supreme dominion through the azure deep of air," but his imagination is not like that of Musset in the service of sensibility. He does not bestow his own emotions upon us but is rather in the Aristotelian sense an imitator. He is indeed at the very opposite pole from Rousseau and the "apostles of affliction." "Let a man," he says, "not darken delight in his life." "Disclose not to strangers our burden of care; this at least shall I advise thee. Therefore is it fitting to show openly to all the folk the fair and pleasant things allotted us; but if any baneful misfortune sent of heaven befalleth man, it is seemly to shroud this in darkness."[5] And one should also note Pindar's hostility towards that other great source of romantic lyricism—nostalgia ("The desire of the moth for the star"), and the closely allied pursuit of the strange and the exotic. He tells of the condign punishment visited by Apollo upon the girl Coronis who became enamoured of "a strange man from Arcadia," and adds: "She was in love with things remote—that passion which many ere now have felt. For among men, there is a foolish company of those who, putting shame on what they have at home, cast their glances afar, and pursue idle dreams in hopes that shall not be fulfilled."[6]

We are not to suppose that Pindar was that most tiresome and superficial of all types—the professional optimist who insists on inflicting his "gladness" upon us. "The immortals," he says, "apportion to man two sorrows for every boon they grant."[7] In general the Greek whom Kipling sings and whom we already find in Schiller—the Greek who is an incarnation of the "joy of life unquestioned, the everlasting

---

*For all the food has been in his heart.—*Publisher's translation.*

†The most desperate songs are most beautiful, and I know some immortal ones that are just pure cries.—*Publisher's translation.*

wondersong of youth"[8]—is a romantic myth. We read in the Iliad:[9] "Of all the creatures that breathe or crawl upon the earth, none is more wretched than man." Here is the "joy of life unquestioned" in Homer. Like Homer the best of the later Greeks and Romans face unflinchingly the facts of life and these facts do not encourage a thoughtless elation. Their melancholy is even more concerned with the lot of man in general than with their personal and private grief. The quality of this melancholy is rendered in Tennyson's line on Virgil, one of the finest in nineteenth-century English poetry:

Thou majestic in thy sadness at the doubtful doom
of human kind.[10]

One should indeed not fail to distinguish between the note of melancholy in a Homer or a Virgil and the melancholy of the ancients, whether Stoic or Epicurean, who had experienced the hopelessness and helplessness of a pure naturalism in dealing with ultimate problems. The melancholy of the Stoic is the melancholy of the man who associates with the natural order a "virtue" that the natural order does not give, and so is tempted to exclaim at last with Brutus, that he had thought virtue a thing and had found that it was only a word. The melancholy of the Epicurean is that of the man who has tasted the bitter sediment (*amari aliquid*) in the cup of pleasure. It is not difficult to discover modern equivalents of both Stoic and Epicurean melancholy. "One should seek," says Sainte-Beuve, "in the pleasures of René the secret of his *ennuis,*" and so far as this is true Chateaubriand is on much the same level as some Roman voluptuary who suffered from the *Taedium vitae* in the time of Tiberius or Nero.[11] But though the Roman decadent gave himself up to the pursuit of sensation and often of violent and abnormal sensation, he was less prone than a Chateaubriand to associate this pursuit with the "infinite"; and so he was less nostalgic and hyperaesthetic. His Epicureanism was therefore less poetical no doubt, but on the other hand he did not set up mere romantic restlessness as a sort of substitute for religion. It was probably easier therefore for him to feel the divine discontent and so turn to real religion than it would have been if he had, like the Rousseauist, complicated his Epicureanism with sham spirituality.

To say that the melancholy even of the decadent ancient is less nostalgic is perhaps only another way of saying what I have said about the melancholy of the ancients in general—that it is not so purely personal. It derives less from his very private and personal illusions and still less from his very private and personal disillusions. In its purely personal quality romantic melancholy is indeed inseparable from the whole conception of original genius. The genius sets out not merely to be unique but unique in feeling, and the sense of uniqueness in feeling speedily passes over into that of uniqueness in suffering—on the principle no doubt laid down by Horace Walpole that life, which is a comedy for those who think, is a tragedy for those who feel. To be a beautiful soul, to preserve one's native goodness of feeling among men who have been perverted by society, is to be the elect of nature and yet this election turns out as Rousseau tells us to be a "fatal gift of heaven." It is only the disillusioned romanticist, however, who assumes this elegiac tone. We need to consider what he means by happiness while he still seeks for it in the actual world and not in the *pays des chimères*. Rousseau tells us that he based the sense of his own worth on the fineness of his powers of perception. Why should nature have endowed him with such exquisite faculties[12] if he was not to have a satisfaction commensurate with them, if he was "to die without having lived"? We have here the psychological origins of the right to happiness that the romanticists were to proclaim. "We spend on the passions," says Joubert, "the stuff that has been given us for happiness." The Rousseauist hopes to find his happiness in the passions themselves. Romantic happiness does not involve any moral effort and has been defined in its extreme forms as a "monstrous dream of passive enjoyment." Flaubert has made a study of the right to happiness thus understood in his "Madame Bovary." Madame Bovary, who is very commonplace in other respects, feels exquisitely; and inasmuch as her husband had no such fineness the right to happiness meant for her, as it did for so many other "misunderstood" women, the right to extramarital adventure. One should note the germs of melancholy that lurk in the quest of the superlative moment even if the quest is relatively successful. Suppose Saint-Preux had succeeded in compressing into a single instant "the delights of a thousand centuries"; and so far as outer circumstances are concerned had had to pay no penalty. The nearer the approach to a superhuman intensity of feeling the greater is likely to be the ensuing languor. The ordinary round of life seems pale and insipid compared with the exquisite and fugitive moment. One seems to one's self to have drained the cup of life at a draught and save perhaps for impassioned recollection of the perfect moment to have no reason for continuing to live. One's heart is "empty and swollen"[13] and one is haunted by thoughts of suicide.

This sense of having exhausted life[14] and the accompanying temptation to suicide that are such striking features of the malady of the age are not necessarily associated with any outer enjoyment at all.

One may devour life in revery and then the melancholy arises from the disproportion between the dream and the fact. The revery that thus consumes life in advance is not necessarily erotic. . . .

The happiness of which Rousseau dreamed, it has been made plain, was not this active and ethical happiness, but rather the passive enjoyment of the beautiful moment—the moment that he would like to have last forever. After seeking for the beautiful moment in the intoxication of love, he turned as we have seen to pantheistic revery. "As long as it lasts," he says of a moment of this kind, "one is self-sufficing like God." Yes, but it does not last, and when he wakes from his dream of communion with nature, he is still solitary, still the prisoner of his ego. The pantheistic dreamer is passive in every sense. He is not working either according to the human or according to the natural law, and so is not gaining either in material or in ethical efficiency. In a world such as that in which we live this seems too much like picnicking on a battlefield. Rousseau could on occasion speak shrewdly on this point. He wrote to a youthful enthusiast who wished to come and live with him at Montmorency: "The first bit of advice I should like to give you is not to indulge in the taste you say you have for the contemplative life and which is only an indolence of the spirit reprehensible at every age and especially at yours. Man is not made to meditate but to act."

The contemplative life is then, according to Rousseau, the opposite of action. But to contemplate is according to an Aristotle or a Buddha to engage in the most important form of action, the form that leads to happiness. To identify leisure and the contemplative life with pantheistic revery, as Rousseau does, is to fall into one of the most vicious of confusions. Perhaps indeed the most important contrast one can reach in a subject of this kind is that between a wise strenuousness and a more or less wise passiveness, between the spiritual athlete and the cosmic loafer, between a Saint Paul, let us say, and a Walt Whitman.

The spiritual idling and drifting of the Rousseauist would be less sinister if it did not coexist in the world of to-day with an intense material activity. The man who seeks happiness by work according to the natural law is to be rated higher than the man who seeks happiness in some form of emotional intoxication (including pantheistic revery). He is not left unarmed, a helpless dreamer in the battle of life. The type of efficiency he is acquiring also helps him to keep at bay man's great enemy, ennui. An Edison, we may suppose, who is drawn ever onward by the lure of wonder and curiosity and power, has little time to be bored. It is surely better to escape from the boredom of life after the fashion of Edison than after the fashion of Baudelaire.[15]

I have already pointed out, however, the peril in a one-sided working of this kind. It makes man efficient without making him ethical. It stimulates rather than corrects a fearless, formless expansion on the human level. This inordinate reaching out beyond bounds is, as the great Greek poets saw with such clearness, an invitation to Nemesis. The misery that results from unrestraint, from failure to work according to the human law, is something different from mere pain and far more to be dreaded; just as the happiness that results from a right working according to the human law is something different from mere pleasure and far more worthy of pursuit.

The present alliance between emotional romanticists and utilitarians[16] is a veritable menace to civilization itself. It does not follow . . . because revery or "intuition of the creative flux" cannot take the place of leisure or meditation, that one must therefore condemn it utterly. It may like other forms of romanticism have a place on the recreative side of life. What finally counts is work according to either the human or the natural law, but man cannot always be working. He needs moments of relief from tension and concentration and even, it should seem, of semi-oblivion of his conscious self. As one of the ways of winning such moments of relaxation and partial forgetfulness much may be said for revery. In general one must grant the solace and rich source of poetry that is found in communion with nature even though the final emphasis be put on communion with man. It is no small thing to be, as Arnold says Wordsworth was, a "priest of the wonder and bloom of the world." One cannot however grant the Wordsworthian that to be a priest of wonder is necessarily to be also a priest of wisdom. Thus to promote to the supreme and central place something that is legitimate in its own degree, but secondary, is to risk starting a sham religion.

Those who have sought to set up a cult of love or beauty or science or humanity or country are open to the same objections as the votaries of nature. However important each of these things may be in its own place, it cannot properly be put in the supreme and central place for the simple reason that it does not involve any adequate conversion or discipline of man's ordinary self to some ethical centre. I have tried to show that the sense of solitude or forlornness that is so striking a feature of romantic melancholy arises not only from a loss of hold on the traditional centres, but also from the failure of these new attempts at communion to keep their promises. The number of discomfitures of this kind in the period that has elapsed since the late eighteenth century suggests that this period was even more than most periods an age of sophistry. Every age has had its false teachers, but possibly no age ever had so many dubious moralists as this, an incomparable series of false prophets from Rousseau himself down to Nietzsche and Tolstoy.

Notes

1 In his *Mal romantique* (1908) E. Seillière labels the generations that have elapsed since the rise of Rousseauism as follows:
  1. Sensibility (*Nouvelle Héloïse*, 1761).
  2. Weltschmerz (Schiller's *Aesthetic Letters*, 1795).
  3. Mal du siècle (Hugo's *Hernani*, 1830).
  4. Pessimism (vogue of Schopenhauer and Stendal, 1865).
  5. Neurasthenia (culmination of *fin de siècle* movement, 1900).

2 *Eckermann,* September 24, 1827.

3 See *La Nuit de Mai.*

4 These lines are inscribed on the statue of Musset in front of the Théâtre Français. Cf. Shelley:
> Our sweetest songs are those that tell of
> saddest thoughts.

5 Translation by J. E. Sandys of fragment cited in Stobaeus, *Flor.* CIX, I.

6 *Pythian Odes,* III, 20 ff.

7 *Pythian Odes,* III, 81–82.

8 *Song of the Banjo,* in the *Seven Seas.*

9 *XVII,* 446–47.

10 A brief survey of melancholy among the Greeks will be found in Professor S. H. Butcher's *Some Aspects of the Greek Genius.*

11 The exasperated quest of novelty is one of the main traits both of the ancient and the modern victim of ennui. See Seneca, *De Tranquillitate animi*: "Fastidio illis esse coepit vita, et ipse mundus; et subit illud rabidorum deliciarum: quousque eadem?" (Cf. La Fontaine: Il me faut du noveau, n'en fût-il plus au monde.)

12 "A quoi bon m'avoir fait naître avec des facultés exquises pour les laisser jusqu'a la fin sans emploi? Le sentiment de mon prix interne en me donnant celui de cette injustice m'en dédommageait en quelque sorte, et me faisait verser des larmes que j'aimais a laisser couler." *Confessions,* Livre IX (1756).

13 *Nouvelle Héloïse,* Pt. VI, Lettre VIII.

14 "Encore enfant par la tête, vous êtes déjà vieux par le coeur." *Ibid.*

15 I scarcely need say that I am speaking of the man of science only in so far as he is purely naturalistic in his point of view. There may enter into the total personality of Edison or any particular man of science other and very different elements.

16 M. René Berthelot has written a book on pragmatism and similar tendencies in contemporary philosophy entitled *Un Romantisme Utilitaire*. I have not read it but the title alone is worth more than most books on the subject I have read.

Questions

1 Were Romanticists the only modern Europeans who relied on escapist crutches?

2 "Romantic protests were just early stirrings of protest against middle-class conformity and mass culture." What is your reaction to this statement?

3 What threats to individual personality-integrity are faced by today's youth? Any resemblance to Romantic times?

4 Is there any significant connection between Romanticism and the hippie movement?

5 Drugs were employed by some Romanticists to induce creativity in their art. Do you think that these experiences added to the creativity of the Romantic artists? Are drugs the ultimate escapist crutch?

6 Are Americans still hung up on eighteenth century cosmopolitonism when they try to export their brand of "truth" and "democracy" to emerging nations without regard for the particular needs of the area?

4

The Alienation
of Many Worlds

The average man doesn't understand his own complex culture very well, and he certainly doesn't understand others. One reason is his lack of perspective and the blinding distortions and oversimplifications of propaganda. An acute case is the lack of understanding between the Communist and Capitalist worlds. The two worlds are not only alienated from one another, they are alienated within. Inhabitants of a planet near the center of the Milky Way are reading the report of a correspondent sent to get an objective view of the conflicts.

Marx Lies Alienated in His London Grave

Frederick Gentles

Planet Earth far out in the Milky Way Galaxy is in deep trouble. To this neutral observer from inner space, something appears to be radically wrong with the Earthlings. They have divided their planet into two main and bitterly contentious groups, each of which is absolutely certain that life should be lived in a certain way. They threaten one another with nasty name-calling, huge military machines, and the planet's biggest bombs. A third force has developed, but it is fragmented and at present cannot compete seriously with the two major powers.

It seems that some of the present trouble began about one hundred years ago when a man named Karl Marx boldly set forth the ideas that workers should be entitled to the full share of the products of their labor, that they should not be tied to a monotonous, degrading job running a machine, and that they should unite to overthrow their enemy, the Capitalists, who were responsible for alienating one man from another with their profit system, their specialized technology, and their class structure that divided men into rich and poor.

The planet had always had upper and lower classes, according to the followers of Marx, and they had always been contending. Typically, however, a small upper class had dominated the masses in what was termed the dialectic (dialogue or argument) of history. There was the thesis or right way of doing things according to rules set up by an establishment class, and an antithesis or another way of doing things sponsored by an alienated antiestablishment class. The oppressors of the thesis or establishment class had been variously called patricians, lords, guildmasters, and bourgeois middle-class men with money. The alienated majority had been called plebeians, serfs, apprentices, and workers of the world. According to Marx, the clash between thesis and antithesis typically resulted in a new and superior culture or synthesis.

The last synthesis Marx envisioned was to result from a clash be-tween the new middle-class, business-oriented community which dominated society and the proletariat or working class. The "good guys," the proletariat, would triumph, of course, and everything would be full of promise. Man would no longer be enslaved by class, machine, or private capital with its lust for profits. In Marx's vision, man could develop himself to his fullest extent and would not be dehumanized by alienating agents. Man, by being one with fellow man and no longer at odds with others, achieves maturity; in turn, the creative and mature life results in freedom.

The Capitalists, however, contend that this maturity is impossible. It is Utopian, they say, and contrary to the nature of the men in-habiting this particular planet. The Capitalists had built a great society based on alienation, free enterprise, and unlimited competi-tion. Theirs was a vigorous culture which resulted in great fortunes for a few at the expense of great poverty for many. Largely because of protest marches and violence by the workers and demands for economic and social justice by farming communities, however, demo-cratic-type governments were prevailed upon to regulate the appetites of the businessmen so that more people had a share in the products of society. They built a great egalitarian society for the majority by curtailing the rugged individualism of a few. But alienated minorities still remained.

The Communist society (actually, it was based neither on true Communism nor on Marxist socialism, despite its claims) developed in the eastern part of the planet and the Capitalistic society in the western portion. Neutral citizens were alienated in both camps. In the Communist world a neutral was called a dirty reactionary, while in the Capitalist world a neutral might be called a Socialist, pinko, or a com-symp (for communist-sympathizer). Both societies placed great emphasis on conformity: the Capitalists, who embraced Chris-tianity, proclaimed the universal brotherhood of man; and the Com-munists, who considered the state a great evil because it—as well as Capitalism—divided and alienated men from one another, advo-cated the universal union of working men. Despite their ideals of brotherhood, both West and East were dearly devoted to their flags and to the separate plots of ground which each inhabited on the planet. At times, the state seemed to be more important than the economic and social theories each promulgated.

They say in the West that God is dead. He isn't, of course; he has just changed for many people. They also say in the West that Marx is dead. Actually, he started to die long before he was placed in his grave. Marx once stated, "One thing I know, I am not a Marxist." Presumably he said this because so many people were interpreting his ideas in ways he hadn't intended. It is also possible that he was thinking quite differently at age sixty-five than he was at age twenty-five.

Marx must lie alienated in his grave at Highgate Cemetery in London if he knows what has been done with his major ideas. He said that specialists were alienated from society because they were educated to experience only a part of life, yet the Communist nations have gone in for specialization as much as their adversaries. Indeed, the higher education in Communist nations consists almost entirely of a specialist nature in the fields of engineering, science, technology, and other practical studies. As far as Marx was concerned, these specialists were the real drop-outs from society because only part of the man was educated to understand the world in which he lived. They alienated themselves from the world of reality.

The highly organized party system and the penetrating police state, both admitted to respectability in the Communist world in the twentieth century, must be at great variance with the sacred words of the Master of communism who advocated freeing man from his many bonds. Communism has come to have more of a political definition than the economic one Marx espoused, and it is quite rigid in restricting freedom of expression, of the press, and of new ideas. But Communism is not monolithic, as Mr. William F. Buckley, Jr. emphasizes in an article toward the end of this chapter. It had become so diverse that in 1968 right-wing Capitalists were rooting for a small Communist state (Czechoslovakia) that had been invaded by one of the two monster Communist states (the Soviet Union and China), who were, in turn, at bitter odds with each other—alienated.

In publicity for its fiftieth anniversary in 1967, one Communist country admitted that there were three classes in its society: "The Soviet society consists of two friendly classes. There are the working class and the collective farm peasantry. Somewhere between them there are the intellectuals who form a social stratum." The publicity did not admit of a fourth class in this so-called classless society, where, as a visitor readily observes, there is alienation between the classes. A new middle class has arisen consisting of bureaucrats, scientists, and management officials seeking a comfortable life filled with gadgets but also with a fear of those who rock the boat and threaten their conservative desire for stability.

Because the Soviet Communists now have many things to conserve and because of their desire for stability, there has been some emphasis on peaceful coexistence with the Capitalist world and even on a peaceful transformation of Capitalism into Communism as an evolutionary, not a revolutionary, goal. Calls to violent revolution have been reduced, at least in several nations in the Eastern part of the world. Therefore, much of the old Marxism is dead.

The radical Marx recognized the inevitability of change, but possibly he did not foresee the inevitability that radical ideas are bound to lose momentum, to be modified by changing conditions, to be mellowed by aging radicals and newer generations, and to soften with the conservatism that almost always accompanies success. Economic and political success has reduced the belligerency, and, hence, the alienation, of the more successful Communist nations. This may suggest that the West can subvert Communism by helping to make it successful. It is the poor and downtrodden of this world, individuals as well as nations, who are especially alienated and, therefore potentially dangerous to others.

Meanwhile, on the other side of the planet, Communism continues to engender fear in some parts. Some Western elitists fear that Communism will make everyone equal, even though Marx never advocated equality very strongly. His friend and colleague, Engels, said it would be ridiculous to think of everyone being equal: "The only equality of the proletariat is the elimination of classes. Any demand for equality that goes beyond that, of necessity passes into absurdity." Thus, "From each according to his ability" has meant inequality in the Communist world with differences in wages and salaries according to the contribution by members of society. "To each according to his needs" has been partly realized so that great pockets of poverty have been eliminated in many Communist countries.

As Capitalism has shown signs of subverting Communism, so Socialism has subverted the old Capitalism. Capitalist countries have implemented various socialistic security measures to reduce the level of alienation, and at least one of them has a guaranteed annual income planned for all families. The creeping socialism which many Capitalists feared arrived full-blown with conservative administrations, and the mixed economy of Capitalism-Socialism has resulted in the most upholstered civilization in the planet's short history.

In some respects both adversaries are fighting windmills, though they don't realize it. There is some Socialism in the Capitalist countries, and there is some Capitalism in Socialist countries. It would be an oversimplification, however, to state that there are no fundamental differences between the two systems. It is not the purpose of this report to go into these differences, but one must suggest that they do not seem great enough to justify war. Both sides seem to have resisted extremist, paranoiac, and super-patriotic elements which oppose participating in cultural exchanges, meeting across conference tables, engaging in trade, and in general creating a basis for harmony and mutual understanding. The Old Marxism and the Old Capitalism are both dead, though some Old and True Believers refuse to recognize the fact. To their dying day they will continue to fear and to hate the opposing dogma, not realizing that much of what they hate has long been dead.

The Communist Manifesto and the Declaration of Independence,
two of the great documents of Western Civilization, are alike in many ways.
Both have a preamble announcing boldly the openness of the documents,
both list their grievances against a common enemy, both express a
desire to free man from his bonds, and both are revolutionary documents
today. Would you also say that both are Utopian and that their objectives
are not likely to be realized in the twentieth century?

Manifesto of the Communist Party

Karl Marx and Friedrich Engles

A specter is haunting Europe—the specter of Communism. All
the powers of Old Europe have entered into a holy alliance to exorcise this specter; Pope and Czar, Metternich and Guizot, French
Radicals and German police-spies.

Where is the party in opposition that has not been decried as
communistic by its opponents in power? Where the opposition that
has not hurled back the branding reproach of Communism, against
the more advanced opposition parties, as well as against its reactionary adversaries?

Two things result from this fact.

I. Communism is already acknowledged by all European powers
to be in itself a power.

II. It is high time that Communists should openly, in the face of
the whole world, publish their views, their aims, their tendencies,
and meet this nursery tale of the specter of Communism with a Manifesto of the party itself.

To this end Communists of various nationalities have assembled
in London, and sketched the following Manifesto to be published in
the English, French, German, Italian, Flemish and Danish languages.

Bourgeois and Proletarians

The history of all hitherto existing society is the history of class
struggles.

Freeman and slave, patrician and plebeian, lord and serf, guild-
master and journeyman, in a word, oppressor and oppressed, stood in
constant opposition to one another, carried on an uninterrupted, now

From *The USSR and Communism* by Alfred Rieber and Robert Nelson
(Glenview, Ill.: Scott, Foresman, 1964), pp. 318–320.

hidden, now open fight, that each time ended, either in a revolutionary reconstitution of society at large, or in the common ruin of the contending classes.

In the earlier epochs of history we find almost everywhere a complicated arrangement of society into various orders, a manifold gradation of social rank. In ancient Rome we have patricians, knights, plebeians, slaves; in the middle ages, feudal lords, vassals, guildmasters, journeymen, apprentices, serfs; in almost all of these classes, again, subordinate gradations.

The modern bourgeois society that has sprouted from the ruins of feudal society, has not done away with class antagonisms. It has but established new classes, new conditions of oppression, new forms of struggle in place of the old ones.

Our epoch, the epoch of the bourgeoisie, possesses, however, this distinctive feature; it has simplified the class antagonisms. Society as a whole is more and more splitting up into two great hostile camps, into two great classes directly facing each other: Bourgeoisie and Proletariat.

From the serfs of the middle ages sprang the chartered burghers of the earliest towns. From these burgesses the first elements of the bourgeoisie were developed.

The discovery of America, the rounding of the Cape, opened up fresh ground for the rising bourgeoisie. The East-Indian and Chinese markets, the colonization of America, trade with the colonies, the increase in the means of exchange and in commodities generally, gave to commerce, to navigation, to industry, an impulse never before known, and thereby, to the revolutionary element in the tottering feudal society, a rapid development.

The feudal system of industry, under which industrial production was monopolized by closed guilds, now no longer sufficed for the growing wants of the new market. The manufacturing system took its place. The guild-masters were pushed on one side by the manufacturing middle class; division of labor between the different corporate guilds vanished in the face of division of labor in each single workshop.

Meantime the markets kept ever growing, the demand ever rising. Even manufacture no longer sufficed. Thereupon steam and machinery revolutionized industrial production. The place of manufacture was taken by the giant, Modern Industry, the place of the industrial middle class, by industrial millionaires, the leaders of whole industrial armies, the modern bourgeois.

Modern Industry has established the world's market, for which the discovery of America paved the way. This market has given an immense development to commerce, to navigation, to communication by land. This development has, in its turn, reacted on the extension of industry; and in proportion as industry, commerce, navigation, railways extended, in the same proportion, the bourgeoisie developed, increased its capital, and pushed into the background every class handed down from the Middle Ages.

We see, therefore, how the modern bourgeoisie is itself the product of a long course of development, of a series of revolutions in the modes of production and of exchange.

Each step in the development of the bourgeoisie was accompanied by a corresponding political advance of that class. An oppressed class under the sway of the feudal nobility, an armed and self-governing association in the mediaeval commune, here independent urban republic (as in Italy and Germany), there taxable "third estate" of the monarchy (as in France), afterwards, in the period of manufacture proper, serving either the semi-feudal or the absolute monarchy as a counterpoise against the nobility, and, in fact, corner-stone of the great monarchies in general, the bourgeoisie has at last, since the establishment of Modern Industry and of the world's market, conquered for itself, in the modern representative State, exclusive political sway. The executive of the modern State is but a committee for managing the common affairs of the whole bourgeoisie.

The bourgeoisie, historically, has played a most revolutionary part.

The bourgeoisie, wherever it has got the upper hand, has put an end to all feudal, patriarchal, idyllic relations. It has pitilessly torn asunder the motley feudal ties that bound man to his "natural superiors," and has left remaining no other nexus between man and man than naked self-interest, than callous "cash payment." It has drowned the most heavenly ecstasies of religious fervor, of chivalrous enthusiasm, of Philistine sentimentalism, in the icy water of egotistical calculation. It has resolved personal worth into exchange value, and in place of the numberless indefeasible chartered freedoms, has set up that single, unconscionable freedom—Free Trade. In one word, for exploitation, veiled by religious and political illusions, it has substituted naked, shameless, direct, brutal exploitation.

The bourgeoisie has stripped of its halo every occupation hitherto honored and looked up to with reverent awe. It has converted the physician, the lawyer, the priest, the poet, the man of science, into its paid wage-laborers.

The bourgeoisie has torn away from the family its sentimental veil, and has reduced the family relation to a mere money relation.

The bourgeoisie has disclosed how it came to pass that the brutal display of vigor in the Middle Ages, which reactionists so much admire, found its fitting complement in the most slothful indolence. It has been the first to show what man's activity can bring about. It has accomplished wonders far surpassing Egyptian pyramids, Roman aqueducts, and Gothic cathedrals; it has conducted expeditions that put in the shade all former Exoduses of nations and crusades.

The bourgeoisie cannot exist without constantly revolutionizing the instruments of production, and thereby the relations of production, and with them the whole relations of society. Conservation of the old modes of production in unaltered form, was, on the contrary, the first condition of existence for all earlier industrial classes. Constant revolutionizing of production, uninterrupted disturbance of all social conditions, everlasting uncertainty and agitation, distinguish the bourgeois epoch from all earlier ones. All fixed, fast-frozen relations, with their train of ancient and venerable prejudices and opinions, are swept away; all new-formed ones become antiquated before they can ossify. All that is solid melts into air, all that is holy is profaned, and man is at last compelled to face with sober senses his real conditions of life, and his relations with his kind.

The need of a constantly expanding market for its products chases the bourgeoisie over the whole surface of the globe. It must nestle everywhere, settle everywhere, establish connections everywhere.

The bourgeoisie has through its exploitation of the world's market given a cosmopolitan character to production and consumption in every country. To the great chagrin of reactionists, it has drawn from under the feet of industry the national ground on which it stood. All old established national industries have been destroyed or are daily being destroyed. They are dislodged by new industries, whose introduction becomes a life and death question for all civilized nations, by industries that no longer work up indigenous raw material, but raw material drawn from the remotest zones, industries whose products are consumed, not only at home, but in every quarter of the globe. In place of the old wants, satisfied by the productions of the country, we find new wants, requiring for their satisfaction the products of distant lands and climes. In place of the old local and national seclusion and self-sufficiency we have had intercourse in every direction, universal interdependence of nations. And as in material, so also in intellectual production. The intellectual creations of individual nations become common property. National onesidedness and narrowmindedness become more and more impossible, and from the numerous national and local literatures, there arises a world-literature.

The bourgeoisie, by the rapid improvement of all instruments of production, by the immensely facilitated means of communication, draws all, even the most barbarian, nations into civilization. The cheap prices of its commodities are the heavy artillery with which it batters down all Chinese walls, with which it forces the barbarians' intensely obstinate hatred of foreigners to capitulate. It compels all nations, on pain of extinction, to adopt the bourgeois mode of production; it compels them to introduce what it calls civilization into their midst, i.e., to become bourgeois themselves. In one word, it creates a world after its own image.

The bourgeoisie has subjected the country to the rule of the towns. It has created enormous cities, has greatly increased the urban population as compared with the rural, and has thus rescued a considerable part of the population from the idiocy of rural life. Just as it has made the country dependent on the towns, so it has made barbarian and semi-barbarian countries dependent on the civilized ones, nations of peasants on nations of bourgeois, the East on the West.

The bourgeoisie keeps more and more doing away with the scattered state of the population, of the means of production, and of property. It has agglomerated population, centralized means of production, and has concentrated property in a few hands. The necessary consequence of this was political centralization. Independent, or but loosely connected provinces, with separate interests, laws, governments, and systems of taxation, became lumped together into one nation, with one government, one code of laws, one national class interest, one frontier, and one customs tariff.

The bourgeoisie, during its rule of scarce one hundred years, has created more massive and more colossal productive forces than have all preceding generations together. Subjection of Nature's forces to man, machinery, application of chemistry to industry and agriculture, steam-navigation, railways, electric telegraphs, clearing of whole continents for cultivation, canalization of rivers . . . what earlier century had even a presentiment that such productive forces slumbered in the lap of social labor?

We see then: the means of production and of exchange on whose foundation the bourgeoisie built itself up, were generated in feudal society. At a certain stage in the development of these means of production and of exchange, the conditions under which feudal society produced and exchanged, the feudal organization of agriculture and manufacturing industry, in one word, the feudal relations of property, became no longer compatible with the already developed productive forces; they became so many fetters. They had to burst asunder; they were burst asunder.

Into their places stepped free competition, accompanied by a social and political constitution adapted to it, and by the economical and political sway of the bourgeois class.

A similar movement is going on before our own eyes. Modern bourgeois society with its relations of production, of exchange, and of property, a society that has conjured up such gigantic means of production and of exchange, is like the sorcerer, who is no longer able to control the powers of the nether world whom he has called up by his spells. For many a decade past the history of industry and commerce is but the history of the revolt of modern productive forces against modern conditions of production, against the property relations that are the conditions for the existence of the bourgeoisie and of its rule. It is enough to mention the commercial crises that by their periodical return put on its trial, each time more threateningly, the existence of the bourgeois society. In these crises a great part not only of the existing products, but also of the previously created productive forces, is periodically destroyed. In these crises there breaks out an epidemic that, in all earlier epochs, would have seemed an absurdity—the epidemic of overproduction. Society suddenly finds itself put back into a state of momentary barbarism; it appears as if a famine, a universal war of devastation, had cut off the supply of every means of subsistence; industry and commerce seem to be destroyed; and why? because there is too much civilization, too much means of subsistence, too much industry, too much commerce. The productive forces at the disposal of society no longer tend to further the development of the conditions of bourgeois property; on the contrary, they have become too powerful for these conditions, by which they are fettered, and as soon as they overcome these fetters, they bring disorder into the whole of bourgeois society, endanger the existence of bourgeois property. The conditions of bourgeois society are too narrow to comprise the wealth created by them. And how does the bourgeoisie get over these crises? On the one hand by enforced destruction of a mass of productive forces; on the other, by the conquest of new markets, and by the more thorough exploitation of the old ones. That is to say, by paving the way for more extensive and more destructive crises, and by diminishing the means whereby crises are prevented.

The weapons with which the bourgeoisie felled feudalism to the ground are now turned against the bourgeoisie itself.

But not only has the bourgeoisie forged the weapons that bring death to itself; it has also called into existence the men who are to wield those weapons—the modern working class—the proletarians.

In proportion as the bourgeoisie, i.e., capital, is developed, in the same proportion is the proletariat, the modern working class, developed; a class of laborers, who live only so long as they find work, and who find work only so long as their labor increases capital. These laborers, who must sell themselves piecemeal, are a commodity, like every other article of commerce, and are consequently exposed to all the vicissitudes of competition, to all the fluctuations of the market.

Owing to the extensive use of machinery and to division of labor, the work of the proletarians has lost all individual character, and, consequently, all charm for the workman. He becomes an appendage of the machine, and it is only the most simple, most monotonous, and most easily acquired knack, that is required of him. Hence, the cost of production of a workman is restricted almost entirely to the means of subsistence that he requires for his maintenance, and for the propagation of his race. But the price of a commodity, and therefore also of labor, is equal to its cost of production. In proportion, therefore, as the repulsiveness of the work increases, the wage decreases. Nay, more, in proportion as the use of machinery and division of labor increases, in the same proportion the burden of toil also increases, whether by prolongation of the working hours, by increase of the work enacted in a given time, or by increased speed of the machinery, etc.

Modern industry has converted the little workshop of the patriarchal master into the great factory of the industrial capitalist. Masses of laborers, crowded into factories, are organized like soldiers. As privates of the industrial army they are placed under the command of a perfect hierarchy of officers and sergeants. Not only are they the slaves of the bourgeois class, and of the bourgeois State, they are daily and hourly enslaved by the machine . . . and, above all, by the individual bourgeois manufacturer himself. The more openly this despotism proclaims gain to be its end and aim, the more petty, the more hateful and the more embittering it is.

The less skill and exertion of strength implied in manual labor, in other words, the more modern industry becomes developed, the more is the labor of men superseded by that of women. Differences of age and sex have no longer any distinctive social validity for the working class. All are instruments of labor, more or less expensive to use, according to age and sex.

No sooner is the exploitation of the laborer by the manufacturer, so far at an end, that he receives his wages in cash, than he is set upon by the other portions of the bourgeoisie, the landlord, the shopkeeper, the pawnbroker, etc.

The lower strata of the Middle class—the small tradespeople, shopkeepers, and retired tradesmen generally, the handicraftsmen and peasant—all these sink gradually into the proletariat, partly because their diminutive capital does not suffice for the scale on which modern industry is carried on, and is swamped in the competition with the large capitalists, partly because their specialized skill is rendered worthless by new methods of production. Thus the proletariat is recruited from all classes of the population.

The proletariat goes through various stages of development. With its birth begins its struggle with the bourgeoisie. At first the contest is carried on by individual laborers, then by the workpeople of a factory, then by the operatives of one trade, in one locality, against the individual bourgeois who directly exploits them. They direct their attacks not against the bourgeois conditions of production, but against the instruments of production themselves; they destroy imported wares that compete with their labor, they smash to pieces machinery, they set factories ablaze, they seek to restore by force the vanished status of the workman of the Middle Ages.

At this stage the laborers still form an incoherent mass scattered over the whole country, and broken up by their mutual competition. If anywhere they unite to form more compact bodies, this is not yet the consequence of their own active union, but of the union of the bourgeoisie, which class, in order to attain its own political ends, is compelled to set the whole proletariat in motion, and is moreover yet, for a time, able to do so. At this stage, therefore, the proletarians do not fight their enemies, but the enemies of their enemies, the remnants of absolute monarchy, the landowners, the non-industrial bourgeois, the petty bourgeoisie. Thus the whole historical movement is concentrated in the hands of the bourgeoisie; every victory so obtained is a victory for the bourgeoisie.

But with the development of industry the proletariat not only increases in number; it becomes concentrated in greater masses, its strength grows and it feels that strength more. The various interests and conditions of life within the ranks of the proletariat are more and more equalized, in proportion as machinery obliterates all distinctions of labor, and nearly everywhere reduces wages to the same low level. The growing competition among the bourgeois, and the resulting commercial crises, make the wages of the workers even more fluctuating. The unceasing improvement of machinery, ever more rapidly developing, makes their livelihood more and more precarious; the collisions between individual workmen and individual bourgeois take more and more the character of collisions between two classes. Thereupon the workers begin to form combinations (Trades' Unions) against the bourgeois; they club together in order to keep up the rate of wages; they found permanent associations in order to make provision beforehand for these occasional revolts. Here and there the contest breaks out into riots.

Now and then the workers are victorious, but only for a time. The real fruit of their battles lies not in the immediate result but in the ever-expanding union of workers. This union is helped by the improved means of communication that are created by modern industry, and that place the workers of different localities in contact with one another. It was just this contact that was needed to centralize the numerous local struggles, all of the same character, into one national struggle between classes. But every class struggle is a political struggle. And that union, to attain which the burghers of the Middle Ages, with their miserable highways, required centuries, the modern proletarians, thanks to railways, achieve in a few years.

This organization of the proletarians into a class, and consequently into a political party, is continually being upset again by the competition between the workers themselves. But it ever rises up again; stronger, firmer, mightier. It compels legislative recognition of particular interests of the workers, by taking advantage of the divisions among the bourgeoisie itself. Thus the ten-hours' bill in England was carried.

Altogether collisions between the classes of the old society further, in many ways, the course of development of the proletariat. The bourgeoisie finds itself involved in a constant battle. At first with the aristocracy; later on, with those portions of the bourgeoisie itself, whose interests have become antagonistic to the progress of industry; at all times with the bourgeoisie of foreign countries. In all these countries it sees itself compelled to appeal to the proletariat, to ask for its help, and thus to drag it into the political arena. The bourgeoisie itself, therefore, supplies the proletariat with weapons for fighting the bourgeoisie.

Further, as we have already seen, entire sections of the ruling classes are, by the advance of industry, precipitated into the proletariat, or are at least threatened in their conditions of existence. These also supply the proletariat with fresh elements of enlightenment and progress.

Finally, in times when the class struggle nears the decisive hour, the process of dissolution going on within the ruling class, in fact, within the whole range of an old society, assumes such a violent glaring character, that a small section of the ruling class cuts itself adrift, and joins the revolutionary class, the class that holds the future in its hands. Just as, therefore, at an earlier period, a section of the nobility went over to the bourgeoisie, so now a portion of the bourgeoisie goes over to the proletariat, and in particular, a portion of the bourgeois ideologists, who have raised themselves to the level of comprehending theoretically the historical movement as a whole.

Of all the classes that stand face to face with the bourgeoisie today the proletariat alone is a really revolutionary class. The other classes decay and finally disappear in the face of modern industry; the proletariat is its special and essential product.

The lower middle class, the small manufacturer, the shopkeeper, the artisan, the peasant, all these fight against the bourgeoisie to save from extinction their existence as fractions of the middle class. They are therefore not revolutionary, but conservative. Nay, more, they are reactionary, for they try to roll back the wheel of history. If by chance they are revolutionary, they are so only in view of their impending transfer into the proletariat; they thus defend not their present, but their future interests, they desert their own standpoint to place themselves at that of the proletariat.

The "dangerous class," the social scum, that passively rotting class thrown off by the lowest layers of old society, may, here and there, be swept into the movement by a proletarian revolution; its conditions of life, however, prepare it far more for the part of a bribed tool of reactionary intrigue.

In the conditions of the proletariat, those of the old society at large are already virtually swamped. The proletarian is without property; his relation to his wife and children has no longer anything in common with the bourgeois family relations; modern industrial labor, modern subjection to capital, the same in England as in France, in America as in Germany, has stripped him of every trace of national character. Law, morality, religion, are to him so many bourgeois prejudices, behind which lurk in ambush just as many bourgeois interests.

All the preceding classes that got the upper hand sought to fortify their already acquired status by subjecting society at large to their conditions of appropriation. The proletarians cannot become masters of the productive forces of society, except by abolishing their own previous mode of appropriation, and thereby also every other previous mode of appropriation. They have nothing of their own to secure and to fortify; their mission is to destroy all previous securities for, and insurances of, individual property.

All previous historical movements were movements of minorities, or in the interest of minorities. The proletarian movement is the self-conscious, independent movement of the immense majority, in the immense majority. The proletariat, the lowest stratum of our present society, cannot stir, cannot raise itself up, without the whole super-incumbent strata of official society being sprung into the air.

Though not in substance, yet in form, the struggle of the proletariat with the bourgeoisie is at first a national struggle. The proletariat of each country must, of course, first of all settle matters with its own bourgeoisie.

In depicting the most general phases of the development of the proletariat, we traced the more or less veiled civil war, raging within existing society, up to the point where that war breaks out into open revolution, and where the violent overthrow of the bourgeoisie lays the foundation for the sway of the proletariat.

Hitherto every form of society has been based, as we have already seen, on the antagonism of oppressing and oppressed classes. But in order to oppress a class certain conditions must be assured to it under which it can, at least, continue its slavish existence. The serf, in the period of serfdom, raised himself to membership in the commune, just as the petty bourgeois, under the yoke of feudal absolutism, man-aged to develop into a bourgeois. The modern laborer, on the con-trary, instead of rising with the progress of industry, sinks deeper and deeper below the conditions of existence of his own class. He becomes a pauper, and pauperism develops more rapidly than popu-lation and wealth. And here it becomes evident that the bourgeoisie is unfit any longer to be the ruling class in society and to impose its conditions of existence upon society as an over-riding law. It is unfit to rule because it is incompetent to assure an existence to its slave within his slavery, because it cannot help letting him sink into such a state that it has to feed him instead of being fed by him. Society can no longer live under this bourgeoisie, in other words its existence is no longer compatible with society.

The essential condition for the existence, and for the sway of the bourgeois class, is the formation and augmentation of capital; the condition for capital is wage-labor. Wage-labor rests exclusively on competition between the laborers. The advance of industry, whose involuntary promoter is the bourgeoisie, replaces the isolation of the laborers, due to competition, by their revolutionary combination, due to association. The development of modern industry, therefore, cuts from under its feet the very foundation on which the bourgeoisie produces and appropriates products. What the bourgeoisie therefore produces, above all, are its own grave-diggers. Its fall and the victory of the proletariat are equally inevitable. . . .

Position of the Communists in Relation to the Various Existing Opposition Parties

. . . The Communists fight for the attainment of the immediate aims, for the enforcement of the momentary interests of the working class; but in the movement of the present they also represent and take care of the future of that movement. In France the Communists ally themselves with the Social-Democrats, against the conservative and radical bourgeoisie, reserving, however, the right to take up a critical position in regard to phrases and illusions traditionally handed down from the great Revolution.

In Switzerland they support the Radicals, without losing sight of the fact that this party consists of antagonistic elements, partly of Democratic Socialists, in the French sense, partly of radical bourgeois.

In Poland they support the party that insists on an agrarian revolution, as the prime condition for national emancipation, that party which fomented the insurrection of Cracow in 1846.

In Germany they fight with the bourgeoisie whenever it acts in a revolutionary way against the absolute monarchy, the feudal squirearchy, and the petty bourgeoisie.

But they never cease, for a single instant, to instill into the working class the clearest possible recognition of the hostile antagonism between bourgeoisie and proletariat, in order that the German workers may straightway use, as so many weapons against the bourgeoisie the social and political conditions that the bourgeoisie must necessarily introduce along with its supremacy, and in order that, after the fall of the reactionary classes in Germany, the fight against the bourgeoisie itself may immediately begin.

The Communists turn their attention chiefly to Germany, because that country is on the eve of a bourgeois revolution that is bound to be carried out under more advanced conditions of European civilization, and with a much more developed proletariat, than that of England was in the seventeenth, and of France in the eighteenth century, and because the bourgeois revolution in Germany will be but the prelude to an immediately following proletarian revolution.

In short, the Communists everywhere support every revolutionary movement against the existing social and political order of things.

In all these movements they bring to the front, as the leading question in each, the property question, no matter what its degree of development at the time.

Finally, they labor everywhere for the union and agreement of the democratic parties of all countries.

The Communists disdain to conceal their views and aims. They openly declare that their ends can be attained only by the forcible overthrow of all existing social conditions. Let the ruling classes tremble at a Communistic revolution. The proletarians have nothing to lose but their chains. They have a world to win.

Working men of all countries, unite!

Writing in the "North American Review" for June, 1889, Andrew Carnegie, conceded the beautiful ideals of Communism, but he said they were not practical in a world dominated by the Law of Competition and Individualism. How did his ideas of the nature of man differ from those of Karl Marx? Which ideas are closer to the Christian ideal?

The Gospel of Wealth

Andrew Carnegie

The price which society pays for the law of competition, like the price it pays for cheap comforts and luxuries, is also great, but the advantages of this law are also greater still, for it is to this law that we owe our wonderful material development, which brings improved conditions in its train. But, whether the law be benign or not, we must say of it, as we say of the change in the conditions of men to which we have referred: It is here; we cannot evade it; no substitutes for it have been found; and while the law may be sometimes hard for the individual, it is best for the race, because it insures the survival of the fittest in every department. We accept and welcome, therefore, as conditions to which we must accommodate ourselves, great inequality of environment, the concentration of business, industrial and commercial, in the hands of a few, and the law of competition between these, as being not only beneficial, but essential for the future progress of the race. Having accepted these, it follows that there must be great scope for the exercise of special ability in the merchant and in the manufacturer who has to conduct affairs upon a great scale. That this talent for organization and management is rare among men is proved by the fact that it invariably secures for its possessor enormous rewards, no matter where or under what laws or conditions. The experienced in affairs always rate the MAN whose services can be obtained as a partner as not only the first consideration, but such as to render the question of his capital scarcely worth considering, for such men soon create capital; while, without the special talent required, capital soon takes wings. Such men become interested in firms or corporations using millions; and estimating only simple interest to be made upon the capital invested, it is inevitable that their income must exceed their expenditures, and that they must accumulate wealth. Nor is there any middle ground which such men can occupy, because the great manufacturing or commercial concern

From "The Gospel of Wealth" by Andrew Carnegie, *North American Review*, June, 1889, pp. 653–657.

which does not earn at least interest upon its capital soon becomes bankrupt. It must either go forward or fall behind: to stand still is impossible. It is a condition essential for its successful operation that it should be thus far profitable, and even that, in addition to interest on capital, it should make profit. It is a law, as certain as any of the others named, that men possessed of this peculiar talent for affairs, under the free play of economic forces, must, of necessity, soon be in receipt of more revenue than can be judiciously expended upon themselves; and this law is as beneficial for the race as the others.

Objections to the foundations upon which society is based are not in order, because the condition of the race is better with these than it has been with any others which have been tried. Of the effect of any new substitutes proposed we cannot be sure. The Socialist or Anarchist who seeks to overturn present conditions is to be regarded as attacking the foundation upon which civilization itself rests, for civilization took its start from the day that the capable, industrious workman said to his incompetent and lazy fellow, "If thou dost not sow, thou shalt not reap," and thus ended primitive Communism by separating the drones from the bees. One who studies this subject will soon be brought face to face with the conclusion that upon the sacredness of property civilization itself depends—the right of the laborer to his hundred dollars in the savings bank, and equally the legal right of the millionaire to his millions. To those who propose to substitute Communism for this intense Individualism the answer, therefore, is: The race has tried that. All progress from that barbarous day to the present time has resulted from its displacement. Not evil, but good, has come to the race from the accumulation of wealth by those who have the ability and energy that produce it. But even if we admit for a moment that it might be better for the race to discard its present foundation, Individualism,—that it is a nobler ideal that man should labor, not for himself alone, but in and for a brotherhood of his fellows, and share with them all in common, realizing Swedenborg's idea of Heaven, where, as he says, the angels derive their happiness, not from laboring for self, but for each other, —even admit all this, and a sufficient answer is, This is not evolution, but revolution. It necessitates the changing of human nature itself—a work of aeons, even if it were good to change it, which we cannot know. It is not practicable in our day or in our age. Even if desirable theoretically, it belongs to another and long-succeeding sociological stratum. Our duty is with what is practicable now; with the next step possible in our day and generation. It is criminal to waste our energies in endeavoring to uproot, when all we can profitably or possibly accomplish is to bend the universal tree of humanity a little in the direction most favorable to the production of good fruit under existing circumstances. We might as well urge the destruction of the highest existing type of man because he failed to reach our ideal as to favor the destruction of Individualism, Private Property, the Law of Accumulation of Wealth, and the Law of Competition; for these are the highest results of human experience, the soil in which society so far has produced the best fruit. Unequally or unjustly, perhaps, as these laws sometimes operate, and imperfect as they appear to the Idealist, they are, nevertheless, like the highest type of man, the best and most valuable of all that humanity has yet accomplished.

Tucker, professor of politics and director of Russian studies at Princeton
University, concludes his book "The Marxian Revolutionary Idea" with a
chapter on man reaching maturity at the end of history. Tucker says
Marx's "enduring value lies especially in his 'futurology.' His vision of a
matured humanity dwelling in a transformed world at the end of
history remains one of the most relevant of human utopias."

Marx and the End of History

Robert C. Tucker

The hundred-and-fiftieth anniversary of Marx's birth is a more
propitious occasion for commemoration of him than the hundredth
would have been.[1] In May 1918, the world was at war, and not
much concerned with such ceremonies. A party of Marxist revolutionaries had just taken power in Russia, but the future of that
revolution, and others like it, was still unclear. And some early philosophical writings of Marx, knowledge of which was destined greatly
to deepen our understanding of the genesis and meaning of Marxism,
were still lying in archives and unknown to all but a very few. It
was still too soon to assess the historical significance of Marx. Now
we are better situated in time to make the assessment.

The most important of the early writings published since 1918
are the *Economic and Philosophical Manuscripts of 1844.* Here the
young Marx set down a first systematic sketch of Marxism in concepts largely derived from post-Kantian German philosophy, Hegel's
in particular. Deciphering what he conceived to be the "esoteric"
meaning of Hegel's *Phenomenology of Mind,* he formulated his own
conception of history as a process of self-development of the human
species culminating in communism. Man, according to this conception, is essentially a producer; and material production is the primary
form of his producing activity, industry being the externalized productive powers of the species. In the course of his history, which
Marx described as a "history of production," a world of created objects gradually arises around man. Original nature is overlaid with
a man-made "anthropological nature" or "nature produced by history."
And Marx believed that this was the true or scientific restatement
of the Hegelian conception. For had not Hegel seen the history of
the world as a production-history on the part of the world-spirit? His

error had been to mystify the process by treating the productive activity as *mental* activity primarily. To move from mystification to reality, from philosophy to science, one had only to turn Hegel on his head. Then it appeared that the Hegelian image of spirit creating a world was simply a philosopher's distorted picture of the reality of history, namely, that man—working man—creates a world in *material* productive activities over the centuries. Inevitably, therefore, Marx later named his transformed Hegelianism the "materialist conception of history."

Still following Hegel's basic scheme, Marx in the manuscripts visualized the human history of production as being also a history of estrangement (*Entfremdungsgeschichte*). Man's nature, he postulated, was to be a "free conscious producer," but so far he had not been able to express himself freely in productive activity. He had been driven to produce by need and greed, by a passion for accumulation which in the modern bourgeois age becomes accumulation of capital. His productive activity had always, therefore, been involuntary; it had been "labor." And since man, when he produces involuntarily, is estranged from his human nature, labor is "alienated labor." Escape from alienated labor finally becomes materially possible in the stage of technological development created by modern machine industry. The way of escape lies in the revolutionary seizure and socialization of the productive powers by the workers. Repossessed through revolution of his organs of material production externalized in industry, man will at last be able to produce in freedom. To Marx communism did not mean a new economic system. It meant the end of economics in a society where man, liberated from labor, would realize his creative nature in a life of leisure. So Marx defined communism in his manuscripts as "transcendence of human self-alienation," and saw it as the real future situation that Hegel had depicted in a mystified manner at the close of his *Phenomenology,* where spirit, having attained absolute knowledge, returns to itself out of its alienation and is fully "at home with itself in its otherness."

Such, very briefly, was Marxism as originally expounded; and it was this view of history that Marx and Engels elaborated in their voluminous later writings. Naturally, much was added and refined. Marx's thought, however, like that of most powerfully original thinkers, showed an underlying continuity. Indeed, *Capital,* published in 1867, was simply the form in which he finally finished and published the book he set out to write in his manuscripts of 1844.

Consequently, we are now able to see in him, far more clearly than anyone could easily have done a half-century ago, an heir and representative of the great age of German philosophy that started with Kant and ran its course through Schelling, Fichte, and Hegel to its diverse later outcomes. I do not mean to say that we should see him only as a philosopher, or Marxism itself exclusively as a philosophical phenomenon. For Marx, as perhaps befitted a descendant of rabbinical forbears, had a prophetic mission. The teaching that he derived from philosophy and saw as science was received widely as a new faith. It became the party ideology of movements for revolution and, in our century, regimes of revolution acting in Marx's name. Here, however, I am not concerned with Marxism as a party ideology, but with Marx as an intellectual and Marxism as *he* understood it. My question is this: What is his most important message to us now? The answer I wish to suggest is that the aspect of Marx with the greatest enduring significance and relevance for our time is the utopian aspect, the part that we today might call his "futurology." In order to explain this view, let me go a few steps further in identifying his position.

If we ask ourselves what kind of philosopher Marx basically was, it is easy to answer that he was a philosopher of history. For all his various attempts at a general definition of his position were statements about the historical process. Yet to describe Marx as a philosopher of history is to express a rather superficial truth, because history per se was not the primary object of his theorizing. The primary object was man, man as a species and "species-being" (*Gattungswesen*); and the theory of man is the matrix of Marx's theory of history. He defines history as the *growth-process* of the human species. In his own succinct statement in the 1844 manuscripts: "And just as all things natural must *become,* man, too, has his act of becoming—*history. . . .* "

Now this way of thinking carried the interesting implication that history has an end. Not in the sense of the world's ending, for Marx assumed, in his pre-nuclear innocence, that man and his world would exist indefinitely if not forever. The end of history meant the end of the growth-process of humanity, its emergence into adulthood. Although life and its vicissitudes would go on, and presumably some sorts of change would still occur, the historical agony of growing up, the long struggle of the species to *become* man—a class struggle in large part—would finally be over. The developmental stages of history, which Marx linked with successive "modes of production" from slave labor in antiquity through serf labor in the feudal period to wage labor in the bourgeois era, would be superseded by a radically new mode of productive activity and, along with it, an entirely new form of human community not subject to the dialectical dissolution and breakdown that had necessarily overtaken all historical forms of society. It was with this central idea in mind that Marx wrote in the preface to *The Critique of Political Economy* that the existing bourgeois social formation would bring to a close the prehistory of human society. It was another way of saying that the coming great revolution would usher in the post-historical phase of man's existence on this planet.

The notion of the adulthood of the species was meant by Marx with utmost philosophical seriousness. History as man's protracted "act of becoming" would give way in post-history to man's *being*, to his maturity on both a collective and individual scale. Only at the end could this occur, although the material conditions for it were developing all along. For alienation dogged humanity in every historical cycle of the growth-process, and indeed reached its lowest depth in the bourgeois era when man in the form of the wretched proletarian factory worker became a totally abased dehumanized being, an *Unmensch*. Thus, self-realization, or becoming fully human, was not for Marx a problem that an individual person could solve on his own. It could be solved only within the framework of the self-realization of the species at the end of history.

The normative concept of man implicit in this theory has already been touched upon. Man was seen as a spontaneously productive being with a need to express himself along a multitude of lines, and as tending in all his productive activities, material production included, to construct things "according to the laws of beauty." Marx's vision of the post-historical future was governed by this idea. Not only would machine industry be liberated to produce enough goods to meet the needs of all, but man himself would be liberated from the acquisitive drive, the obsession with wealth that had made him an alienated being. He would consequently be emancipated from the twin tyranny of need and specialization, from his age-old imprisonment in a life of labor and from the various enslaving forms of division of labor inherent in that life. The radically new mode of production coming in post-history would be the free creativity of individuals producing in cooperative association.

Marx not only conceived man as an artistic being in essence, but envisaged his post-historical relationship with "anthropological nature" in artistic terms. Unlike most modern Western philosophers, for whom the subject-object relation has presented primarily the problem of knowing, Marx hardly recognized this problem. Having translated Hegel materialistically, he saw the objects outside man as so many congealments of human productive activity combined with the stuff that the earth provided wherewith to make things. Consequently, their existence and knowability were not really in question. The posture of Cartesian doubt was not for Marx. How could it be for one whose imperative need was not to establish that a world exists but to explain why it appeared so unbearably ugly and oppressive—and to change it? Marx approached the problem of the subject-object relation from an aesthetic viewpoint.

The self-realization of the species would involve the humanization of the world that man had created, the "resurrection of nature." Having been produced in alienated labor and appropriated as private property, the world of objects made by human hand and machine confronted its makers during history as an "alienated world." The end of history would bring its de-alienation. After acquiring mastery of his productive powers and freedom to produce in a human way, man would refashion his own objectified nature according to the laws of beauty. Instead of confronting him as negations of himself, alien and hostile beings, the objects of his production would bring him self-confirmation. In addition to developing his productive talents in all directions, he would develop his capacity for aesthetic experience. His five senses would be cleansed gradually of the possessiveness, the "sense of having," that had always in the past defiled them and prevented him from perceiving and appreciating the intrinsic aesthetic quality of objects outside him. Consequently, reasoned Marx in his manuscripts of 1844, post-historical man would finally leave even communism behind. For communism, too, was a kind of ownership and possession—communal possession. With the complete humanization of man, even this form of possessiveness would be transcended. So we read in the manuscripts that "communism is the necessary form and energetic principle of the immediate future, but communism is not as such the goal of human development, the form of human society." Not communism as such but "positive humanism" was the goal of human development.

The idea of history having an end is not something new with Marx. In essence it as an eschatological idea with roots extending deep into the Judeo-Christian tradition. The heavenly afterlife was brought down to earth in the utopias of the Renaissance, the eighteenth-century Enlightenment, and the early nineteenth-century socialists. Marx built upon these foundations as well as upon German philosophy. But because of the Hegelian philosophical perspective from which he worked, and of the genius that he brought to the task, he created one of the most *relevant* of modern utopias.

What makes his futurology so pertinent to present problems is, I think, first of all the world scope of his conception of man's post-historical future. Marx was not a community-builder. He had no use for small-scale utopian community ventures carried out, as he once scornfully put it, "behind the back of society." That, to him, was utopianism in the pejorative sense. Being a philosopher of Hegelian formation, for whom history was meaningful only as world-history, he insisted from the start of his theorizing that the goal of human development could only be a new state of the world (*Weltzustand*). So he envisaged utopia on a global scale: man fully matured, master at last of his own powers and those of nature, exercising conscious control of the collective life-process, living the freely creative life in a universal human society.

Marx has been criticized for having little to say about community structures and institutional arrangements in post-historical society.[2] But such criticism may be misdirected in the final analysis, and in any event there is something to be said on the other side. A growing number of human problems have become or are fast becoming world problems, not resolvable within the confines of a single community or country or region, however large, although solutions may and should often *begin* locally. Not only war-and-arms-competition fall in this category, but also unchecked population growth, economic lag and food shortage, racialism, denial of human rights and freedoms, the squandering of mineral resources, the pollution of soil, water, and the earth's atmosphere, and so on. Progress can be made on such problems in nations and regions, but adequate solutions cannot be found within any national or hemispheric or European or Atlantic or communist community but only within a universal human community. In our time, any serious utopia must be, like Marx's, a new state of the world.

His futurology also has relevance for us in its concrete envisagement of a future human life-style. Marx's concept of the "abolition of labor" in post-historical society anticipated certain present developments that are taking place owing to a technological revolution rather than the proletarian revolution forecast in the *Communist Manifesto*. Automation and the unlocking of the productive powers of the atom have begun to pose the question of a profound reorientation of man's existence, a reorientation from the work-centered life to a different kind of life. With the elimination of a great deal of economic labor, the problem of the *good* life may become inescapable for a growing proportion of mankind. What kind of living will then take the place of a large part of what has been called working for a living?

Marx's aesthetic utopia, has vision of a post-historical world where human existence takes on the character of creative leisure and artistic expression, represents at least one conceivable answer. Since men in the mass may not have as much artistic bent as he imputed to human nature and may not regard leisure as the unmitigated blessing he thought it would be, we cannot take his utopia as a statement of the inevitable. It still has value, however, as a preview of what is possible. And his notion of the entire environment as a field for aesthetic effort, of "anthropological nature" itself as man's supreme work of art, is particularly pertinent in an age that has seen so much spoliation of nature, destruction of natural beauty, and spread of urban blight. Who in our time, living in big cities, can doubt the imperative need for what Marx called the "true resurrection of nature"?

There is possible guidance for us, finally, in his fundamental concept of the growing up of the race, the graduation of man from his historical growth-process into adulthood. Not that we can take a happy ending of history for granted any longer. Living in the final third of the twentieth century, with great tragedies behind and dangers ahead, we cannot anticipate the future in a Marxian spirit of millenarian optimism. We can see that man may not achieve a universal community, that he may not gain mastery of his powers, that the world's population may go on exploding, that racialism and nationalism may continue to flourish, that life may grow poorer in an increasingly crowded, impersonal, coercive, and regimented society, and that—in the warning words of Erik H. Erikson—"Reactionary rage equipped with atomic weapons may mean the end of man just when for the first time he has a chance to become one species."[3] But the very hugeness of these dangers suggests that *without* some such breakthrough to human maturity as Marx was talking about, the cause may be lost. What I mean to say is that the least likely future may be one in which man muddles through more or less as he has been doing, governments show no more imagination and moral leadership than they have been showing, and history goes on as usual.

The precondition of successful human adaptation and even survival may be radical change—not so much in the organizational arrangements for living as in the consciousness of people, their attitudes to others and themselves, their sense of responsibility to distant peoples and future generations, their patterns of feeling and identity. This is to say that further growth is essential, that the species may now be in a "maturation crisis." If so, one of the most serious aspects of the crisis is the general lack of awareness of it, the tendency of most people and even the leaders of nations to assume that no great change is called for, that no enlargement of the human spirit is necessary, that we immature humans are already grown up. Marx therefore may be at his most relevant in telling us that this is not so, that the species is still engaged in its historical act of becoming and has not yet fully achieved the condition of *being* human.

It must be said, in conclusion, that he was far more effective in grasping these fundamentals and envisaging a fully human future than he was in specifying the means of bringing it about. He greatly overestimated material and technological development as the prerequisite of human maturation, failing to see the immense psychological difficulties and the consequent critical role of leadership and education in the process. He imagined, mistakenly, that revolutionary force and violence could be the means of achieving not only a new society but the new adult human being as its inhabitant; and so he left to such teachers as Gandhi and Martin Luther King, Jr., the task of showing men how to change society, nonviolently, by changing themselves. Finally, and as a result, Marx thought that the revolutionary process of man's maturation could take place very rapidly once the conditions were ripe. He did not understand that the growing up of collective man is bound to be—like the growing up of individuals—a protracted process marked by partial advances, occasional breakthroughs, inevitable setbacks, and only eventual success.

But he was not the first prophet to be more successful in pointing out the promised land than in leading people to it. His genius lay in his powers of visualizing the end. In an age when utopianism has become the only realism, these powers are needed as never before.

Notes

1 An address presented at a symposium held in Trier on May 5, 1968, by the German UNESCO Commission to commemorate the hundred-and-fiftieth anniversary of Marx's birth.

2 For example, by Martin Buber, in *Paths in Utopia,* ch. 8, and in my *Philosophy and Myth in Karl Marx,* ch. 13.

3 R. I. Evans, *Dialogue with Erik Erikson* (New York, Evanston, and London: Harper & Row, 1967), p. 33.

William F. Buckley, Jr., conservative columnist and author, elucidates on the fragmentation of the Communist idea. It's getting so one cannot easily generalize about anything any more—whether Communists, capitalists, Christians, conservatives, or even liberals.

What Is a Communist?

William F. Buckley, Jr.

In the old days, a Communist or for that matter a pro-Communist was thought to be someone who, in his practical political life, took orders from the Soviet Union. For decades, when someone said that Jones was a "Communist" he meant that he took his instructions from Lenin, or after that from Stalin, or after that from Khrushchev.

There were always some people who styled themselves as "Communists" who disagreed with the Soviet Union's party line, but they were thought of as deviates, even as for instance, Father Feeney of Boston who styles himself a true "Catholic" is a deviate, the Pope having the last word to say on who is and who isn't a Catholic.

After all, a follower of Robert Owen, the 19th century socialist, could think of himself as a "Communist," as could a follower of Daniel De Leon, or for that matter of any number of communitarian utopianists.

But the real test was: did you take your orders from the Soviet Union. So rigidly did that test apply that even followers of Leon Trotsky, who considered himself a Marxist-Leninist purer by far than Stalin, had a hard time convincing the world at large that they were "Communists." Instead, for the sake of intelligible communication, they were called "Trotskyists," and their party in the United States is called the Socialist Workers Party.

But now—George Kennan and others are in effect saying—how do you apply that test? And even if you find that the test does apply, i.e., that the particular person you have in mind follows the line laid down in Moscow, don't you even then come out with something rather different from the old hobgoblin? Even if you do follow the Moscow line it isn't so bad as it used to be.

Nowadays (the argument goes) you have buttoned-down bureaucrats like Kosygin and Brezhnev who, sure, are unamiable creatures, but they don't execute or send to concentration camps everyone who disagrees with them, they don't dispatch the tanks to crush every dissenter everywhere.

And as for applying the term internationally, how do you do it? When you see states like Albania defying Moscow to side with Mao Tse-tung. And Yugoslavia 20 years now independent of Moscow's line. And no less than three parties in the Dominican Republic, all of them styling themselves as Communist, all of them disagreeing with each other, one of them Muscovite, another Maoist, another something else. How does one account for the apparent freedom of even Bulgaria? The old monolith is gone . . .

It is all very interesting, and the centrifugal explosion is certainly in many aspects encouraging. Leave alone, for a moment, the bearing of it all on foreign policy, and smile a bit at the lengths some intellectuals are willing to run with the position (one of them on television recently wondered whether Ho Chi Minh was really a Communist). Isn't it interesting what the implications of the position are on political controversy in the United States?

For instance in 1947 the highest court in New York State declared that to call someone a Communist or a pro-Communist was libelous per se (Mencher v. Chesley, 297 N.Y. 94), i.e., that the term was defamatory in the sense, say, that to call someone a prostitute or a thief is defamatory, as opposed to, say, calling someone a Democrat or a politician.

If nobody now knows what "Communist" means any more—and who dares to know if Kennan does not—then mustn't the courts remove "Communist" or "pro-Communist" from the category of per se libel?

Another way to put it: when, recently, did even an acknowledged Communist, say Bettina Aptheker, suffer as the result of her avowed views? Are we crawling back from the days when to be a "Communist" was automatically to be isolated from the range of respectable opinion? What will the laws of controversy say on the subject?

True believers convince themselves there can be no middle course between capitalism and communism. Dogmatists operating in both societies may serve only to slow what is the inevitable process of change. Is convergence necessary for a peaceful world? Is the answer an unqualified yes or no?

Convergence: The Uncertain Meeting of East and West

Time Essay

> The only choice is either bourgeois or socialist ideology. There is no middle course.
>
> —LENIN

Should Lenin be taken at his word? Some Western political theorists and even a few Russians think not, and in defense of their belief they have propagated what has become known as the convergence theory. In essence, the theory proposes that capitalism and Communism—driven by the irresistible scientific and technological forces that control modern industrial states—will eventually coalesce into a new form of society, blending the personal freedom and profit motive of Western democracies with the Communist system's government control of the economy.

Convergence prophets argue that the theory has universal application, but contend that it applies particularly to the United States and Russia. Despite their manifest differences, both nations are post-industrial powers grappling with the problems of advanced technology. According to the convergence theory, Moscow and Washington should meet some day at the omega point somewhere on the outskirts of Belgrade, the capital of a nation that has—so far, successfully—introduced elements of capitalism into a doctrinally Marxist society.

Perhaps the most dramatic endorsement of the convergence theory has come from behind the Iron Curtain. In a 10,000-word essay that was widely but illicitly circulated in Russia before being smuggled out to the West in 1968, the distinguished Soviet physicist Andrei Sakharov held that the only hope for world peace was a rapprochement between the socialist and capitalist systems. Suggesting that Sakharov's clandestine ideas still have a certain appeal for Russian intellectuals, another Soviet physicist, Pyotr Kapitsa, gave an oblique endorsement to convergence while on a tour last fall of U.S. universities. "There should not be one multiplication table for Russians and another for Americans," he told a Washington press conference. "I believe that a bringing together of the two systems is correct."

Major Heresy

Kapitsa's approval of the Sakharov thesis was a trifle ambiguous, and with good reason: convergence is regarded by Soviet ideologues as a major heresy. In essence, the theory is a variation on a Marxist theme—namely, that economic developments govern political and social evolution. But it challenges the conviction of Soviet orthodoxy that Communism alone is the road to human development. After publication of his essay in the West, Sakharov was dismissed as chief consultant to the state committee for nuclear energy, and hardly a month goes by without a denunciation of convergence appearing in the Soviet press.

The convergence theory has only recently become the hope of a few Russian thinkers: the idea if not the term has been a persistent but chimerical dream in the West for decades. During World War II, when the Soviet Union was cast as an ally of Western democracies, convergence was widely propagated by a pair of émigré Russian sociologists, Nikolai Timasheff of Fordham and the late Pitirim Sorokin of Harvard. Both professors theorized that the Soviet Union would eventually develop into a less repressive and more democratic society as it progressed economically.

More recently, convergence has been taken up with considerable enthusiasm by economists—notably the Dutch Nobel prizewinner Jan Tinbergen and Harvard's John Kenneth Galbraith. In *The New Industrial State,* Galbraith states with his customary *élan* that technology has an imperative all its own. On the Russian side, advanced industrialization will inevitably lead to greater intellectual curiosity and freedom; in the U.S., it will inexorably lead to more planning and centralized economic controls.

Industrialization v. Ideology

The convergence theory rests on three basic assumptions. One is that industrialization by necessity leads to urbanization and a common culture with uniformities in skills, techniques, organizations and even problems—like the alienation of factory workers from jobs and machines. Because workers and managers in Gary, Ind., and Magnitogorsk perform similar tasks, the argument goes, they tend to develop similar ways of life. The second premise is that industrialization leads to increased diversity and complexity in a society—to a pluralistic condition that overrides all ideologies. The third is that industrialization creates affluence, which undermines political discipline and ideological conformity.

In some areas, especially economics, there is evidence that the U.S. and Russia have a great deal more in common today than they did a generation ago. America now accepts a degree of "socialism," bureaucratic regulation and welfare statism that would have been considered unthinkable not so long ago. The large corporations that dominate the U.S. economy often resemble branches of government far more than they do textbook examples of free-enterprise capitalism.

Since Stalin, Russia has been subjected to a rising tide of consumer expectations, which party planners have periodically had to acknowledge by modifying priorities. In order to make its economy work better, the Soviet government has reluctantly undertaken certain quasi-capitalist reforms. Russia's current five-year plan, for example, provides some managerial incentives and gives individual factories greater freedom from centralized planning.

Despite the surface similarities of Russia and the U.S., critics of convergence answer that economic factors have never played a dominant role in the evolution of societies. Recent history suggests that industrialization and economic progress are compatible with liberty or tyranny, and do not necessarily override cultural or political differences between nations. Witness, for example, parliamentary Britain and autocratic Germany at the turn of the century, or Detroit in the Roosevelt era and Essen under Hitler. The postwar economic progress of Japan has undoubtedly contributed to the viability of its democratic political system: but East Germany, the most technologically advanced of any Eastern European nation, has achieved economic success under the most rigid and doctrinaire of Communist tyrannies.

The convergence theory, in the words of Kremlinologist Bertram Wolfe, is "vulgar Marxism." It posits a fundamentalist belief in economic determinism that Marx himself would probably have disavowed. It ignores or underrates the role played by traditions, value systems and even national characteristics in deciding the future of societies. The concepts that people have of national characteristics, of course, are often mere caricatures, but they generally contain some truth, of a subtler variety than meets the eye. The American devotion to individualism and freedom can be exaggerated; yet the Lockean principles of individual liberty and ordered freedom that underlie the U.S. Constitution and indeed U.S. society are related to the American character and the American ideal. The line leading from the czars to Stalin to the Kremlin's present rulers is by no means straight. Still, it is no accident that the Russians—for whom a ruling father-figure rather than the individual is the central symbol in the national mystique—have a history of autocracy.

In the limited sense that capitalist societies are heading inexorably for more state planning and control and that socialist ones must inevitably allow for more decentralization, the convergence theory is true. It may well be that both Russia and the U.S. will come still closer to sharing a common economic model. But broad, perhaps unbridgeable differences will remain, particularly over the philosophic questions of the dreams and goals of the two societies.

Orthodoxy in Tatters

Especially among the young there is always a tendency to extol opposites. Just as many American youths seem to yearn for the collective, non-materialistic life, many young people in Communist countries seem to admire some (but by no means all) of the individualism and the material benefits of Western society. Today, Communism is splintered, Marxism orthodoxy in tatters. Nevertheless, the Communist view of man still has a powerful and self-perpetuating hold in those societies where it has become part of the culture—and it is still a vast distance removed from anything that American society would accept in the foreseeable future. The definitions of "bourgeois" and "socialist" ideologies have changed over the years—and no doubt will continue to change—but in the long run Lenin may well prove to be right.

The future is always problematical, but the weight of evidence suggests that Communist and non-Communist societies will continue to develop on separate but parallel tracks. Fortunately, though, basic differences no longer imply the inevitability of a cataclysmic showdown. The pragmatics of survival may well be the one respect in which the U.S. and Soviet Russia are really meeting. That may be a more helpful and hopeful prospect than the euphoric vision of convergence.

Is it possible for a meeting ground to exist between Christians and Marxists? Yes, says Father Girardi, an Italian priest who has been active in Marxist-Christian dialogues in Europe. Doctrinaire Christians, Capitalists, Marxists, and Nationalists will no doubt express horror at the thought. But not all people are doctrinaire. Those with open minds are able to explore areas of agreement and disagreement, even in relation to the ideas of atheists and Third Worlders. Perhaps if more people would examine the issues openly, we could begin to reduce the profound alienation penetrating all societies today.

Toward a New Humanism

Giulio Girardi

One of the most fascinating and, for some, alarming dialogues taking place is that between Christians and Marxists. After only a few years of contacts between the two groups, there has been a change in their perspectives that disturbs and scandalizes some, while it fills others with hope. No one seems to be indifferent. For many Christians, the Marxist is no longer enemy No. 1 but, rather, today's favorite partner in dialogue and perhaps tomorrow's collaborator. The attitude of many Marxists toward part of the Christian world has evolved in the same way.

Dialogue includes objective aspects—meetings, conferences, debates—and subjective aspects, those of the evolution of mutual attitudes and frames of mind. Dialogues actually take place only if, beyond external contacts and public or official stands, new attitudes and states of mind can be discerned. This is precisely what is being questioned by some who say that meetings for dialogue are really only juxtaposed monologues and that dialogues between Marxists and Christians are really impossible. However, those who have witnessed the enriching experience of dialogue and been touched by the dynamism that dialogue gives to reflection no longer wonder about its possibility. Nor do they have any doubt about the spiritual evolution that is taking place in many Christians and Marxists.

What gives the character of dialogue to meetings between Christions and Marxists is the spirit in which they approach problems and examine each other's positions. One sees in such meetings an effort

From "Toward a New Humanism" by Giulio Girardi, *The Center Magazine,* March, 1970, pp. 9–13. Reprinted, by permission, from the March 1970 issue of *The Center Magazine,* a publication of The Center for the Study of Democratic Institutions in Santa Barbara, California.

to understand, a critical attitude with respect to one's own positions, and a dynamism not only in opposing one another but in approaching and enriching one another. The critical spirit tends to make the man of today refuse to adhere to a doctrine and, above all, to a faith only because it represents a sacred heritage of his family, his milieu, his class, or his party. He feels the need of realizing personally the importance of everything that is proposed to him. He may wish to submit his positions to the proof of argument. Aware of the various cultures, ideologies, and religions that divide man, not inclined to "excommunicate" anyone, the man of today looks on his own doctrinal orientation as a personal choice, able to stand the test of confrontation with other points of view.

By virtue of his individualistic feeling, the man of today recognizes the right of everyone to orient his life according to the needs of his conscience. By virtue of his feeling for community, he knows that the movement toward truth is not merely a simple relation between subject and object but an intersubjective community relationship. By virtue of his sense of the historic actuality of truth, he is not likely to think that he possesses the totality of truth or that "the other" is sunk in error; instead, his attitude is one of inquiry and openness to the perspectives of others.

It is not only doctrinal dialogue that affects the dynamism of our age but also—and perhaps in an even more urgent and obvious way—what might be called operative dialogue, that is, dialogue concerned with pressing human problems. The problems of our age, especially those of war and poverty, penetrate so acutely to the conscience of humanity that all men of good will, whatever their religious and political orientation, are profoundly concerned. Humanity finds itself at a turning point in its history. The time has come for men to take their destiny in hand and to assume responsibility for their own history. Far from appearing as a possible solution to human problems, war is now recognized as the most serious and menacing problem of all.

Other necessities of our time—for example, the unification of humanity, the pluralist conscience, the secularization movement—are being assumed by Marxists and Christians not extrinsically but through an internal evolution, so that the working hypothesis at the basis of their dialogue can be stated in this way: in a more profound fidelity to their own inspirations, the participants in the dialogue discover among themselves a certain ideal community. For the Christian, dialogue becomes one of the fundamental expressions of his love for others; it lies at the very heart of the Christian message.

If it is true that some Christians find this dialogue impossible, it is no less true that others are convinced that Marxists are, for Christians, ideal participants, and vice versa. This latter conviction is not based simply on the fact that Marxism is a worldwide movement with great historical force. For it is more than that. From the doctrinal point of view, Marxism represents an organic and total view of the world and of life. Therefore, doctrinal dialogue with Marxists is for the Christian, who has his own organic and universal view, a splendid opportunity. It forces the Christian to reconsider all his positions (and his problems) in the light of the demands of the contemporary world. This is not to confer on Marxism an exclusive claim to modernity. But certainly Marxism is rich with perspectives, aspirations, and challenges. I will even say that doctrinal Marxism represents a synthesis of secular values that historic Christianity has neglected and that the modern world has rediscovered, in spite of that neglect.

Like Christianity, Marxism wishes to be both a doctrine and a way of life, a living synthesis of thought and action. It looks at all individual and community action in the light of an ideal. It breathes life into reflection. For that reason, Marxism and Christianity must inevitably find each other in every domain, whether it be to clash and accuse, or to join and collaborate. Beyond a profound opposition between them, there is an historic complementarity. Marxists and Christians are beginning to see in one another values that they themselves lack and, to some degree, are now obliged to take account of. More and more their positions are manifesting resemblances and, at least by hypothesis, even certain ideal convergences.

Here we must meet one of the principal objections to dialogue, the charge that it is sterile. "What was your conclusion?" one is asked upon returning from a conference. It is clear that those who pose the question feel that no end has been reached because no end could be reached. Information has been exchanged, positions examined, the game played, but in the end, they feel, nothing significant has changed on either side. For such questioners, rapprochements are possible only if Marxists stop being wholly Marxist, or Christians being wholly Christian, or both.

It seems to me that the results of dialogue can be reduced to some basic elements. First, from the point of view of human relations, the reciprocal confidence, even friendship, which has flourished between Marxists and Christians is fundamental. This is not a matter of romanticizing dialogue, but, rather, of seeing that dialogue, insofar as it unites diverse groups, results in a transformation of attitudes. This transformation goes beyond the integralist attitude toward a humanist attitude. The theme of humanism, with all it implies, is at the center of the doctrinal dialogue. The humanist theme conditions the very possibility of dialogue for both Marxists and Christians. It also gives this dialogue its richest substance.

In contrast, Christian integralism holds that all values are essentially dependent on religious values and that no encounter is possible in the secular sphere except on the basis of a religious convergence. Marxist integralism holds that all values are essentially dependent on the socioeconomic sphere—more precisely on revolutionary action led by the proletariat class, particularly by the Communist Party—and that no encounter is possible unless one adopts *praxis* [practice] as a criterion of truth and value. At the center of every integralist vision there is the view that the individual person is totally relative, that he has no value in himself and for himself. Religious integralism sees man only in his relation to God; Marxist integralism sees him only in his relation with nature, society, class, and party.

Dialogue, however, becomes possible to the degree that Christians and Marxists, without renouncing their original values, can discover a humanist inclination in themselves. Christian humanism consists essentially in affirming the relative autonomy of man and secular values. For the Christian humanist, the value of man and the secular order does not consist exclusively in their relation to God and religion. Christianity, though it admits of a humanist dimension, cannot be reduced to humanism, nor is humanism the center of its perspective. Christianity is not a humanism, no strictly religious view can be merely humanist. Nor does Christianity identify itself with any particular form of humanism, culture, or society. But this is not an obstacle to dialogue; it widens the possibilities for dialogue. The Christian can study without prejudice the kinds of humanism to be understood in our age. In that connection, we see the Christian attitude in dialogue shifting, becoming less and less centered on the problem of God and more and more on the problem of man. Thus, atheism in itself is not an obstacle to dialogue with the Christian when it is not reduced to undermining the human richness of the Christian or challenging his freedom. As a matter of fact, atheism can be one of the objects of dialogue. And as for the debate on religious freedom, it is still fundamentally important, but in the Marxist-Christian dialogue it is taken in the widest context of the debate on human liberty.

In the Marxist world, we are seeing a rediscovery of the individual, his problems, his value, his autonomy with respect to nature and society. And we are seeing a reaffirmation of the autonomy of super-structures—especially culture—in relation to infrastructures. Obviously, this is a matter of the relative autonomy of man because Marxism must continue to regard man's relation to society as essential and, also as essential, the relation of superstructural values to their foundation. But for the Marxist humanist in dialogue, the individual person is not reduced to society and infrastructures; he has a value in himself. The structuralist interpretation of Marxism—now very much in vogue in France—is the antithesis of the humanist interpretation; it is a type of Marxism closed in on itself and inaccessible to dialogue.

The humanist point of view allows Christians to recognize authentic human values in systems and communities that challenge the religious dimension of existence. It allows Marxists to recognize authentic human values outside their own institutions, and, by affirming the relative autonomy of culture, Marxists discover an interest in research and strictly doctrinal dialogue, and respect the demands of both.

There is no doubt that religious and atheist orientations evoke profoundly different views of the world and consequently different judgments of the particular options open to man. Dialogue does not have the role of wiping out this opposition but of specifying the scope of it. But specifying the scope of divergences does not exclude all possibility of convergence. I should like to try to indicate some of those convergences between Marxists and Christians, at least as a working hypothesis:

• Man has a basic relationship to nature but he cannot be reduced to that relationship. Man's being is essentially different and superior in relation to all other beings of the universe, especially because of his power to initiate change. Strongly conditioned by the evolution of nature, human history is nevertheless governed by original laws that respect man's initiative and cannot be thought of as a simple transposition of natural laws.

• Every man has a basic relationship to society but he cannot be reduced to that relation. He can fulfill himself only in and through society but his value is not reduced to that society. The ideal community permits the flourishing of all individuals; the freedom of each individual is the condition of freedom for all. In that society, man will have achieved such a mastery over nature that he will fulfill himself as ruler and architect of his own history.

• Man is essentially an historic being; that is, he is constantly developing and, in developing, changing his reality. But this developmental process does not exclude the continuity which permits us to characterize history as human. In that precise sense, we can still speak of "human nature."

• The history of man and the world is not a chaotic succession of events, nor is it a circular movement. It is a continuing ascent toward an ever-richer humanization; it is a movement of liberation. This ascent is neither determined nor inevitable; it is accomplished through man's own free and active intervention.

• All of man's life and history is conditioned by socioeconomic substructures to such an extent that we can infer historic laws from economic dynamism. Nevertheless, other sectors of human activity, mainly culture, enjoy a certain autonomy. Human liberty, though conditioned by economic freedom, cannot be reduced to it. Economic liberation facilitates the solution of human problems but it does not automatically resolve them. Man will still have to face the problem of the meaning of life and death, of suffering and solitude.

• Today, most men find themselves in a condition of political, social, and economic alienation. Most of the time, human independence and equality are purely formal matters. The riches of the earth and the reins of power are still in the hands of a minority who exploit the rest of humanity. The present political and economic structures in the world canonize immoral and unjust relationships among men. They create and nourish an egoistic attitude. It is in this objective and subjective situation of humanity—that is, in the oppressive structures and in the egoistic attitude—that we must especially study the causes of war.

• This situation is not, however, inevitable, and no one should be resigned to it. We have the right, duty, and power to change it by responsible action on a worldwide scale. Love of man for man remains sterile as long as it does not penetrate social, political, and economic institutions and put them at the service of humanity. Peace does not consist in the tranquility of an existing order but in the establishing of a new order. In that sense, peace comes through revolution. Total revolution tends to create a new humanity.

• A commitment to the realization of the future City is a basic ingredient of a moral life. Actually constructing such a City with its structural, cultural, objective, and subjective components may be considered as a rule of the moral life, a criterion of value. Thus, all of human action and revolutionary *praxis* are a criterion of morality. It is not the success of any particular institution, considered by itself, that is the criterion of morality. Rather, the demands of the new order that must be built are manifested to the human conscience as a function of the development of a social reality.

• The alienation of most men is inevitably the result of an economy centered on the principle of free competition. What is needed, therefore, is vigorous intervention by national and international public authority to order economic life—especially property—to the service of all men, and to make the interest of community prevail over that of individuals. Private ownership of property should be suppressed wherever it confers on individuals preponderant power and wealth to the detriment of the common good.

• When the intervention of public authority in economic life goes beyond certain limits, it causes new forms of alienation: economic initiative then passes into the hands of a new minority—politicians and bureaucrats—thus stifling the initiative of individuals and creating and stabilizing a dictatorial regime. Therefore the intervention of the public authority in economic life should reflect the real interests and will of the community. Such intervention should be submitted to control by the people; it should permit to workers the greatest possible sharing of decision-making power at every level.

• The authentic revolution is capable of profoundly transforming structures and attitudes. Recourse to violence may sometimes be justified as an extreme solution for stopping violence. But the most persuasive revolutionary method is non-violent action. Although dictatorship may be justified as an exceptional and temporary solution, the only successful revolution is the one which results in a stability based on the free support of all the people.

• To the degree that religion diverts man from a revolutionary commitment, sanctifies the existing order, and allies itself with power, religion has been and remains an alienating force. To the extent that religion in that sense is a conservative force, it can and must be combated. However, the attitude described above is not essential to religion. Religion—notably Christianity—has also challenged the established order. Today, many Christians are showing an awareness of the revolutionary implications of their faith. The old static categories of Greek philosophical and theological thought are being challenged. One sees in many Christians the formation of a theology and a philosophy of revolution, and this is necessarily accompanied by a certain revolution in theology and philosophy itself.

• The future of humanity will be marked for a long time by the competitive coexistence of East and West, of socialism and capitalism. This does not necessarily mean there must be a competition between religious belief and unbelief. An authentically human revolutionary ideal does not need to have either an atheist or a religious outlook. To achieve the revolutionary ideal, believers and non-believers must work together in a framework of equality, without discrimination. It is therefore inexact to say—as some have done, in order to cut short the possibility of a dialogue—that atheism and Christianity, or materialism and Christianity, have nothing in common. There is no doubt that human life is seen quite differently by atheists and religious believers. But this divergence does not necessarily imply a difference in political, social, and economic orientation. Certainly a Christian cannot collaborate on a project planned by atheists if its purpose is atheistic, and vice versa. But both atheists and believers can work together to achieve a project that is simply human and that can be viewed in different doctrinal contexts. This principle does not become operative, of course, unless one recognizes the secular nature of the state and all that it implies. The lay state must respect all ideologies but grant privileges to none. Because of its very mission, the state is neither Christian nor atheist, it is simply human. In the lay state, believers and non-believers should be able to feel themselves citizens to the fullest.

• Because the secular order enjoys relative autonomy with respect to religion, there can be common research between believers and non-believers in various areas: anthropological, moral, political, social, economic. Within those areas there are possibilities for quite wide convergences to develop and for the elaboration of a common plan for a community, even for a common humanism.

• Among the many problems in the modern world, the problem between Christians and Marxists is not necessarily one of opposing positions. Neither Christians nor Marxists have a prefabricated solution which can be deduced from their respective world views. Christians and Marxists meet, therefore, not to find a common solution to their problems, but with a common attitude of inquiry. They undertake dialogue not to present opposing ideologies, but they meet merely as men anxious to contribute to the solution of the problems of man. Many theoretical and practical difficulties are inherent in the problems of the world, in the objective situation. These difficulties are not related to either the Marxist or Christian context within which one reflects. Many difficulties arise, not from the fact that one side or the other refuses to accept a solution, but from the fact that solutions do not yet exist; they must be discovered, or invented. For such problems, dialogue between Marxists and Christians has lost the character of a confrontation. It has, instead, become a mutual search for new solutions.

Questions

1 Catholics, Irish, Poles, Italians, and other minorities have felt alienated in America. How and why did they achieve equality with the majority?

2 What groups are still alienated? Why?

3 Considering the long history of the earth (about four and one-half billion years) and the even longer history of the universe with its billions of galaxies, why should a person get hungup on petty problems that alienate him in a small place, on a small planet, in an infinitely small amount of time? Why not be broad-minded, think big, be galactic? Be way-out, be extra galactic!

4 If Marx were to return today, would he find alienation within the Communist world? Would he be alienated?

5 By the way, do you feel alienated? Why?

6 Will communism and capitalism eventually merge into one system if there is no third world war? If so, what will that new political and economic system be like?

7 "The future belongs to the bureaucrats no matter what the economic system may be." Do you agree or disagree?

8 Is avarice, ambition, and the desire to "get ahead" innate in man or culturally learned? What are the implications for a classless society?

9 Why have past attempts at forming a perfect society (either in religious or economic terms) ended up as a repressive police state?

5

The Significance of
Darwin, Freud, and Einstein

The essay below deals with the Second Scientific Revolution. The first Scientific Revolution, which occurred during the sixteenth and seventeenth centuries, had profound consequences for Western cultural canons. Now, as a result of the scientific innovations of the past century, Western man is once more caught up in a sweeping transformation of values. And once more, it is theoretical science that has provoked the change. Is it possible that the Scientific Revolution which culminated in Newton will be as insignificant as the crime rate in Antarctica when compared with the Second Scientific Revolution as represented by Darwin, Freud, and Einstein?

The Transformation of Enlightenment Mythology

Melvin Steinfield

During the mid-1950s the generally barren wasteland of American commercial television programming was brightened up by a satirical gem. In a comedy skit spoofing abstract art, the well-known comedian Red Skelton played the part of an avant-garde sculptor. His work entitled *Undifferentiated Mass of Clay* was being displayed on a table which he accidentally jostled. His masterpiece fell to the ground and split into two parts. The prize-winning sculpture which had been acclaimed in newspaper headlines was now ruined! But only for a moment. Suddenly Skelton got a brainstorm. Placing both pieces of the broken *objet d'art* back onto the display table, he hastily changed the sign to read: *Two Undifferentiated Masses of Clay*. The following day, newspaper headlines once more hailed the artist for creating a new masterpiece that was even better than the previous one.

Sound absurd? If so, don't blame Red Skelton. Comedy often presents the raw edge of truth. No wonder it sometimes hurts. Skelton's timely television satire mirrored all too accurately a growing feeling of the average mid-twentieth century citizen: art had become too far removed from everyday life. It had become exotic, esoteric, and obscure. The degree of specialization, new techniques, and outrageous approaches differed so radically from previous art forms that artists seemed to be communicating only with themselves. The circle of those who could comprehend, let alone appreciate, their work was being circumscribed ever more narrowly.

These radical departures from artistic traditions in the twentieth century were not confined to painting or sculpture. Music, poetry, and drama also underwent a flurry of unprecedented developments. In addition to the flaunting of artistic, musical, and literary canons, other cultural areas experienced revolutionary change. The development of existentialist philosophy, for instance, seemed related somehow to the malaise of the age. Something was definitely in the twentieth century air, and it was affecting diverse corners as well as main sections of the cultural scene.

Was there some connection between existentialism and abstract art? Were cubist paintings related in any way to the atonality and dissonance of contemporary musical composition? Why the surge of symbolism and myth in modern poetry? What historical forces caused the theater-of-the-absurd to flourish at the same time that "stream-of-consciousness" novels prevailed? Were those strange configurations of melodic patterns in music any more unnerving than the curious formations of glass and steel that were supposed to be functional buildings? Was Dali's surrealistic paintings merely Freudian confessions on canvas? What was bothering modern artists?

These kinds of questions had been faced before. Whenever there were fundamental changes in the myth-system, radical changes in cultural canons and patterns soon followed. Think of the Scientific Revolution and its effects, for instance. Science was the single most important determiner of the eighteenth century myth-system. The Scientific Revolution of the sixteenth and seventeenth centuries had challenged the foundations of the medieval outlook. The credibility of the God-oriented scheme of the universe as well as that of the Church was questioned and found wanting. The authority of traditional experts was exposed and debunked, and a new set of beliefs emerged. The new myth-system, eighteenth century rationalism, was largely the result of that first Scientific Revolution.

In a like manner, there are many reasons to believe that science was again largely responsible for the directions taken by art, literature, philosophy, and other cultural areas in the twentieth century. In fact, it is not farfetched to state that the collective result of the contributions of such scientists as Darwin, Freud, and Einstein was to set men adrift with irrational drives on a competitive planet in a disorderly universe that was pulsating with irregular and unpredictable rhythm.

This abrasive new view of man, life, and the cosmos contradicted the neat, orderly, tranquil world of universal natural law which had set the tone for Enlightenment life style and behavior patterns. It led to an anxious search for objective meaning in a world where everything was relative, where men were motivated by irrational forces beyond their control, and where life was one big competitive rat-race for ephemeral, material, and hedonistic goals that had no foundation in classical philosophy. New developments such as existentialism, surrealism, and cubism were merely some of the more obvious signs of the relativity that resulted from the destruction of faith in absolute values.

Twentieth century man was a tormented witness to the most devastating blows any Western mythology had ever been forced to undergo. The changes of the twentieth century were even more traumatic than the ones caused by Newton. The Scientific Revolution had certainly shaken the medieval outlook to its archaic foundations. But what was destroyed was replaced by another myth-system with a similar hierarchy of values. That is, the specifics of the medieval mythology were altered since it was believed that natural laws and not a divine being directed the movements of the universe, but the faith in the new mythology founded on Newtonian science was just as strong as the faith in the God-oriented universe. "Absolute Truth" as revealed by Enlightenment mythology enjoyed the same firm acceptance in the eighteenth century as medieval versions of Absolute Truth had enjoyed in their time.

Something different occurred with the Second Scientific Revolution, however. This time the work of Darwin, Freud, Einstein and others who participated in the trend could not produce a replacement for the dethroned canons. Instead of a mythology, whether directed by natural law or a divine being, that was orderly and dependable, the new science could only project doubt and uncertainty about man and the workings of the universe. Gone was the faith in the old specifics, but gone also was the faith that there could ever be a new version of Absolute Truth in a world of relativity.

Caught with his myths in disarray, Western man scurried for cover. Everyone found his own kind of shelter. Propelled by even more frantic pressures than those which led to Romantic escapism, twentieth century man began to fashion whatever myths seemed to make the most sense to him personally. Few retained any sort of faith in absolute values. How could they, after the work of Darwin, Einstein, and Freud?

Darwin's theories, and those of other biologists that have come to be associated with Darwinism, challenged the doctrine of the immutability of species. By overthrowing the religious theory of special creation it repeated what Copernicus had done in postulating his heliocentic theory in place of an earth-centered universe. Copernicus and Darwin both presented theories which, bolstered by later scientific discoveries, had the effect of destroying fundamental views supported by all the reputable Establishment authorities of their time. The effect of the theory of evolution was stunning. Debates about the origin of man and life were stimulated; respect for religious authority was further undermined; new concepts of the nature of man emerged; and Social Darwinism was used to justify economic and political competition as part of the new law of nature. In effect, Darwin's theory, like so many other scientific revelations, was applied to social, religious, political, economic, as well as scientific realms.

Translating Darwin's theories in ways Darwin himself never envisioned, advocates of Social Darwinism used the new notion of life as a continuous struggle to support their pet system of economics, such as imperialism. Others found in Social Darwinism justification for a particular political idea, such as nationalism. Instead of the harmonious world of eighteenth century rationalism, the nineteenth century Darwinian world was a dynamic one in which the most deserving specimens would emerge triumphant after a bloody struggle.

With the Enlightenment rationale for egalitarianism destroyed by the implications of evolutionary theory, and with the Romantic and nationalistic trends seeking to emphasize differences between men rather than their likenesses, a natural marriage took place. Laissez-faire capitalism, expansionist imperialism, racism, and super-nationalism were all given a powerful shove by the work of Charles Darwin, whether he realized it or not. As a shy scientist living in a quite restricted world, he of course did not intend his biological theories to be applied to humanistic realms. But, as we have seen again and again, it is virtually impossible to isolate scientific ideas; the impact of science in modern Western civilization is indeed extensive.

The impact of Freud was likewise much greater than in the field of psychology alone. Some of the major applications of his theories and those that have come to be associated with him are as revolutionary as those of Darwin. Freud opened up an infinity of cynical questions about what motivates man. In general, the answers indicate that the Enlightenment view of man as a rational being has been invalidated. Man is now viewed as motivated by irrational passions beyond his control. Assorted irrational drives cause him to behave the way he does. Man is neither good nor evil, he merely responds to forces that direct his actions and should not feel guilty about his uncontrollable behavior patterns. Thus, Freud further weakened traditional Christian beliefs by undermining the concept of original sin. Guilt, in his view, should be eliminated.

Man is not to be blamed for following the dictates of his drives. There is a lot of Rousseau in Freud. Both shared a sensitivity to the dilemma of repressed instincts. Man lives in society and must restrain many of his natural instincts, but that causes him all sorts of personal mental anguish. The problem of modern man is to develop a pattern that will enable him to express his natural feelings without harming others. But many of his feelings seem to depend on harming others in some way, even if only psychologically. Western man absorbed some of the personal torment of Rousseau and Freud, for he is still groping passionately for the proper balance between individual self-expression and order in society. It is a psychological problem with grave sociological and political implications.

If Freud altered the Enlightenment concept of human nature, Einstein altered the concept of physical nature. His theory of relativity was destined to spill over into many cultural areas outside the limits of physics. The universal acceptance of mechanistic science was replaced by the incredible notions of the universe as a four-dimensional space-time continuum in which matter and energy are just two different forms of the same thing and in which time is relative.

This was such a stunning overthrow of the earlier unlimited faith in the Newtonian world scheme that minds were sent reeling. If the notion of the universe itself was challenged, what else could possibly withstand the onslaught of future theories? What element of Absolute Truth would survive the latest trends of modern science? As a result of Einstein's work, as well as of the work of other famous physicists and chemists in the twentieth century, there never again would exist a total faith in "absolute" categories. Nuclear physics, thermonuclear weapons, the mutability of elements—twentieth century science had achieved the wildest dreams of the most fanatical alchemists or deranged Romanticists.

The net effect of the work of Darwin, Freud, Einstein, and all the others who participated in the development of these new theories was to produce a Second Scientific Revolution that staggered the imagination. The distance between abstract art and the public's comprehension of it was tiny compared with the distance between the new symbolic language of science and the average man's ability to understand it through conventional sense impressions. The extent and depth of the new scientific theories were beyond fathoming by anyone but the relatively small number of specialists who had devoted their lives to studying small corners of the new knowledge. The big need was for synthesis of the new information, for the age of specialization was threatening to make conversation about anything other than the weather and the football scores impossible.

There were many other effects of the work of Darwin, Freud and Einstein, such as the Scopes Monkey Trial, the Atomic Bomb, and a loosening of sexual mores, among other things. Likewise, there were numerous others who contributed to the Second Scientific Revolution. Darwin, Freud, and Einstein were the giants in their fields just as Copernicus, Galileo, and Newton were in theirs, but there were also Bruno, Brahe, Kepler and others in the first revolution, and Planck, Michelson and Morley among others in the latter one. Hopefully, your study of the two scientific revolutions will not end with this essay.

As you read more about the men, the theories, and the events of the twentieth century, it will be interesting to see if your study confirms the hypothesis that present-day Western culture cannot be fully comprehended without an awareness of the scientific revolution which transformed its mythology. Judging from the length of time it took for the full effects of the first Scientific Revolution to make themselves felt on the eighteenth century, it seems safe to predict that your study may not even have the opportunity to take into account the onslaught of effects we can expect to be forthcoming in the next century.

But you can try.

As recently as 1965 three American states continued to ban the teaching of evolution in all public educational institutions. A relatively moderate element of the American Establishment considered that situation to be very much in need of change, as the following editorial indicates.

An Evolution Law and Some Archaic Voices

Life Editorial

In case you thought the Scopes Trial put an end to Monkey Laws, you're dead wrong. Tennessee—where William Jennings Bryan and Clarence Darrow fought their mighty forensic battle on the lawn outside the Dayton courthouse 40 years ago—still has a statute banning the teaching of evolutionary theory in all public schools and colleges. Mississippi has one too. So does Arkansas. A number of other state laws permit similar bans on a local-option basis. Even now the whole subject is controversial enough to make most textbook publishers chary of "Darwinism," and a 1956 survey showed less than half of all U.S. high school students willing to accept evolution as a valid theory.

In Arkansas, a progressive pedagogue can be nicked up to $500 for teaching any "theory or doctrine that mankind ascended or descended from a lower order of animals." A month ago the teachers there struck back. Charging that the law impugned the judgment, integrity and competence of teachers, besides being unenforceable, the executive secretary of the 15,000-member state teachers' association demanded its repeal.

At that, the Arkansas Baptist Bible Fellowship, which represents 13 churches in nine cities, came to the law's defense. "We firmly believe," its statement ran, "that man was created in the image of God by the direct and immediate act of God without process of evolution." Then Governor Orval Faubus, eschewing theology for the sake of a more earthy argument, allowed as how he didn't think the law was especially needed, "but it's all right as a safeguard to keep 'way out' teachers in line."

This brought forth a comment that could well stand as an epitaph to all such bad law-making. "The issue is not whether or not the theory of evolution is true. . . . The issue is whether or not a man can say what he wants, teach what he wants, think what he wants." Wise words from John Scopes, former biology teacher of Dayton, Tenn., now living in retirement in Shreveport, La.

Editorial from *Life* Magazine, October 8, 1965. © 1965 Time Inc.

More than four years after the "Life" Magazine editorial poked fun at the archaic opposition to the teaching of evolution (see preceding article), an incredible relic of "monkey law" mentality pierced the smog-covered skies of America's most populous state. In late 1969 the California Board of Education voted to overrule its own carefully-appointed committee of curriculum experts and to insert remarks which implicitly endorsed the validity of the theory of special creation. With the intention of granting equal space for a nonscientific theory in the guidelines for teachers of science, the Board unintentionally created a storm of controversy. Two letters to the editor of a major California daily newspaper by respected authorities in the field were published on the same day. They reveal the continuing conflict originally set into motion by Darwin's ideas. Dr. Gerard, one of the world's foremost physiologists, is dean of the graduate division at the University of California at Irvine; Rev. Grispino is an assistant professor of sacred scripture at Loyola University in Los Angeles.

Some Things Should Not Be Mixed

R. W. Gerard

The State Board of Education has voted to have inserted into a long and meticulously prepared document on the teaching of science an utterly irrelevant statement concerning the Biblical version of man's origin.

Some things should not be mixed. The Bible itself enjoins man, "Render therefore unto Caesar the things that are Caesar's and unto God the things that are God's." (Matthew xxii: 21.) And the Supreme Court has concurred.

I wonder if Dr. Max Rafferty was really serious when he said that both views of the origin of man should be presented and the children allowed to decide.

Should a scientific course on reproduction also mention the stork "theory"? Did it require the Apollo 11 mission to prove that the moon is not made of green cheese? Is the soothsaying of astrology really to be considered along with the precise content of astronomy that allowed man to plan his unerring trip to and from the moon? And the behavior of the propelling rockets was based on what we still call "the atomic theory."

Science is cautious in calling its understandings "laws," for new evidence may always alter them—usually by enrichment rather than discard. Even the "law" of gravitation, so precisely and magnificently developed by Newton, was given new dimension by Einstein.

From "Monkey Law Mentality Under Fire Again," *Los Angeles Times*, December 6, 1969. Copyright, Los Angeles Times. Reprinted with permission.

In the case of evolution, I know of no responsible person who has examined the evidence who questions that species arose by a continuing series of changes from ancestral ones. This is the essence of evolution and is as much a fact as atoms and gravity. Darwin's theory as to the mechanism of evolution has been supported by vast amounts of evidence over the century since it was presented, but some other mechanism might still prove important.

Although I am a member of the committee that prepared the "guide lines," I was unable to attend the unfortunate board meeting, but I am informed that two physicians on the board, claiming scientific expertise, followed the prodding of some speakers at the hearing and agreed that evolution is "only a theory" and that the view of special creation should also be presented. As a newspaper article put it, "God to get equal time."

What an undignified approach to God! An article also quoted one of the insistent ladies: "We feel we started this controversy by first bringing it to public attention but we want to give full credit to Gov. Reagan for appointing men to the board who are open minded on this subject."

I have several comments to make. First, most doctors, but not all, have had an education that helps them understand the nature of scientific evidence as well as knowing many scientific facts; very few have really studied the evidence concerning evolution.

I know. Besides being a biologist I am a physician and have helped teach medical students and doctors for half a century. I would trust most physicians to do a reasonable job of diagnosing and treating my body illnesses, but not much beyond this.

Second, there may be many citizens of this state who do not "believe" in evolution. I think of the surgeon who asked the five students in his clinic to examine a patient and recommend whether or not to operate. The first entirely missed the acute appendicitis and said, "Do not operate." The other four took the easy path and agreed. The surgeon then said, "I'm sorry, gentlemen, you are all wrong. I shall operate at once." But the patient got into the conversation at this point, "The hell you are, doc; five to one odds are good enough for me."

Third, I shudder at the judgment of an official who does not distinguish between "open mindedness" and professional incompetence in making appointments to an important body that determines what "operations" are performed on our children.

Finally, I ask how easy it will be in the future to induce busy people to devote much valuable time and expert knowledge to the service of the state if their honest and thoughtful efforts are cavalierly distorted by a group of people neither qualified nor inclined to make responsible judgments.

A committee of a dozen or so was carefully chosen from outstanding science teachers and administrators at all levels of the public school system plus a few established scientists from institutions of higher education. These men and women contributed truly great amounts of time and effort to the task of developing guide lines for a coherent and meaningful science education in the schools of California, with no recompense whatsoever except the satisfaction of serving their state and contributing to the education of its future citizens.

The board, overruling the committee and its own science advisory body, has in effect changed one letter, from "not" to "now."

The Ghost of the Scopes Trial

Rev. Joseph A. Grispino

As an active member of the Society of Biblical Literature and of the Catholic Biblical Society of America, may I voice an unofficial plea in the name of America's two most learned Biblical societies which represent Protestant-Jews-Catholics? May I assume to speak for the vast silent majority of scholars who are not fundamentalists?

If so, I want to thank the members of the California State Board of Education for their laudable Biblical intentions, but, behold, I see the ghost of the Scopes trial again! The Board's manner of Biblical interpretation permeating the two added paragraphs, in the basic outline for new textbooks, is blatantly fundamentalist. The board's dichotomy of Bible vs. science is antiquated and unnecessary.

The teaching found in the books and publications of the Biblical nonfundamentalists is simply that the main intention of the writers of Genesis, chapters 1 to 3, was not to speak about the scientific questions of creation and evolution but about a religious question— that God made everything! *How* He made everything was beyond their knowledge and intention.

Now if scientists present theories of the origin of the material universe and if they present strong arguments in favor of a gradual evolution from lower forms of life to human life, we welcome these theories and arguments. We thereby interpret the Biblical creation story to mean that God gave the first impulse to the creation of the material universe and to the lowest form of life. We thank the scientists for making mankind see God's tremendous power in his initial act of creation.

Freud had much to say about the nature of man. In one of his last books, written a few years before his death, Freud stresses the innate aggressiveness of pleasure-seeking man. His views seem to reinforce the concept of life as a never-ending struggle for supremacy; in effect, the harmonious Newtonian order is a Freudian impossibility. Other Enlightenment concepts, such as the basic goodness of man and the perfectibility of society, are also discredited by Freud's picture of human nature.

Man's Instinct for Aggression

Sigmund Freud

The element of truth behind all this, which people are so ready to disavow, is that men are not gentle creatures who want to be loved, and who at the most can defend themselves if they are attacked; they are, on the contrary, creatures among whose instinctual endowments is to be reckoned a powerful share of aggressiveness. As a result, their neighbour is for them not only a potential helper or sexual object, but also someone who tempts them to satisfy their aggressiveness on him, to exploit his capacity for work without compensation, to use him sexually without his consent, to seize his possessions, to humiliate him, to cause him pain, to torture and to kill him. *Homo homini lupus.*[1] Who, in the face of all his experience of life and of history, will have the courage to dispute this assertion? As a rule this cruel aggressiveness waits for some provocation or puts itself at the service of some other purpose, whose goal might also have been reached by milder measures. In circumstances that are favourable to it, when the mental counter-forces which ordinarily inhibit it are out of action, it also manifests itself spontaneously and reveals man as a savage beast to whom consideration towards his own kind is something alien. Anyone who calls to mind the atrocities committed during the racial migrations or the invasions of the Huns, or by the people known as Mongols under Jenghiz Khan and Tamerlane, or at the capture of Jerusalem by the pious Crusaders, or even, indeed, the horrors of the recent World War [1914–1918]—anyone who calls these things to mind will have to bow humbly before the truth of this view.

The existence of this inclination to aggression, which we can detect in ourselves and justly assume to be present in others, is the factor which disturbs our relations with our neighbour and which forces civilization into such a high expenditure [of energy]. In consequence of this primary mutual hostility of human beings, civilized society is perpetually threatened with disintegration. The interest of work in common would not hold it together; instinctual passions are stronger than reasonable interests. Civilization has to use its utmost efforts in order to set limits to man's aggressive instincts and to hold the manifestations of them in check by psychical reaction-formations. Hence, therefore, the use of methods intended to incite people into identifications and aim-inhibited relationships of love, hence the restriction upon sexual life, and hence too the ideal's commandment to love one's neighbour as oneself—a commandment which is really justified by the fact that nothing else runs so strongly counter to the original nature of man. In spite of every effort, these endeavours of civilization have not so far achieved very much. It hopes to prevent the crudest excesses of brutal violence by itself assuming the right to use violence against criminals, but the law is not able to lay hold of the more cautious and refined manifestations of human aggressiveness. The time comes when each one of us has to give up as illusions the expectations which, in his youth, he pinned upon his fellow-men, and when he may learn how much difficulty and pain has been added to his life by their ill-will. At the same time, it would be unfair to reproach civilization with trying to eliminate strife and competition from human activity. These things are undoubtedly indispensable. But opposition is not necessarily enmity; it is merely misused and made an *occasion* for enmity.

The communists believe that they have found the path to deliverance from our evils. According to them, man is wholly good and is well-disposed to his neighbour; but the institution of private property has corrupted his nature. The ownership of private wealth gives the individual power, and with it the temptation to ill-treat his neighbour; while the man who is excluded from possession is bound to rebel in hostility against his oppressor. If private property were abolished, all wealth held in common, and everyone allowed to share in the enjoyment of it, ill-will and hostility would disappear among men. Since everyone's needs would be satisfied, no one would have any reason to regard another as his enemy; all would willingly undertake the work that was necessary. I have no concern with any economic criticisms of the communist system; I cannot enquire into whether the abolition of private property is expedient or advantageous.[2] But I am able to recognize that the psychological premisses on which the system is based are an untenable illusion. In abolishing private property we deprive the human love of aggression of one of its instruments, certainly a strong one, though certainly not the strongest; but we have in no way altered the differences in power and influence which are misused by aggressiveness, nor have we altered anything in its nature. Aggressiveness was not created by property. It reigned almost without limit in primitive times, when property was still very scanty, and it already shows itself in the nursery almost before property has given up its primal, anal form; it forms the basis of every relation of affection and love among people (with the single exception, perhaps, of the mother's relation to her male child[3]). If we do away with personal rights over material wealth, there still remains prerogative in the field of sexual relationships, which is bound to become the source of the strongest dislike and the most violent hostility among men who in other respects are on an equal footing. If we were to remove this factor, too, by allowing complete freedom of sexual life and thus abolishing the family, the germ-cell of civilization, we cannot, it is true, easily foresee what new paths the development of civilization could take; but one thing we can expect, and that is that this indestructible feature of human nature will follow it there.

It is clearly not easy for men to give up the satisfaction of this inclination to aggression. They do not feel comfortable without it. The advantage which a comparatively small cultural group offers of allowing this instinct an outlet in the form of hostility against intruders is not to be despised. It is always possible to bind together a considerable number of people in love, so long as there are other people left over to receive the manifestations of their aggressiveness. I once discussed the phenomenon that it is precisely communities with adjoining territories, and related to each other in other ways as well, who are engaged in constant feuds and in ridiculing each other— like the Spaniards and Portuguese, for instance, the North Germans and South Germans, the English and Scotch, and so on.[4] I gave this phenomenon the name of 'the narcissism of minor differences', a name which does not do much to explain it. We can now see that it is a convenient and relatively harmless satisfaction of the inclination to aggression, by means of which cohesion between the members of the community is made easier. In this respect the Jewish people, scattered everywhere, have rendered most useful services to the civilizations of the countries that have been their hosts; but unfortunately all the massacres of the Jews in the Middle Ages did not suffice to make that period more peaceful and secure for their Christian fellows.

When once the Apostle Paul had posited universal love between men as the foundation of his Christian community, extreme intolerance on the part of Christendom towards those who remained outside it became the inevitable consequence. To the Romans, who had not founded their communal life as a State upon love, religious intolerance was something foreign, although with them religion was a concern of the State and the State was permeated by religion. Neither was it an unaccountable chance that the dream of a Germanic world-dominion called for anti-semitism as its complement; and it is intelligible that the attempt to establish a new, communist civilization in Russia should find its psychological support in the persecution of the bourgeois. One only wonders, with concern, what the Soviets will do after they have wiped out their bourgeois.

If civilization imposes such great sacrifices not only on man's sexuality but on his aggressivity, we can understand better why it is hard for him to be happy in that civilization. In fact, primitive man was better off in knowing no restrictions of instinct. To counterbalance this, his prospects of enjoying this happiness for any length of time were very slender. Civilized man has exchanged a portion of his possibilities of happiness for a portion of security. We must not forget, however, that in the primal family only the head of it enjoyed this instinctual freedom; the rest lived in slavish suppression. In that primal period of civilization, the contrast between a minority who enjoyed the advantages of civilization and a majority who were robbed of those advantages was, therefore, carried to extremes. As regards the primitive peoples who exist to-day, careful researches have shown that their instinctual life is by no means to be envied for its freedom. It is subject to restrictions of a different kind but perhaps of greater severity than those attaching to modern civilized man.

When we justly find fault with the present state of our civilization for so inadequately fulfilling our demands for a plan of life that shall make us happy, and for allowing the existence of so much suffering which could probably be avoided—when, with unsparing criticism, we try to uncover the roots of its imperfection, we are undoubtedly exercising a proper right and are not showing ourselves enemies of civilization. We may expect gradually to carry through such alterations in our civilization as will better satisfy our needs and will escape our criticisms. But perhaps we may also familiarize ourselves with the idea that there are difficulties attaching to the nature of civilization which will not yield to any attempt at reform. Over and above the tasks of restricting the instincts, which we are prepared for, there forces itself on our notice the danger of a state of things which might be termed 'the psychological poverty of groups'.[5] This danger is most threatening where the bonds of a society are chiefly constituted by the identification of its members with one another, while individuals of the leader type do not acquire the importance that should fall to them in the formation of a group.[6] The present cultural state of America would give us a good opportunity for studying the damage to civilization which is thus to be feared. But I shall avoid the temptation of entering upon a critique of American civilization; I do not wish to give an impression of wanting myself to employ American methods. . . .

In all that follows I adopt the standpoint, therefore, that the inclination to aggression is an original, self-subsisting instinctual disposition in man, and I return to my view that it constitutes the greatest impediment to civilization. At one point . . . I was led to the idea that civilization was a special process which mankind undergoes, and I am still under the influence of that idea. I may now add that civilization is a process in the service of Eros, whose purpose is to combine single human individuals, and after that families, then races, peoples and nations, into one great unity, the unity of mankind. Why this has to happen, we do not know; the work of Eros is precisely this.[7] These collections of men are to be libidinally bound to one another. Necessity alone, the advantages of work in common, will not hold them together. But man's natural aggressive instinct, the hostility of each against all and of all against each, opposes this programme of civilization. This aggressive instinct is the derivative and the main representative of the death instinct which we have found alongside of Eros and which shares world-dominion with it. And now, I think, the meaning of the evolution of civilization is no longer obscure to us. It must present the struggle between Eros and Death, between the instinct of life and the instinct of destruction, as it works itself out in the human species. This struggle is what all life essentially consists of, and the evolution of civilization may therefore be simply described as the struggle for life of the human species.[8] And it is this battle of the giants that our nurse-maids try to appease with their lullaby about Heaven.[9]

Notes

1 ['Man is a wolf to man.' Derived from Plautus, Asinaria II, iv, 88.]

2 Anyone who has tasted the miseries of poverty in his own youth and has experienced the indifference and arrogance of the well-to-do, should be safe from the suspicion of having no understanding or

good will towards endeavours to fight against the inequality of wealth among men and all that it leads to. To be sure, if an attempt is made to base this fight upon an abstract demand, in the name of justice, for equality for all men, there is a very obvious objection to be made —that nature, by endowing individuals with extremely unequal physical attributes and mental capacities, has introduced injustices against which there is no remedy.

3 [Cf. a footnote to Chapter VI of *Group Psychology* (1921c), *Standard Ed.,* 18, 101n. A rather longer discussion of the point occurs near the end of Lecture XXXIII of the *New Introductory Lectures* (1933a).]

4 [See Chapter VI of *Group Psychology* (1921c), *Standard Ed.,* 18, 101, and 'The Taboo of Virginity' (1918a), ibid., 11, 199.]

5 [The German *'psychologisches Elend'* seems to be a version of Janet's expression *'misère psychologique'* applied by him to describe the incapacity for mental synthesis which he attributes to neurotics.]

6 Cf. *Group Psychology and the Analysis of the Ego* (1921c).

7 [See *Beyond the Pleasure Principle* (1920g) passim.]

8 And we may probably add more precisely, a struggle for life in the shape it was bound to assume after a certain event which still remains to be discovered.

9 [*'Eiapopeia vom Himmel.'* A quotation from Heine's poem *Deutschland,* Caput I.]

The following excerpts from a book written for the layman try to show how the work of Einstein produced a fundamental revolution in scientific thinking. Particularly worthy of attention are the passages dealing with what we now understand "reality" to be and what our hopes are for bringing the physical phenomena of our universe into the realm of "understanding." Is the picture of what may be possible a bright one or a discouraging one?

The Universe and Dr. Einstein

Lincoln Barnett

$E = mc^2$ provides the answer to many of the longstanding mysteries of physics. It explains how radioactive substances like radium and uranium are able to eject particles at enormous velocities and to go on doing so for millions of years. It explains how the sun and all the stars can go on radiating light and heat for billions of years, for if our sun were being consumed by ordinary processes of combustion, the earth would have died in frozen darkness eons ago. It reveals the magnitude of the energy that slumbers in the nuclei of atoms, and forecasts how many grams of uranium must go into a bomb in order to destroy a city. Finally it discloses some fundamental truths about physical reality. Prior to Relativity scientists had pictured the universe as a vessel containing two distinct elements, matter and energy—the former inert, tangible, and characterized by a property called mass, and the latter active, invisible, and without mass. But Einstein showed that mass and energy are equivalent: the property called mass is simply concentrated energy. In other words matter is energy and energy is matter, and the distinction is simply one of temporary state.

In the light of this broad principle many puzzles of nature are resolved. The baffling interplay of matter and radiation which appears sometimes to be a concourse of particles and sometimes a meeting of waves, becomes more understandable. The dual role of the electron as a unit of matter and a unit of electricity, the wave electron, the photon, waves of matter, waves of probability, a universe of waves—all these seem less paradoxical. For all these concepts simply describe different manifestations of the same underlying reality, and it no longer makes sense to ask what any one of them "really" is. Matter and energy are interchangeable. If matter sheds its mass and travels with the speed of light we call it radiation or energy. And conversely if energy congeals and becomes inert and we can ascertain its mass we call it matter. Heretofore science could only note their ephemeral properties and relations as they touched the perceptions of earthbound man. But since July 16, 1945 man has been able to transform one into the other. For on that night at Alamogordo, New Mexico, man for the first time transmuted a substantial quantity of matter into the light, heat, sound, and motion which we call energy.

Yet the fundamental mystery remains. The whole march of science toward the unification of concepts—the reduction of all matter to elements and then to a few types of particles, the reduction of "forces" to the single concept "energy," and then the reduction of matter *and* energy to a single basic quantity—leads still to the unknown. The many questions merge into one, to which there may never be an answer: what is the essence of this mass-energy substance, what is the underlying stratum of physical reality which science seeks to explore?

Thus Relativity, like the Quantum Theory, draws man's intellect still farther away from the Newtonian universe, firmly rooted in space and time and functioning like some great, unerring, and manageable machine. Einstein's laws of motion, his basic principles of the relativity of distance, time, and mass, and his deductions from these principles comprise what is known as the Special Theory of Relativity. In the decade following the publication of this original work, he expanded his scientific and philosophical system into the General Theory of Relativity, through which he examined the mysterious force that guides the whirling of the stars, comets, meteors, and galaxies, and all the moving systems of iron, stone, vapor, and flame in the immense inscrutable void. Newton called this force "universal gravitation." From his own concept of gravitation Einstein attained a view of the vast architecture and anatomy of the universe as a whole. . . .

Today the outer limits of man's knowledge are defined by Relativity, the inner limits by the Quantum Theory. Relativity has shaped all our concepts of space, time, gravitation, and the realities that are too remote and too vast to be perceived. The Quantum Theory has shaped all our concepts of the atom, the basic units of matter and energy, and the realities that are too elusive and too small to be perceived. Yet these two great scientific systems rest on entirely different and unrelated theoretical foundations. They do not, as it were, speak the same language. The purpose of the Unified Field Theory is to construct a bridge between them. Believing in the harmony and uniformity of nature, Einstein has evolved a single edifice of physical laws to encompass both the phenomena of the atom and the phenomena of outer space.

What unexpected new aspects of nature the Unified Field Theory may uncover and how many old mysteries it may resolve is still too early to predict. But its obvious minimum achievement is that it unites the laws of gravitation and the laws of electromagnetism within one basic superstructure of universal law. In the same way that Relativity reduced gravitational force to a geometrical property of the space-time continuum, the Unified Field Theory reduces electromagnetic force—the other great universal force—to equivalent status. "The idea that there are two structures of space independent of each other, the metric-gravitational and the electromagnetic," Einstein once observed, "is intolerable to the theoretical spirit." Yet despite all his efforts he could not incorporate electromagnetic field laws into General Relativity. Now after thirty-three years of exploring endless gambits of mathematical logic he appears to have achieved his purpose. One may ask if this proves then that electromagnetic and gravitational force are physically the "same thing." It would be no more accurate to make such a statement than to assert that steam, ice, and water are the "same thing"—though all are manifestations of the same substance. What the Unified Field Theory does do is to show that gravitational and electromagnetic force are not independent of each other—that they are in a very real physical sense inseparable. More specifically it describes gravitational and electromagnetic force in terms of a deeper reality that undergirds both—a basic universal field within which gravitational and electromagnetic fields are merely particular ephemeral forms or conditions of state.

If the fullest implications of the Unified Field Theory are sustained by the tests of the future—if the laws of quantum physics can also be derived from its equations—crucial new insights will doubtless be attained into the composition of matter, the structure of the elementary particles, the mechanics of radiation, and other enigmas of the subatomic world. Yet these will be essentially by-products. For the great philosophical triumph of the Unified Field Theory is implicit in the first word of its title. It carries to logical fulfillment the long course of science towards the unification of man's concepts of the physical world. Through the centuries the varied currents of discovery, theory, research, and reason have steadily converged, mingled, and flowed onward into ever widening and deepening channels. The first long advance was the reduction of the world's multifarious substances into 92 natural elements. Then these elements were reduced to a few fundamental particles. Concurrently the various "forces" in the world came to be recognized one by one as varying manifestations of electromagnetic force, and all the different kinds of radiation in the universe—light, heat, X-rays, radio waves, gamma rays—as nothing more than electromagnetic waves of varying wave length and frequency. Ultimately the features of the universe distilled down to a few basic quantities—space, time, matter, energy, and gravitation. But in Special Relativity, Einstein demonstrated the equivalence of matter and energy, and in General Relativity he showed the indivisibility of the space-time continuum. The Unified Field Theory now culminates and climaxes this coalescing process. For from its august perspective the entire universe is revealed as one elemental field in which each star, each atom, each wandering comet and slow-wheeling galaxy and flying electron is seen to be but a ripple or tumescence in the underlying space-time unity. And so a profound simplicity supplants the surface complexity of nature. The distinctions between gravitational force and electromagnetic force, matter and energy, electric charge and field, space and time, all fade in the light of their revealed relationships and resolve into configurations of the four-dimensional continuum which is the universe. Thus all man's perceptions of the world and all his abstract intuitions of reality merge finally into one, and the deep underlying unity of the universe is laid bare.

The Unified Field Theory touches the "grand aim of all science," which, as Einstein once defined it, is "to cover the greatest number of empirical facts by logical deduction from the smallest possible number of hypotheses or axioms." The urge to consolidate premises, to unify concepts, to penetrate the variety and particularity of the manifest world to the undifferentiated unity that lies beyond is not only the leaven of science; it is the loftiest passion of the human intellect. The philosopher and mystic, as well as the scientist, have always sought through their various disciplines of introspection to arrive at a knowledge of the ultimate immutable essence that undergirds the mutable illusory world. More than twenty-three hundred years ago Plato declared, "The true lover of knowledge is always striving after *being*. . . . He will not rest at those multitudinous phenomena whose existence is appearance only."

But the irony of man's quest for reality is that as nature is stripped of its disguises, as order emerges from chaos and unity from diversity, as concepts merge and fundamental laws assume increasingly simpler form, the evolving picture becomes ever more remote from experience —far stranger indeed and less recognizable than the bone structure behind a familiar face. For where the geometry of a skull predestines the outlines of the tissue it supports, there is no likeness between the image of a tree transcribed by our senses and that propounded by wave mechanics, or between a glimpse of the starry sky on a summer night and the four-dimensional continuum that has replaced our perceptual Euclidean space.

In trying to distinguish appearance from reality and lay bare the fundamental structure of the universe, science has had to transcend the "rabble of the senses." But its highest edifices, Einstein has pointed out, have been "purchased at the price of emptiness of content." A theoretical concept is emptied of content to the very degree that it is divorced from sensory experience. For the only world man can truly know is the world created for him by his senses. If he expunges all the impressions which they translate and memory stores, nothing is left. That is what the philosopher Hegel meant by his cryptic remark: "Pure Being and Nothing are the same." A state of existence devoid of associations has no meaning. So paradoxically what the scientist and the philosopher call the world of appearance—the world of light and color, of blue skies and green leaves, of sighing wind and murmuring water, the world designed by the physiology of human sense organs—is the world in which finite man is incarcerated by his essential nature. And what the scientist and the philosopher call the world of reality—the colorless, soundless, impalpable cosmos which lies like an iceberg beneath the plane of man's perceptions—is a skeleton structure of symbols.

And the symbols change. While physicists of the last century knew, for example, that the crimson of a rose was a subjective, aesthetic sensation, they believed that "in reality" the quality they termed crimson was an oscillation of the luminiferous ether. Today it is conventional to identify crimson as a wave length. But it is equally proper to think of it as the value of the energy content of photons. Such considerations led a famous physicist to remark cynically that on Mondays, Wednesdays, and Fridays one uses the quantum theory, and on Tuesdays, Thursdays, and Saturdays the wave theory. In either case the concepts employed are abstract constructions of theory. And upon examination such concepts as gravitation, electromagnetism, energy, current, momentum, the atom, the neutron, all turn out to be theoretical substructures, inventions, metaphors which man's intellect has contrived to help him picture the true, the objective reality he apprehends beneath the surface of things. So in place of the deceitful and chaotic representations of the senses science has substituted varying systems of symbolic representation. While these systems are distinguished by constantly increasing mathematical accuracy, it would be difficult today to find any scientist who imagines himself, because of his ability to discern previous errors, in a position to enunciate final truths. On the contrary, modern theorists are aware, as Newton was, that they stand on the shoulders of giants and that their particular perspective may appear as distorted to posterity as that of their predecessors seemed to them.

For all the promise of future revelation it is possible that certain terminal boundaries have already been reached in man's struggle to understand the manifold of nature in which he finds himself. In his descent into the microcosm he has encountered indeterminacy, duality, paradox—barriers that seem to admonish him he cannot pry too inquisitively into the heart of things without altering and vitiating the processes he seeks to observe. And in exploring the macrocosm he comes at last to a final featureless unity of space-time, mass-energy, matter-field—an ultimate, undiversified, and eternal ground beyond which there appears to be nowhere to progress. "The prison house," said Plato, "is the world of sight." Every seeming avenue of escape from this prison house that science has surveyed leads only deeper into a misty realm of symbolism and abstraction.

It may be that the extreme and insurmountable limit of scientific knowledge will be reached in the attainment of perfect isomorphic representation—that is, in a final flawless concurrence of theory and natural process, so complete that every observed phenomenon is accounted for and nothing is left out of the picture. In its approach to this goal, science has hitherto achieved its most notable pragmatic and operational triumphs. For while telling nothing of the true "nature" of things, it nevertheless succeeds in defining their relationships and depicting the events in which they are involved. "The event," Alfred North Whitehead declared, "is the unit of things real." By this he meant that however theoretical systems may change and however empty of content their symbols and concepts may be, the essential and enduring facts of science and of life are the happenings, the activities, the events. The implications of this idea can best be illustrated by contemplating a simple physical event such as the meeting of two electrons. Within the frame of modern physics one can depict this event as a collision of two elementary grains of matter or two elementary units of electrical energy, as a concourse of particles or of probability waves, or as a commingling of eddies in a four-dimensional space-time continuum. Theory does not define what the principals in this encounter actually are. Thus in a sense the electrons are not "real" but merely theoretical symbols. On the other hand the meeting itself is "real"—the event is "real." It is as though the true objective world lies forever half-concealed beneath a translucent, plastic dome. Peering through its cloudy surface, deformed and distorted by the ever changing perspectives of theory, man faintly espies certain apparently stable relationships and recurring events. A consistent isomorphic representation of these relationships and events is the maximal possibility of his knowledge. Beyond that point he stares into the void.

In the evolution of scientific thought, one fact has become impressively clear: there is no mystery of the physical world which does not point to a mystery beyond itself. All highroads of the intellect, all byways of theory and conjecture lead ultimately to an abyss that human ingenuity can never span. For man is enchained by the very condition of his being, his finiteness and involvement in nature. The farther he extends his horizons, the more vividly he recognizes the fact that, as the physicist Niels Bohr puts it, "we are both spectators and actors in the great drama of existence." Man is thus his own greatest mystery. He does not understand the vast veiled universe into which he has been cast for the reason that he does not understand himself. He comprehends but little of his organic processes and even less of his unique capacity to perceive the world about him, to reason and to dream. Least of all does he understand his noblest and most mysterious faculty: the ability to transcend himself and perceive himself in the act of perception.

Man's inescapable impasse is that he himself is part of the world he seeks to explore; his body and proud brain are mosaics of the same elemental particles that compose the dark, drifting dust clouds of interstellar space; he is, in the final analysis, merely an ephemeral conformation of the primordial space-time field. Standing midway between macrocosm and microcosm he finds barriers on every side and can perhaps but marvel, as St. Paul did nineteen hundred years ago, that "the world was created by the word of God so that what is seen was made out of things which do not appear."

The role of science in reducing the influence and credibility of organized religion is precisely delineated by one of the twentieth century's most brilliant minds. In keeping with the unorthodox approach of "Hangups From Way Back," however, it should be pointed out that even the most brilliant minds have often been wrong. With due respect, but also with our usual amount of irreverence toward canonized authority, may we inquire of you: How perceptive is Whitehead's analysis of the declining influence of religion in a science-oriented society?

Science and the Modern World

Alfred North Whitehead

But on the whole, during many generations, there has been a gradual decay of religious influence in European civilisation. Each revival touches a lower peak than its predecessor, and each period of slackness a lower depth. The average curve marks a steady fall in religious tone. In some countries the interest in religion is higher than in others. But in those countries where the interest is relatively high, it still falls as the generations pass. Religion is tending to degenerate into a decent formula wherewith to embellish a comfortable life. A great historical movement on this scale results from the convergence of many causes. I wish to suggest two of them . . . for consideration.

In the first place for over two centuries religion has been on the defensive, and on a weak defensive. The period has been one of unprecedented intellectual progress. In this way a series of novel situations have been produced for thought. Each such occasion has found the religious thinkers unprepared. Something, which has been proclaimed to be vital, has finally, after struggle, distress, and anathema, been modified and otherwise interpreted. The next generation of religious apologists then congratulates the religious world on the deeper insight which has been gained. The result of the continued repetition of this undignified retreat, during many generations, has at last almost entirely destroyed the intellectual authority of religious thinkers. Consider this contrast: when Darwin or Einstein proclaim theories which modify our ideas, it is a triumph for science. We do not go about saying that there is another defeat for science, because its old ideas have been abandoned. We know that another step of scientific insight has been gained.

Religion will not regain its old power until it can face change in the same spirit as does science. Its principles may be eternal, but the expression of those principles requires continual development. This evolution of religion is in the main a disengagement of its own proper ideas from the adventitious notions which have crept into it by reason of the expression of its own ideas in terms of the imaginative picture of the world entertained in previous ages. Such a release of religion from the bonds of imperfect science is all to the good. It stresses its own genuine message. The great point to be kept in mind is that normally an advance in science will show that statements of various religious beliefs require some sort of modification. It may be that they have to be expanded or explained, or indeed entirely restated. If the religion is a sound expression of truth, this modification will only exhibit more adequately the exact point which is of importance. This process is a gain. In so far, therefore, as any religion has any contact with physical facts, it is to be expected that the point of view of those facts must be continually modified as scientific knowledge advances. In this way, the exact relevance of these facts for religious thought will grow more and more clear. The progress of science must result in the unceasing codification of religious thought, to the great advantage of religion.

The religious controversies of the sixteenth and seventeenth centuries put theologians into a most unfortunate state of mind. They were always attacking and defending. They pictured themselves as the garrison of a fort surrounded by hostile forces. All such pictures express half-truths. That is why they are so popular. But they are dangerous. This particular picture fostered a pugnacious party spirit which really expresses an ultimate lack of faith. They dared not modify, because they shirked the task of disengaging their spiritual message from the associations of a particular imagery.

Let me explain myself by an example. In the early medieval times, Heaven was in the sky, and Hell was underground; volcanoes were the jaws of Hell. I do not assert that these beliefs entered into the official formulations: but they did enter into the popular understanding of the general doctrines of Heaven and Hell. These notions were what everyone thought to be implied by the doctrine of the future state. They entered into the explanations of the influential exponents of Christian belief. For example, they occur in the *Dialogues* of Pope Gregory,[1] the Great, a man whose high official position is surpassed only by the magnitude of his services to humanity. I am not saying what we ought to believe about the future state. But whatever be the right doctrine, in this instance the clash between religion and science, which has relegated the earth to the position of a second-rate planet attached to a second-rate sun, has been greatly to the benefit of the spirituality of religion by dispersing these medieval fancies.

Another way of looking at this question of the evolution of religious thought is to note that any verbal form of statement which has been before the world for some time discloses ambiguities; and that often such ambiguities strike at the very heart of the meaning. The effective sense in which a doctrine has been held in the past cannot be determined by the mere logical analysis of verbal statements, made in ignorance of the logical trap. You have to take into account the whole reaction of human nature to the scheme of thought. This reaction is of a mixed character, including elements of emotion derived from our lower natures. It is here that the impersonal criticism of science and of philosophy comes to the aid of religious evolution. Example after example can be given of this motive force in development. For example, the logical difficulties inherent in the doctrine of the moral cleansing of human nature by the power of religion rent Christianity in the days of Pelagius and Augustine—that is to say, at the beginning of the fifth century. Echoes of that controversy still linger in theology.

So far, my point has been this: that religion is the expression of one type of fundamental experiences of mankind: that religious thought develops into an increasing accuracy of expression, disengaged from adventitious imagery: that the interaction between religion and science is one great factor in promoting this development.

I now come to my second reason for the modern fading of interest in religion. . . . We have to know what we mean by religion. The churches, in their presentation of their answers to this query, have put forward aspects of religion which are expressed in terms either suited to the emotional reactions of bygone times or directed to excite modern emotional interests of nonreligious character. What I mean under the first heading is that religious appeal is directed partly to excite that instinctive fear of the wrath of a tyrant which was inbred in the unhappy populations of the arbitrary empires of the ancient world, and in particular to excite that fear of an all-powerful arbitrary tyrant behind the unknown forces of nature. This appeal to the ready instinct of brute fear is losing its force. It lacks any directness of response, because modern science and modern conditions of life have taught us to meet occasions of apprehension by a critical analysis of their causes and conditions. Religion is the reaction of human nature to its search for God. The presentation of God under the aspect of power awakens every modern instinct of critical reaction. This is fatal; for religion collapses unless its main positions command immediacy of assent. In this respect the old phraseology is at variance with the psychology of modern civilisations. This change in psychology is largely due to science, and is one of the chief ways in which the advance of science has weakened the hold of the old religious forms of expression.

Note

1 Cf. Gregorovius' *History of Rome in the Middle Ages,* Book III, Ch. III, Vol. II, English Trans.

Questions

1 Who affected your life more: Einstein or Edison?

2 Why is the prestige accorded technological achievements generally less than that accorded theoretical achievements in science?

3 Who are some of the scientific giants upon whose shoulders Darwin, Freud, and Einstein stood? Did any of them exert as much influence?

4 What is your position on the question, discussed in the magazine editorial and the two letters to the editor, concerning the teaching of evolution and special creation in public schools?

5 Do you appreciate contemporary art? Can you see the connection between art and mythology today?

6

Nationalism
and Two World Wars

The twentieth century has experienced more large-scale warfare than any other century in history. The species is as violent as it has ever been. Romantic nationalism, inherited from the nineteenth century, has taken hold and spread like the flu bug. What is the chemistry of this new germ that carries such a deadly effect?

The Chemistry of Nationalism

Frederick Gentles

CAUCHON, BISHOP OF BEAUVAIS . . . . Call this side of her Nationalism if you will: I can find no better name for it. I can tell you that it is essentially anti-Catholic and anti-Christian; for the Catholic Church knows only one realm, and that is the realm of Christ's kingdom. Divide that kingdom into nations and you dethrone Christ. Dethrone Christ, and who will stand between our throats and the sword? The world will perish in a welter of war.
—BERNARD SHAW, *Saint Joan*[1]

The world has experienced a welter of war since the Bishop of Beauvais spoke at the trial of Joan of Arc in 1431, and it may well perish in a third or fourth holocaust following the first two world wars of this century. Nationalism has been a factor, perhaps the most important factor, in the wholesale slaughter of hundreds of millions since Joan had a glimmer of that intoxicating idea, the nation. The nation that emerged from the God-oriented Middle Ages, however, was not the modern version of that institution but a nation centered around a divine right king with God on the side of the monarch and his people. The Christian world was divided.

The concept of nationalism was pushed beyond the limitations of divine monarchy by the Italian nationalist Niccolo Machiavelli. Within one hundred years of the burning of Joan as a heretic, Machiavelli published *The Prince* in which he suggested a new morality, or a new amorality, of warring, lying, cheating, and stealing if only to benefit and preserve the nation. The prince should, Machiavelli asserted, make himself expert in the use of arms; he should have the strength of a lion. He should have the wit of a fox, because so often peace has been broken and promises made worthless by faithless princes.

But since a Prince should know how to use the beast's nature wisely, he ought of beasts to choose both the lion and the fox;

for the lion cannot guard himself from traps, nor the fox from wolves. He must therefore be a fox to discern traps and a lion to drive off wolves. . . . Thus, it is well to seem merciful, faithful, humane, religious, and upright, and also to be so; but the mind should remain so balanced that were it needful not to be so, you should be able and know•how to change to the contrary. . . . A Prince should therefore be very careful that nothing ever escapes his lips which is not full of the five qualities above named, so that to see and hear him, one would think him the embodiment of mercy, good faith, integrity, kindliness, and religion. And there is no virtue which it is more necessary for him to seem to possess than this last. . . . A certain Prince of our own days, whom it is well not to name, is always preaching peace and good faith, although he is the mortal enemy of both; and both, had he practised as he preaches, would oftener than once, have lost him his kingdom and authority.[2]

In Machiavelli's view, the first principle of foreign policy for any nation is self-interest. This has often resulted in force and fraud, because goodness does not always prevail in a world where so many are not good. One must learn how not to be good, says Machiavelli. Every major nation has its broken bodies and treaties from frequent war; they are just one of the many features of the institution of nationalism.

Modern romantic nationalism emerged out of the American and French revolutions with the emphasis shifting from the king to the people, who possessed a somewhat common culture, language, religion, political establishment, boundaries, and goals. The new idea was a man-made one, but it caught on and became exhilarating when it was wrapped up in stirring national anthems, tricolor flags, bombastic speeches, literature, and, of course, God—because the nation was divine, too. In God We Trust. God and Country. Myth, canon, and hangup were rolled into the chemistry of one romantic idea.

Machiavelli recognized that the *symbol* was necessary in uniting people. So did Mussolini and Hitler. People are also willing to die for symbols. Give them something to love and something to hate, but you don't have to be consistent, said Machiavelli and Hitler. Memories are short. Red and white are common colors in flags, one for war and one for peace. The dove stands for peace. Men die for their colors and for their lions, bears, eagles, swastikas, rising suns, hammers and sickles. They even die for the dove. Remember the war to end all wars? Actually, all wars are fought for peace.

The variety of nationalism that originated in revolutionary America and France adapted itself to the conditions of the twentieth century and proved its vigor by surviving injections of permanent peace serum —the League of Nations and the United Nations. Already in this century over ninety million people have been killed as a result of war, civil as well as international. (It is well to note that there is also a nationalism within a nationalism, such as the north versus south type found in Germany, Italy, the Congo, Great Britain, the Soviet Union, and the United States.)

At the end of World War I, the Allies blamed Germany for being the aggressor. When any nation enters into a war, it must appear to be a defensive move because the peace symbol is supposed to be more moral than the war symbol. Some time after the hysteria and hate died down a bit, a Harvard professor, Sidney Bradshaw Fay, published a revisionist history in which he contended that the blame did not rest with Germany alone but with a number of nations. There were certain fundamental causes which were common to all the great powers, he said. There was the system of secret alliances which divided Europe into two hostile camps and which guaranteed a larger conflict if any two of the opposite allies declared war. There was the infectious militarism which demanded ever-increasing monies for soldiers, sailors, and the modern accessories of war. There was nationalism, which nourished old hatreds between many peoples of Europe, and there was economic imperialism with the struggle for markets, materials, and colonies. Finally, there was the newspaper press which poisoned public opinion in all the major countries. Fay stated: "Too often newspapers in all lands were inclined to inflame nationalistic feelings, misrepresent the situation in foreign countries, and suppress factors in favor of peace."[3]

These were the basic causes and the species, *homo sapiens nationalisticum,* willingly followed the leaders toward Armageddon in 1914. Obviously the germ of nationalism—in the guise of words, dynamic symbols and institutions—was taking firmer hold and, as usual in time of danger, it inspired fears and hatreds together with stronger bonds of unity with one's own kind. Few were immune to the contagion in any country. The love, the hate, the excitement, the music, and the drama of it all were just as pervasive as words, symbols, and institutions. It was a penetrating experience beyond all description. It was sheer romanticism, but it was also down-to-earth realism at the same time. Four years of it!

Ironically, the Allies at the Versailles Peace Conference (and at later conferences) were plotting their own destruction in dictating the terms of peace to the defeated Germans, who believed they had surrendered on the basis of Wilson's Fourteen Points, the first of which provided for a negotiated peace. Germany was burdened with a huge indemnity, deprived of her colonies, forced to agree to German majorities in parts of newly created Poland and Czechoslovakia, and compelled to sign on the dotted line that she had caused the great war. Instead of preparing for a permanent peace, the 1919 Conference was setting up a second round which would feature Adolf Hitler and his own mixture of volatile chemicals.

Before going on to Round Two, however, it is necessary to suggest that the Western Allies outfoxed themselves a second time by insisting that the moderate but weakened Provisional Government in Russia—which had resulted from the overthrow of the Tsar—continue the war against the Germans when it was in no condition to do so. With the army at the front, Petrograd and Moscow contained no strong forces to maintain Alexander Kerensky in power, and thus the Bolsheviks found it relatively easy to overthrow the moderates. Except for the Bolshevik success, communism might not have taken hold in any large country in the twentieth century. Russia spawned communism in other lands, and this has been the *bête noire* of Western nations since. The Western Allies were not outfoxed by their enemies as much as they outfoxed themselves. Not only were they responsible for Hitler, they were largely responsible for Lenin as well.

But the German leaders, in order to win the war for the great German nation, also outfoxed themselves. They ferreted Nikolai Lenin out of exile in Switzerland and across Germany to the northern border. Lenin made his way to Petrograd, and the world, especially Germany, later experienced the venom of Communist fury.

War I gave rise to fascism as well as to communism. Mixed with nationalism, the brew was dynamite and a war-torn world suffered both tyrannies. The frightening thing is that it could happen here in the U.S.A. Depending on their politics, many people are convinced that either communism or fascism is becoming entrenched in American life. It is no secret that partisans of the New Left are convinced that our police and military are fascist when they use unnecessarily rough and brutal methods to break up demonstrations by long-haired, bearded youth with sideburns. It smacks of totalitarianism, they say, when police can pick up three students for such a petty thing as hitchhiking and when the judge can set one of them free after getting a haircut but sentence the other two to jail because their hair was still too long after a second visit to the barber. And, on the other side, it is not classified information that partisans of the far right see nascent communism in the youth communes, the Students for a Democratic Society, and the violent demonstrations in which some carry the American flag but others the North Vietnamese flag. The words commie, pinko, com-symp have been used frequently since Senator Joseph McCarthy split the American public by wrapping himself in the American flag and blanketing unnamed Democrats under the term "Commicrats." Yes, it (communism or fascism) is happening here, at least in the minds of many concerned people.

It was believed that the war to end all wars, the holocaust of 1914–1918, would indeed be the last. Hopes for a new antiwar vaccine were raised by the Locarno treaties in 1925 and by the Pact of Paris in 1928, which condemned recourse to war for the settlement of international controversies. The Pact was signed by sixty nations, but there were a number of reservations, of course, and no provisions were made to enforce its dovelike declaration. A few years before, the people of the United States had demonstrated greater interest in baseball than they did in Woodrow Wilson's pleas for ratification of the Versailles Treaty and the League of Nations. These were positive steps toward mature settlement of disputes and steps away from international anarchy. It was America's failure to enter the League, stated Winston Churchill in the first chapter of *The Gathering Storm,* that dealt it an almost mortal blow.

It did not take long for the storm to gather. The countdown for Round Two began with the Japanese invasion of Manchuria in 1931. It is amazing how quickly the Japanese caught on to the game Western civilization was playing when they awoke from feudal isolation after 1868. They saw immediately that a robust military establishment, industry, and empire were necessary accoutrements to a vital spirit of nationalism. They set out to out-Machiavelli their Machiavellian competitors. They did. The Japanese considered the League of Nations an effete corps of intellectuals; when the League slapped Japan's wrist for the aggression in Manchuria, her delegates picked up their briefcases and walked out. The lesson did not escape Mussolini and Hitler, and a few years later they stuck their daggers into the dying world body. The United States looked on as Britain and France vainly tried to contain the aggressors who were now termed "have-not" nations because they lacked the vast colonies of Britain and France.

Britain and France tried appeasement with Hitler and his counterpart, Mussolini. They thought injections of love, understanding, and kindness ought to pacify the little bullies from the deprived nations of Europe. But the lesson they failed to learn is that the bully always wants more, and the Allies did not want to give up too much. As far as possible, and in the interests of world peace, they decided, the status quo should prevail. British Prime Minister Neville Chamberlain and French Premier Edouard Daladier agreed at Munich in the fall of 1938 to give up the Sudetenland of Czechoslovakia to Germany because of Hitler's demands and the heavy German majority in that nation's mountain area bordering Germany. This partitioning was supported on the basis of Wilson's Fourteen Points which provided for people to determine for themselves which country they preferred. Hitler, playing the role of both lion and fox, signed the agreement with the promise that he had no more territorial aims in Europe. The following spring Nazi troops drove into the rest of Czechoslovakia without even a warning. Immediately, Hitler started demanding the incorporation into Germany of the Polish Corridor with its German majority. Treaties are made only to be broken, said Machiavelli; Hitler was not original, only more flamboyant.

The world was obviously going mad with its huge standing armies, broken treaties, and nationalistic hysteria, myopia, and paranoia. Surely there must be a superior species somewhere in the Solar System. Hitler thought the superior species was right here on earth in the genes of the "Aryan race." Stalin thought it was in the learned behavior of Marxism-Leninism-Stalinism. Both were wrong, and their Machiavellian actions only proved them to be members of the fallible human species torn between hate and love, war and peace.

Hitler was defeated, as were the Japanese; but as War I gave rise to fascism, communism, and War II, so War II spawned a welter of war in the second half of the century. Are our memories so short as to forget Greece, Turkey, Hungary, the Berlin Wall, Laos, Indonesia, Korea, India, Pakistan, Israel, the many Arab states, the Soviet Union, Honduras, El Salvador, Algeria, France, Cuba, Nigeria, Congo, Guiana, Czechoslovakia, Cambodia, China, the United States, Malaya, Great Britain, and even the Belfast Wall separating bitter Protestants from bitter Catholics? Lion, fox, and the elusive dove have been involved in these nationalistic civil and uncivil wars on Planet Earth since 1945.

The romantic nationalism that germinated with the American and French revolutions flowered during the nineteenth century and is still vigorously alive in the twentieth. It would seem to be an archaic, anachronistic, childish institution for a species that considers itself moral, mature, Christian, Hindu, or whatever. Modern man has been threatened by anarchy at home, and he fears the thought of a lawless society, yet he has not fully appreciated the fact there has been *international* anarchy, at least since the fifteenth century when Saint Joan had that certain feeling of romantic love, not for all mankind but only for those inhabiting a certain plot of ground.

Something else must be done now, Miss Joan, because the balance of terror in the world is maintained by a bunch of hung-up juveniles huffing and puffing up their egos in the cause of national self-interest and ready to make the bugle call to arms if that interest is threatened. The elements causing bloody conflict, including Machiavelli's two beastly symbols, must be incinerated. But what will rise from the pyre?

Notes

1 Bernard Shaw, *Saint Joan* (Baltimore, Md.: Penguin, 1952), p. 99. By permission of The Society of Authors, on behalf of the Bernard Shaw Estate.

2 Niccolo Machiavelli, *The Prince,* from *The Western Tradition,* edited by Eugen Weber (Boston: D.C. Heath, 1959), pp. 277–278.

3 Sidney Bradshaw Fay, *The Origins of the World War* (New York: Macmillan, 1930), p. 47.

Hans Kohn, noted authority on nationalism, says that the institution is a state of mind, an act of consciousness. Nationalism—which has become more and more common to mankind since the French Revolution—is difficult to define, he asserts, because there are so many changing factors connected with it. In the selection that follows, Professor Kohn discusses some aspects of this phenomenon which far too few of us have studied.

The Idea of Nationalism

Hans Kohn

Nationalism as we understand it is not older than the second half of the eighteenth century. Its first great manifestation was the French Revolution, which gave the new movement an increased dynamic force. Nationalism had become manifest, however, at the end of the eighteenth century almost simultaneously in a number of widely separated European countries. Its time in the evolution of mankind had arrived, and although the French Revolution was one of the most powerful factors in its intensification and spread, this did not mark the date of its birth. Like all historical movements, nationalism has its roots deep in the past. The conditions which made its emergence possible had matured for centuries before they converged at its formation. These political, economic, and intellectual developments took a long time for their growth, and proceeded at a different pace in the various countries. It is impossible to grade them according to their importance or to make one dependent upon another. All are closely interconnected, each reacting upon the others; and although their growth can be traced separately, their effects and consequences cannot be separated otherwise than in the analysis of the scholar; in life, they are indissolubly intertwined.

Nationalism is inconceivable without the ideas of popular sovereignty preceding—without a complete revision of the position of ruler and ruled, of classes and castes. The aspect of the universe and of society had to be secularized with the help of a new natural science and of natural law as understood by Grotius and Locke. The traditionalism of economic life had to be broken by the rise of the third estate, which was to turn the attention away from the royal courts and their civilization to the life, language, and arts of the people. This new class found itself less bound by tradition than the nobility or clergy; it represented a new force striving for new things; it was ready to break with the past, flouting tradition in its opinion even more than it did in reality. In its rise, it claimed to represent not only a new class and its interests, but the whole people. Where the third estate became powerful in the eighteenth century—as in Great Britain, in France, and in the United States —nationalism found its expression predominantly, but never exclusively, in political and economic changes. Where, on the other hand, the third estate was still weak and only in a budding stage at the beginning of the nineteenth century, as in Germany, Italy, and among the Slavonic peoples, nationalism found its expression predominantly in the cultural field. Among these peoples, at the beginning it was not so much the nation-state as the *Volksgeist* and its manifestations in literature and folklore, in the mother tongue, and in history, which became the center of the attention of nationalism. With the growing strength of the third estate, with the political and cultural awakening of the masses, in the course of the nineteenth century, this cultural nationalism soon turned into the desire for the formation of a nation-state.

The growth of nationalism is the process of integration of the masses of the people into a common political form. Nationalism therefore presupposes the existence, in fact or as an ideal, of a centralized form of government over a large and distinct territory. This form was created by the absolute monarchs, who were the pacemakers of modern nationalism; the French Revolution inherited and continued the centralizing tendencies of the kings, but at the same time it filled the central organization with a new spirit and gave it a power of cohesion unknown before. Nationalism is unthinkable before the emergence of the modern state in the period from the sixteenth to the eighteenth century. Nationalism accepted this form, but changed it by animating it with a new feeling of life and with a new religious fervor.

For its composite texture, nationalism used in its growth some of the oldest and most primitive feelings of man, found throughout history as important factors in the formation of social groups. There is a natural tendency in man—and by "natural tendency" we mean a tendency which, having been produced by social circumstances from time practically immemorial, appears to us as natural—to love his birthplace or the place of his childhood sojourn, its surroundings, its climate, the contours of hills and valleys, of rivers and trees. We are all subject to the immense power of habitude, and even if in a later stage of development we are attracted by the unknown and by change, we delight to come back and to be at rest in the reassuring sight of the familiar. Man has an easily understandable preference for his own language as the only one which he thoroughly understands and in which he feels at home. He prefers native customs and native food to alien ones, which appear to him unintelligible and indigestible. Should he travel, he will return to his chair and his table with a feeling of relaxation and will be elated by the joy of finding himself again at home, away from the strain of a sojourn in foreign lands and contact with foreign peoples.

Small wonder that he will take pride in his native characteristics, and that he will easily believe in their superiority. As they are the only ones in which civilized people like himself can apparently feel at home, are they not the only ones fit for human beings? On the other hand, contact with alien men and alien customs, which appear to him strange, unfamiliar, and therefore threatening, will arouse in him a distrust of everything foreign. This feeling of strangeness will again develop in him sentiments of superiority, and sometimes even of open hostility. The more primitive men are, the stronger will be their distrust of strangers, and therefore the greater the intensity of their group feeling. Rudyard Kipling, in his poem "The Stranger," forcefully expressed this general feeling:

> The Stranger within my gate,
>   He may be true or kind,
> But he does not talk my talk—
>   I cannot feel his mind.
> I see the face and the eyes and the mouth,
>   But not the soul behind.
>
> The men of my own stock
>   They may do ill or well,
> But they tell the lies I am wonted to,
>   They are used to the lies I tell;
> And we do not need interpreters
>   When we go to buy and sell.
>
> The Stranger within my gates,
>   He may be evil or good,
> But I cannot tell what powers control—
>   What reasons sway his mood;
> Nor when the Gods of his far-off land
>   May repossess his blood.*

---

*"The Stranger" copyright 1908 by Rudyard Kipling, from *Rudyard Kipling's Verse: Definitive Edition.* Reprinted by permission of Mrs. George Bambridge, Doubleday & Co., and Macmillan & Co.

These feelings have always existed. They do not form nationalism; they correspond to certain facts—territory, language, common descent—which we also find in nationalism. But here they are entirely transformed, charged with new and different emotions, and embedded in a broader context. They are the natural elements out of which nationalism is formed; but nationalism is not a natural phenomenon, not a product of "eternal" or "natural" laws; it is a product of the growth of social and intellectual factors at a certain stage of history. Some feeling of nationality, it may be said, existed before the birth of modern nationalism—a feeling varying in strength and in frequency from time to time: at some epochs almost completely extinguished, at others more or less clearly discernible. But it was largely unconscious and inarticulate. It did not influence the thought and actions of men in a deep and all-pervading way. It found a clear expression only occasionally in individuals, and in groups only at times of stress or provocation. It did not determine their aims or actions permanently or in the long run. It was no purposeful will welding together all the individuals into a unity of emotions, thoughts, and actions.

Before the age of nationalism, the masses very rarely became conscious of the fact that the same language was spoken over a large territory. In fact, it was not the same language; several dialects existed side by side, sometimes incomprehensible to the man of a neighboring province. The spoken language was accepted as a natural fact. It was in no way regarded as a political or cultural factor, still less as an object of political or cultural struggle. During the Middle Ages, people deduced from the Bible that the diversity of languages was the result of the sinfulness of man, and God's punishment for the building of the Tower of Babel. Consciousness of language was aroused only at times of expeditions and travel or in frontier districts. There, the alien character of the group speaking the alien language was felt, and many national groups were first recognized as different and named by those of alien tongue. The Greek word *barbaros* (which meant "strange" or "foreign," and in consequence "rude" and "ignorant") probably had its source in the idea of stammering or inability to speak in a comprehensible way—a word akin to the Sanskrit expression *barbara,* which meant "stammering" or "non-Aryan." The Slavs called the Germans with whom they came into contact *niemci,* "the mutes," people who cannot make themselves understood. A man speaking an incomprehensible tongue seemed outside the pale of civilization. But language was accepted by the Slavs and by other peoples as a natural fact, not as a cultural inheritance. The language in which the treasures of civilization were inherited and transferred—in medieval Europe as well as in Islam, in India as well as in China—was generally not the language spoken by the people: it was a learned language accessible only to the educated class. Even if it was not a language of different origin, it was generally so archaic and so rich in many purely literary, classical associations that it was understood only by a small minority.

Before nationalism, language was very rarely stressed as a fact on which the prestige and power of a group depended. Alien languages remained until the very recent centuries the languages used by official bodies, in the scholarly world, or among the upper classes. To mention only one fact which stands for a large number, the Breton estates, which were very jealous of their independence, nevertheless spoke French, and in the Act of Union for the Defense of the Liberties of Brittany of 1719 the Breton spokesmen did not mention language grievances. The translations of the Bible in Protestant countries were not undertaken from any motives of nationalism, but purely for the spreading of the true religion. Queen Elizabeth had the Bible and the Prayer Book translated into Welsh, and divine service held in Welsh, to liberate the Welsh from the "ignorance of popery." With the growth of nationalism in the following centuries, still dominated by religion but already harboring the seeds of the new growth, the translations of the Bible certainly were effective in rousing national feeling and in giving a new importance to the national language—which through the spread of popular education and the wider use of the printing press became more and more an element of growing cultural importance. At the same time, the language became uniform, obliterating the vernacular dialects or pushing them into the background, and covering a greater territory as its undisputed domain.

This large territory became an object of love to its inhabitants as a result of a long and difficult process. This love of the homeland, which is regarded as the heart of patriotism, is not a "natural" phenomenon, but an artificial product of historical and intellectual development. The homeland which a man "naturally" loves is his native village or valley or city, a small territory well known in all its concrete details, abounding in personal memories, a place in which his life was generally lived throughout its whole span. The whole territory inhabited by what we should consider today a nationality—a territory frequently distinguished by great diversity of landscape and climate —was practically unknown to the average man, and could become known only by instruction or travel, which before the age of nationalism were limited to a very small minority. Voltaire, who lived before this age, pointed out that "plus cette patrie devient grande, moins on l'aime, car l'amour partagé s'affaiblit. Il est impossible d'aimer tendrement une famille trop nombreuse qu'on connaît à peine.*"

Nationalism is not, as some scholars under the influence of Aristotle suggest, a harmonious natural growth qualitatively identical with the love for family and home. It is frequently assumed that man loves in widening circles—his family, his village, his tribe or clan, the nation, and finally humanity and the supreme good. But love of home and family is a concrete feeling accessible to everyone in daily experience, while nationalism, and in an even higher degree cosmopolitanism, is a highly complex and originally an abstract feeling. It gains the emotional warmth of concreteness only through the effects of an historical development which, by means of education, economic interdependence, and corresponding political and social institutions, brings about the integration of the masses and their identification with a body far too great for any concrete experience. Nationalism— our identification with the life and aspirations of uncounted millions whom we shall never know, with a territory which we shall never visit in its entirety—is qualitatively different from the love of family or of home surroundings. It is qualitatively akin to the love of humanity or of the whole earth. Both belong to what Nietzsche called (in *Thus Spoke Zarathustra*) *Fernstenliebe,* love of those far away, and which he distinguished from the *Nächstenliebe,* love of those near by.

Life in a common territory, subject to the same influences of nature and, to an important although lesser degree, to the same influences of history and legal systems, produces certain common attitudes and traits, often called national character. We find in the literature of all peoples throughout history frequent characterizations of national groups such as the Gauls or the Greeks, the Germans or the English. Some of these traits seem to persist for a long time, and are mentioned by observers in different centuries. Other traits seem to change under the influence of historical developments. There are known instances of change, within a few decades, in what was considered at a certain time the most essential character trait of a nation. In the beginning of the eighteenth century, when the English were considered a nation most inclined to revolution and to change, while the French seemed a most stable and stolid nation, Voltaire wrote: "The French are of the opinion, that the government of this island is more tempestuous

*The bigger this party gets, the less you get to love it because the love that you share gets weaker. It is impossible to love tenderly a family so large that you scarcely know it.—*Publisher's translation.*

than the sea which surrounds it, which indeed is true." One hundred years later, just the opposite opinion about the English and the French was generally held. The English were then, and are today, considered—by themselves and others—as a stolid nation, proud in their disinclination to violent revolution; while the French were considered a people easily given to and delighting in revolutionary upheavals.

A similar change took place in opinion about the Germans. One hundred years ago, they were thought a very lovable and most impractical people, fit for metaphysics and music and poetry but unfit for modern industry and business. Now* the Germans produce very few, if any, metaphysicians, musicians, or poets of renown; but on the other hand they have become successful and ruthless bullies and hard and efficient masters in modern industry and business. The Mongols under Genghis Khan were warriors famous for their belligerence, and brought all Asia and half of Europe under their yoke. In the sixteenth century, through the adoption of Lamaist Buddhism, their old spirit was completely broken and they were turned into peaceful and pious men. Under the influence of the Soviet government and its revolutionary propaganda the wild instincts of the race have been reawakened, and a new and different consciousness has started to animate the Mongol people and to break their religious inhibitions.

The judgments of observers concerning the character of national groups are colored in varying degrees by the political exigencies of the situation and the sentimental attitudes of the observer. Between the extremes—which may be illustrated by a statement of Henry Morley that "in the literature of any people we perceive under all contrasts of form produced by variable social influences the one national character from first to last," and the opposite by J. M. Robertson that "the nation considered as a continuous and personalized organism is in large measure a metaphysical dream"—we may accept the position of Sir Francis Galton that "different aspects of the multifarious character of man respond to different calls from without, so that the same individual, and much more the same race, may behave very differently at different epochs." Men and men's character are extremely complex; the more so, the less primitive men are. This holds true even more of a highly complex group like the nation. An immense diversity of individuals goes into making up a nation, and during the lifetime of a nation the most diverse influences are exercised upon it, molding and transforming it. For growth and change are the laws under which all historical phenomena fall.

*Eds. note: Recall that Kohn's book was published in 1944.

As a youth, Hitler was looking for relevancy in education. He found it in what he called popular nationalism as opposed to dynastic patriotism. He updated Machiavelli by emphasizing propaganda, fanaticism, intolerance, and racial purity in the achievement of national goals. But he himself became a victim—a victim of his own propaganda; a victim by apparently believing everything he said; a victim in a dismal bunker in 1945.

Mein Kampf

Adolf Hitler

One thing was certain: my apparent failure in school. I learned what I liked, but above all I learned what in my opinion might be necessary to me in my future career as a painter. In this connection I sabotaged all that which seemed unimportant or that which no longer attracted me. At that time my marks were always extreme depending upon the subject and my evaluation of it. 'Praiseworthy' and 'Excellent' ranked with 'Sufficient' and 'Insufficient.' My best efforts were in geography and perhaps even more so in history. These were my two favorite subjects and in them I led my class.

Now, after so many years, when I examine the results of that period, I find two outstanding facts of particular importance:

First, *I became a nationalist.*

Second, *I learned to grasp and to understand the meaning of history.*

Old Austria was a 'State of nationalities.' . . .

At a comparatively early age I, too, was given the opportunity to participate in the national struggle of old Austria. Money was collected for the *Südmark* and the school club; our conviction was demonstrated by the wearing of cornflowers and the colors black, red, and gold; the greeting was 'Heil'; *'Deutschland über alles'* was preferred to the imperial anthem, despite warnings and punishments. In this manner the boy was trained politically at an age when a member of a so-called national State knows little more of his nationality than its language. It is obvious that already then I did not belong to the lukewarm. In a short time I had become a fanatical 'German nationalist,' a term which is not identical with our same party name of today.

My development was quite rapid, so that at the age of fifteen I already understood the difference between dynastic 'patriotism' and popular 'nationalism'; at that time the latter alone existed for me. . . .

Even today, courses in world history in the so-called secondary schools are still badly neglected. Few teachers realize that the aim of history lessons should not consist in the memorizing and rattling forth of historical facts and data; that it does not matter whether a boy knows when this or that battle was fought, when a certain military leader was born, or when some monarch (in most cases a very mediocre one) was crowned with the crown of his ancestors. Good God, these things do not matter.

To 'learn' history means to search for and to find the forces which cause those effects which we later face as historical events.

Here, too, the art of reading, like that of learning, is *to remember the important, to forget the unimportant.* . . .

The art of historical thinking, which had been taught me in school, has never left me since. More and more, world history became a never-failing source of my understanding of the historical events of the present, that is, politics. What is more, I do not want to 'learn' it, but I want it to teach me. . . .

During the years of my unruly youth nothing had grieved me more than having been born at a time when temples of glory were only erected to merchants or State officials. The waves of historical events seemed to have calmed down to such an extent that the future appeared really to belong to the 'peaceful competition of nations,' that means a quiet mutual cheating, excluding forceful measures. The individual States began more and more to resemble enterprises which cut the ground from under each other, stole each other's customers and orders, and tried to cheat each other by every means, setting this in a scene which was as noisy as it was harmless. This development, however, not only seemed to endure, but it was intended to transform the world (with general approval) into one big department store, in the lobbies of which the busts of the most cunning profiteers and the most harmless administration officials were to be stored for eternity. The business men were to be supplied by the English, the administration officials by the Germans; the Jews, however, would have to sacrifice themselves to being proprietors, because, as they themselves admitted, they never earn anything but only 'pay,' and, besides, they speak most of the languages.

Why could one not have been born a hundred years earlier? For instance, at the time of the Wars of Liberation when a man really was worth something, even without 'business'?!

I was often filled with annoying thoughts because, as it appeared, of the belated entrance of my journey into this world, and I looked upon this period of 'quiet and order' that awaited me as an unmerited mean trick of Fate. Even as a boy I was not a 'pacifist,' and all attempts at an education in this direction came to naught.

The Boer War appeared to me like summer lightning.

Every day I was on the lookout for the newspapers; I devoured dispatches and reports, and I was happy that I was being allowed to witness this heroic struggle, if only from afar.

The Russo-Japanese War already found me much more mature and also more attentive. At that time I had taken sides more for national reasons, and when settling my opinions I had at once taken the side of the Japanese. In the defeat of the Russians I saw also a defeat of the Austrian Slavic nationalities. . . .

The fight of the year 1914 was certainly not forced upon the masses, good God! but desired by the entire people itself.

One wanted at last to make an end to the general uncertainty. Only thus is it understandable that for this most serious of all struggles more than two million German men and boys joined the flag voluntarily, ready to protect it with their last drop of blood.

To me personally those hours appeared like the redemption from the annoying moods of my youth. Therefore I am not ashamed today to say that, overwhelmed by impassionate enthusiasm, I had fallen on my knees and thanked Heaven out of my overflowing heart that it had granted me the good fortune of being allowed to live in these times.

A struggle for freedom had broken out, greater than the world had ever seen before; because, once Fate had begun its course, the conviction began to dawn on the great masses that this time the question involved was not Serbia's or Austria's fate, but the existence or non-existence of the German nation. . . .

I had left Austria primarily for political reasons: but what was more natural that now that the fight had begun that I had to act according to this conviction? I did not want to fight for the Habsburg State, but I was ready to die at any time for my people and the Reich it constituted.

On August 3 I submitted a direct petition to His Majesty King Ludwig III with the request that I be permitted to serve in a Bavarian regiment. The cabinet office was certainly more than busy in those days; my joy was the greater when on the following day I received the reply to my request. My joy and my gratitude knew no end when I had opened the letter with trembling hands and read that my request had been granted and that I was summoned to report to a Bavarian regiment. A few days later I wore the uniform which I was not to take off again for six years.

Thus, as probably for every German, there began for me the most unforgettable and the greatest period of my mortal life. In the face of the events of this mighty struggle the entire past fell back into shallow oblivion. It is now ten years since this mighty event happened, and with proud sadness I think back to those weeks of the beginning of the heroic fight of our people which Fate had graciously permitted me to share.

As if it were yesterday, one picture after the other passes before my eyes: I see myself donning the uniform in the circle of my dear comrades, turning out for the first time, drilling, etc., till finally the day came when we marched.

There was only one thing that worried me at that time, like so many others also: that was whether we would not arrive at the front too late. This alone disturbed my peace again and again. Thus in every jubilation over a new heroic deed there seemed to be a hidden drop of bitterness as with every new victory the danger of our being delayed seemed to increase.

Finally, the day came when we left Munich in order to start fulfilling our duty. Now for the first time I saw the Rhine as we were riding towards the west along its quiet waters, the German river of all rivers, in order to protect it against the greed of the old enemy. When through the delicate veil of the dawn's mist the mild rays of the early sun set the Niederwalddenkmal shimmering before our eyes, the 'Watch on the Rhine' roared up to the morning sky from the interminably long transport train and I had a feeling as though my chest would burst.

Then at last came a damp, cold night in Flanders through which we marched silently, and when the day began to emerge from the fog, suddenly an iron salute came whizzing over our heads towards us and with a sharp report the small bullets struck between our rows, whipping up the wet earth; but before the small cloud had dispersed, out of two hundred throats the first hurrah roared a welcome to the first messenger of death. But then it began to crackle and roar, to sing and howl, and with feverish eyes each one of us was drawn forward faster and faster over turnip fields and hedges till suddenly the fight began, the fight of man against man. But from the distance the sounds of a song met our ears, coming nearer and nearer, passing from company to company, and then, while Death busily plunged his hand into our rows, the song reached also us, and now we passed it on: '*Deutschland, Deutschland über alles, über alles in der Welt!*'

The art of war Machiavelli spoke of nearly five hundred years ago has now been institutionalized by the planet's nations. War—past, present, and future—consumes a major portion of national budgets around the world. By 1970, the worldwide total spent on the military was reported to be 40 percent greater than that spent on education. The budget for the United Nations is less than that of the University of Michigan. Who demands increasing military expenditures—government hierarchies or the people? Why? What would happen if the U.S. and the U.S.S.R. disarmed?

Peace Is Hell: Report From Iron Mountain

Editors of **Trans-Action**

In August of 1963, if we can believe Leonard C. Lewin, a Special Study Group was set up, under Government auspices and with melodramatic secrecy, in order (1) to determine what problems the United States would face if permanent peace broke out; and (2) to draw up a program to deal with these problems. The Study Group's sponsor was probably an *ad hoc* Government committee at, or near, the cabinet level. Included among the Group's 15 members were an economist, a sociologist, a cultural anthropologist, a psychologist and a psychiatrist, and one literary critic. The 15 met once a month, usually for two days, over a period of two and a half years, the first and final meetings being held in an underground nuclear shelter inside Iron Mountain, in upstate New York (near war-gamer Herman Kahn's Hudson Institute). A report was unanimously agreed upon, then submitted to the Government "interagency committee," along with an urgent recommendation that its contents be kept secret.

There the matter rested—until winter 1966, when a member of the Study Group, "John Doe," came to New York, looked up Leonard Lewin, and handed him a copy of the report, explaining that while he himself accepted all of the *Report's* conclusions, he also strongly believed that its findings should be made public. Lewin promptly found a publisher, wrote an introduction, included an interview with John Doe, and refused to say another word about the report's origins.

Report from Iron Mountain on the Possibility and Desirability of Peace, with Introductory Material by Leonard C. Lewin (The Dial Press, New York, 1967) says, in essence, that while permanent peace may be possible, it probably would not be desirable. To quote the

From "Peace is Hell: Report From Iron Mountain," *Trans-action,* February, 1968, pp. 7–8. Copyright © Jan./Feb., 1968 by TRANS-action, Inc. New Brunswick, New Jersey.

Report: "It is uncertain, at this time, whether peace will ever be possible. It is far more questionable, by the objective standard of continued social survival rather than that of emotional pacifism, that it would be desirable even if it were demonstrably attainable."

Peace, the *Report* concludes, is hell. If society is to remain stable, wars must continue. "War itself is the basic social system, within which other secondary modes of social organization conflict or conspire." The indispensable functions that war and war preparedness serve are assigned to various categories, perhaps the key ones being economic, political, sociological, and ecological.

1. *Economic.* Military spending, by virtue of its independence from the normal supply-demand economy, acts as a balance wheel. "It is, and has been, the essential economic stabilizer of modern societies." Among possible substitutes offered are a comprehensive social-welfare program; a fantastically elaborate disarmament-inspection system; and an even more enormous investment in space research. Social-welfare programs, however, would not, in the long run, eat up enough resources, and in addition would not remain very long outside the normal economy. A disarmament-inspection system would also not prove "wasteful" enough, and would be incongruous in a world permanently at peace. Space-research programs, the *Report* decides, appear to be the only realistic substitute. (It is the *only* substitute the Study Group warmly endorses.)

2. *Political.* It is only because of the threat of war that individual nations, and stable governments, can exist. " . . . 'war' is virtually synonymous with nationhood. The elimination of war implies the inevitable elimination of national sovereignty and the traditional nation-state." Furthermore, military spending serves to keep a certain portion of the population poor, thus maintaining "necessary class distinctions" and a ready supply of unskilled labor. As a possible substitute, new external enemies might be created—like invaders from outer space, "fictitious alternate enemies," or air and water pollution (which would have to be deliberately intensified). According to the *Report,* only the creation of "fictitious alternate enemies" offers any promise.

3. *Sociological.* The army and the draft serve to remove antisocial members from society. War itself catharsizes aggressive impulses. And the existence of an external menace induces citizens to become patriotic and subservient to the state. "Allegiance requires a cause; a cause requires an enemy." Possible substitutes: programs like the Peace Corps; "Socially oriented blood games"; and "A modern, sophisticated form of slavery." Of the substitutes, only slavery, the *Report* concludes, may prove "efficient" and "flexible."

4. *Ecological.* War has been the chief evolutionary mechanism for maintaining a proper balance between the population and the supplies the population needs to survive. Here, at least, war has a drawback: It is not eugenic. Nuclear wars, for example, kill off the superior as well as the inferior. A possible substitute *and* improvement: " . . . a universal requirement that procreation be limited to the products of artificial insemination," along with "A comprehensive program of applied eugenics."

What the *Report* does, then, is to legitimize war. The Special Study Group's key conclusion is: "If it were necessary at this moment to opt irrevocably for the retention or dissolution of the war system, common prudence would dictate the former course."

The bulk of the available evidence suggests that the book is a hoax. As for the perpetrator, nominees have included Richard Rovere, John Kenneth Galbraith (who told *Trans-action,* archly, "If I had been a member of the Study Group, I would have been sworn to secrecy"), Kenneth Boulding (whose *Disarmament and the Economy* is quoted), Vance Bourjaily, and—anticlimax of the anticlimaxes—Leonard Lewin. All roads, however, lead to Leonard Lewin: he is a freelance journalist who has reviewed a book on think-tanks, he edited *A Treasury of Political Humor,* and he loaned a working draft of the *Report* to a *Trans-action* informant.

The *Report* is far from being "just a hoax," though, and it cannot be dismissed out of hand. Despite its many specious arguments and its spotty knowledge of social science, it is also an acutely accurate satire. What it satirizes is explained by John Doe: " . . . what they wanted from us was a different kind of *thinking.* It was a matter of approach. Herman Kahn calls it 'Byzantine'—no agonizing over cultural and religious values. It is the kind of thinking that Rand and the Hudson Institute and [the Institute for Defense Analysis] brought into *war* planning. . . . " War-gaming has become peace-gaming.

The fact is that the *Report* could have been compiled entirely from authentic sources. There are many social scientists doing this kind of investigation; there are members of the Defense Department who think like this. As one reader has observed, "This provides a better rationale of the U.S. Government's posture today than the Government's official spokesmen have provided. A better title for the book, in fact, would have been the same as Norman Mailer's novel: *Why Are We in Vietnam?*"

The threat that the *Report* holds is not so much that it will be believed and acted upon, but that it *has* been believed and acted upon. Significantly, *Trans-action* has found that those readers who take the book seriously tend to be Government officials. Upon inquiry, sources very close to the White House were authorized to say that the files and libraries of the Executive Office of the President have been reviewed, and although some reports in the general subject area covered by the *Report* were found, there was no record of this particular report. These sources believed, therefore, that no comment was appropriate at this time. Informally, they observed that their statement does not rule out the possibility that the *Report* was sponsored either in the White House, by some Congressional committee, or by some other agency within the Federal Establishment.

More important than the need to know whether *Report from Iron Mountain* is authentic or not, the public needs to know what the current thinking of U.S. Government agencies is in regard to (1) what problems the United States would face in the event of peace and disarmament and (2) what programs should be devised to deal with these problems.

One Defense Department informant has admitted that some of his colleagues have agreed with the *Report's* conclusion that the Vietnam war is sound because at least it helps preserve stability at home. Another informant, who works at the highest levels in strategic planning within the Pentagon, asserted after reading the *Report* that he saw no reason to consider it a hoax, since he often comes upon reports that read in much the same way. Yet a third person—a recent alumnus of the defense Establishment—found the *Report* quite credible. All this testifies to the enormous gap between secret Governmental assessments of questions of war and peace, of disarmament, and of the "war system" and official public stances—as much as it testifies to Mr. Lewin's skill as a creator of social-science fiction.

The publication of *Report from Iron Mountain,* whatever its source, should become an occasion for a new public demand for a penetrating examination and evaluation of Government reports on strategic planning for disarmament and peace. The extent to which a belief in the desirability and inevitability of "the war system" is built into the operational conceptions of the Government is of deepest public concern, not to be thwarted by claims that these are matters of state that require secrecy.

Some observers have suggested that nationalism has peaked out and given way to ideology—that is, communism, fascism, democracy, or some other political dogma. Some have even suggested the end of ideology with the world heading toward great collective societies. But for millions of people nationalism has not yet bowed out; people still have a compelling love affair with their flag. The affair is an age-old hangup. It belonged to the ancient Sumerian, Joan of Arc, Machiavelli, Hitler, the writer, and, no doubt, the reader. As late as June 1970, five older people at a Republican Club meeting in San Diego declared they would rip to pieces and even kill anyone tearing up the American flag. A member of the panel discussion on the subject of student militancy, dissent, and campus violence declared this only proved that there are also violence-prone individuals outside the campus.

New Patriotic Feeling Rises

Associated Press

From its lofty isolation on a windless moon to an endless, earthly vigil over a thousand city halls, the American flag is getting around nowadays.

On car bumpers, car windows, car aerials, car doors.

In stores, in homes, in churches, in halls.

It's there, almost everywhere, a mute symbol of America . . . and some highly contradictory ideas.

"I consider the flag as sacred as the sacraments of my church," says an Elks lodge official. "Anyone who would destroy it is stupid."

"The flag," counters a Negro poverty worker, "never did anything for anybody. Try to find one in the black ghetto."

The alienated, peace-beaded hippie?

"Countries cause all our problems," says one. "I don't believe in flags."

Adds Up to Patriotism

Sacred, suspected and a little over-simplified. It all adds up to that perplexing expression called patriotism.

Patriotism?

For some, it is supporting the government in the face of criticism, and for others it is criticizing the government to speed reforms.

For some, it is mounting the drive for law and order, and for others it's breaking the law to further a cause.

From "New Patriotic Feeling Rises," *San Diego Union,* December 14, 1969. Reprinted by permission.

Historically, a patriot was that person who loved his country and promoted and defended its interests. And historically, as now, almost anyone could qualify as long as national interest remained a matter of personal persuasion.

Who, then, is a patriot?

The next best question, with more available answers, is how and why are Americans patriotic.

"I've always gone back to the fundamental that action brings reaction," says Frank Wetzel, a director of the U.S. Flag Foundation in New York.

"There's a new feeling of patriotism today because people are tired of protests. They're starting to collect their ideas and take a stand."

Patriotism in the past two years has been a highly visual expression. And it has been something of a phenomenon.

Reader's Digest, in a spectacularly successful campaign started last February, distributed more than 18 million flag decals to its subscribers, then was flooded with requests for 32 million more.

Most of the additional decals went to large corporations, including Gulf Oil Co., which is handing out more than 20 million of the flag stickers as a service station promotion.

Love It or Leave

Another popular decal—an Elks' sticker bearing the slogan "Our Flag—Love It or Leave"—was first distributed through local lodges a year ago and has topped one million in circulation.

New York's Daily News has distributed more than one million flag stickers to its readership, including one designed in honor of the Apollo 11 moon mission and carrying the slogan, "Good Old USA."

Since most of the decals were distributed at no cost and without request, it is difficult to measure public response to the flag campaigns. However, it is overwhelming if it is anything like the demand for cloth flags.

New York's Annin Flag Co., one of the country's oldest and largest flag manufacturers, has had its orders doubled in the last year.

"The demand is incredible, especially for flags that you attach to car aerials," said a spokesman. "I suppose it's all part of the new conservative trend in the country, a reaction to all the protests."

"Patriotism is a word monopolized by the right, and in the rightest view, it involves a sort of mindless allegiance based on accident of birth," says Ira Glasser, staff attorney for the American Civil Liberties Union in New York.

"It's translated into a belief that unpopular views must be suppressed," he said. "And it has little to do with values underlying the Bill of Rights."

Glasser, who specializes in court action involving student protestors, is most concerned about application of patriotic symbols to law and order issues.

Symbols Misused

"It's frightening that good people can end up subscribing to totalitarianism through misuse of patriotic symbols," he said, "but that is exactly what's happening."

Whether or not the ambitions of the New Left are patriotic concerns practically no one inside the movement.

But, for the sake of argument, young radicals see nothing about their thinking that isn't patriotic.

"The New Left is an authentically American development," says Dave Gelber, 28, an editorial associate of New York's Liberation magazine, a forum for leftist organizations.

"American radicals couldn't conceive of any other country to live in other than their own," he said. "They want to stay in this country. They want to make something that is decent and livable."

Then there is Barbara Crane, a Clinton, N.Y., mother who has decals on her car, plus an aerial flag, and who organized a counter-protest to protest the anti-Vietnam war protest.

Questions

1 Does Professor Fay's analysis of the fundamental causes of World War I apply as well to the second world war? Explain.

2 Some ninety million people are said to have been killed in twentieth century war, internal and external. Some look upon this death toll lightly and mention that at least it is a form of population control. Comment.

3 Is world federalism a practical alternative to ultranationalism?

4 In what ways does the American federation support the idea of world federalism? What factors would be different on a world scale?

5 Even if communism and fascism had not arisen after

World War I, would the world's nations have found excuses for another great war?

6 What are some of the benefits to mankind from nationalism? Could these be kept in some sort of a world federation?

7 Would you say that nationalism has declined in the major nations even in light of the conflicts between China and Russia, and America and DeGaullist France? Considering democracy and the rise of communism and fascism after World War I, do you feel ideology is more important today in linking people together than national boundaries?

7

A New Africa
in an Old World

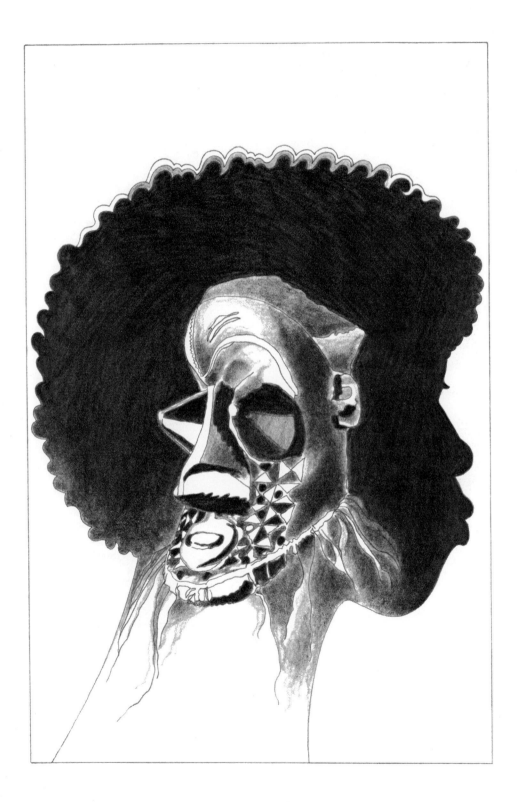

Civilizations and cultures are not superior or inferior to one another, they are only different, say the anthropologists. Contrary to his expectations, Adolf Hitler failed to prove the existence of a master race, and likewise, Western civilization with its record of imperialistic atrocities has failed to establish its moral superiority to other patterns of culture—whether in Africa or anywhere else. But Western imperialism has managed to interrupt the mosaic of hundreds of cultural images in Africa, where only a common continent confines the wonderful diversity.

Images of the Black Man's Burden

Frederick Gentles

Basically, we are all Africans. "Not in innocence, and not in Asia, was mankind born," says Robert Ardrey in *African Genesis.* "The home of our fathers was that African highland reaching north from the Cape to the Lakes of the Nile. Here we came about—slowly, ever so slowly—on a sky-swept savannah glowing with menace."[1]

For thousands of years there have been rich cultures in Africa displaying the hues of varied life styles. If there have been no apparently superior cultures, it is because not everyone can agree on the definitions of "superior." There were brilliant Mali, Ghana, and Songhay empires in Africa while Europeans were still bogged down in the Middle Ages. Who is to say, therefore, what is superior?

Western man claimed he was superior:

We are Anglo-Saxons, and must obey our blood and occupy new markets, and, if necessary, new lands. . . . [This is] the Anglo-Saxon instinct of empire.

. . . Like England, we will establish trading posts throughout the world, we will cover the oceans with our merchant marine, we will build a navy to the measure of our greatness; great colonies will grow about our posts of trade, and American law, American order, American civilization and the American flag will plant themselves on shores hitherto bloody and benighted.

. . . If it means Anglo-Saxon solidarity; if it means an English-American understanding upon the basis of a division of the world's markets, and English-speaking people's league of God for the permanent peace of this war-worn world, the stars will fight for us, and countless centuries will applaud.[2]

This happened to be an American patriot, Senator Albert Beveridge of Indiana, singing out praises of an American dream in 1898 to rousing applause from the Senate floor. It could as easily have been a German reacting to the Kaiser's "Deutschland Über Alles," a Frenchman thundering out the "Marseillaise," a Britisher thrilling to "Rule Britannia," or any other supernationalist tingling to the strains of his nation's concepts of territorial imperative and racial supremacy. These were the vibrations of nationalism and imperialism as the nineteenth century gave way to the twentieth. At that time, they were considered to be good vibrations. They were the vibrations of Rudyard Kipling's *White Man's Burden*:

> Take up the White Man's burden
> Send forth the best ye breed,
> Go bind your sons to exile
> To serve your captives' need;
> To wait in heavy harness
> On fluttered folk and wild,
> Your new-caught sullen peoples,
> Half-devil and half-child. . . .
>
> Take up the White Man's burden
> The savage wars of peace,
> Fill full the mouth of Famine
> And bid the sickness cease. . . .

Ye dare not stoop to less—*

These vibrations turned bad, however, and the twentieth century has not yet recovered from the shock waves created by the followers of those tuneful ditties. Africans in particular suffered from the humility of being partitioned, ruled, exploited, enslaved, preached at, indoctrinated, judged, jailed, and dehumanized. The imperialists brought their weapons, troops, religion, government, engineers, and economists to redo the face of Africa, not exactly in their image, but in an image they considered profitable for themselves and "best" for the Africans. In much of Africa, the white man was actually the black man's burden.

Both black and white peoples had various reactions to the imperialism that permeated the entire continent. Besides black and white manifestations, there were various shades of gray, and a more accurate picture of the consequences of imperialism must lie among the grays rather than with an absolutist one-color representation. After all, millions of people were involved over a period of decades in this

*"The White Man's Burden" copyright 1908 by Rudyard Kipling, from *Rudyard Kipling's Verse: Definitive Edition*. Reprinted by permission of Mrs. George Bambridge, Doubleday & Co., and Macmillan & Co.

land of many images. Images—insofar as they are symbolic of basic attitudes and orientations—change with place, time, individuals, and value systems. Whatever the images, there is no question that European imperialism has provided a foundation for much of the activity and turmoil in Africa today.

It is a fact that Europeans came in great numbers after the Berlin Conference of 1875, which divided much of Africa into dozens of colonies, most with boundary lines arbitrarily dividing races and cultures. It is a fact that there was exploitation, cruelty, and many of the other tyrannies mentioned earlier. And it is a fact that many Westerners do not understand what imperialism has done to Africa and Africans. Westerners have only vague images of an Africa where images abound.

One image of the new Africa is that of the Third World movement discussed by the black psychiatrist Frantz Fanon in several books that are recommended reading for partisans of the New Left. In *The Wretched of the Earth* and *Black Skin, White Masks,* Fanon described the violence of colonialism and what it did to the black man's psyche. It ground him under to make him feel dirty and inferior to his overlord. It also left him with a residue of bitterness years after the end of most colonial rule in Africa. Colonialism took its toll physically and mentally, and the Third World—composed mainly of devotees in Africa and Asia who want to avoid alignment with either of the two major power blocs and who want to remain distinct from many values of capitalist and communist systems—is bitter about the tyranny of one people over another. Fanon says the world cannot long remain half capitalist, half communist. It must become oriented toward people in a new socialist humanism. "The Third World," he writes, "ought not to be content to define itself in the terms of values which have preceded it. On the contrary, the underdeveloped countries ought to do their utmost to find their own particular values and methods and a style which shall be peculiar to them."[3]

The old humanism failed, and capitalist and communist totalitarian values did not result in freedom for all. Psychic alienation of the black man continues in the Portuguese colonies of Angola and Mozambique, and in Rhodesia and the Republic of South Africa. Where is there justice in the fact that the rich cities of white-dominated southern Africa continue to be built on the servile labor of blacks working underground in gold and diamond mines? The Republic of South Africa leads the world in the production of gold, gem diamonds, and antimony, and is among the world's leaders in the extraction of other minerals. The blacks do the hard, dirty work and live on the edge of poverty in subservience to the whites whom they maintain in comparative luxury. To condone the myths and canons built up around this economic and social slavery after 5000 years of civilization is an insult to the intelligence of man. The Third World wants a new morality that is not racist or dominated by economic greed.

Justice will come only through protest and violence says Fanon, because those who have most of the world's wealth will not willingly give it up to share with the poor. According to the Third World view, the rich nations maintain themselves through violence in the form of police, military, and governmental establishments, and it will take violence to overthrow these regimes. That one gets only what one fights for is a lesson learned from the West. The Third World movement, the New Left around the world, looks to Fanon and others like him to find its morality, justice, and love for all men of good will.

There are other images of Africa and imperialism than that of the Third World, however. These images may or may not encompass elements of Fanon's philosophy. One is tribalism. Africans, like other people around the planet, are oriented to the tribe, with its special language, habits, beliefs, music, and so on. The tribe is as dear to the Ibo, Kikuyu, Masai, and Shanti as it is to the Scotsman, Walloon, Yankee, and the man from Dixie. When the newly independent nations maintained colonial boundary lines, many tribal leaders struck for their independent rights. The movement for local self-government was not entirely unlike movements that had occurred down through history in Europe and America. In several African countries political parties were formed that sponsored a new federalism as opposed to other parties which favored strong national governments. Bitter conflicts resulted on the order of those that separated Jefferson and Hamilton, and Wallace and Nixon and Humphrey.

Tribalism is powerful in Africa because it is one of the primary images people have of themselves. But the new nationalism is a powerful image, too, and many Africans have built up a romantic image of being a Nigerian, Ghanan, Kenyan, or whatever. Over thirty new nationalities were created within a ten-year period beginning in 1957. "Instant nationalism" broke out with its accoutrements of troops, foreign policy, bureaucracy, economic planning, and pride. It takes time to mold a nation, and thus it is amazing how quickly some Africans have taken up the national idea despite strong tribal ties.

Obviously, there is more to a line than meets the eye, because already one detects a fierce nationalism within borders in Africa. What is there in a line that stirs the imagination of people to build an image around it? Gamal Abdel Nasser, for instance, dreamed of creating a United Arab Republic out of the bonds of race, religion, language, and culture in North Africa and the Middle East. Instead, those strong ties gave way to the arbitrary lines that separate Moroccans, Algerians, Tunisians, Libyans, Egyptians, Sudanese, Syrians, etc. In the central part of Africa, Guinea, Ivory Coast, Ghana, Cameroon, Uganda, Tanzania, Kenya, and others have been successful in maintaining law and order within the arbitrary lines. To the south, Kenneth Kaunda and Dr. Hastings Banda have succeeded in keeping many tribes in line in their new nations of Zambia and Malawi, despite proximity to white-ruled Rhodesia, the Portuguese colonies and the Republic of South Africa—all of which so fear the new African nationalism that they supported Katanga, Biafra, and other tribal and regional defections. It is likely, however, that the Congo and Nigerian civil wars will be a warning to other tribal and separatist movements that they cannot succeed against the stronger national order.

In essence, then, we have a new Africa in an old world of nations. But many in Africa want to move on from the hangups of the old world. Instead of the boundaries of nationalism, they want to create the image of a united African people by drawing a longer line around the shores of that great continent. The dream of Pan-Africanism is not a new one. Actually, some of the roots of the movement appeared in the United States early in this century with Dr. W. E. B. Du Bois— one of the great black leaders who inspired others in the founding of the NAACP—advocating the regeneration of the black peoples in America in association with a freed and independent African people. Another black leader early in the twentieth century, Marcus Garvey, preached a back-to-Africa movement for black people all over the world. They would return to a United States of Africa. The seed of a united Africa germinated, and the dream has finally come true, according to one authority, because it is now universal throughout the continent. Only practical obstacles stand in the way of full realization of the dream.

Despite strong nationalistic power blocs, fears, rivalries, and the glamour of power at home, abroad, and in the United Nations for some leaders, the Pan-African dream is alive. Kwame Nkrumah, former president of Ghana, was one of the first leaders of the movement when African nations began to break free of their colonial ties. In *Africa Must Unite,* he said:

> There are those who maintain that Africa cannot unite because we lack the three necessary ingredients for unity, a common race, culture and language. It is true that we have for centuries been divided. The territorial boundaries dividing us were fixed long ago, often quite arbitrarily, by the colonial powers. Some of us are Moslems, some Christians; many believe in traditional, tribal gods. Some of us speak French, some English, some Portuguese, not to mention the millions who speak only one of the hundreds of different African languages. We have acquired cultural differences which affect our outlook and condition our political development.
>
> All this is inevitable, due to our historical background. Yet in spite of this I am convinced that the forces making for unity far outweigh those which divide us. In meeting fellow Africans from all parts of the continent I am constantly impressed by how much we have in common. It is not just our colonial past, or the fact that we have aims in common, it is something which goes far deeper. I can best describe it as a sense of one-ness in that we are *Africans.**

Although Africans have had to settle for something less than unity in these first years after independence, Pan-African conferences continue to be held, political and economic proposals are made, and regional tariff agreements concluded. Nationalism came to Africa, as it came to Europe in the late Middle Ages, from the urban areas oriented to trade, to commerce, and to the larger unit of the nation for protection. Pan-Africanism, like one-worldism in the West, stems from a small corps of intellectuals who are not predominant in the national power structure. Africa may already be too bogged down with the many hangups of what passes for civilization: nationalism, competition for prestige, power, profits, and politics as usual. Can it escape these strong ties to find the larger unity or will it continue to emulate the other two worlds?

"I am alone in the African street," says Robert Ardrey, "lost, afraid, and without allies. I understand nothing. Yet this is the street where I was born."[4] How far have we come, brothers?

*From *Africa Must Unite* by Kwame Nkrumah (New York: International Publishers, 1963), p. 132. By permission of International Publishers and Heinemann Educational Books Ltd., London.

Notes

1 Robert Ardrey, *African Genesis* (New York: Dell, 1961), p. 9.

2 R. W. Leopold and A. S. Link, *Problems in American History* (Englewood Cliffs, N.J.: Prentice-Hall, 1957), p. 492. The selection was taken from the *Boston Herald,* April 28, 1898.

3 Frantz Fanon, *The Wretched of the Earth* (New York: Grove Press, 1968), p. 99. Translated by Constance Farrington.

4 Ardrey, *op. cit.,* p. 356.

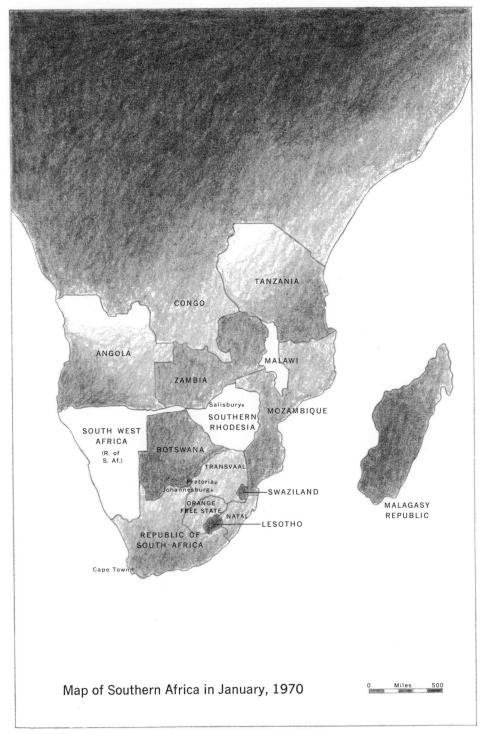

Map of Southern Africa in January, 1970

0   Miles   500

The Republic of South Africa is a tinderbox generating racial unrest inside and outside the country. The white ruling caste has kept the nation divided into several rather sharp racial classes. At the top is the Dutch-descended group which prevails upon most of the British-descended people to support "apartheid." Next on the scale of segregation are the hundreds of thousands of East Indians who are only a notch removed from a few million Cape Coloreds, a mixture of races. At the bottom of this caste society stands the huge Bantu population, which receives the full brunt of apartheid. Here Professor Karis describes the evolution of the problems that now confront much of Africa and the world.

South Africa: The End Is Not Yet

Thomas Karis

The importance of the Republic of South Africa in the contemporary world is unrelated to its relatively modest size or power. In an age in which legally sanctioned racial discrimination is almost universally condemned, South Africa stands out as a champion of *apartheid* (racial separation) and white supremacy within its borders. Ignoring the affirmation of human rights contained in the Charter of the United Nations and in the Universal Declaration of Human Rights adopted by the General Assembly in 1948, South African governments have strengthened legal and institutional barriers to minimize contacts between whites and nonwhites and to divide them into separate communities.

The overwhelming majority of nations in the world have rejected the repeated contention of successive South African governments that apartheid is a domestic matter. Within the UN, apartheid has become a burning issue; outside, it has evoked the passionate hostility of the peoples of Africa and of their leaders, who are committed to bring about the downfall of the Republic's regime of white domination and the eradication of its policies of apartheid. The struggle that has been joined, if South Africa continues on its present course, promises to be long; and the outcome could have fateful consequences both for those immediately involved and for the world as a whole.

The Beloved Country

"Fly to the unspoiled land of contrasts," reads the headline of an advertisement for South African Airways. "There is no other country

Excerpted from Thomas Karis, "South Africa: The End Is Not Yet," *Headline Series* No. 176. New York: Foreign Policy Association, April 1966.

like it." South Africa is indeed a land of contrasts. Alan Paton in
Cry, the Beloved Country, probably the most widely known South
African novel, has drawn the contrast between the loveliness of the
countryside and the ugliness of the city for the African newcomer,
between the overpowering attraction of modern society and the price
in conflict and disintegration paid by the African, who is not allowed
fully to share it.

South Africa is a far-flung country, about one-sixth the size of the
United States. Americans who live in the western part of the United
States would feel at home on the high veld, the grassy plateau of the
interior, 4,000 to 6,000 feet above sea level. The climate is healthy
throughout most of the country. To the south, the climate of the
Cape and its fruit-growing areas is similar to that of southern California. Near the northeast coast, separated from the high veld by the
spectacular Drakensberg Mountains, are the lush and subtropical
valleys of Paton's Natal.

But almost half the country is semidesert and only about 15 percent is arable. There are no arterial rivers or lakes. The rainbearing
winds from the Indian Ocean make a pattern of rainfall that is
heaviest—about 30 to 50 inches a year—along the eastern coast.
Rain decreases steadily as one moves to the desert areas of the west.
Droughts occur periodically, the soil is generally poor, agricultural
productivity is low and erosion is a major and continuing problem.

Some of the most fertile areas are heavily populated African reserves near the east coast, notably the Transkei, which the government is promoting as a "self-governing" homeland for the Xhosa
people. Erosion there is so serious, however, that large numbers of
Africans must be drawn off the land if soil conservation measures
are to be effective.

Riches lie under the soil, however, far from the Transkei. Mining
and the industrial development which began in the 1870's account
for the heavy concentration of whites on the Witwatersrand (literally,
ridge of the white waters), the gold-bearing reef running roughly
east and west of Johannesburg. South Africa is not only rich in gold
and diamonds, but it also possesses in abundance and proximity to
each other the metals needed for heavy industry. In the Transvaal, the
Orange Free State and northern Natal are found, for example, iron
ore, limestone, manganese, chrome, copper, vast reserves of uranium
and probably the world's most cheaply mined coal, which provides
inexpensive power and some of which is converted to oil. Natural
oil, however, is lacking.

The People: Numbers and Beginnings

The 4 to 1 ratio of nonwhite to white in the world's population is mirrored in South Africa. Of its 18 million people (excluding South-West Africa), less than 20 percent are white; nearly 70 percent are Africans, 9 percent are Coloreds (a term different from American usage and meaning racially mixed) and 3 percent are Asians.

When the Dutch East India Company established a halfway revictualing station at the Cape in 1652, only the short, yellowish Bushmen and Hottentots were there and in the hinterland. Government spokesmen often say that the Bantu tribes entered South Africa from the north at about the same time the whites arrived in the south. But there is evidence that these tribes, probably migrating southward from central and east Africa, were in the area that is now the Transvaal and Natal at least by 1500 and perhaps centuries earlier. They did not confront whites, the frontiersmen who were trekking east and north from the Cape, until the 1770's, when they met in the area between present-day Port Elizabeth and East London. Meanwhile, before contact was made with the Bantu, miscegenation between whites and slaves, Hottentots or others had already produced a Colored population.

The three-fifths of the white population known as Afrikaners trace their ancestry to the small group of whites (Dutch, French and German) which settled at the Cape in the latter part of the 17th century. They speak Afrikaans, a distinctive language derived from Dutch, which is one of South Africa's two official languages (the other is English). By 1800 they numbered only about 16,000 within the borders of the settlement. In addition, there were about 17,000 slaves and possibly 20,000 Hottentots, Bushmen and Coloreds. Beyond the company's effective control was a small number of cattle farmers moving eastward as had their ancestors more than a century earlier. Not until 1820, when the British government assisted emigration because of unemployment at home, did a substantial number of English-speaking people—about 5,000—settle in South Africa. Many more came later.

Indians were brought to Natal in the 1860's as indentured labor to work on the sugar plantations. Many remained after serving their indentures. The Indian government prohibited recruitment in 1911, and shortly afterwards the South African government banned the free immigration of Indians. But by then an Indian community of about 150,000 was already established with half a century of history as South Africans.

Dependence and Independence

It is useful at this point to sketch the major shifts in political control and constitutional status. The rule of the Dutch East India Company lasted until 1795, when the British temporarily occupied the Cape. A second British occupation in 1806 became permanent. During the decade after 1836, some 10,000 Boers (literally, farmers) migrated from the Cape into the interior to escape British rule and color-blind practices. This migration, known as the Great Trek, led to the establishment of Boer republics (the Orange Free State and the Transvaal), and further insulated the Boers from new and alien ideas.

British policy in the second and third quarters of the 19th century responded in a vacillating manner to conflicting domestic pressures of evangelicalism and liberalism and to the need for economy. But with the beginning of diamond and gold mining, the economic motivations behind British imperialism increased in southern Africa. Tensions grew sharp between *Uitlanders* (foreigners or outsiders, as the British were called) and Boers and between Whitehall and Pretoria (the capital of the Transvaal). The result in 1899 was the Anglo-Boer war.

The Transvaal and Orange Free State republics were defeated in 1902, became crown colonies, and soon were granted the powers of self-government that Cape Colony and Natal already had. Economic and political pressures for closer union and a common anxiety about a united front in governing the African population culminated in the formation of the Union of South Africa on May 31, 1910, as a self-governing British Dominion.

The Union's independence within the British Commonwealth was recognized in 1926 and given formal legal effect by British and South African statutes in 1931 and 1934 respectively. South Africa continued to be a member of the Commonwealth until May 31, 1961, when the Republic of South Africa was proclaimed.

Neighbors—Friendly and Otherwise

South Africa is separated from the hostility of independent black Africa by a buffer of white-controlled states: Portuguese Angola, Rhodesia and Portuguese Mozambique. South Africa's mandated territory of South-West Africa, south of Angola and bordering the Atlantic Ocean, provides an additional buffer. There is one gap, however: Bechuanaland, a British territory that is now self-governing but will become independent, under the name of Botswana, on September

30 [1966]. Bechuanaland has long, common borders with South-West Africa and the Republic and is not far from South Africa's major industrial area. It also touches Zambia for seven miles at the confluence of the Zambezi and Chobe rivers, which travelers can cross in a pontoon ferry. Bechuanaland has served in recent years as a corridor for South African political refugees moving north to Zambia or even to Rhodesia or by air to Tanzania.

Bechuanaland's usefulness as a guerrilla or military base against South Africa is limited, however. The terrain is open; but more important is the fact that the country, an impoverished and largely semi-desert territory of about 500,000 to 600,000 people, is economically dependent upon South Africa and anxious to maintain proper relations.

Even more dependent is the British territory of Basutoland, a mountainous enclave within South Africa, due to become independent next July [1966] under the name of Lesotho. Bechuanaland, Basutoland and Swaziland (also a British territory lying between South Africa and Mozambique) are sources of labor for South Africa's gold mines and industry and, in effect, "native reserves" of the Republic. For more substantial bases against South Africa, revolutionary leaders await the fall of white rule in Rhodesia and Mozambique. . . .

Dominating and Dividing the Africans

"The present government believes in the domination of the white man in his own area," Dr. Verwoerd said in 1963, quoting a statement he had made to the Natives' Representative Council in 1950, "but it equally believes in the domination of the Bantu in his area." By 1961 only some legislative tidying up remained in the process of reducing the status of Africans in the so-called white areas to that of labor without rights or security. On the other hand, in response to pressure both at home and abroad, the timetable of domestic colonialism was accelerated after January 23, 1962. On that day, Dr. Verwoerd announced that the government intended to grant "self-government" to the Transkei, the impoverished rural reserve between Basutoland and the Indian Ocean.

The Transkei is an almost unbroken black territory, roughly the size of Switzerland, with few "spots" of white residence and a long history of separate regional consciousness. Its land is eroded and overstocked; subsistence farming is unable to support its 1.4 million African inhabitants; there are few wage-paying jobs; and at any time, perhaps half or more of the adult males are working outside. The

Transkei and all the other Bantu areas, consisting of over 250 scattered reserves, contain about 37 percent of the African population (1960) and 12.9 percent of the land. Presumably they are to be consolidated, enlarged and developed as tribal "homelands"—Bantustans—for eight "national units."

In most respects the trend of legislation affecting Africans outside the reserves since 1948 has been in line with traditional policies. Customary social and residential segregation, for example, and segregation in the use of public facilities have been made mandatory, more rigid and deliberately conspicuous. Penalties for violation of the traditional master-servant relationship by the subordinate party have been stiffened. The hated pass system has been extended to African women. The 1926 legislative color bar against skilled work by African mine workers has, potentially, been extended to all jobs. In order to protect whites against nonwhite competition, legislation has empowered officials to reserve particular jobs for a particular race.

Not only are African trade unions not recognized and Africans prohibited from striking, but, under an act passed shortly after Sharpeville, anyone who intimidates others to stay away from work, or jeers at them for working, or breaks a contract of employment in essential services may be penalized by ten strokes of a cane, or five years' imprisonment, or a fine of $1,400 or a combination of any two of these. (For various offenses, 16,887 persons, nearly all of them Africans, were subjected to lashing in 1964.) The Bantu Laws Amendment Act of 1964 treats all Africans in urban areas, no matter how long resident or even if born there, as "temporary sojourners," in Dr. Verwoerd's phrase. They are subject to expulsion if not properly employed or if considered troublesome and are consigned to a tribal area they may have never seen.

In some respects, however, policy has broken with the past by removing nearly all rights and opportunities that pointed toward individual participation and eventual equality in a nonracial society. Thus, for example, ownership of land outside the reserves has been abolished; interracial contacts (everyone being required to register by race) have been reduced to a minimum; private schools for Africans may exist only with governmental approval; and admittance [of Africans] to the previously nonracial classrooms of the University of Cape Town and Witwatersrand University has been forbidden. Even the University College of Fort Hare for nonwhites, whose reputation extended beyond the Republic, has been converted into one of several tribal-related and government-controlled colleges.

Within the doctrinaire framework that treats urban Africans as citizens of tribal homelands, the government has sought to improve housing, community facilities and police behavior. Some new commercial and job opportunities have been opened. As noted earlier, the government has tacitly accepted or sometimes actively cooperated with white labor unions in allowing the fuller use of African labor.

At the same time, official policy seeks to uproot any sense of permanent belonging outside the reserves and to treat Africans as a migrant labor force, preferably working on contract away from their families. Migrant laborers are, in fact, very widely used in mining and often in other employment. For example, near Cape Town, 18,311 African men, of whom 12,390 were married, were housed in bachelor quarters in January 1963. Nevertheless, probably about two-thirds of the more than 4 million Africans in urban areas are "permanently" urbanized. While their orientation to modern life becomes stronger and their material expectations grow, their political aspirations are expected to find expression in the homelands. . . .

Realism and the National Interest

South Africa's government is firmly in control and its anticommunism is fervent. The opportunities offered American businessmen by South Africa's flourishing economy are lucrative. And, according to some observers, the country's location and facilities are strategic. In view of these factors, there are those who, even though they may disapprove of apartheid, feel that United States policy toward South Africa should be based on our "real" national interests; and that, consequently, the United States should not intervene in "domestic" South African affairs; or, if it does, it should at least not take any action that will be disruptive. This approach to the problem is reinforced by an analysis that sees African states continuing to be weak and unstable; the African activities of Communist China and the Soviet Union, inept; organized resistance within South Africa or large-scale infiltration by saboteurs and guerrillas, remote; a frontal attack on South Africa, inconceivable; and an African alternative government to the present regime, chaotic or Communist.

On the other hand, a strong argument can be made that South Africa's strategic and economic value to the United States is much less than vital. Strategically, the importance of the Cape route to Asia as an alternative to Suez has declined, partly as a result of changing military technology and long-range air transport. The United States missile tracking and deep-space probe installations now located in South Africa could be relocated elsewhere in Africa. Economically, the reduction or severing of ties with South Africa would undoubtedly have some impact, but this could be easily absorbed. Nor would a ban on imports, even including gold, from South Africa create problems that could not be resolved. For those advocating a tougher policy, the real issue is whether or not the advantages the United States derives from its present relations with South Africa are far outweighed by the political and moral costs of identification with a racist regime.

'Hopeless but Not Serious'

The wry remark that the situation is hopeless but not serious may well apply to South Africa. But if hopelessness means that racial war is inevitable, as pessimists believe, the prospect is indeed bleak. Not only could such a conflict be incredibly bitter and violent, but it also could profoundly damage United States relations with the nonwhite peoples of the world. Violations of human rights in South Africa, therefore, are significantly different from violations in Haiti or those which occurred in Ghana under Nkrumah, for example, since they may lead to consequences that could vitally affect United States interests. The consequences would be especially grave—were violence to erupt—if the United States appeared guilty of tacitly supporting the South African regime or if, in a time of crisis, it intervened to bolster white rule.

United States spokesmen in the UN have repeatedly stated this country's opposition to apartheid and have expressed confidence that it eventually will come to an end. "How and when the South African government will abandon its hateful racial policies we cannot know," Ambassador Francis Plimpton said in 1961, "but abandon them it will." What hopefully would follow, in the United States view, is the development of a "democratic and equal society" with "majority rule and minority rights." Future relationships, it is assumed, would be multiracial, since, unless there is to be a mass exodus of whites, large numbers of them will continue to live in the area now ruled by the Republic. (A 1965 estimate of population in the year 2000 is 6.2 million whites, 7.6 million Coloreds and Indians, and 28.5 million Africans.) . . .

Current United States Policy

Current United States policy is a mixture that probably satisfies no one. On the one hand, the United States has manifested its abhorrence of apartheid in a variety of ways. It has invited nonwhites to diplomatic functions in South Africa since 1963, has embargoed the sale of all military equipment since the end of that year (losing an estimated $435 million in arms and aircraft sales during the following two years), has expressly praised men like Luthuli and Mandela, and supports educational and training programs for South African and South-West African political exiles. United States sensitivity to racial issues that bear directly upon Americans was illustrated in 1965, when Dr. Verwoerd insisted that aircraft carrier flight crews landing in South Africa should not be racially mixed. The United States, therefore, cancelled a visit to Cape Town by the carrier *Independence,* on its way to Vietnam, and sent an oiler on a 14,000-mile round trip at a cost of nearly $300,000 to refuel the *Independence* 250 miles off Cape Town.

On the other hand, the United States continues to hope that "the steady and repeated impact of the conscience of the world community" will do more to bring about a change in policy "than any dramatic action." Meanwhile, it maintains missile tracking and space stations in South Africa, includes South Africa in world sugar quotas, and actively assists (if perhaps, it no longer actively encourages) American businessmen interested in South Africa, some of whose statements have been grist for the South African propaganda mill. Thus in 1965 Lauris Norstad, former NATO supreme commander turned businessman, extolled "South Africa's importance as an ally and as an economic force in the free world."

In recent years, United States policy has tended to move slowly from cordiality to correctness and may be moving toward coldness. Nevertheless, the United States has failed to convince the South African government that it means what it says. What is urgently necessary, in the judgment of many independent observers, is continuing but more dramatic disengagement from the South African embrace.

Too Little and Too Late?

The problem, however, is extraordinarily complex, and partial disengagement is only a first step. Carrots as well as sticks, multilateral as well as unilateral initiatives, in the author's view, are necessary. Any policy which offers a chance for success must provide concrete measures of reassurance for fearful whites. Minimum essentials of desired change and minimum timetables for achieving them should be defined. And the United States and other powers must consider the continuing obligations they incur in sponsoring change that may lead to violence.

Above all, the time has come for Washington to put South Africa high on its agenda of priority issues. A policy of drift and temporizing is understandable, given urgent preoccupations in Southeast Asia and elsewhere. But such a policy or lack of one is both dangerous and short-sighted. The end of hope is not yet, but the time is late.

With each passing day white South Africans who are open-minded and seek to bridge the racial gulf become more despairing, and the bitterness and frustration of African leaders inside and outside the Republic increase. And within the United States, we may surely antici-pate a time when Negro and civil rights groups add the South African issue to the list of their urgent concerns.

Perhaps the United States and Britain in cooperation with like-minded allies could still exercise their power to influence white South Africans to change the direction of their country's policy. But will they act in time? If not, any lingering hope that the "beloved country" will become an example of multiracial goodwill and the motor of con-tinental prosperity may at last be dead.

Despite some scattered discrimination against whites and East Indians, black African leaders are generally determined not to encourage the racism found in the white societies they know. Africa, it is said, is experiencing in a few years what Western man experienced in centuries—modernization within a world of nationalities. The following selection traces the emergence of African nations into the modern world.

The New Nationalism

Louis L. Snyder

Emergence: The Historical Pattern

The continent of Africa, more than 11,530,000 square miles in extent, three times the size of Europe, only recently became an active partner in world history. With the exception of Egypt, one of the cradlelands of Western civilization, Africa has remained—alone among the great continents—silent and passive through the course of history. Its coastline was explored and settled by small European groups in the fifteenth-century Age of Exploration, but not until the third quarter of the nineteenth century was Africa south of the Sahara integrated into modern world society.

European conquerors carved up the giant continent into colonies and protectorates. They exploited its natural resources. At the same time they halted tribal wars, reduced the toll of disease, improved transportation and communication, and constructed roads, power plants, plantations, and mines. Even so, comparatively few Europeans came to Africa. By the middle of the twentieth century, of a total population of two hundred million, only six million, or approximately 3 per cent, were of European background. As late as 1945 there were only four independent states in Africa (Ethiopia, Liberia, Egypt, and South Africa); 90 per cent of the continent was still under colonial control.

World War II marked the beginning of the end of colonialism in Africa. During the war, Allied leaders, anxious for African support, hinted at eventual self-government. But the global prestige of the white man began to decline when reverses were inflicted by the Japanese. African troops who had served overseas and who had learned new skills returned home to demand more political power. In what has been called "a revolution of rising expectations," all Africa exploded in a drive for emancipation that turned into a wild scramble. The process began in the north in the relatively progressive Arab-Muslim states, which were geographically associated with the Mediterranean world and better prepared for self-rule.

The cry "Uhuru" ("Freedom!" in Swahili) was heard south of the Sahara. The white minority was overwhelmed, as one new independent state after another appeared. The colonial powers began to leave Africa, sometimes in haste. The older map with its colored outlines of European possessions was supplanted by one that depicted a patchwork of independent states. By 1964 there were thirty-four independent African states, surpassing Europe (thirty-one) and Asia (twenty-nine).

During the rapid liquidation of European rule, the receding colonialism took on a variegated pattern. Although the British were not altogether aware of the pace of nationalism in Africa, they wisely predicted developments there. From the beginning they based their African policy on eventual self-rule. They trained Africans for the responsibilities of government; they placed African chiefs in charge of local affairs under the guidance of British officials in a kind of indirect rule. They gave more power to African leaders, and more voting privileges to the people. Eventually, the British were able to withdraw from most of their African colonies without the ignominy of being pushed out.

The French colonial policy was "assimilation": the colonies were to be absorbed into a national French framework. France still dominated her African possessions at the end of World War II, but liquidation was soon inaugurated. Between 1958 and 1960, some twelve million people in the hinterland of the Sahara were given their independence, although they remained loosely joined to France in the French Union.

The fever of independence appeared in the Belgian Congo in the late 1950's. After an uprising in January 1959, the Belgians, on June 30, 1960, suddenly granted full independence to the Congo. With no preparation for this unexpected concession, the Congolese descended to chaos. The Italians lost their African possessions as a consequence of the war, but retained administration of Somaliland through the United Nations.

Only Portugal and Spain remained outside the periphery. Both continued to designate their African possessions as "overseas provinces," in theory holding the same rights as metropolitan provinces but in fact remaining colonies. Both tried to resist the pressures that had brought freedom to some two hundred million Africans. Although the Portuguese in Angola on the Atlantic coast and Mozambique on the

Indian Ocean were outnumbered by about fifty to one, Portugal refused to grant independence to her colonies. Spain gave up her protectorate in Morocco but not the rest of her African possessions.

Africa was the last continent to enter the age of nationalism, and thereby, the modern era.[1] This marked the culmination of a long historical process whereby society was transformed after the English and French revolutions.

> In this transformation which is fundamentally one and the same everywhere, the unity of mankind, long postulated by universal religions by the Stoics, by the rational humanism of the age of Enlightenment, is for the first time becoming a reality. The rise of nationalism, the quest for equality and human dignity, which now transform ancient and primitive tribal societies in sub-Saharan Africa, put the capstone to the growing edifice of humanity. We are at the beginning of a new era of history, in which all formerly isolated and secluded parts of the globe are entering into communication and intercourse on a footing of legal equality.[2]

The process had been accelerated by the time it reached Africa, the last great home of empire. Rapid liquidation took place. But the Africans had much less experience and training in self-government than had the peoples of such former colonial dependencies as India and the Philippines.[3] The transition was beset with perplexities and filled with critical tensions, though they were not much more severe than the bitter struggles which took place in Europe and the Americas before their peoples were able to achieve and maintain nationhood.

Africa presented a unique situation because both the nation and the state had to be created. African nationalism, stemming from Negro-African resentment of white colonialism, was promoted by a small elite of leaders whose job it was to create nations in areas where nations, as we know them, seldom existed. It was not an easy task, for controversy marked the path of development.

Nationalism was both blessing and curse for the new African nations—a blessing because it won their hotly desired freedom. But independence did not automatically bring with it either efficient government, social equality, or economic prosperity. Africans learned, as had others in the past, that the road to justice was a thorny one.

Characteristics of Ethnic Nationalism

To those Westerners who forget the development of their own nations, African nationalism seems baffling, paradoxical, and crude. Its outstanding characteristic was its ethnic or racial quality.[4] Dominant racial overtones reflected hatred for the white man—a residue of colonialism. Each new state was affected by antiwhite sentiment. African nationalists denounced the white man as a demagogue who tried to maintain the *status quo.* Mbonu Ojike, a Nigerian, put it plainly: "They [the European imperialists] employ their hush-hush policy of gradualism and of the you-will-never-get-there technique to retard progress in Africa. They speak of democracy but act imperialistically. They say 'we fight for freedom,' but they give Africa political servitude and ignoble tutelage. They proclaim religious tolerance, but are themselves the worst example of religious bigotry and proselytism."[5]

The euphoria produced by independence could not obliterate the feeling of resentment against the white man. At the ceremony marking the independence of the Congo, Patrice Lumumba spoke of

> the mockery, the insults, the blows submitted to morning, noon, and night because we were *"Nègres."* We have known the law was never the same, whether dealing with a white or a Negro; that it was accommodating for one, cruel and inhuman to the other. . . . We have known that in the cities there were magnificent houses for the whites and crumbling hovels for the Negroes, that a Negro was not admitted to movie theaters or restaurants, that he was not allowed to enter so-called "European" stores, that when the Negro traveled, it was on the lowest level of a boat, at the feet of the white man in his de luxe cabin.[6]

The retained anger was expressed in this poem:

Young Africa's Plea

> Don't preserve my customs
> As some fine curios
> To suit some white historian's tastes.
> There's nothing artificial
> That beats the natural way,
> In culture and ideals of life.
> Let me play with the white man's ways,
> Let me work with the black man's brains,
> Let my affairs themselves sort out.
> Then in sweet re-birth
> I'll rise a better man,
> Not ashamed to face the world.
> Those who doubt my talents
> In secret fear my strength;

> They know I am no less a man.
> Let them bury their prejudice,
> Let them show their noble sides,
> Let me have untrammelled growth.
> My friends will never know regret
> And I, I will never forget.[7]

The thinking was essentially xenophobic—an angry protest against foreign encroachment and interference by the white man. Most African nationalists pointed to the continent as the black man's land. The black man would do with it what he wanted, and he would no longer allow the white man to profit exclusively from it. No matter what the argument, it eventually boiled down to the basic issue, black versus white man.

All Africa was gripped by the acute problem of the plural society ("a society comprising two or more elements of social orders which live side by side, yet without mingling, in one political unit").[8] People of different color had to learn to live in the same society. Africa became a laboratory for one of the world's most disturbing problems, that of race relations.[9]

To the white man, reduced from his superior status or even expelled, nationalism in Africa meant simply a return to primitivism. The black man, it was said, was constitutionally incapable of industrializing or modernizing his society. The white man's favorite question was: "What would have happened in North America had the rich land been left to the backward, lazy Indian?" The European minority was worried about its future. Predictions were made both inside and outside Africa that there would be a mass slaughter of whites in the new nations. Skeptics pointed to the Mau Mau uprising in Kenya, disorders in Uganda and Tanganyika, and violence in the Congo as precedents for the outbreak of racial war.

Despite the angry tone of nationalist leaders, there was no mass slaughter. Once they had achieved their independence, black Africans were inclined to accept social differences. Relations between the races became even easier in some areas than they had been under colonial regimes. For example, white settlers in Kenya, who had given way to despair and had sold their homes, eventually returned to live side by side with the four other ethnic groups—Bantu, Nilotic, Nilot-Hamitic, and Hamitic.[10]

It is not yet clear what direction nationalism and racialism will take in the new Africa. The peoples there have been subjected to the power and efficiency of Western culture, and they are impressed. It remains to be seen whether or not they will surrender to the ways of the white man. The assimilative process may be cultural, but almost certainly it will not be biological. Racial barriers will remain. Moreover, it is unlikely that the new African will reject altogether his tribal loyalty, his old gods, and his traditional family customs in the process of cementing national ties.

Notes

1 Hans Kohn, "Changing Africa in a Changing World," *Current History,* XLI (Oct. 1961), p. 194.

2 Hans Kohn and Wallace Sokolsky, *African Nationalism in the Twentieth Century* (Princeton, 1965), pp. 15–16.

3 T. Walter Wallbank, *Contemporary Africa: Continent in Transition* (rev. ed.; Princeton, 1964), p. 11.

4 Some observers use the designation "black nationalism" to refer to the African states. As used here it is to be distinguished from the extremist sense it has taken on in the United States (Black Muslims).

5 Mbonu Ojike, in *Africa, Today and Tomorrow* (New York, 1945), pp. 45–46; courtesy of African Academy of Arts and Research.

6 Patrice Lumumba, in *Africa Speaks,* ed. James Duffy and Robert Manners (Princeton, 1961), pp. 90–91.

7 *An Anthology of West African Verse,* compiled by Olembe Bassir (Ibadan, Nigeria, 1957), p. 57.

8 Cf. John S. Furnivall, *Colonial Policy and Practice: A Comparative Study of Burma and Netherlands India* (Cambridge, England, 1948), p. 446.

9 Wallbank, *op. cit.,* p. 12.

10 *Ibid.* See Ch. 6.

Alex Quaison-Sackey of Ghana, former president of the U.N. General
Assembly, says that Fanon's "The Wretched of the Earth" must be read
by all who wish to understand what it means to fight for freedom, equality,
and dignity. In this selection, Fanon condemns the imperialists for raping
Africa and then leaving it. The Allies, he says, expected reparations from
Germany after both world wars; Africa can expect no less. What do the
Western nations owe Africa?

The Wretched of the Earth

Frantz Fanon

Colonialism and imperialism have not paid their score when they
withdraw their flags and their police forces from our territories. For
centuries the capitalists have behaved in the underdeveloped world
like nothing more than war criminals. Deportations, massacres, forced
labor, and slavery have been the main methods used by capitalism
to increase its wealth, its gold or diamond reserves, and to establish
its power. Not long ago Nazism transformed the whole of Europe
into a veritable colony. The governments of the various European
nations called for reparations and demanded the restitution in kind
and money of the wealth which had been stolen from them: cultural
treasures, pictures, sculptures, and stained glass have been given back
to their owners. There was only one slogan in the mouths of Europeans on the morrow of the 1945 V-day: "Germany must pay." Herr
Adenauer, it must be said, at the opening of the Eichmann trial, and
in the name of the German people, asked once more for forgiveness
from the Jewish people. Herr Adenauer has renewed the promise
of his people to go on paying to the state of Israel the enormous
sums which are supposed to be compensation for the crimes of the
Nazis.[1]

In the same way we may say that the imperialist states would
make a great mistake and commit an unspeakable injustice if they
contented themselves with withdrawing from our soil the military
cohorts, and the administrative and managerial services whose function it was to discover the wealth of the country, to extract it and
to send it off to the mother countries. We are not blinded by the
moral reparation of national independence; nor are we fed by it. The
wealth of the imperial countries is our wealth too. On the universal

plane this affirmation, you may be sure, should on no account be taken to signify that we feel ourselves affected by the creations of Western arts or techniques. For in a very concrete way Europe has stuffed herself inordinately with the gold and raw materials of the colonial countries: Latin America, China, and Africa. From all these continents, under whose eyes Europe today raises up her tower of opulence, there has flowed out for centuries toward that same Europe diamonds and oil, silk and cotton, wood and exotic products. Europe is literally the creation of the Third World. The wealth which smothers her is that which was stolen from the underdeveloped peoples. The ports of Holland, the docks of Bordeaux and Liverpool were specialized in the Negro slave trade, and owe their renown to millions of deported slaves. So when we hear the head of a European state declare with his hand on his heart that he must come to the aid of the poor underdeveloped peoples, we do not tremble with gratitude. Quite the contrary; we say to ourselves: "It's a just reparation which will be paid to us." Nor will we acquiesce in the help for underdeveloped countries being a program of "sisters of charity." This help should be the ratification of a double realization: the realization by the colonized peoples that *it is their due* and the realization by the capitalist powers that in fact *they must pay*.[2] For if, through lack of intelligence (we won't speak of lack of gratitude) the capitalist countries refuse to pay, then the relentless dialectic of their own system will smother them. It is a fact that young nations do not attract much private capital. There are many reasons which explain and render legitimate this reserve on the part of the monopolies. As soon as the capitalists know—and of course they are the first to know—that their government is getting ready to decolonize, they hasten to withdraw all their capital from the colony in question. The spectacular flight of capital is one of the most constant phenomena of decolonization.

Private companies, when asked to invest in independent countries, lay down conditions which are shown in practice to be inacceptable or unrealizable. Faithful to the principle of immediate returns which is theirs as soon as they go "overseas," the capitalists are very chary concerning all long-term investments. They are unamenable and often openly hostile to the prospective programs of planning laid down by the young teams which form the new government. At a pinch they willingly agree to lend money to the young states, but only on condition that this money is used to buy manufactured products and machines: in other words, that it serves to keep the factories in the mother country going.

In fact the cautiousness of the Western financial groups may be explained by their fear of taking any risk. They also demand political stability and a calm social climate which are impossible to obtain when account is taken of the appalling state of the population as a whole immediately after independence. Therefore, vainly looking for some guarantee which the former colony cannot give, they insist on garrisons being maintained or the inclusion of the young state in military or economic pacts. The private companies put pressure on their own governments to at least set up military bases in these countries for the purpose of assuring the protection of their interests. In the last resort these companies ask their government to guarantee the investments which they decide to make in such-and-such an under-developed region.

It happens that few countries fulfill the conditions demanded by the trusts and monopolies. Thus capital, failing to find a safe outlet, remains blocked in Europe, and is frozen. It is all the more frozen because the capitalists refuse to invest in their own countries. The returns in this case are in fact negligible and treasury control is the despair of even the boldest spirits.

In the long run the situation is catastrophic. Capital no longer circulates, or else its circulation is considerably diminished. In spite of the huge sums swallowed up by military budgets, international capitalism is in desperate straits.

But another danger threatens it as well. Insofar as the Third World is in fact abandoned and condemned to regression or at least to stagnation by the selfishness and wickedness of Western nations, the underdeveloped peoples will decide to continue their evolution inside a collective autarky [economic independence]. Thus the Western industries will quickly be deprived of their overseas markets. The machines will pile up their products in the warehouses and a merciless struggle will ensue on the European market between the trusts and the financial groups. The closing of factories, the paying off of workers and unemployment will force the European working class to engage in an open struggle against the capitalist regime. Then the monopolies will realize that their true interests lie in giving aid to the underdeveloped countries—unstinted aid with not too many conditions. So we see that the young nations of the Third World are wrong in trying to make up to the capitalist countries. We are strong in our own right, and in the justice of our point of view. We ought on the contrary to emphasize and explain to the capitalist countries that the fundamental problem of our time is not the struggle between the socialist regime and them. The Cold War must be ended, for it leads nowhere. The plans for nuclearizing the world must stop, and large-scale investments and technical aid must be given to under-developed regions. The fate of the world depends on the answer that is given to this question.

Moreover, the capitalist regime must not try to enlist the aid of the socialist regime over "the fate of Europe" in face of the starving multitudes of colored peoples. The exploit of Colonel Gargarin doesn't seem to displease General de Gaulle, for is it not a triumph which brings honor to Europe? For some time past the statesmen of the capitalist countries have adopted an equivocal attitude toward the Soviet Union. After having united all their forces to abolish the socialist regime, they now realize that they'll have to reckon with it. So they look as pleasant as they can, they make all kinds of advances, and they remind the Soviet people the whole time that they "belong to Europe."

They will not manage to divide the progressive forces which mean to lead mankind toward happiness by brandishing the threat of a Third World which is rising like the tide to swallow up all Europe. The Third World does not mean to organize a great crusade of hunger against the whole of Europe. What it expects from those who for centuries have kept it in slavery is that they will help it to rehabilitate mankind, and make man victorious everywhere, once and for all. But it is clear that we are not so naive as to think that this will come about with the cooperation and the good will of the European govern-ments. This huge task which consists of reintroducing mankind into the world, the whole of mankind, will be carried out with the in-dispensable help of the European peoples, who themselves must re-alize that in the past they have often joined the ranks of our com-mon masters where colonial questions were concerned. To achieve this, the European peoples must first decide to wake up and shake themselves, use their brains, and stop playing the stupid game of the Sleeping Beauty.

Notes

1 It is true that Germany has not paid all her reparations. The in-demnities imposed on the vanquished nation have not been claimed in full, for the injured nations have included Germany in their anti-communist system of defense. This same preoccupation is the perma-nent motivation of the colonialist countries when they try to obtain from their former colonies, if not their inclusion in the Western system, at least military bases and enclaves. On the other hand they have decided unanimously to forget their demands for the sake of

NATO strategy and to preserve the free world; and we have seen Germany receiving floods of dollars and machines. A Germany once more standing on its feet, strong and powerful, was a necessity for the Western camp. It was in the understood interests of so-called free Europe to have a prosperous and reconstructed Germany which would be capable of serving as a first rampart against the eventual Red hordes. Germany has made admirable use of the European crisis. At the same time the United States and other European states feel a legitimate bitterness when confronted with this Germany, yesterday at their feet, which today metes out to them cutthroat competition in the economic field.

2 "To make a radical difference between the building up of socialism in Europe and our relations with the Third World (as if our only relations with it were external ones) is, whether we know it or not, to set the pace for the distribution of the colonial inheritance over and above the liberation of the underdeveloped countries. It is to wish to build up a luxury socialism upon the fruits of imperialist robbery —as if, inside the gang, the swag is more or less shared out equally, and even a little of it is given to the poor in the form of charity, since it's been forgotten that they were the people it was stolen from." Marcel Péju, "To die for De Gaulle?" *Temps Modernes,* No. 175–6, October-November 1960.

In the following selection, Bohannan, professor of anthropology at Northwestern University, dissolves the myths Western peoples have of Africa and Africans. This first chapter of his fascinating book on African social, political, and economic life discusses a continent little understood by the rest of the world.

Africa and Africans

Paul Bohannan

The Myth and the Fact

Africa has, for generations now, been viewed through a web of myth so pervasive and so glib that understanding it becomes a two-fold task: the task of clarifying the myth and the separate task of examining whatever reality has been hidden behind it. Only as it is stated and told can the myth be stripped away. Only if the myth is stripped away can the reality of Africa emerge.

Africa splashed into the consciousness of the rest of the world in July of 1960 with the eruption of the newly independent Congo, all but forgotten since the days of the slave trade. In the century between 1860 and 1960 Africa had been the province of Africans, and of a few missionaries, colonial government officials, and scholars. Occasionally the isolation was pierced by travelers: yet men like André Gide, when they broke the dark barrier, admitted that they saw problems and moral questions of which they had sooner remain ignorant. For the rest, there was Dr. Schweitzer and there were the maunderings of moralistic and naïve romantics like Laurens van der Post to stand between Martin Johnson's *Lion* and today's New York *Times*. All of them, for one reason or another, had an interest in preserving the myths.

Africa was the "Dark Continent," but the darkness had much more to do with the European and American visitors to it, and workers in it, than it had to do with Africans. It was in the interests of officials to say, in their reports to their governments and indeed in their letters home, that Africa was peaceful and was progressing along predetermined lines. It was in the interests of missionaries, in emphasizing their undoubted victories, to exaggerate the depravity of the base line from which their ministrations had brought their converts. It was, on the other hand, in the interest of physical and biological scientists either to disregard Africans or to treat them as specimens. It was in the interests of many anthropologists who were studying alien cultures to look only at Africa's bright side.

It was, therefore, into a profoundly ignorant Western world that Africa was plunged in 1960. Some colonial governments had mountains of data—almost all of it the wrong kind to cope with the new situation. The professional association in America, the African Studies Association, had far fewer than three hundred fellows in that year and was nevertheless hailed as the largest national organization of its sort. The International African Institute was thirty years old—and it was almost the sole bastion of information and of facts about Africa: but it was run by a director, a librarian, an executive secretary, and a small editorial and office staff.

In the years since the Congo blew up, all this has changed drastically. But a new difficulty has been encountered: all the students who are going into African studies want to study the same thing. They follow the subjects and problems of pioneers like James S. Coleman in his study of Nigerian nationalism, and David Apter in his work on the political structure of the Gold Coast, which was soon to become Ghana, instead of following the pioneering spirit of inquiry that these men represent. Too many scholars follow the headlines, or else they follow the noble savage. Problems of Nigerian political parties; Mau Mau; the "emergence of elites" in eastern and central Africa or in Senegal; race in the Republic of South Africa. But less attention to French-speaking Africa, to Chad and Niger—indeed, the Central African Republic has never been studied (until a few months before the writing of these words, it had never even received a UNESCO visitation. How backward and forgotten can a country get?)

Moreover, organizations like The Peace Corps, Cross-Roads Africa and many other smaller operations are suddenly providing us with a large number of Americans who know something about Africa, and perhaps more important, who know something about cross-cultural living. The business and industrial worlds, as well as the academic and artistic worlds, must make ready to receive these people and utilize their talents and their experience: not just as foreign representatives, but as analytical and constructive critics of world economy and world society.

There has, in fact, been a notable change in information about and attitudes toward Africa on the part of the general American public—led, perhaps, by high school students and their teachers. In 1956, when anyone heard I was interested in Africa he would say,

"Oh, do you know Dr. Schweitzer?" By the end of 1960, the question had become, "Do you know Tom Mboya?" naming the American press's favorite African politician. By the fall of 1962, things had changed even further: a high school audience began a discussion session after a short preliminary lecture with, "What are the precise differences in the platforms of KANU and KADU?" We have come a long way.

Yet, our information is scattered and disorganized. Nobody has, as yet, found a way to bring together systematically what is known to scholars, what the missionaries have learned, and what business and industrial representatives know.

Although it is of a limited sort, missionaries have amassed a tremendous knowledge about Africa that should be utilized. Missionaries speak the languages of the peoples they missionize. They tend to stay in these places from three to twenty-five years (with breaks, of course, because one cannot stay away from one's own culture for too long without its becoming diluted). However, lack of utilization of missionaries by scholars is only part of the problem. Missionaries, with all of their knowledge, have garnered it for specific purposes. I do not question these purposes, but only state that they are not the purposes of statesmanship or scholarship.

Businessmen who have been in and out of Africa know an amazing amount about it—people in the copper companies, trading companies, and more recently the banks and the flour mills. Their knowledge is about very different subjects from that of the missionaries or the scientists, but they do have a tremendous fund of untapped information. There is little opportunity for businessmen, missionaries, and scholars to forgather and talk.

Because informed people were rare, and because those who did exist did not pool their knowledge, Americans and other Westerners became aware and conscious of Africa with all the myths intact.

Some of the most pervasive myths are the simpest: the myth of the lions in the jungles. Lions do not live in jungles. In the first place, only about 5 percent of the African continent can be called jungle in any case. What few lions there are live in the grasslands. But darkness goes with jungles and wild beasts, and the lions in the jungles persist as a symbol for the unrecognized fear that Americans have for Africa.

The myth that Africa is the dark continent is, actually, a subject-object confusion. Europe was certainly isolated—as isolated as Africa has ever been, and was much more so than Africa during the Middle

Ages. Africans and Arabs and Indians, during this time, had an active trade across the Indian Ocean and across the Sahara—even across the Mediterranean. Morocco leather was made south of the Sahara—it was bought from the Moroccans by Europeans, who did not ask further where it came from. In the twelfth and thirteenth centuries the whole subcontinent of Africa south of the Sahara was flooded with cowrie shells, which became a currency—and they came from the Maldive Islands, via Venice and the Arabs. Africa was in touch with the rest of the world while most of Europe slept. Africa was even in touch with the fringes of Europe. There are portraits of Africans on Greek vases; there are portrait busts of Negroes in Roman art. Europe must recognize the fact that it was *Europe* that woke up only in the fifteenth century.

The next myth—and it is one that will be met everywhere—is that Africa was "savage." The myth began in the seventeenth and eighteenth centuries when savages became a philosophical necessity for the emergence of Europe. Savages, both depraved and noble, explained historical as well as psychic problems—but the ideas concerning savages were buttressed with few facts. Savages were next to "missing links," mythical creatures of a cosmographic theory known as the "chain of being" outliving the theory that spawned them. Savages were clean, and unriddled by the problems of industrialization and vast (and vastly painful) social change. Savages, on the other hand, could not speak, knew not fire, and were at the mercy of the destructive forces of brute nature. Such savages were what we all might have been, except for the grace of God. It must also be admitted that missionaries, probably more than any other single group, kept the myth of savagery alive. The more "savage" a place, the greater the missionaries' mundane as well as supermundane rewards. Their undeniable fortitude and the hardships they bore were translated into the imagery of "savagery" by congregations and mission societies at home, even if they did not themselves write them so (and many were level-headed observers who did not). They knew better, as their papers show: yet the image they cast before them was that of heroes doing battle with cannibalism, lust, and depravity—the forces of "darkness."

Today, we can admit the facts on which such a myth was based, at the same time that we can be objective about them. African culture shares more of its traits, its history, its social organization with Europe than Asia shares with Europe and certainly more than the North American Indians and the Australian aborigines share with

Europe. Economically, Africa and Europe are a single sphere. Methods of production of food in Africa are pretty much the same as they were in Europe a few centuries, and in some instances a few millennia, ago. Market organization was the same. The religions are variations on the same basic themes. Family organization—pretty much the same values, although Africans tend to be polygynous and Europeans tend to be monogamous. But the values are quite the same. Such could not be said of the Chinese or the Aztecs.

Moreover, there were in 1960 literally thousands of Africans who were trained and ready to take over the administration of their countries: not as many as they themselves would desire, but in most of British and French Africa—particularly those without European settlers—there were enough to start with. Along with their traditionalism, there is a very broad streak of modernism in all Africans. Unlike some peoples of the Pacific and the Americas, Africans have shown comparatively little resistance to change and so-called modernization. This again may stem largely from the fundamental similarity of African and European (including American) cultures. They share anciently a great common pool of culture, and although the African manifestations of it are different from those of Europeans, the differences are superficial when set beside the gulfs that separate either from Australian aborigines, Malays, or even the Japanese. Perhaps even more important, they share Europe's diseases and so were not decimated on contact.

But there are other myths to be exploded: one is the more generalized myth, in America, about race. Africans are "supposed" to be Negroes—but there are lots of Africans who are not. There are Caucasians and there are Bushmen.

The whole subject of race has been torn asunder and "exposed" by modern genetics, yet the very term has encapsulated connotations from false scientific claims and ethical judgments of centuries. The word "race" means, to geneticists, an interbreeding population with distinct and heritable characteristics. The difficulty comes in properly delimiting the relevant characteristics. For a century and more, race and language were confused—race and culture are still confused. Language is often a characteristic of an interbreeding population, but it is not a biotic characteristic, and therefore has nothing to do with "race." The same is true of culture. In the guise of differential intelligence (whatever that may eventually come to mean) and therefore "cultural potential," the old problem is still with us, and is still given a false biological base. Like witchcraft to the Age of Reformation, the concept of race seems to be the non sequitur by which the modern world explains forces that it does not understand. Race as a social problem is still with us—and it is the social problem that must be dealt with.

The racial myth leads us to another: that is the myth among American Negroes about what Africa is and what its nature is. American Negroes came to this country, as we are all constantly aware, as slaves. The first Negro arrived in the New World in 1494. Negroes provided as much of the heritage of the American continent as any other group. They have been here just as long. American Negroes, toward the end of the nineteenth century, when they were being more systematically closed out from the dominant culture than they had ever been before, turned back to Africa in search of security. There were two reactions: one was to deny any kind of association with Africa. The other was to embrace it as a fatherland. Pan-Africanism started as a movement among American Negroes; they were its driving force from the late nineteenth century until the end of World War II. Since then, they have been grossly disappointed, because African aims are nationalistic and their own are equalitarian. Today, none can any longer deny Africa, even culturally. Many Negroes have nevertheless turned against Africans. Yet they dare not deny them too loudly today, for to deny Africa is to deny the blackness of their skins, and to deny that is to be a traitor to the great force that French-speaking Africans call *negritude,* and that burns vibrantly in the Negro revolution in the United States. Educated and upper middle-class American Negroes are caught between Black Muslims and Africans —wishing to deny both, but able to deny neither.

American Negroes are as American as American Swedes, and their African heritage has made great contributions to American culture: from attitudes toward child care to southern cooking. Africanisms came into America the way that Polishisms came into it. People came in, and people always react to new situations according to the dictates of their old fundamental experience. If that experience was African or Swedish, this is "the way they do things." People bring up their children basically as they themselves were brought up. When one starts being a nursemaid or a mother or a father or an uncle, only a narrow part of the whole arc of culture is in Dr. Spock's book [*Baby and Child Care*]. The rest was learned in the social relationships in which one was involved when young. Therefore, there is a tendency for all basic values and ways of behavior to persist, even as they may be reinterpreted, or even superficially rejected.

The American Negro myth of Africa is one of the most dominant —and one of the most false, precisely because Negroes too were subject to the dominant myths about Africa. For many an American Negro, the myth that he has not contributed to American culture is compounded with—and confounded by—that other myth that Africans were "savages." The Negroes' problem was that cultural forces were at play making it necessary for them to subscribe to the myths about Africa at the same time that psychic forces of *amour-propre* [self-esteem] forced them to dissociate from Africa. They had either to dissociate and give the lie to the first myth or turn their African background into a Golden Age. The contradiction was blatant, and often destructive.

Another wrongheaded myth, very like the ones we have already examined for all that the subject matter is different, is the myth of the 1960s: African nations must be either for us or against us in the Cold War. Since the Cold War is the major problem for Americans, as for Communists, it seems all but incredible that some peoples do not see the world as opposed camps. Africans are neither for nor against the West—neither for nor against the Communist bloc. They are *for Africa,* sometimes just for their own country or even their own tribe. If we are for Africa, they are for us, and if we are against Africa, they are against us.

And finally, one last position must be made clear. The West does not so much have an African problem, as Africa has a European problem. South Africa is enough a European country to appear to have a native problem, but the "natives" think of it as a European problem. East Africans have a European problem. So do the Katangese. It was only half in jest that Kwame Nkrumah suggested building a monument in Accra to the Anopheles mosquito, the carrier of the malaria that made Europeans reject West Africa as "unsuitable for colonization." In the long run, unless Europeans in Africa change their ways, their future there is a dim one.

The European nations began in the fourteenth and fifteenth centuries an expansion that is only now being reversed. This expansion against the rest of the world was intrinsic to Euro-American culture, an integral part of its growth. Europeans combined classical and Judaeo-Christian ideas to provide the basis of an emergent morality. Christianity made such demands after the Middle Ages that there was only one thing to do: to push outwards in all directions. The rest of the peoples of the world were hit from outside. With the settling of the Europeans in America and Australia and South Africa, the people who were already there either collapsed as the Australian aborigines did or turned themselves into dependent remnant tribes as the American Indians did in the face of white power. But Africans adapted and adopted.

After the West expanded and collided with all these people, the new society needed clerks and catechists and laborers in order to carry on business and achieve its purposes. Europeans started teaching people to use shovels and pencils, to figure and to read. When a man learns to read, the door has been opened. People see culture that in a colonial situation they are by definition not allowed to have. They are perfectly capable of practicing it, but are not allowed it. In such a situation, colonial people become deprived people. Africans, when they were living a tribal life, were not deprived people. Lives of tremendous dignity and valued rewards can be lived away from the trappings of Western civilization. But once the consciousness of those trappings seeps into awareness, a new day has arrived, and a new struggle must ensue.

In his Foreign Policy Report of February 18, 1970, President Nixon stated: "Clearly there is no question of the United States condoning, or acquiescing in, the racial policies of the white-ruled regimes. For moral as well as historical reasons, the United States stands firmly for the principles of racial equality and self-determination." The address was followed by the closing of the American consulate in Salisbury, Rhodesia, where a white supremacy regime rules a country of 240,000 whites and 4,500,000 blacks. Black African leaders want to negotiate an end to white minority dominance in Rhodesia, the Republic of South Africa, and the Portuguese colonies. United States foreign policy is involved.

U.S. Hopes to Help Avert Bloody Race War in Africa

Stanley Meisler

America's new Africa policy of speaking softly and carrying a small stick will be tested severely in the years ahead by the racial conflict between whites and blacks in southern Africa.

State Department officials recognize this but they believe there is enough time for American gentle persuasion to play a role in averting a bloody race war.

They could be wrong. On his two-week tour of Africa which ended last Sunday, Secretary of State William P. Rogers was told by President Kenneth Kaunda of Zambia:

"Definitely, an explosion is going to take place, based on ideology and color."

If an explosion ever does take place, it will be very difficult for the United States to stick to its pronouncements about low profile, aloofness, and nonintervention.

There are large American investments in South Africa and the United States has a population that is more than 10% black. Thus, there would be enormous pressures for involvement. The Nixon Administration might resist them, but it would be difficult.

That is why American officials are quick to support any movement toward a peaceful solution, no matter how slight or improbable.

At the moment, the United States is continually proclaiming its approval of the Lusaka Manifesto. This document, written largely by Kaunda and President Julius Nyerere of Tanzania and endorsed by the Organization of African Unity, insists that black Africa, in its confrontation with white Africa, "would prefer to negotiate rather than destroy, to talk rather than kill.

"If peaceful progress to emancipation were possible," the manifesto goes on, "or if changed circumstances were to make it possible in the future, we would urge our brothers in the resistance movements to use peaceful methods of struggle even at the cost of some compromise on the timing of change."

In his visit to Zambia, Secretary Rogers took every chance he had to praise the manifesto, which was issued there last April [1969]. A strong endorsement came, as well, from President Nixon in his recent statement to Congress on American foreign policy.

"Though we abhor the racial policies of the white regimes," the President said, "We cannot agree that progressive change in southern Africa is furthered by force . . .

"The United States warmly welcomes, therefore, the recent Lusaka Manifesto . . . That statesmanlike document combines a commitment to human dignity with a perceptive understanding of the depth and complexity of the racial problem in the area."

But what can the United States do to make the Lusaka Manifesto meaningful?

Some U.S. officials believe the United States can help by counseling black African countries to maintain their patience while pressuring the white regimes to give black Africa a signal that they are ready to negotiate.

The black Africans insist that they have received no signal at all in the 10 months since they issued the manifesto.

"We realize this is essentially a human problem," Kaunda told American newsmen who accompanied Rogers to Zambia, "but I'm afraid that the response (to the manifesto) has been nil up to now."

The great problem is that the white regimes feel very strong these days and see no reason to compromise with the black countries. Although African guerrillas try to infiltrate southern Africa, they have made very little headway in their campaign to wrest control from the whites in Rhodesia, South Africa, South African-controlled South West Africa, and Portuguese Angola and Mozambique.

At the moment, the black leaders feel their only hope of compromise lies with Portugal, the weakest of the white powers in southern Africa. Unlike the South Africans, the Portuguese are not powered by any white supremacist ideology.

Drained financially by the guerrilla fighting in Angola and Mozambique, Portugal, in the view of men like Kaunda, conceivably could reach an accommodation some day with black Africa—at least on setting a distant date for African independence. The Lusaka Manifesto is clearly aimed at the Portuguese first.

In this, Kaunda believes the United States can have a major role. Maintaining that Portugal, as a member of NATO, is susceptible to American influence, Kaunda told newsmen, "The United States is about the only world power that could help us solve the unfolding ideological and racial conflict with southern Africa."

It is not certain, however, that Portugal feels as drained by its troubles in Africa or as susceptible to American influence as Kaunda believes.

Certainly South Africa and Rhodesia have shown no sign that they are in the mood to compromise these days. Confident and powerful, they do not see black Africa and its guerrillas as a real threat, at least not now.

The South Africans, however, are a troubled and far-sighted people who might accept and even encourage black rule in neighboring Angola and Mozambique, if they believe that would satisfy black Africa to the point where campaigns against the other white regimes would be called off.

But Portugal may be stubborn. If it is, the Lusaka Manifesto will prove a rather weak reed on which to hang an American policy.

Questions

1 What is the Black Man's Burden?

2 Kenyans have discriminated against Asians. Ibos in Nigeria were involved in a tribal discrimination situation which resulted in what was called the Biafran War. Do all men have a need at one time or another to hate and/or to dominate an "out-group"?

3 How does your answer to question two relate to conditions in southern Africa?

4 Do you regard apartheid as a matter of domestic concern for South Africa or as a matter of international concern? If the latter, what policies should the United States adopt?

5 Does the South African experience suggest the course American history might have taken had the Confederate States of America been successful in the War Between the States?

6 How much does the presence of white rule in southern Africa serve as a common rallying point for cooperation and perhaps even unity among black African states? Would the downfall of white supremacy in those states hinder the movement toward African unity?

7 Frantz Fanon says in "Black Skin, White Masks" that the Peloponnesian War is as much his as the invention of the compass in China, simply because he is a man. Skin color has nothing to do with it. "I am man," he says, "and what I have to recapture is the whole past of the world." Explain.

8

An Old Asia in a New World

The West has long looked upon Asia with its huge populations and land areas as venerable, quiet, and submissive, but suddenly it is no longer any of these things. Western imperialism jolted the giant from its sleep, and now the world must take note. Basically, it is an old Asia in modern dress that has appeared in what to it is a new world.

Story of East Wind Prevailing Over West Wind

Frederick Gentles

Western civilization with its imperialism, nationalism, religion, and industrialism did not, as a butterfly, light delicately on the shoulders of Oriental society; it tromped heavily, and progress with its hydroelectric plants, transistor radios, assembly lines, and smog is one of the most pervasive results, according to one version of the Eastside-Westside story. But the progress in Asia is not entirely Western in nature, as many people believe. There are trappings resulting from Western imperialism, of course, but these trappings are given a flavor uniquely Indian, Chinese, Japanese, Cambodian, or whatever. Asia will continue to be Asia, and East and West will meet only when each finds it mutually beneficial to do so. The global diversity of our crowded village will continue despite any overall political, social, and economic institutions that might be created. Nevertheless, Western imperialism acted as a catalyst to inspire change in Asia. How and why did an old Asia come to life in what appeared to be a new world?

The change in Asia began, it seems, just the other day. It began with a reaction to the aggressive nineteenth and twentieth century imperialism that did much to crush the freedom and independence of virtually all Asiatic peoples. In all of East Asia only Thailand remained nominally independent, and this only at the discretion of Britain and France, because they did not wish to share a common colonial border for fear of conflict.

The familiar superiority complex of a technically-advanced system when dealing with a so-called primitive society was inherent in Western imperialism as it spread toward Asia. At the turn of the last century Lord Kitchener stated the racist attitude of imperialism quite concisely: "It is this consciousness of the inherent superiority of the European which has won for us India. However well educated and clever a native may be, and however brave he may have proved himself, I believe that no rank we can bestow on him would cause him to be considered an equal of the British officer."[1]

Actually, the arrogance of the white man from the West began to manifest itself as soon as Vasco da Gama found his way around the Cape of Good Hope to India in 1498. The Portuguese da Gama, a hero to the West, a pirate to the East, destroyed shipping at will in the Indian Ocean, and he believed he had the right because the Pope's Line of Demarcation gave Portugal control of the Eastern hemisphere. He insolently refused to pay port taxes at the Indian port of Calicut, and his successor Alvarez Cabral introduced violence Western style on a grand scale when he sailed to India with a large fleet outfitted for military duty. This was to be the beginning of over four hundred years of violence and conquest imposed by Western civilization upon Eastern civilization. The European conquerors came for spices, precious stones, and silks, but they also came to impose their own true faith on the natives. Thousands risked their lives for pepper, other thousands for the cross.

People do not suffer the ignominies of racial myths forever (witness minority uprisings in America), and the tyranny of imperialism eventually inspired active opposition in Asiatic lands. In India a long fight for freedom began with the Sepoy uprising in 1857, which the British called a rebellion but which Indian patriots considered the First War of Independence. It was crushed, but a greater feeling of national purpose arose to make itself felt in the organization of a Congress Party in 1885. The Congress Party worked for more Indian representation in all governmental bodies—local, provincial, and central—to alleviate poverty and to educate the masses.

Another phase of the struggle for national identity became evident after World War I. When war broke out, India cooperated with the British by mobilizing over a million men to fight on fronts as far removed as the Western, Macedonian, German East African, Iraq, Jerusalem, and Suez. Despite massive losses, she was not represented directly at the Versailles Peace Conference, and in 1919 the British extended martial law throughout India because of general unrest. This reversion to old imperial ways shocked Indians, who had expected gratitude and at least some concessions toward independence as a result of their sacrifices in the war. A nasty "incident" arose at Amristar, the Sikh capital in the Punjab, when some 10,000 unarmed men, women, and children gathered in a park to protest the British tyranny, despite a recent order prohibiting large meetings. General Reginald E. H. Dyer issued to his troops 1650 rounds of ammunition with orders to use up the supply. Some 400 were killed and 1200 wounded. Fifty rounds may have gone astray.

General Dyer testified later that the killings were essential to produce "a sufficient moral effect, from a military point of view, not merely on those present but more especially throughout the Punjab."[2] When Dyer returned to England he was presented with a jeweled sword with the inscription, *Savior of the Punjab*. Even Mahatma Gandhi could not remain very passive after this action. He dedicated the rest of his life to freeing his people from their barbaric rule. The world knows the work of his unconquerable soul.

British rule, in its political examples as well as in its imperialistic atrocities, inspired Indian nationalism; in its humane aspects it also inspired a Hindu movement for social and religious reform. The faith was made more compassionate with moves to abolish suttee—where a widow felt compelled to throw herself on the funeral pyre of her husband—and the caste system, where there were even untouchable untouchables. Suttee has now been pretty much done away with, but the caste system lingers on in Indian life, particularly in the villages. The caste system is a rather ridiculous system, is it not? But Westerners do not often recognize their own caste systems which continue to operate well into the twentieth century; witness "untouchable" neighborhoods, restaurants, schools, clubs, fraternal organizations, and society pages. All civilizations are built upon some kind of discrimination as a perpetuation of the myths underlying their culture, and frequently this discrimination is only a variety of "untouchability." *N'est ce pas?*

The English language is widespread throughout the Far East, but nowhere is it more entrenched than in India; there peoples speaking dozens of languages find English the only common one. In recent years there has been much controversy over which language should prevail in India's Parliament, and riots have occurred in various parts of the country over which language should prevail in certain provinces. Rioting over language may seem a rather small matter to an outsider, yet there have also been language riots in Belgium, Wales, Quebec, and Brittany in recent years.

India's progress, before and after the achievement of independence in 1947, owes much to the legacy Britain left in parliamentary institutions, education, science, engineering, and social values. But India is adapting the inheritance in her own way. She has been the leader of a Third World movement that rejected lining up with either of the two goliaths. She has opted for a mixed economy of socialism and free enterprise capitalism and for five-year plans outlining the state's progress. Her gross national product has increased as expected over the last two decades, but the rapid growth of population—in 1970 estimated at about 550,000,000—has resulted in only a small per capita increase of the new wealth. India needs help in solving her economic problems. United States aid has been substantial, but a recent Congressional proviso limits our aid to private businesses only. (The American psyche has a hangup about giving aid to socialist institutions. The proviso seems to say that there is something sacred about private enterprise and something evil about social enterprise.)

As populations increase, social controls seem to be more necessary. The anarchy of free enterprise run wild cannot be permitted in the twentieth century as it was in the nineteenth. India is finding this to be true, and this was also the reaction of Mao Tse-tung to the free-wheeling capitalism and imperialism that engulfed China. The details of the China story read a bit different from India's, but the broad outline is the same—Western imperialist arrogance and tyranny over peoples oriented to other values.

China, like India, suffered the Portuguese and the British and a good many more. John Bull insisted on bringing in opium from India to supply the Chinese market despite an imperial Manchu edict forbidding this despicable trade. The Opium War of the 1840s resulted not only in defeat for the Chinese but in further entrenchment of the British—and later the French, Germans, Russians, and Japanese—in spheres of influence all over China. By 1900 China was no longer independent. She had been forced to sign what she now calls the Unequal Treaties, which compelled her to turn over to Russia territory in Siberia north of the Amur River and territory along the Pacific Coast down to the Korean border. She was humiliated by being coerced to open up "treaty ports" for the exclusive use of the imperialist powers and to concede to France, Great Britain, Japan, and the United States the right of those countries to try their own citizens in China under the foreign laws. Foreign soldiers were stationed in China, and gunboats, including American ones, patrolled the rivers. The Western predators were just as violent and certainly more exploitative than the Eastern predators who had invaded Europe over a thousand years before—the Huns.

Lord Kitchener's slur on the intelligence of the Indians and his assertion of British superiority was matched by a sign on park grounds around the Foreign Settlement in Peking: *No dogs or Chinese allowed.* The psychic effects of the white man's claims to superiority may not have been as damaging to the Asian as other aspects of imperialism, but there is no question that the impact of colonialism was much more than economic exploitation. The spell of Western civilization was felt on political, cultural, and social levels as well as on the economic. As a young person might put it today, colonialism was a bad scene despite the hospitals, Christian missions, schools, roads, telegraph lines, and oil for the lamps of China.

Of course, the Chinese reacted in various ways to the "master race" of the "master culture." Some joined the Western bandwagon because of self-interest or conviction. One even became a brother of Jesus, a certain Hung Hsiu-ch'uan (1814–1864), who led the Taiping Rebellion against the Manchu dynasty, which had dominated China for over two hundred years. His followers worshipped God, Jesus, and Hung as the new Son of Heaven come to save the world from the forces of evil represented by the Manchu. Hung put together a combination of the militant teaching of the Old Testament, the love of the New Testament, and Chinese nationalism to crusade against prostitution, slavery, adultery, gambling, alcohol, opium, tobacco, and, of course, the Manchu. His followers were known as the "long-haired rebels" because they let their hair grow. The Taiping rebels controlled several provinces in the 1850s, but when another leader began to get vibrations from God, the rebellion broke up in bloody purges, nepotism, profligacy, and corruption.[3]

Other Chinese reacted to colonialism with shame, with humility, and some, finally, with violence. After deep humiliations by war with France in the 1880s and with Japan in 1894–1895, many were disgusted with the antiquated, conservative, and passive teachings of Confucius. In 1900, the secret Patriotic Order of Loyal Harmonious Fists—Boxers—rose up against the tyranny of the white devil, particularly the French Catholic missionaries who sought to extend their rights of extraterritoriality and other special privileges.

The Boxers slaughtered thousands of Chinese Christians and a number of missionaries before Russian, British, American, and Japanese soldiers crushed what Westerners have termed the Boxer Rebellion. Professor Fairbank calls it a war—the fourth largest, he says —which China fought against imperialist powers in the nineteenth century. (It is interesting to remember that the British called the Sepoy uprising in 1857 a mutiny; Indians called it the First War for Independence.) If it was a rebellion, it was not against the Manchu dynasty, because the Dowager Empress supported the Boxers at first; it was in Western eyes, then, actually a rebellion against foreign control of China. Afterward, Peking was sacked by the armies of the imperialist powers with all the looting, rape, and murder that has so often resulted from soldiers intoxicated with victory.

China's twentieth century has been torn by a 1911 revolution overthrowing the Manchu dynasty, twenty-one insulting "Demands" by

Japan, warlords dividing the land, loss of Manchuria, civil war between Communists and the Nationalist Kuomintang Party, war with Japan, civil war again, and finally in 1949 the triumph of a Communist regime intent on giving Confucius the *coup de grâce* by replacing him with something called Maoism.

Historically, China's ideals have held the scholars in highest repute because they perpetuated the heritage of the culture; farmers were second because they fed and clothed the nation; artisans were third because they processed what the farmers produced, and merchants were last because they were regarded as exploiters of society. Two other lower classes were sometimes added: soldiers were lowly because they destroyed things and killed people, and the so-called "mean people" were lowly because they were domestic slaves, prostitutes, and entertainers. Mao seems to have elevated what he calls the poor and middle peasant (indicating some difference in wealth?) to the top rung in the new order, the worker to the second, and members of the People's Liberation Army to the third. The scholar may be on the fourth rung, but merchants and "mean people" have been pretty well eliminated in the new People's Democratic Republic of China. In a so-called classless society, then, there are classes. (Western society has quite a different order of precedence in rating its classes. What is the order?)

Whereas the Taiping Rebellion was inspired by Western nationalism and Christianity, Chinese Communism has been swayed by Western Marxism-Leninism. Yet Taiping-type morality has been transmitted to Maoism in the form of a deified national leader, a puritanical people's program, equality of the sexes, and fanatic dedication to the truth with no myths or hangups—just canons, the "correct way" of doing things. The correct way is marked in the Little Red Book (the Quotations of Mao Tse-tung, probably more ubiquitous in China than the Bible is in the West), which says that the East Wind prevails over the West Wind and that the imperialist nations are really paper tigers. The Book says nothing about China herself being a paper tiger (or dragon), yet it would still be an error for Westerners to suggest that China cannot and will not achieve her goal of building a great economic, social, and cultural state. She may, for the leaders and people continue to have the patience of China of old. Confucius may be dead in modern China, but one of his sayings still holds true: "It is not system that makes man great. It is man that makes system great."

And speaking of systems, Japan—in seeing European nations tromp all over India, China, and Southeast Asia—determined after the overthrow of the Tokogawa Shogunate in 1868 that the Western system of imperialism would not crush her. She saw the blow coming and made haste to build national, imperial, military, and industrial institutions not only to protect herself but also to be equipped to compete in the game with the Western powers. The game was rough, the stakes were high, and the rewards were great; and by strength of will, by bluff, and by guile (Machiavelli?), Japan succeeded in building a strong, Western-type culture. She was ruthless in carving out a great empire at the expense of her neighbors. She had the opportunity of creating a great oriental unity, but because of corruption stemming from wealth, power, and *hubris*—the Greek word for pride—she marched on to destruction just as in a Greek tragedy. Although she has suffered for this arrogance, the story from 1868 to 1945 is a remarkable one in many ways.

Within twenty-five years of her destruction in 1945, Japan has risen from the ruins to become the third greatest industrial power in the world. This is another remarkable episode in the story of a remarkable people who lack natural resources, cooperative neighbors, and nearby markets. Japan must trade to live, and the world is her market place.

Why have the Japanese been able to create a great industrial and commercial nation twice over within one hundred years? For one thing, the Japanese intended to. They have placed emphasis on self-discipline, will power, and Spartan virtues of doing much with little. Also, as former U.S. ambassador to Japan Edwin O. Reischauer points out, since the last war Japan, especially its youth, has been strengthened by the ideals of domestic and international democracy, and he sees hope for continuing vigor and prosperity. All that has happened to Japan has not been due to Westernization. As Reischauer observes:

> The experience of modern Japan suggests that the common concept that the whole world is becoming Westernized is not correct. In the early phases of Western influence, this may seem to be the case, but now we can see that a very large percentage of the changes that have swept Japan during the past century are better described as modernization than as Westernization. Industrialization has developed in the West too only during the past two centuries. Transistor radios or air travel are as natural a part of contemporary Japanese society as of our own. So also are such strictly modern institutions as universal education, universal suffrage, or labor unions. A highly modernized Japan remains distinctively Japanese and the West today

seems as ready to make cultural borrowings from Japan as Japan from the West. All this gives hope to other less modernized non-Western countries that they too can modernize without losing their cultural distinctiveness.[4]

Much of the traditional Japanese music, art, dance, drama, and literature has regained its old vigor, states Reischauer, and the cultural flow is now very much in two directions. Japan borrows from the West, and the West is discovering Zen Buddhism, Haiku poetry, and the Japanese canons of design, interior decoration, and landscape gardening.

Institutions and values are changing all over Asia, but roots of the old cultures persist. Is China the exception? She has changed because of Western influence, but has she completely severed the roots of the Confucianist heritage? Will Mao prove the school of learned behaviorists correct (as opposed to the Lorenz, Ardrey, Morris, *et al.* school) in that man can be trained to love his brothers, all of them all of the time, beginning of course, with 700,000,000 Chinese? It is a matter of will and reason which orientals certainly possess in as great an amount as occidentals.

Notes

1 K. M. Panikkar, *Asia and Western Dominance* (New York: Collier, 1969), p. 116.

2 Stanley Wolpert, *India* (Englewood Cliffs, N.J.: Prentice-Hall, 1965), p. 127.

3 John K. Fairbank, Edwin O. Reischauer, Albert M. Craig, *East Asia: The Modern Transformation* (Boston: Houghton Mifflin, 1965), pp. 158–163.

4 Edwin O. Reischauer, *The United States and Japan* (Cambridge, Mass.: Harvard University Press, 1965), p. 334. Reprinted by permission.

From "The Nehru Era" one gains an insight into the enormous economic and political problems that beset India after independence. Her problems continue to be enormous, and India needs help if she is to modernize the life style of centuries past.

The Nehru Era

Stanley Wolpert

Just as Gandhi personified India's Nationalist movement after 1921, Nehru,[1] India's first prime minister, symbolized his nation during its first fifteen years of independent rule. The symbol was often misleading, for Nehru was in many respects atypical of India, and what he represented in word and deed was the ideal, the loftiest aspiration of his countrymen, rather than the reality of their condition. Yet his popularity and power from 1947 through 1962 were unique, and few monarchs or dictators of world history have so affected their governments' world images and policies as did this democratically elected, responsible leader of modern India. The reasons for Nehru's success seem more obvious to Western observers than did Gandhi's. Jawaharlal was, after all, the typical hero-figure of modern times: high-born, wealthy, handsome, brilliant, yet idealistic, self-sacrificing, dedicated to national service rather than individual pleasure; dreamer and doer; the artist with a touch of the poet in his soul, yet a practical man of the world.

A Kashmiri Brahman of Allahabad, the only son of Motilal Nehru, young Jawaharlal, born on November 14, 1889, was enrolled at Harrow in 1905, and two years later at Trinity College, Cambridge, where he took his degree in 1910. In 1912 he became a barrister of the Inner Temple, returning to Allahabad to practice law for some eight years. He joined Congress in 1913, and became a disciple of Gandhi in 1920, following his father as president of Congress in 1929. Intellectually and temperamentally Nehru was more Western than Indian; his mental makeup was a unique mixture of Liberalism, Fabian Socialism, and Marxism, and his personality was dynamic, impulsive, passionate. In some respects he was the antithesis of Gandhi, yet he recognized The Mahatma as the heart of India, and always remained a loyal son of his spiritual father. By the time India attained independence Nehru was fifty-eight, yet his freshness of

Stanley Wolpert, *India,* © 1965. Reprinted by permission of Prentice-Hall, Inc., Englewood Cliffs, New Jersey.

mind and amazing physical vitality made him seem young. Youthfulness was part of the secret of his appeal and political success. He captured the imagination of India's new generation of intellectuals. He was an inexhaustible political campaigner in a country so vast and so poorly equipped with rapid transport that few men could match his pace. His writings, his speeches, his mere presence, all exuded vigor and fresh life. He cared as intensely about minute details as he did about matters of momentous import. He went everywhere, spoke to everyone, concerned himself with everything. He was one of the great stylists of the English language in modern times, a brilliant public speaker and charming conversationalist. All Indians could identify with Gandhi; most wished they could be like Nehru.

From August 15, 1947 until January 26, 1950, India was a dominion; thereafter she became a totally independent republic. The first months of freedom were darkened by mass migrations to and from Pakistan, economic dislocation, war in Kashmir, and the murder of Mahatma Gandhi on January 30, 1948.[2] Never was so new a nation so quickly burdened with such tragic and weighty problems. An estimated ten million Hindus, Muslims, and Sikhs crossed the borders of the Punjab and Bengal in a matter of months, with somewhere between one-half and one million killed in the bloody process. The resettlement of immigrants from Pakistan still remained unfinished, especially in Calcutta, after eighteen years of independence. In addition, personal property, public monetary, and natural resource (primarily Indus water) disputes plagued India for more than a decade after partition. The integrated economy of British India was shattered overnight by political fiat. West Pakistan, the bread-basket of the subcontinent, was suddenly divorced from the coal and iron-producing India it had long helped to feed. East Pakistan, the jute plantation for Hughli factories, was arbitrarily severed from the major industrial market for its major product. Landowners in Calcutta were stripped of their property across the newly delineated border. Bombay mill-owners lost their raw cotton supply from Sind. Trade collapsed as tariff barriers rose like forbidding walls to seal off the new neighboring states from economic intercourse.

Internally, India was faced with integrating over 500 princely states into the new dominion. Sardar Patel and his gifted assistant, V. P. Menon,[3] successfully cajoled, convinced, and coerced a multitude of maharajas into joining the new union. Hyderabad and Kashmir, the two largest states, presented the only serious obstacles to this process of peaceful integration. Hyderabad, most populous of the Indian states with over sixteen million subjects, less than 15 per

cent of whom were Muslim, was still ruled by the Muslim *nizam**
and his noble courtiers. The *nizam* hoped to retain internal autonomy, and refused to sign an "Instrument of Accession" to India for
more than a year. Finally, in September 1948, Indian troops invaded
the *nizam's* territory to "restore order" there, and in less than a week
all armed resistance collapsed. Kashmir proved a thornier problem.

Politically, India's first major objective was to draft a constitution.
The Constituent Assembly, convened in December 1946, labored
almost three years at this monumental assignment. Nehru himself
delineated his nation's constitutional "objectives" in a Resolution
presented to the newly formed Assembly on December 13, 1946,
affirming that India was to become "an Independent Sovereign
Republic"[4] and "Union" of British India and surrounding states, in
which "all power and authority" would be "derived from the people."
Within that republic everyone would be guaranteed "justice, social,
economic and political: equality of status, of opportunity, and before
the law; freedom of thought, expression, belief, faith, worship, voca-
tion, association and action, subject to law and public morality." Dr.
B. R. Ambedkar, leader of the untouchables, was elected chairman
of the drafting committee as proof of Congress' intention to implement fully these democratic and egalitarian objectives. The constitution was approved by the Assembly in November 1949, to be effective from January 26, 1950. A year later India held its first national election, with some 173 millions enfranchised by universal
adult suffrage, the largest electorate in world history. Nearly 4,000
seats for elective office were contested by more than 17,000 Indian
candidates, representing some sixty different political parties. Though
approximately 80 per cent of the enfranchised population was totally
illiterate, more than one hundred million Indians took the trouble to
vote for their official representatives in an impressive display of national consciousness; for most voters this was the first lesson in democratic process.

With Nehru as its leading campaigner (he personally reached an
estimated thirty million people, traveling over 30,000 miles in little
more than forty days), Congress won a popular plurality (some 45
per cent of the total votes cast), and impressive majority (362 out
of 489 seats) in the ruling lower house of Parliament. As president of
its dominant party and prime minister of the republic, Nehru held
the reins of power firmly. Determined to use his five-year mandate to

---

**Ed. note*: One of a line of sovereigns of Hyderabad, India, reigning from
1713 to 1950.

good advantage, Nehru led his government in a program of energetic reform, economic and social as well as political.

As an intellectual Socialist, Nehru had stressed the need for governmental direction in economic planning as early as 1931, when he moved the Karachi Congress to pass a resolution calling for nationalization of key Indian industries. Since then Congress was committed to the development of a "Socialist democracy" in India, and in January 1948 Nehru became chairman of the economic program committee of Congress, which laid down the broad policy lines for future planning. In March 1950 a national Planning Commission was created, with Nehru at its head, to draw up a master plan for the "most effective and balanced utilization of the country's resources." During his entire tenure as prime minister, Nehru remained chairman of this Planning Commission. The first Five Year Plan, inaugurated in April 1951, was a fairly modest proposal, calling for an 11 per cent growth in national income by 1956, or an overall increase of from about eighteen to twenty million dollars worth of goods and services. Transportation and communications, especially the grossly depleted rolling stock of India's railroads (heavily overworked during the war), received the largest single share of planned expenditure, though agricultural development was also stressed, above all the need for irrigation through multipurpose dam, irrigation, and hydroelectric projects. For lack of resources, government almost entirely ignored heavy industry until the inauguration of the second Plan. Economic planning was the Indian government's official attack upon the devastating problem of poverty, which at the start of the first Plan kept India's predominantly peasant population of some 360 millions hovering on the brink of starvation. The estimated per capita annual income in 1951 was less than sixty dollars, and for approximately fifty million untouchables and another forty million landless laborers it was far less. Despite concerted national effort, insufficient capital, inadequate concentration of savings, lack of technical skills, mass illiteracy, endemic diseases of every kind and the grinding inertia of poverty all conspired, together with the inexorable growth in population, to hinder any dramatic improvement in the economic situation as a whole. Therefore, though the goals of the first Plan were achieved, Nehru and Congress agreed that the pace was not swift enough. At its Avadi session in 1955, Congress resolved to plan in the future "with a view to the establishment of a socialistic pattern of society, where the principle means of production are under social ownership of control, production is progressively speeded up and there is equitable distribution of the national wealth."

   The second Plan (1956–61), therefore, allotted a much larger share (about 20 per cent) of total expenditure to the development of heavy industry and mineral extraction. Nehru never favored sweeping nationalization of existing industry, but rather a "socialization of the vacuum" approach, which in view of India's industrial underdevelopment was, of course, potentially most significant. Private enterprise in India, however, recognized that the Congress government was highly flexible in interpreting the "socialistic pattern" it was resolved to develop, and India's economy, like Hinduism itself, remained singularly tolerant and eclectic. The second Plan's expenditure was to be almost three times that of the first, an estimated ten billion dollars, about half of which was, it was hoped, to come from private investment. The major goals were: an 18 per cent increase in per capita income, to somewhere around seventy dollars per annum; a 150 per cent boost in heavy industrial production; about a 25 per cent rise in agricultural output; and the creation of some ten million new jobs to absorb the equivalent expansion in the labor market during this period. By 1961 the Planning Commission hoped "to rebuild rural India, to lay the foundations of industrial progress, and to secure to the greatest extent feasible opportunities for weaker and under-privileged sections of our people and the balanced development of all parts of the country." Lack of capital and several years of poor rain obliged the government to cut back expenditure in 1958, and the Plan fell short of its anticipated goals. Population pressure proved to be far more serious a drain on Indian resources than anyone in the cabinet seems to have anticipated. V. K. Krishna Menon, for example, a close friend and trusted adviser of Nehru's, who served as ambassador to the United Nations and minister of defense (1957–62) as well as a member of the Planning Commission after 1957, used to counter advise on India's urgent need for more family planning and population control by saying that new Indians were born with two hands capable of work and only one mouth to feed. By 1961 India's population had jumped to about 440 millions; what would have been a 42 per cent per capita income increase for the population of 1951 became only 16 per cent for the new total. Added population meant that the level of Indian unemployment, perhaps the greatest in the world today, actually increased rather than diminished despite protracted and concerted national economic effort.

   By the end of the second Plan India's national income had been raised to the equivalent of about thirty billion dollars. India was able to produce about three and one-half million tons of steel ingots, and fifty-five million tons of coal, but the value of her exports remained little more than about one billion dollars, and without continuing and substantial foreign aid even modest planning on a national scale would have been almost impossible. Congress and Nehru, however, had made the Plans and continued dynamic economic growth under government stimulus the key plank in their platform, and all nations of the world concerned with the preservation of democratic self-government in India, as well as the plight of her vast population, took a vital interest in helping India to help itself. It was generally realized that, although the urgent and compelling problem of Indian poverty is as much an international as an internal Indian problem, its resolution must ultimately be worked out by Indians themselves and that aid must be given freely. Suspicions, doubts, and anxieties are as real a legacy of Western intrusion and British rule for millions of Indian minds as the English language itself. National pride, self-determination, and the importance of self-help are in turn vital and valuable legacies of the Nationalist struggle. Nehru fully appreciated all of these forces in the mental makeup of modern India, and his power within India was based in good measure upon his unique capacity for articulating the "Indian position" to the world at large.

Throughout his premiership, Nehru served as his own foreign minister. Indeed, until 1962 India's foreign policy was primarily Nehru's. He tried to make India a "third force" of nonalignment in a world polarized by the cold war. The pillars of Indian foreign policy in the Nehru era were naturally based on national self-interest, but because of the peculiar nature of recent Indian and indeed world history, they acquired a highly moralistic and often broadly attractive tone. Anticolonialism and antiracism dominated most of Prime Minister Nehru's pronouncements on foreign affairs, and his genuine concern and sensitivity about both were shared by India's intellectual elite. The positive side of these reactions against British autocracy and prejudice was expressed in terms of India's pro-Asian and -African position in world councils, and though Nehru denied any ambitions of ever becoming the head of an Afro-Asian power bloc, he was in fact looked to by leaders in many emerging nations of both continents as their natural spokesman. Even before independence, in March and April 1947, India sponsored an Asian Relations Conference in Delhi, attended by representatives of some twenty-eight African and Asian countries. Early in 1949 India convened a second conference of fifteen African and Asian powers to consider the Dutch "police action" in Indonesia. The following year, Nehru told India's *Lok Sabha* that "The biggest fact of the modern world is the resurgence of Asia."[5] Despite national disagreements and regional as well as cultural differences, there was, he insisted "such a thing as Asian sentiment." At the Afro-Asian Conference of twenty-nine states held at Bandung, Indonesia, in 1955, Nehru played a leading role, though the challenge for Afro-Asian leadership posed by China became more apparent during those sessions through the personal popularity and aggressiveness of Chou En-lai.

Sino-Indian relations became, in good measure, the practical testing ground for Nehru's policy after 1954. In April of that year a Sino-Indian trade treaty was concluded over Tibet which articulated the five principles that Nehru hoped might become the basis of all future agreements among major world powers. Those were: mutual respect for each other's territorial integrity and sovereignty; nonagression; noninterference in each other's internal affairs; equality and mutual benefit; and peaceful coexistence. Here was India's alternative to the martial confrontation and "mutual distrust" of the United States and the Soviet Union. If the two greatest powers of Asia, one governed by the principles of democratic liberalism, the other by communism, could arrive at so equable an international agreement and live up to it, why could not the nations of Europe and America do the same? Nehru recognized, of course, that China not only shared much of India's great cultural heritage, but also had experienced a protracted recent period of Western imperial oppression, and hence felt the same revulsion for colonialism and racism. Yet, on the other hand, had not Russia and America, both offsprings of Western civilization, so recently fought as allies against Axis tyranny? Surely the same five principles might apply equally well, if only given a fair trial. From India's vantage point the sole alternative seemed mutual destruction and possible world annihilation. The era of *"Hindu-Chin Bhai Bhai"* ("Indians and Chinese are Brothers") was, however, short-lived, and Chinese "cartographic aggression" against India's northern tier became a massive military invasion in 1962. The Chinese action profoundly shocked Nehru personally, and was a tragic warning to India. She has since recognized that a treaty of nonaggression alone may not suffice to deter every international aggressive impulse.

Peace was one of the pillars of India's pre-1962 policy, and as the leading Asian power within the Commonwealth, India was able to play a unique mediating role in the settlement of several major world conflicts, including the Korean War, the war in French Indochina, and the conflict in the Congo. India has strongly supported United Nations efforts to secure world peace, and has served on U.N. commissions created for precisely that purpose. India's decision to remain in the Commonwealth has, moreover, helped that remarkable association of free nations to set an example for mankind of the potential for harmonious international intercourse among peoples of the most diverse racial, religious, and cultural backgrounds which may well prove to be the most important historical legacy of British imperial expansion. In view of the primary value Gandhi placed upon *ahimsa* [literally, "noninjury"], India's stress on nonviolence as part of her foreign policy is perhaps less surprising than the several instances in which she resorted instead to violent solutions. Though India initially brought the Kashmir conflict before the Security Council for peaceful resolution, recent Indian intransigence on the question of a plebiscite, despite insistence that the "Pakistani aggression" first be "vacated," has reduced that struggle to a stalemate based on military confrontation. Sporadic violence continues along the Kashmir "cease-fire" line, and it may at any time drag India and Pakistan into war. The December 1961 invasion of Goa by Indian troops was another instance in which the Nehru government abandoned its policy of striving to seek peaceful solutions to international problems. Admittedly, India had been impressively patient in her negotiations and entreaties to Portugal for more than a decade preceding the military action. There was, moreover, understandably strong feeling among India's population at large, as well as perhaps the majority of Goa's more than 600,000 residents, in favor of integrating Goa within the new Indian Union. After the British withdrawal, lesser European powers, which had obviously retained toeholds in India by British sufferance, were expected to follow Britain's example and quit India as well. The French did so in 1954, when they gave up Pondicherry, their last and major remaining Indian enclave. The Portuguese, however, stubbornly insisted after 1950 that Goa, Diu, and Daman were "integral" parts of their nation. Since under 2,000 residents of Goa were Portuguese by birth, over 60 per cent were Hindu by religion, and most of the population spoke Konkani, a dialect of Marathi, as their native language, Indians had little difficulty in refuting these claims. Within Goa, moreover, a "liberation committee" led several *satyagraha* [passive resistance] campaigns in 1954 and 1955. Portuguese troops were far less considerate than the British had been, and many of these *satyagrahis* were killed during their nonviolent demonstrations and marches. Nehru had been almost alone for several years before 1961 in withstanding mounting Indian pressure within his own country to move troops across the hostile border and reclaim by force what had been taken by force so many centuries ago. As the most outspoken advocate of peaceful settlement of international disputes in the world at large, India's prime minister was naturally aware of how damaging to India's peacemaking prestige any forceable seizure of Goa was bound to be. Why then did he finally capitulate? Perhaps he was simply tired of saying no to those who so long urged him to say yes. Perhaps he abandoned all hope of ever changing Portugal's "state of heart" on this issue. Possibly he sensed that Congress desperately needed the acclaim which so popular an action was bound to bring to a Party that was often and openly criticized within India for having lost the "spirit of the Freedom Struggle" now that it had long held political power. For whatever reasons, Nehru reversed himself. India's army moved in and took full control, almost without fighting. Goa, Diu, and Daman came under Delhi's central administration as India's newest "Union territory."

Constitutionally committed to the development of a "secular and welfare" state, the government of India embarked under Nehru's direction upon a comprehensive program of social reform. Thanks to Gandhi's encouragement, millions of Hindu women had enlisted in the ranks of his *satyagraha* movements, many enduring long prison terms and violence. Nehru's elderly mother had been struck down in a police charge in 1932, only a few years before she died. In 1929 government had taken the first major step since 1891 against infant marriage, by passing the Child Marriage Restraint Act. This Act raised the minimum legal age of marriage to eighteen for males and fourteen for females. After independence, more vigorous legislation was proposed by Liberal leaders of Congress to reform the Hindu Code, and the Hindu Marriage Act of 1955 raised the age of marriageable females to fifteen, made bigamy and polygamy criminal offenses, and introduced divorce initiated by a wife into Hindu law. A year later the Hindu Succession Act gave females, including widows, claims to shares in property inheritance equal to those of their male siblings. The Hindu Adoption and Maintenance Act of 1956, moreover, gave women as well as men the power to adopt children, and called for maintenance of widows as well as separated wives as long as they did not convert to another faith. Orthodox Hindu opposition to these measures was strident, yet Nehru's popularity and the continued power of Congress made their enactment, if not rigid enforcement, possible. In the second national elections of 1957, Congress won a slightly larger percentage of the popular vote than it had amassed in 1951–52, receiving in all some fifty-one million out of 113 million votes cast.

Partition of the subcontinent had removed one major source of disunity from the Indian scene, yet the linguistic provinces controversy, reflecting a deeper sort of cultural "communalism" within India, soon became a very urgent issue confronting Nehru's government. Viewed from the perspective of history, the concept of national unity for India may be recognized as a relatively recent growth, stimulated greatly by united opposition (predominantly Hindu) to the consolidation of British rule. By and large "Indian" history is the patchquilt product of numerous regional histories, with more of a continental than national character, at least until the nineteenth century. The substitution of English for Sanskrit and Persian as the official language of administration, law, and university education was one of the most important factors facilitating this growth of national awareness among Indians. Until 1920 all sessions of Congress were conducted in English, and even the most ardently anti-British leaders of Congress like Tilak were obliged to use English when they spoke at "Nationalist" meetings outside the linguistic borders of their own region. Gandhi, however, recognized that without a national language indigenous to India Congress would perforce remain the debating society of a minority intellectual elite. Though his own native tongue was Gujarati, The Mahatma sponsored Hindi, spoken by a plurality of Indians, as the national linguistic substitute for English. At the Nagpur Congress in 1920 thousands of Hindi-speaking members attended and listened to speeches in their own language. For every non-Hindi speaker (like Jinnah) who was thus alienated from Congress meetings, hundreds of hitherto apolitical Indians were lured into the arena of struggle. The Congress constitution was revised that same year with some twenty-one provincial committees established along regional linguistic lines rather than existing territorial divisions, thus committing Congress implicitly to the redrawing of India's provincial borders on a linguistic basis. While striving to develop an indigenous national language for India, Gandhi was at the same time eager to attract mass support in all non-Hindi speaking regions by popularizing the Congress program through the major regional languages. The program of national education stimulated substitution of regional languages and Hindi for English in secondary schools and colleges throughout the country. The Indian constitution designated Hindi in the Devanagri script the "official language of the Union," though English would "continue to be used" for all official purposes until 1965. (This time limit has subsequently been removed, and English remains in practice as "official" a national language of India as Hindi.) The constitution also provided for the creation of a special commission in 1955 to study the entire language problem of India.

Those agitating for the creation of new linguistic provinces refused, however, to wait for official action. The Telugu-speaking population of Madras, conscious of its glorious history under the ancient Andhra Empire (which flourished at about the dawn of the Christian era) and chafing under the provincial control of a predominantly Tamil-speaking bureaucracy, launched a vigorous campaign for the administrative separation of *Andhra Pradesh* (Andhra State) from Madras in 1952. Potti Sriramalu, the aged leader of this nonviolent struggle, emulated Gandhi by undertaking a fast-unto-death on behalf of this demand. Sriramalu's death in December 1952 brought a change of heart in Delhi, and within a year Andhra State was born. A "Pandora's box"[6] of regional linguistic demands for the geographical reapportionment of India had been flung open. The States Reorganization Commission, created in 1955, submitted its proposal for the redrawing of India's internal map in 1956, recommending the creation of fourteen linguistic states. Instead of resolving the divisive regional agitation, however, this report served only to provoke violent agitation in Bombay, where Marathi- and Gujarati-speaking factions were irate at being left under one administrative unit. The Samyukta Maharastra Samiti (United Maharastra Party) and Maha Gujarat Parishad (Great Gujarat Party) launched mass demonstrations calling for Bombay's partition along linguistic lines. Political differences were subordinated to regional language loyalties by leaders throughout the state, and the 1957 elections were fought in this region on the overriding issue of linguistic regional loyalty versus national unity. The latter lost, and Congress candidates who called for cool heads in averting factional strife that could lead to India's fragmentation were defeated by a united front of Hindu Communalists, Socialists, and Communists, who made language and regional culture their political battlecry. Bombay was finally divided into Gujarat and Maharashtra in 1960. Similar agitation for the creation of a Punjabi-speaking province out of the predominantly Hindi-language state of India's Punjab continued unsuccessfully throughout the Nehru era. The central government resisted this demand, while yielding to others, on the grounds that religious communalism, rather than linguistic consciousness, primarily inspired the movement and so far has remained adamantly unyielding.

Notes

1 See Nehru, *Toward Freedom;* and Michael Brecher, *Nehru. A Political Biography* (London: Oxford University Press, 1959).

2 For a fictional account of the assassination see Stanley Wolpert, *Nine Hours to Rama* (New York: Random House, 1962).

3 V. P. Menon, *The Story of the Integration of the Indian States* (New York: Macmillan, 1956).

4 Speech: Pandit Nehru (extract), December 13, 1946, in *India, 1947–50. Internal Affairs,* ed. S. L. Poplai (London: Oxford University Press, 1959). I, pp. 65ff.

5 Speech in Parliament, March 17, 1950, *Jawaharlal Nehru's Speeches,* 1949–1953 (Delhi: Publications Division, Ministry of Information and Broadcasting, 1954), Second Impression, p. 144.

6 See Selig S. Harrison, *India. The Most Dangerous Decades* (Princeton: Princeton University Press, 1960).

In this selection Mao Tse-tung relates how the modernization in China was due largely to Western capitalist and socialist influences. He agrees that if there were no Soviet Union or no World War II to weaken the imperialist powers there would be no communism in China. Would you believe that Mao, nevertheless, is working to destroy the Communist Party in China and, indeed, China as a nation? This is what he says in the first paragraph below. He describes how this Utopia will come about with the help of the Soviet Union. Times have changed a bit since this was written in 1949!

The People's Democratic Dictatorship

Mao Tse-tung

In Commemoration of the Twenty-Eighth
Anniversary of the Communist Party of China

The first of July 1949 marks the fact that the Communist Party of China has already lived through twenty-eight years. Like a man, a political party has its childhood, youth, manhood and old age. The Communist Party of China is no longer a child or a lad in his teens but has become an adult. When a man reaches old age, he will die; the same is true of a party. When classes disappear, all instruments of class struggle—parties and the state machinery—will lose their function, cease to be necessary, therefore gradually wither away and end their historical mission; and human society will move to a higher stage. We are the opposite of the political parties of the bourgeoisie. They are afraid to speak of the extinction of classes, state power and parties. We, on the contrary, declare openly that we are striving hard to create the very conditions which will bring about their extinction. The leadership of the Communist Party and the state power of the people's dictatorship are such conditions. Anyone who does not recognize this truth is no Communist. Young comrades who have not studied Marxism-Leninism and have only recently joined the Party may not yet understand this truth. They must understand it—only then can they have a correct world outlook. They must understand that the road to the abolition of classes, to the abolition of state power and to the abolition of parties is the road all mankind must take; it is only a question of time and conditions. Communists the world over are wiser than the bourgeoisie, they understand the laws governing the existence and development of things, they understand dialectics and they can see farther. The bourgeoisie does not welcome this truth

From *Selected Works of Mao Tse-tung* (Peking: Foreign Language Press, 1969), Vol. 4, pp. 411–423.

because it does not want to be overthrown. To be overthrown is painful and is unbearable to contemplate for those overthrown, for example, for the Kuomintang reactionaries whom we are now overthrowing and for Japanese imperialism which we together with other peoples overthrew some time ago. But for the working class, the labouring people and the Communist Party the question is not one of being overthrown, but of working hard to create the conditions in which classes, state power and political parties will die out very naturally and mankind will enter the realm of Great Harmony. We have mentioned in passing the long-range perspective of human progress in order to explain clearly the problems we are about to discuss.

As everyone knows, our Party passed through these twenty-eight years not in peace but amid hardships, for we had to fight enemies, both foreign and domestic, both inside and outside the Party. We thank Marx, Engels, Lenin and Stalin for giving us a weapon. This weapon is not a machine-gun, but Marxism-Leninism. . . .

From the time of China's defeat in the Opium War of 1840, Chinese progressives went through untold hardships in their quest for truth from the Western countries. Hung Hsiu-chuan, Kang Yu-wei, Yen Fu and Sun Yat-sen were representative of those who had looked to the West for truth before the Communist Party of China was born. Chinese who then sought progress would read any book containing the new knowledge from the West. The number of students sent to Japan, Britain, the United States, France, and Germany was amazing. At home, the imperial examinations were abolished and modern schools sprang up like bamboo shoots after a spring rain; every effort was made to learn from the West. In my youth, I too engaged in such studies. They represented the culture of Western bourgeois democracy, including the social theories and natural sciences of that period, and they were called "the new learning" in contrast to Chinese feudal culture, which was called "the old learning". For quite a long time, those who had acquired the new learning felt confident that it would save China, and very few of them had any doubts on this score, as the adherents of the old learning had. Only modernization could save China, only learning from foreign countries could modernize China. Among the foreign countries, only the Western capitalist countries were then progressive, as they had successfully built modern bourgeois states. The Japanese had been successful in learning from the West, and the Chinese also wished to learn from the Japanese. The Chinese in those days regarded Russia as backward, and few wanted to learn from her. That was how the Chinese tried to learn from foreign countries in the period from the 1840s to the beginning of the 20th century.

Imperialist aggression shattered the fond dreams of the Chinese about learning from the West. It was very odd—why were the teachers always committing aggression against their pupil? The Chinese learned a good deal from the West, but they could not make it work and were never able to realize their ideals. Their repeated struggles, including such a countrywide movement as the Revolution of 1911, all ended in failure. Day by day, conditions in the country got worse, and life was made impossible. Doubts arose, increased and deepened. World War I shook the whole globe. The Russians made the October Revolution and created the world's first socialist state. Under the leadership of Lenin and Stalin, the revolutionary energy of the great proletariat and labouring people of Russia, hitherto latent and unseen by foreigners, suddenly erupted like a volcano, and the Chinese and all mankind began to see the Russians in a new light. Then, and only then, did the Chinese enter an entirely new era in their thinking and their life. They found Marxism-Leninism, the universally applicable truth, and the face of China began to change.

It was through the Russians that the Chinese found Marxism. Before the October Revolution, the Chinese were not only ignorant of Lenin and Stalin, they did not even know of Marx and Engels. The salvoes of the October Revolution brought us Marxism-Leninism. The October Revolution helped progressives in China, as throughout the world, to adopt the proletarian world outlook as the instrument for studying a nation's destiny and considering anew their own problems. Follow the path of the Russians—that was their conclusion. In 1919, the May 4th Movement took place in China. In 1921, the Communist Party of China was founded. Sun Yat-sen, in the depths of despair, came across the October Revolution and the Communist Party of China. He welcomed the October Revolution, welcomed Russian help to the Chinese and welcomed co-operation with the Communist Party of China. Then Sun Yat-sen died and Chiang Kai-shek rose to power. Over a long period of twenty-two years, Chiang Kai-shek dragged China into ever more hopeless straits. In this period, during the anti-fascist Second World War in which the Soviet Union was the main force, three big imperialist powers were knocked out, while two others were weakened. In the whole world only one big imperialist power, the United States of America, remained uninjured. But the United States faced a grave domestic crisis. It wanted to enslave the whole world; it supplied arms to help Chiang Kai-shek slaughter several million Chinese. Under the leadership of the Communist Party of China, the Chinese people, after driving out Japanese imperialism, waged the People's War of Liberation for three years and have basically won victory.

Thus Western bourgeois civilization, bourgeois democracy and the plan for a bourgeois republic have all gone bankrupt in the eyes of the Chinese people. Bourgeois democracy has given way to people's democracy under the leadership of the working class and the bourgeois republic to the people's republic. This has made it possible to achieve socialism and communism through the people's republic, to abolish classes and enter a world of Great Harmony. Kang Yu-wei wrote *Ta Tung Shu,* or the *Book of Great Harmony,* but he did not and could not find the way to achieve Great Harmony. There are bourgeois republics in foreign lands, but China cannot have a bourgeois republic because she is a country suffering under imperialist oppression. The only way is through a people's republic led by the working class. . . .

Twenty-four years have passed since Sun Yat-sen's death, and the Chinese revolution, led by the Communist Party of China, has made tremendous advances both in theory and practice and has radically changed the face of China. Up to now the principal and fundamental experience the Chinese people have gained is twofold:

(1) Internally, arouse the masses of the people. That is, unite the working class, the peasantry, the urban petty bourgeoisie and the national bourgeoisie, form a domestic united front under the leadership of the working class, and advance from this to the establishment of a state which is a people's democratic dictatorship under the leadership of the working class and based on the alliance of workers and peasants.

(2) Externally, unite in a common struggle with those nations of the world which treat us as equals and unite with the people of all countries. That is, ally ourselves with the Soviet Union, with the People's Democracies and with the proletariat and the broad masses of the people in all other countries, and form an international united front.

"You are leaning to one side." Exactly. The forty years' experience of Sun Yat-sen and the twenty-eight years' experience of the Communist Party have taught us to lean to one side, and we are firmly convinced that in order to win victory and consolidate it we must lean to one side. In the light of the experiences accumulated in these forty years and these twenty-eight years, all Chinese without exception must lean either to the side of imperialism or to the side of socialism. Sitting on the fence will not do, nor is there a third road. We oppose the Chiang Kai-shek reactionaries who lean to the side of imperialism, and we also oppose the illusions about a third road.

"You are too irritating." We are talking about how to deal with domestic and foreign reactionaries, the imperialists and their running dogs, not about how to deal with anyone else. With regard to such reactionaries, the question of irritating them or not does not arise. Irritated or not irritated, they will remain the same because they are reactionaries. Only if we draw a clear line between reactionaries and revolutionaries, expose the intrigues and plots of the reactionaries, arouse the vigilance and attention of the revolutionary ranks, heighten our will to fight and crush the enemy's arrogance can we isolate the reactionaries, vanquish them or supersede them. We must not show the slightest timidity before a wild beast. We must learn from Wu Sung on the Chingyang Ridge. As Wu Sung saw it, the tiger on Chingyang Ridge was a man-eater, whether irritated or not. Either kill the tiger or be eaten by him—one or the other.

"We want to do business." Quite right, business will be done. We are against no one except the domestic and foreign reactionaries who hinder us from doing business. Everybody should know that it is none other than the imperialists and their running dogs, the Chiang Kai-shek reactionaries, who hinder us from doing business and also from establishing diplomatic relations with foreign countries. When we have beaten the internal and external reactionaries by uniting all domestic and international forces, we shall be able to do business and establish diplomatic relations with all foreign countries on the basis of equality, mutual benefit and mutual respect for territorial integrity and sovereignty.

"Victory is possible even without international help." This is a mistaken idea. In the epoch in which imperialism exists, it is impossible for a genuine people's revolution to win victory in any country without various forms of help from the international revolutionary forces, and even if victory were won, it could not be consolidated. This was the case with the victory and consolidation of the great October Revolution, as Lenin and Stalin told us long ago. This was also the case with the overthrow of the three imperialist powers in World War II and the establishment of the People's Democracies. And this is also the case with the present and the future of People's China. Just imagine! If the Soviet Union had not existed, if there had been no victory in the anti-fascist Second World War, if Japanese imperialism had not been defeated, if the People's Democracies had not come into being, if the oppressed nations of the East were not rising in struggle and if there were no struggle of the masses of the people against their reactionary rulers in the United States, Britain, France, Germany, Italy, Japan and other capitalist countries—if not for all these in combination, the international reactionary forces bearing down upon us would certainly be many times greater than now. In such circumstances, could we have won victory? Obviously not. And even with victory, there could be no consolidation. The Chinese people have had more than enough experience of this kind. This experience was reflected long ago in Sun Yat-sen's deathbed statement on the necessity of uniting with the international revolutionary forces.

"We need help from the British and U.S. governments." This, too, is a naive idea in these times. Would the present rulers of Britain and the United States, who are imperialists, help a people's state? Why do these countries do business with us and, supposing they might be willing to lend us money on terms of mutual benefit in the future, why would they do so? Because their capitalists want to make money and their bankers want to earn interest to extricate themselves from their own crisis—it is not a matter of helping the Chinese people. The Communist Parties and progressive groups in these countries are urging their governments to establish trade and even diplomatic relations with us. This is goodwill, this is help, this cannot be mentioned in the same breath with the conduct of the bourgeoisie in the same countries. Throughout his life, Sun Yat-sen appealed countless times to the capitalist countries for help and got nothing but heartless rebuffs. Only once in his whole life did Sun Yat-sen receive foreign help, and that was Soviet help. Let readers refer to Dr. Sun Yat-sen's testament; his earnest advice was not to look for help from the imperialist countries but to "unite with those nations of the world which treat us as equals". Dr. Sun had experience; he had suffered, he had been deceived. We should remember his words and not allow ourselves to be deceived again. Internationally, we belong to the side of the anti-imperialist front headed by the Soviet Union, and so we can turn only to this side for genuine and friendly help, not to the side of the imperialist front.

"You are dictatorial." My dear sirs, you are right, that is just what we are. All the experience the Chinese people have accumulated through several decades teaches us to enforce the people's democratic dictatorship, that is, to deprive the reactionaries of the right to speak and let the people alone have that right.

Who are the people? At the present stage in China, they are the working class, the peasantry, the urban petty bourgeoisie and the national bourgeoisie. These classes, led by the working class and the Communist Party, unite to form their own state and elect their own government; they enforce their dictatorship over the running dogs of imperialism—the landlord class and bureaucrat-bourgeoisie, as well as the representatives of those classes, the Kuomintang reactionaries and their accomplices—suppress them, allow them only to behave themselves and not to be unruly in word or deed. If they speak or act in an unruly way, they will be promptly stopped and punished. Democracy is practised within the ranks of the people, who enjoy the rights of freedom of speech, assembly, association and so on. The right to vote belongs only to the people, not to the reactionaries. The combination of these two aspects, democracy for the people and dictatorship over the reactionaries, is the people's democratic dictatorship.

Why must things be done this way? The reason is quite clear to everybody. If things were not done this way, the revolution would fail, the people would suffer, the country would be conquered.

"Don't you want to abolish state power?" Yes, we do, but not right now; we cannot do it yet. Why? Because imperialism still exists, because domestic reaction still exists, because classes still exist in our country. Our present task is to strengthen the people's state apparatus —mainly the people's army, the people's police and the people's courts —in order to consolidate national defence and protect the people's interests. Given this condition, China can develop steadily, under the leadership of the working class and the Communist Party, from an agricultural into an industrial country and from a new-democratic into a socialist and communist society, can abolish classes and realize the Great Harmony. The state apparatus, including the army, the police and the courts, is the instrument by which one class oppresses another. It is an instrument for the oppression of antagonistic classes; it is violence and not "benevolence". "You are not benevolent!" Quite so. We definitely do not apply a policy of benevolence to the reactionaries and towards the reactionary activities of the reactionary classes. Our policy of benevolence is applied only within the ranks of the people, not beyond them to the reactionaries or to the reactionary activities of reactionary classes.

The people's state protects the people. Only when the people have such a state can they educate and remould themselves on a countrywide scale by democratic methods and, with everyone taking part, shake off the influence of domestic and foreign reactionaries (which is still very strong, will survive for a long time and cannot be quickly destroyed), rid themselves of the bad habits and ideas acquired in the old society, not allow themselves to be led astray by the reactionaries, and continue to advance—to advance towards a socialist and communist society.

Here, the method we employ is democratic, the method of persuasion, not of compulsion. When anyone among the people breaks the law, he too should be punished, imprisoned or even sentenced to death; but this is a matter of a few individual cases, and it differs in principle from the dictatorship exercised over the reactionaries as a class.

As for the members of the reactionary classes and individual reactionaries, so long as they do not rebel, sabotage or create trouble after their political power has been overthrown, land and work will be given to them as well in order to allow them to live and remould themselves through labour into new people. If they are not willing to work, the people's state will compel them to work. Propaganda and educational work will be done among them too and will be done, moreover, with as much care and thoroughness as among the captured army officers in the past. This, too, may be called a "policy of benevolence" if you like, but it is imposed by us on the members of the enemy classes and cannot be mentioned in the same breath with the work of self-education which we carry on within the ranks of the revolutionary people.

Such remoulding of members of the reactionary classes can be accomplished only by a state of the people's democratic dictatorship under the leadership of the Communist Party. When it is well done, China's major exploiting classes, the landlord class and the bureaucrat-bourgeoisie (the monopoly capitalist class), will be eliminated for good. There remain the national bourgeoisie; at the present stage, we can already do a good deal of suitable educational work with many of them. When the time comes to realize socialism, that is, to nationalize private enterprise, we shall carry the work of educating and remoulding them a step further. The people have a powerful state apparatus in their hands—there is no need to fear rebellion by the national bourgeoisie.

The serious problem is the education of the peasantry. The peasant economy is scattered, and the socialization of agriculture, judging by the Soviet Union's experience, will require a long time and painstaking work. Without socialization of agriculture, there can be no complete, consolidated socialism. The steps to socialize agriculture must be co-ordinated with the development of a powerful industry having state enterprise as its backbone. The state of the people's democratic dictatorship must systematically solve the problems of industrialization. . . .

We must overcome difficulties, we must learn what we do not know. We must learn to do economic work from all who know how, no matter who they are. We must esteem them as teachers, learning from them respectfully and conscientiously. We must not pretend to know when we do not know. We must not put on bureaucratic airs.

If we dig into a subject for several months, for a year or two, for three or five years, we shall eventually master it. At first some of the Soviet Communists also were not very good at handling economic matters and the imperialists awaited their failure too. But the Communist Party of the Soviet Union emerged victorious and, under the leadership of Lenin and Stalin, it learned not only how to make the revolution but also how to carry on construction. It has built a great and splendid socialist state. The Communist Party of the Soviet Union is our best teacher and we must learn from it. The situation both at home and abroad is in our favour, we can rely fully on the weapon of the people's democratic dictatorship, unite the people throughout the country, the reactionaries excepted, and advance steadily to our goal.

Mao Tse-tung has experimented with the whole population of China in
one of the most remarkable revolutions in history. When has any one man
attempted to destroy the ancient cultural myths of over 700,000,000
people and impose on them his own ideas, some of which would, according
to one school of thought, remake man in an image contrary to his own
self-centered nature? Will Mao be successful in creating the selfless man,
and, if he is, will this make man free? Professor Gurley of the Economics
Department at Stanford University, presents a penetrating and uncommon
Western view of Maoist society in contrast to other writers who describe
China as comparable to a 1984 or a Brave New World.

The New Man in the New China

John W. Gurley

While capitalist and Maoist processes of economic development
have several elements in common, the differences between the two
approaches are nevertheless many and profound. It is certainly not
evident that one approach or the other is always superior, either in
means or ends. What is evident, however, is that most studies by
American economists of Chinese economic development are based on
the assumption of capitalist superiority, and so China has been dealt
with as though it were simply an underdeveloped United States—an
economy that "should" develop along capitalist lines and that "should"
forget all that foolishness about Marxism, Mao's thought, great leaps,
and cultural revolutions, and get on with the job of investing its savings efficiently. This unthinking acceptance by American economists
of the view that there is no development like capitalist development
has resulted in studies of China that lack insight.

The practice of capitalism has not, of course, met the ideal specifi-
cation for it as theorized by Adam Smith. In general, the theory
holds that an economy can develop most rapidly if every person,
whether as entrepreneur, worker, or consumer, is able to pursue his
own self-interest in competitive markets without undue interference
from government. Progress is best promoted, not by government, but
by entrepreneurs owning the material means of production, whose
activities, guided by the profit motive, reflect consumers' demands
for various goods and services. Labor productivity is enhanced by

From "Maoist Economic Development: The New Man in The New China"
by John Gurley, *The Center Magazine*, May, 1970, pp. 25–33. Reprinted by
permission from the May 1970 issue of *The Center Magazine,* a publication
of The Center for the Study of Democratic Institutions in Santa Barbara,
California.

material incentives and the division of labor (specialization); economic progress is made within an environment of law and order, harmony of interests, and stability. It is by these means that economic development, according to the theory, can best be attained, and its attainment can best be measured by the national output.

In practice, many markets have been more monopolistic than competitive, government has interfered in numerous and extensive ways in competitive market processes in pursuit of greater equity in income distribution, higher employment of labor, and better allocation of economic resources. Capitalism of the individualist, competitive type has to some extent given way in most parts of the industrial capitalist world to a state welfare capitalism, in which government plays a larger role and private entrepreneurs and consumers somewhat smaller ones than envisaged by Adam Smith and his disciples. Despite these departures from the ideal model of capitalism, however, it is fair to say that the main driving force of the capitalist system remains private entrepreneurs who own the means of production, and that competition among them is still widespread and worldwide.

There is no doubt that capitalist development, whatever importance its departures from the Smithian model have had, has been highly successful in raising living standards for large numbers of people. It has been relatively efficient in using factors of production in ways best designed to provide all the goods that consumers by and large have demanded. It has also encouraged new ways of doing things—innovative activity and technological advances.

At the same time, however, there is a heavy emphasis in capitalist development—as there now is throughout most of the world—on raising the national output, on producing "things" in ever-increasing amounts. Implicit is the view that man is merely an input, a factor of production, a means to an end. Moreover, capitalist development has almost always been uneven in several crucial ways—in its alternating periods of boom and bust; in enriching some people thousands of times more than others; in developing production facilities with much more care than it has devoted to the welfare of human beings and their environment; in fostering lopsided development, both in terms of geographical location within a country and, especially in low-income countries, in terms of a narrow range of outputs, such as in one- or two-crop economies. The lopsided character of capitalist development has been evident historically in those nations that today have advanced industrial economies, but it is especially evident in the underdeveloped countries (with their mixture of feudal and capitalist features) that are tied in to the international capitalist system —those countries that, by being receptive to free enterprise and foreign capital, regardless of whether they are also receptive to freedom, are in the "free world." . . .

The Maoists' disagreement with the capitalist view of economic development is profound. Their emphasis, values, and aspirations are quite different from those of capitalist economists. Maoist economic development occurs within the context of central planning, public ownership of industries, and agricultural cooperatives or communes. While decision-making is decentralized to some extent, decisions regarding investment versus consumption, foreign trade, allocation of material inputs and the labor supply, prices of various commodities—these and more are essentially in the hands of the state. The profit motive is officially discouraged from assuming an important role in the allocation of resources, and material incentives, while still prevalent, are downgraded.

Perhaps the most striking difference between the capitalist and Maoist views concerns goals. Maoists believe that while a principal aim of nations should be to raise the level of material welfare of the population, this should be done only within the context of the development of human beings, encouraging them to realize fully their manifold creative powers. And it should be done only on an egalitarian basis—that is, on the basis that development is not worth much unless everyone rises together; no one is to be left behind, either economically or culturally. Indeed, Maoists believe that rapid economic development is not likely to occur *unless* everyone rises together. Development as a trickle-down process is therefore rejected by Maoists, and so they reject any strong emphasis on profit motives and efficiency criteria that lead to lopsided growth.

In Maoist eyes, economic development can best be attained by giving prominence to men rather than "things."

Recently, capitalist economists have begun to stress the importance for economic growth of "investment in human capital"—that is, investment in general education, job training, and better health. It has been claimed that expenditures in these directions have had a large "payoff" in terms of output growth. Although this might seem to represent a basic change in their concept of man in the development process, actually it does not. "Investment in human capital" means that economic resources are invested for the purpose of raising the skill and the educational and health levels of labor, not as an end in itself but as a means of increasing the productivity of labor. Thus economists are concerned with the "payoff" to investment in human capital, this payoff being the profit that can be made from such an expenditure. Indeed, the very term "human capital" indicates what these economists have in mind: man is another capital good, an input in the productive engine that grinds out commodities; if one invests in man, he may become more productive and return a handsome profit to the investor—whether the investor is the state, a private capitalist, or the laborer himself. Thus the preoccupation of capitalist economists is still with man as a means and not as an end.

The Maoists' emphasis, however, is quite different. First of all, while they recognize the role played by education and health in the production process, their emphasis is heavily placed on the transformation of ideas, the making of the Communist Man. Ideology, of course, may be considered as part of education in the broadest sense, but it is surely not the part that capitalist economists have in mind when they evaluate education's contribution to economic growth. Moreover, ideological training does not include the acquisition of particular skills or the training of specialists—as education and job training in capitalist countries tend to do. The Maoists believe that economic development can best be promoted by breaking down specialization, by dismantling bureaucracies, and by undermining the other centralizing and divisive tendencies that give rise to experts, technicians, authorities, and bureaucrats remote from or manipulating "the masses." Finally, Maoists seem perfectly willing to pursue the goal of transforming man even though it is temporarily at the expense of some economic growth. Indeed, it is clear that Maoists will not accept economic development, however rapid, if it is based on the capitalist principles of sharp division of labor and sharp (meaning unsavory or selfish) practices.

The proletarian world-view, which Maoists believe must replace that of the bourgeoisie, stresses that only through struggle can progress be made; that selflessness and unity of purpose will release a huge reservoir of enthusiasm, energy, and creativeness; that active participation by "the masses" in decision-making will provide them with the knowledge to channel their energy most productively; and that the elimination of specialization will not only increase workers' and peasants' willingness to work hard for the various goals of society but will also increase their ability to do this by adding to their knowledge and awareness of the world around them.

It is an essential part of Maoist thinking that progress is not made by peace and quietude, by letting things drift and playing safe, or, in the words of Mao Tse-tung, by standing for "unprincipled peace, thus giving rise to a decadent, philistine attitude. . . . " Progress is made through struggle, when new talents emerge and knowledge advances in leaps. Only through continuous struggle is the level of consciousness of people raised, and in the process they gain not only understanding but happiness.

Mao sees man engaged in a fierce class struggle—the bourgeoisie against the proletariat—the outcome of which, at least in the short run, is far from certain. The proletarian world outlook can win only if it enters tremendous ideological class struggles.

Maoists believe that each person should be devoted to "the masses" rather than to his own pots and pans, and should serve the world proletariat rather than, as the *Peking Review* has put it, reaching out with "grasping hands everywhere to seek fame, material gain, power, position, and limelight." They think that if a person is selfish he will resist criticisms and suggestions and is likely to become bureaucratic and elitist. He will not work as hard for community or national goals as he will for narrow, selfish ones. In any case, a selfish person is not an admirable person. Thus Maoists deemphasize material incentives, for they are the very manifestation of a selfish, bourgeois society. While selflessness is necessary to imbue man with energy and the willingness to work hard, Maoists believe this is not sufficient; man must also have the ability as well. And such ability comes from active participation—from seeing and doing. To gain knowledge, people must be awakened from their half slumber, encouraged to mobilize themselves and to take conscious action to elevate and liberate themselves. When they actively participate in decision-making, when they take an interest in state affairs, when they dare to do new things, when they become good at presenting facts and reasoning things out, when they criticize and test and experiment scientifically—having discarded myths and superstitions—when they are aroused, then, says the *Peking Review*, "the socialist initiative latent in the masses [will] burst out with volcanic force and a rapid change [will take] place in production."

Finally, if men become "selfless," there will be discipline and unity of will, for these "cannot be achieved if relations among comrades stem from selfish interests and personal likes and dislikes." If men become "active," then along with extensive democracy they will gain true consciousness and ultimately freedom, in the Marxian sense of intelligent action. Together, selflessness and active participation will achieve ideal combinations of opposites: "a vigorous and lively political situation . . . is taking shape throughout our country, in which there is both centralism and democracy, both discipline and freedom, both unity of will and personal ease of mind."

It is important to note the "discipline" and "unity of will." As for the basic framework of Marxism-Leninism, Maoists believe that everyone should accept it, and they are quick to "work on" those who lag behind or step out of line. But, within this framework, the Maoists energetically and sincerely promote individual initiative, "reasoning things out and not depending on authorities or myths," "thinking for oneself," and so forth. Outside of this framework, an individual stands little chance; inside the framework, an individual is involved in a dynamic process of becoming "truly free," in the sense of being fully aware of the world around him and an active decision-maker in that world. Mao's thought is meant to lead to true freedom and to unity of will based on a proletarian viewpoint. So everyone must think alike—the Maoist way—to attain true freedom.

For Marx, specialization and bureaucratization were the very antithesis of communism. Man could not be free or truly human until these manifestations of alienation were eliminated, allowing him to become an all-round communist man. Maoists, too, have been intensely concerned with this goal, specifying it in terms of eliminating the distinction between town and countryside, mental and manual labor, and workers and peasants. The realization of the universal man is not automatically achieved by altering the forces of production, by the socialist revolution. Rather, it can be achieved only after the most intense and unrelenting ideological efforts to raise the consciousness of the masses through the creative study and creative use of Mao's thought. Old ideas, customs, and habits hang on long after the material base of the economy has been radically changed, and it takes one mighty effort after another to wipe out the bourgeois superstructure and replace it with the proletarian world outlook. This transformation of the "subjective world" will then have a tremendous impact on the "objective world."

In many ways Maoist ideology rejects the capitalist principle of building on the best, even though the principle cannot help but be followed to some extent in any effort at economic development. However, the Maoist departures from the principle are the important thing. While capitalism, in their view, strives one-sidedly for efficiency in producing goods, Maoism, while also seeking some high degree of efficiency, at the same time and in numerous ways builds on "the worst": experts are pushed aside in favor of decision-making by "the masses"; new industries are established in rural areas; the educational system favors the disadvantaged; expertise (and hence work proficiency in a narrow sense) is discouraged; new products are domestically produced rather than being imported "more efficiently"; the growth of cities as centers of industrial and cultural life is discouraged; steel, for a time, is made by "everyone" instead of by only the much more efficient steel industry.

Of course, Maoists build on "the worst" not because they take great delight in lowering economic efficiency; rather, their stated aims are to involve everyone in the development process, to pursue development without leaving a single person behind, to achieve a balanced growth rather than a lopsided one. Yet if Maoism were only that, we could simply state that, while Maoist development may be much more equitable than capitalist efforts, it is surely less efficient and thus less rapid; efficiency is being sacrificed to some extent for equity. But that would miss the more important aspects of Maoist ideology, which holds that the resources devoted to bringing everyone into the socialist development process—the effort spent on building on "the worst"—will eventually pay off not only in economic ways by enormously raising labor productivity but, more important, by creating a society of truly free men who respond intelligently to the world around them, and who are happy.

The sharp contrast between the economic development views of capitalist economists and those of the Chinese communists cannot be denied; their two worlds are quite different. The difference is not mainly between being Chinese and being American, although that is surely part of it but, rather, between Maoists in a Marxist-Leninist tradition and being present-day followers of the economics first fashioned by Adam Smith and later reformed by John Maynard Keynes. Whatever the ignorance and misunderstanding on the Chinese side regarding the doctrines of capitalist economics, it is clear that many Western economic experts on China have shown little interest in, and almost no understanding of, Maoist economic development. Most of the economic researchers have approached China as though it were little more than a series of tables in a yearbook which could be analyzed by Western economic methods and judged by capitalist values. The result has been a series of unilluminating studies, largely statistical or institutional in method, and lacking analysis of the really distinctive and interesting features of Maoist development. . . .

The truth is that China over the past two decades has made very remarkable economic advances (though not steadily) on almost all fronts. The basic, overriding economic fact about China is that for twenty years she has fed, clothed, and housed everyone, has kept them healthy, and has educated most. Millions have not starved; sidewalks and streets have not been covered with multitudes of sleeping, begging, hungry, and illiterate human beings; millions are not disease-ridden. To find such deplorable conditions, one does not look to China these days but, rather, to India, Pakistan, and almost anywhere else in the underdeveloped world. These facts are so basic, so fundamentally important, that they completely dominate China's economic picture, even if one grants all of the erratic and irrational policies alleged by her numerous critics.

The Chinese—all of them—now have what is in effect an insurance policy against pestilence, famine, and other disasters. In this respect, China has outperformed every underdeveloped country in the world; and, even with respect to the richest one, it would not be far-fetched to claim that there has been less malnutrition due to maldistribution of food in China over the past twenty years than there has been in the United States. If this comes close to the truth, the reason lies not in China's grain output far surpassing her population growth—for it has not—but, rather, in the development of institutions to distribute food evenly among the population. It is also true, however, that China has just had six consecutive bumper grain crops (wheat and rice) that have enabled her to reduce wheat imports and greatly increase rice exports. On top of this, there have been large gains in the supplies of eggs, vegetables, fruits, poultry, fish, and meat. In fact, China today exports more food than she imports. The Chinese are in a much better position now than ever before to ward off natural disasters, as there has been significant progress in irrigation, flood control, and water conservation. The use of chemical fertilizers is increasing rapidly, the volume now over ten times that of the early nineteen-fifties; there have been substantial gains in the output of tractors, pumps, and other farm implements; and much progress has been made in the control of plant disease and in crop breeding.

In education, there has been a major breakthrough. All urban children and a great majority of rural children have attended primary schools, and enrolments in secondary schools and in higher education are large, in proportion to the population, compared with pre-communist days. If "school" is extended to include as well all part-time, part-study education, spare-time education, and the study groups organized by the communes, factories, street organizations, and the army, then there are schools everywhere in China.

China's gains in the medical and public-health fields are perhaps the most impressive of all. The gains are attested to by many fairly recent visitors to China. For example, G. Leslie Wilcox, a Canadian doctor, a few years ago visited medical colleges, hospitals, and research institutes, and reported in "Observations on Medical Practices" (*Bul-*

letin of the Atomic Scientists, June, 1966) that everywhere he found good equipment, high medical standards, excellent medical care—almost all comparable to Canadian standards. As William Y. Chen, a member of the U.S. Public Health Service, wrote in "Medicine in Public Health" (*Sciences in Communist China*), "the prevention and control of many infectious and parasitic diseases which have ravaged [China] for generations" was a "most startling accomplishment." He noted, too, that "the improvement of general environmental sanitation and the practice of personal hygiene, both in the cities and in the rural areas, were also phenomenal."

While all these gains were being made, the Chinese were devoting an unusually large amount of resources to industrial output. China's industrial production has risen on the average by at least eleven per cent per year since 1950, which is an exceptionally high growth rate for an underdeveloped country. Furthermore, industrial progress is not likely to be retarded in the future by any lack of natural resources, for China is richly endowed and is right now one of the four top producers in the world of coal, iron ore, mercury, tin, tungsten, magnesite, salt, and antimony. In recent years, China has made large gains in the production of coal, iron, steel, chemical fertilizers, and oil. In fact, since the huge discoveries at the Tach'ing oilfield, China is now self-sufficient in oil and has offered to export some to Japan.

From the industrial, agricultural, and other gains, I would estimate that China's real Gross National Product (G.N.P.) has risen on the average by at least six per cent per year since 1949, or by at least four per cent on a per-capita basis. This may not seem high, but it is a little better than the Soviet Union did over a comparable period (1928–40), much better than England's record during her century of industrialization (1750–1850), when her income per capita grew at one half of one per cent per year, perhaps a bit better than Japan's performance from 1878 to 1936, certainly much superior to France's one per cent record from 1800 to 1870, far better than India's 1.3 per cent growth during 1950 to 1967; more important, it is much superior to the postwar record of almost all underdeveloped countries in the world.

This is a picture of an economy richly endowed in natural resources, but whose people are still very poor, making substantial gains in industrialization, moving ahead more slowly in agriculture, raising education and health levels dramatically, turning out increasing numbers of scientists and engineers, expanding the volume of foreign trade and the variety of products traded, and making startling progress in the development of nuclear weapons. This is a truer picture, I believe, than the bleak one drawn by some of our China experts.

The failure of many economic experts on China to tell the story of her economic development accurately and fully is bad enough. Even worse has been the general failure to deal with China on her own terms, within the framework of her own goals and methods for attaining those goals, or even to recognize the possible validity of those goals. Communist China is certainly not a paradise, but it is now engaged in perhaps the most interesting economic and social experiment ever attempted, in which tremendous efforts are being made to achieve an egalitarian development, an industrial development without dehumanization, one that involves everyone and affects everyone. All these efforts seem not to have affected Western economists, who have proceeded ahead with their income accounts and slide rules, and their free-enterprise values, to measure and judge. One of the most revealing developments in the China field is the growing belief among the economic experts that further research is hardly worthwhile in view of the small amount of economic statistics that have come out of China since 1958. Apparently, it does not matter that seven hundred and seventy-five million people are involved in a gigantic endeavor to change their environment, their economic and social institutions, their standard of living, and themselves; that never before have such potentially important economic and social experiments been carried out; that voluminous discussions of these endeavors by the Maoists are easily available. No, if G.N.P. data are not forthcoming, if numbers can't be added up and adjusted, then the economy must be hardly worth bothering about.

. . . It is possible that Maoist economic development, by deemphasizing labor specialization and reliance on experts and technicians, reduces the quality of the labor force and so slows the rate of economic growth. On the other hand, as Adam Smith once suggested, labor specialization, while increasing productivity in some narrow sense, is often at the expense of the worker's general intelligence and understanding. It was his view that "the man whose whole life is spent in performing a few simple operations . . . generally becomes as stupid and ignorant as it is possible for a human creature to become." The difference between the most dissimilar of human beings, according to Smith, is not so much the cause of division of labor as it is the effect of it. Consequently, while an economy might gain from the division of labor in some small sense, it could lose in the larger sense by creating men who are little more than passive and unreasoning robots. A major aim of the Maoists is to transform man from this alienated state to a fully aware and participating member of society. The emphasis on "Reds" rather than experts is just one part of this transformation which, it is felt, will release "an atom bomb" of talents and energy and enable labor productivity to take great leaps.

In addition to this argument, which is based on Maoists' interpretation of their own history and experience, it is also possible that the "universal man" in an underdeveloped economy would provide more flexibility to the economy. If most people could perform many jobs moderately well, manual and intellectual, urban and rural, the economy might be more able to cope with sudden and large changes; it could with little loss in efficiency mobilize its labor force for a variety of tasks. Further, since experience in one job carries over to others, a person may be almost as productive, in the job-proficiency sense, in any one of them as he would be if he specialized—a peasant who has spent some months in a factory can more easily repair farm equipment, and so on. Finally, a Maoist economy may generate more useful information than a specialist one and so lead to greater creativity and productivity. When each person is a narrow specialist, communication among such people is not highly meaningful. When, on the other hand, each person has basic knowledge about many lines of activity, the experiences of one person enrich the potentialities of many others.

The point is that this issue—which, I should stress, includes not only labor productivity (that is, the development of material things by human beings) but also the development of human beings themselves—this issue of generalists versus specialists, communist men versus experts, the masses versus bureaucrats, or whatever, is not to be laughed away, as it has been, in effect, by some China experts. How men, in an industrial society, should relate to machines and to each other in seeking happiness and real meaning in their lives has surely been one of the most important problems of the modern age. There is also another basic issue here: whether modern industrial society, capitalist or socialist, does in fact diminish man's essential powers, his capacity for growth in many dimensions, even though it does allocate them "efficiently" and increases his skills as a specialized input. Is man Lockean in nature—reactive to outside forces, adjusting passively to disequilibrium forces from without? Or is he essentially Leibnitzian—the source of acts, active, capable of growth, and having an inner being that is self-propelled? If the latter, how are these powers released?

The Maoists claim that the powers exist and can be released. If they are right, the implications for economic development are so important that it would take blind men on this side of the Pacific to ignore them.

The twenty-first century will belong to Japan, according to growth trends compared with the rest of the world. The Japanese have molded a great society out of business and technical knowledge, much of it borrowed from the West. Is Japan simply remolding the myths, canons, and hangups of Western man or is she offering to the world something totally new and unique?

Toward the Japanese Century

Time Article

In the gentle Senri Hills just outside Osaka, under a pall of dust visible for miles away, helmeted workmen are bustling to put the finishing touches on what looks like a giant's toy box. Here, three weeks hence [March, 1970], Japan's Expo '70 will begin a six-month run. It is the first world's fair ever to be held in Asia, but amid its architectural anarchy the occasional pagoda or the batwing sail of a Chinese junk seems oddly out of place—and time. From one end of the 815-acre site to the other, the skyline is a futurescape of spires and saucers, globes and polyhedrons, sweeping carapaces and shimmering towers of aluminum, glass and steel.

The scene strongly suggests the movie *2001,* and well it might. No country has a stronger franchise on the future than Japan. No developed nation is growing faster. Its economy quadrupled in the past decade, and will triple again in the next. Powered by a *boomu* (the word is a typical Japanese neologism) that has been picking up speed for a full ten years, Japan whistled past Britain in gross national product in 1967, then France in 1968. Last year it surpassed West Germany. With a G.N.P. that is expected to reach $200 billion this year, Japan now ranks third in the world, behind only the U.S. ($932 billion) and the Soviet Union ($600 billion). U.S. Commerce Secretary Maurice Stans says that Japan "could very well" move to the head of the class in the next 20 years. Says Economist Peter Drucker: "It is the most extraordinary success story in all economic history."

At $1,100 a year, Japan's per capita income still ranks only 19th, just ahead of Italy's and far behind the U.S.'s $4,600. But that gap is closing fast as Japanese workers begin to make up for past sacrifices with fat pay increases. "It would not be surprising," says the Hudson Institute's Herman Kahn, "if the 21st century turned out to be the Japanese century."

Miniskirt and Kimono

Not bad for a war casualty with paltry natural resources, few close allies, and hardly enough room to breathe. The four spiny main islands of Nippon house the most crowded society in the world. Japan has half as many people (102 million) as the U.S., and a smaller area than Montana. Only 20% of the spectacularly mountainous land is habitable, and the Japanese are packed into coastal plains at a density of 2,365 to the square mile—about twice that of The Netherlands, the second most densely populated country.

Besides being the most crowded society, Japan is, as Kahn says, "the most achievement-minded society in the world." The Japanese possess a keen sense of competition, sharpened by the fact that their shoulder-to-shoulder existence invariably makes for many rivals and few openings. The competitive spirit extends beyond Nippon's borders and instills a deep concern among the Japanese over their ranking in the world. They intend to move higher. To that ambition they bring a machinelike discipline, an ability to focus with fearful energy on the task at hand, and an almost Teutonic thoroughness in all pursuits, whether business or pleasure.

For all their confidence, the Japanese are enduring acute modernization pangs. Until a century ago, Japan was semifeudal, primarily agricultural and almost totally insulated. Today it is a sometimes baffling blend of West and East, of old and new. Some of its rebellious young radicals would not dream of sitting down to dinner without a deep bow to their honorable grandfathers. The campuses are torn by challenges to authority, but 70% of Japan's marriages are still "arranged." Along the streets of the teeming cities, miniskirts and high heels vie with ankle-length kimonos and wooden clogs. The glass-and-steel sheaths of modern commerce along the main arteries give way to delicate wooden teahouses on cobblestoned side streets, and the skyline juxtaposes industry's mammoth cranes and chimneys with the softly curving roofs of Buddhist temples.

The past still pervades Japan, but it does not crimp its future. Already, the heirs presumptive to the 21st century own a big share of the 20th. A human cliché everywhere is the bespectacled Japanese salesman, quick to bow, to smile and, after consulting his pocket dictionary and his neatly arranged attaché case, to quote a cut-rate price. He is seen even in the lobbies of the Alcron in Prague and the Gellért in Budapest.

The salesman is a more pallid—but also more successful—descendant of two other Japanese prototypes. One was the swashbuckling *wako*, or warrior-trader, who began plundering Asia as early as the 14th century. The second was the soldier-bureaucrat who went to war a generation ago to develop a "Greater East Asia Co-Prosperity Sphere," stretching from Manchuria to Burma. His slogan was "Asia for the Asiatics," but his purpose was really to furnish Japan's factories not only with raw materials but also with vast markets for their goods. Today the Japanese have come closer to establishing an informal Co-Prosperity Sphere than ever before. The difference is that the latter-day *wako* carries a *soroban* (abacus) instead of a sword and wears blue serge instead of the khaki of General Hideki Tojo's Imperial Army.

Equal Slices

Diplomatically, if not commercially, Tokyo has been so discreet since the U.S. occupation ended in 1952 as to be almost invisible. The most prestigious branch of the Japanese government is the Finance Ministry, not the Foreign Ministry. Japan's embassy in Djakarta is symbolic: there is a low, two-story wing for the diplomatic staff and a highrise office tower housing Japanese trading companies.

Diplomatic discretion has meshed wonderfully well with the country's ecumenical trading patterns. Each day Japan exports $44 million worth of goods—one-third to Asia, one-third to the U.S., and one-third to the rest of the world. Few nations can match Japan's prices—not because of cheap labor, which is no longer all that cheap, but because of efficient production and shipping techniques. Incredibly, the Japanese can deliver finished pipeline to Alaska at a total cost that is less than the freight charges alone from Pittsburgh's steel mills. Small wonder that since 1955 Japan's share of world trade has tripled, to 7%, while the U.S. share has declined a few points, to 18%; some economists predict that by 1980 each country will command an identical 15% slice of the market.

The price of Japan's reach for that sizable slice of world trade has been years of national self-denial. "We have sold everything, including the kitchen sink," laments Economist Kiichi Miyazawa, head of the influential Ministry of International Trade and Industry (MITI). "We have left nothing for ourselves." There are shortages of roads, railways, parks, hospitals, sewers and schools. "There is much to be done," says Premier Eisaku Sato, singling out two problems in particular. "The housing shortage is extreme, and pollution is serious."

More than in most countries, urbanization has overwhelmed Japan. Only 20 years ago, 60% of the population was tied to the farm, and Japan still had to import rice; today, as a result of agricultural advances, only 18% of the Japanese people are needed to feed the country and produce a surplus. The dispossessed farmers cram the cities, and the cities have been woefully short-changed. The "Tokaido Corridor," a slender, 366-mile coastal belt running along the Pacific from Tokyo to Kobe, was long celebrated for its beauty in misty wood-block prints and delicate, 17-syllable haiku. Today, with 50% of the population crammed into the corridor, it is a smog-covered slurb.

Travelers jetting in by night first see Tokyo from miles out, an explosion of light against Honshu's black mountain ridges. By day, the world's largest metropolis (pop. 11.4 million) is a hazy brown and gray sprawl. Prosperity has only worsened Tokyo's housing short-age, its snarled traffic, and the soot that boils in across the brown Sumida River from the blast furnaces of Kawasaki, which has 3,000 industrial plants and a population of 940,000. Two-thirds of Tokyo is still without sewers; residents are served by "honeybucket" men, trucks and a "night-soil fleet" of disposal ships, some as big as 1,000 tons, that make daily dumping trips offshore. "Don't worry," a crew-man smiles, "the Black Current will take it all toward the U.S."

When the wind blows in from Tokyo Bay, the downtown area is enveloped in the aroma from "Dream Island," an ironically named landfill project that grows by 7,800 tons of waste a day. The city is trying to reduce its overhanging pall of smog by persuading home-owners and industrialists to switch from coal to fuel oil (at a cost of increased carbon monoxide). But a 15th century samurai's poem boasting that the city "commands a view of soaring Fuji" is now a wry joke.

Tokyo's ebullient *konton* (confusion) can be attractive, and the city has proved an irresistible magnet to Japanese and foreigners alike. It has vitality, diversity and unexpected touches of beauty everywhere —in a tiny rock garden, a sprig of cherry blossoms, a full moon re-flected in the still waters of the imperial moat. Manhattan-style mug-gings are virtually unknown. Still, the city's main problem, says Mayor Ryokichi Minobe, is "too many people." New York City, with 128 sq. ft. of park space per resident, is a verdant paradise compared with Tokyo, which has 7 sq. ft. Real estate values have risen 670% in a decade in some parts of town, and now rival Manhattan's—despite fears that anything built on the land may one day come tumbling down. Mild tremors hit the city almost every day, and experts fret that 3,000,000 would die in another earthquake like the one that flattened the city in 1923. Yet since the 100-ft. limitation on build-ings was done away with in 1962, because of new, supposedly quake-resistant construction techniques, the Japanese have been challenging fate; now abuilding is one office tower of 40 stories, another of 46. Why not? "We Japanese never consider cities solid, lasting existences as the Europeans or Americans do," says Architect Arata Isozaki, 38. "Ours have been destroyed so often by wars, fires and earthquakes that we believe that when it comes to cities, change is the sole permanent characteristic."

The Salary Man

Certainly change has characterized the life-styles of virtually every age group and class, except for those at the very bottom and the very top. The *eta,* descended from the practitioners of such despised occupations as leatherworking and butchering, are Japan's closest equivalent to India's untouchables; there are 1,000,000 of them, living in slums, working as ragpickers or worse, and rarely able to marry outside their class. At the top is Emperor Hirohito, who lives serenely in Tokyo's Imperial Palace with Empress Nagako and devotes most of his time, as ever, to his studies in marine biology.

Perhaps most affected are the people in the middle—the country's 17.6 million "salary men." They are the silent, white-collar backbone of the Land of the Rising G.N.P. Take, for instance, Tokyo Salary Man Iwao Nakatani, 27. He is typically middle-sized (5 ft. 4 in.), middle-income ($222 a month), middle-management. In his three-room, $6,900 flat ($833 down, $41 a month), Nakatani, his wife and two children all sleep in the same room.

Nakatani, who studied business administration at Berkeley, spends 2½ hours each day commuting to his company, Taiyo Kogyo Co., a tent firm that made the translucent roof of the U.S. exhibit at Osaka. Paternalism and lifetime employment are still features of Japanese corporations, and Taiyo Kogyo keeps Nakatani happy with a six-month salary bonus every year and a new-car loan every two years. Corporate entertainment allowances total $2 billion a year in Japan, and Nakatani spends a good chunk of his $1,600 share taking foreign customers to geisha parties. But he is not a kimono chaser. That tradition is beginning to fade, albeit slowly, as Japan's women become more assertive.

Nakatani runs counter to tradition in a number of other ways. He occasionally considers quitting for a better post, though job-hopping is still largely unheard of in a land where people usually stay with the same firm for life. He drives home in his Toyota Corolla every day at 5 p.m., whether his boss has left the office or not. And he thought nothing of voting for the Communists in the last election, though he describes himself as "a conservative's conservative," because he was certain they were going to lose and he wanted to help keep the long-entrenched Liberal Democrats on their toes.

The greatest change in the Nakatanis' life has been in the increased conveniences, but the Japanese salary man is fast learning a lesson absorbed by his Western counterpart long ago. "Now that all of us have a car, color TV and a stereo," says Nakatani, "we Japanese have begun to hanker for a mink coat for the wife and a foreign-made car." Already, Japanese housewives are complaining about "the servant problem."

Then there are Japan's two ages of discontinuity—elder and younger. Older Japanese, used to the rigors of life before the *boomu,* find the relative abundance of contemporary Japan confusing and empty. Eight years ago, as Tokyo's sprawl reached his small farm, Dyusaku Ohno sold his three acres to a development company for $280,000. Now 60, Ohno has his money in good stocks, his children in good schools, his wife in a modern house. But he has lost, he says, "the smell of the earth, the satisfaction of a good crop, the scalding bath at the end of a hard day's work."

Taming the Thunderbolts

Yoshikazu Maeda, 54, a Tokyo bank executive, remembers that day when "the family was more closely knit, living quarters were more cramped, and there was much more mutual personal consideration." He says sadly: "The whole pace of life seems to have speeded up. Human relationships seem to be getting colder." Moreover, the problem of caring for the elderly is growing, if only because there are so many more of them. Improvements in diet and medical care have increased life expectancy for men from only 50 years in 1945 to 69 years today.

A youth problem has already arrived—and how. In a country where children traditionally are coddled up to the age of nine or ten, then are expected to begin facing society's rigorous demands without complaint, Japanese youths are baffling their elders by taking to the streets to protest everything from the "dehumanization" of life to air pollution. In few lands is communication between generations breaking down more rapidly. The suicide rate among 15- to 24-year-olds is one of the highest in the world. So is the record for campus chaos. Last year, 3,500 students were jailed in clashes that closed 100 of Japan's 377 universities, some for as long as twelve months.

The catalogue of student complaints is familiar, and in many respects well justified. Competition for admission is fierce, especially to Tokyo and Kyoto universities, the Oxbridge-like axis that produces most of Japan's ruling establishment of businessmen, bureaucrats and politicians; according to one estimate, 20% of Japan's Diet (parliament) members and 30% of its corporation presidents are Tokyo U. alumni. Jammed with 1.5 million students, a 100% increase since 1960, the understaffed universities strike many youths as diploma factories geared to feed industry. Tokyo's Nihon University has 75,000 students; in its 7,000-student school of economics, there are but 27 professors.

Westerners accustomed to the atmosphere of improvisation at U.S. or French demonstrations are apt to find the Japanese protest scene quite different. Clashes between helmeted students and shield-carrying riot cops seem as stylized—and puzzling—as a No play. Moreover, the rioters, often led by members of the radical *Zengakuren* (a student federation), are usually higher on doctrine than drugs (pot has yet to spread far in Japan). Before long, however, Japanese dissent may be taking on a Western character.

Thousands of students and hippie-style dropouts are being drawn to a Viet Nam protest movement called *Beheiren,* which often draws 5,000 "folksong guerrillas" to monthly protest meetings in Tokyo's swinging Shinjuku area. When the cops come, the kids give them flowers and songs instead of staves and curses. Sample:

> *Oh, the sad, sad riot-squad men*
> *Withering away their finest years*
> *Like wintry shrubs under duralumin shields*

Beheiren's founder is Novelist Makoto Oda, 38. He launched the new wave in dissent two years ago in Sasebo Harbor, where he circled the U.S. carrier *Enterprise* in a small launch, calling out "Don't fight for Uncle Sham!" on a megaphone. If Oda's style has a familiar American quality, it may be due to the fact that he once studied at Harvard, on a Fulbright scholarship.

The rise of dissent—or rather, the decline of Confucian decorum —has stunned Japan's elders. A measure of their confusion is the advice on handling students contained in a manual circulated among the faculty of Tokyo's Chuo University. They should be treated "as foreigners," the handbook advises, "with all their different sets of modes, customs and thoughts." Still, older Japanese take comfort from the fact that so far most of the young *kaminari* (thunderbolts) have dutifully taken "their proper place" in the service of company and country after graduation. A few businessmen are in fact trying to recruit campus activists, valuing their "volatile and creative minds."

Control and Release

Life-styles change more rapidly than character—and the Japanese character bewilders many Westerners. It is shot through with contradictions, as Cultural Anthropologist Ruth Benedict noted in a pioneering study of the Japanese mind that was written in 1946 but is still pertinent. "Both the sword and the chrysanthemum are part of the picture. The Japanese are, to the highest degree, both aggressive and unaggressive, both militaristic and resentful of being pushed around, loyal and treacherous, brave and timid, conservative and hospitable to new ways. They are terribly concerned about what other people will think of their behavior, and they are also overcome by guilt when other people know nothing of their missteps. Their soldiers are disciplined to the hilt but are also insubordinate."

Except for small children and old people, the Japanese lives constantly in a state of near-total control or near-total release. A man may be a perfectly decorous office worker at 4:55 p.m., but by 5:05, after one drink at the bar around the corner, he may be a giggling buffoon. Extremely rigid codes define proper behavior in virtually every social situation, but there are no codes at all to cover many modern contingencies. That is why so much bodychecking and elbowing go on in a Tokyo subway or department store. As Author-Translator Edward Seidensticker puts it in his recent *Japan:* "They are extremely ceremonious toward those whom they know, and highly unceremonious toward others. Few urban Japanese bother to say 'Excuse me' after stepping on a person's toes or knocking a book out of his hand—provided the person is a stranger. If he is known, it is very common to apologize for offenses that have not been committed."

The guideline for the Japanese abroad is "No shame away from home." Japan's neighbors learned the meaning of that aphorism from the appalling atrocities committed during the war; in a very different way, they are learning it again today.

At home, however, extreme overcrowding has led to an overpowering sense of "proper place." Individuality is not a quality sought by most Japanese; even artists usually belong to a group, submerging or sharing their identity. The Japanese are fond of saying that there is a place for every person in their country—but manifestly not for foreigners, who are known as *gaijin* (literally, outside people) and who are discouraged from seeking citizenship or marrying Japanese. The concept of a slot for everyone is best reflected in industry's paternalism. Keeping people in their jobs for life and maintaining a virtually full-employment economy are practices that do not seem to jibe with Japan's emphasis on efficiency. But the Japanese figure shrewdly that they are gaining in social stability whatever they may be losing in wasted salaries.

Fads and Frivolity

Things get done in Japan not by the impulse of a forceful individual but by a process of consensus. The process can be time-consuming, but not always. One result is that fads are epidemic. Paris fashions and the latest rock beats reach Tokyo almost as quickly as they reach New York. The current singing sensation is Osamu Minagawa, a Tokyo six-year-old whose recording of something called *Kuro Neko No Tango* (Black Cat Tango) has sold 2,000,000 records, mostly on the basis of his imitation of a mewing cat. Baseball has been booming since Babe Ruth's visit 35 years ago, but now there are also booms in skiing, golf and gambling; wagers on horse, auto and hydroplane races totaled $3 billion last year.

Sex, too, is enjoying a boom as a spectator sport, with scores of strip joints and nude theaters—but not, as yet, topless waitresses. The Ginza is still Tokyo's main entertainment street, but the rising sin district is Akasaka, where ground-floor bar patrons in the Biblos bend not only their elbows but also their necks—to leer at couples dancing on a transparent plastic floor above. Of the 493 movies that Japan produced last year, 250 were adults-only "eroductions." The hottest flick right now is—what else?—*Sexpo 70.*

Tea and Origami

Though Japan's biggest daily, the *Asahi Shimbun,* has suggested that the country be renamed "Kindergarten Nippon," not all the fads are frivolous. Theater and concert performances are usually S.R.O., especially if the bill is Western. The Berlin Opera's six month appearance in Osaka during Expo has been sold out for a year. Music lessons are all the rage, and at one Tokyo music school four-year-olds learn to play Bach on miniature pianos and violins. At the Tokyo Culture Hall, children flock to the orchestra pit at intermission time to ogle their heroes—cellists and bassoon players.

Despite their hunger for the new, Japanese still show a marked interest in their heritage. Housewives flock to schools to learn origami (paper folding), flower arrangement and the ancient tea ceremony just as unmarried girls fill charm and beauty schools. More flags are out on holidays, and the man's formal kimono is making a modest comeback. Novelist Yukio Mishima (*Forbidden Colors*) has formed his own private army of 100 men to help restore discipline, patriotism and pride in young Japanese. But many artists are exceptions to the growing preoccupation with Japanese identity. They consider their work to be their passports. Says Novelist (*The Ruined Map*) Kobo Abé: "We have nothing left to mark ourselves as particularly Japanese, and we tend to regard ourselves as people with the same aspirations as our counterparts in the U.S. and Europe. Who asks if Kafka was Czech, Austrian or German? His main mark was that he was modern."

The boom that is propelling Japan toward superpower status has been aided hugely by an unparalleled era of free trade that has prevailed virtually everywhere—except in Japan. Pleading postwar poverty and a paucity of resources, Tokyo's bureaucrats created a hothouse economy, sheltered from foreign competition by a network of quotas, tariffs and other trade barriers.

Some rough spots remain. Japan suffers from a labor shortage. Unemployment runs a mere .8%. Those born in the post-1945 baby boom are already at work; those who arrived afterward tend to spend more time in school. As a result, companies have pushed the retirement age from 55 to 60, are hiring housewives for part-time jobs, and are resisting moves to cut the 48-hour work week to 40 hours. With salaries soaring (a high school graduate who started out at $45 a month two years ago now gets $70), and with workers growing scarcer, some firms have built plants in Seoul and Taiwan in search of that vanishing national asset, cheap labor. Inflation, now running at an annual rate of 5.6%, looms as a serious problem, but the Japanese have not done much to slow down their fast-paced economy. The colorful kimono that went for $170 last year now costs $185, a quarter-pint of home-delivered milk has gone from 50¢ to 64¢, and a 28¢ can of tuna is up to 34¢.

Western economists argue that the yen (360 to $1 at the official rate, 354 on the open market) is undervalued, thus giving Japanese exports an unfair price advantage in world markets. The U.S., with its ailing textile industry, and other Western governments are putting strong pressure on Tokyo either to revalue the yen or to liberalize trade. Reluctant to tamper with their currency, the Japanese are expected to carry out a gradual, grudging reduction of barriers against foreign trade and capital over the next couple of years.

The Weaning Process

Ultimately, a far more vexatious issue than any of Japan's economic problems is the nation's future role in Asia and the world. Japan today simply stands too tall and too rich to maintain a low profile—or no profile—for many more years. "This country," says Finance Minister Takeo Fukudá, "can no longer be permitted to think of our own problems without paying attention to the outside world." Foreign Minister Kiichi Aichi agrees. Writing in *Foreign Affairs* recently, he spoke of the need for "gradually weaning the public away from 'little-Japanism.' "

Events may hasten the process. Britain will complete its east-of-Suez withdrawal next year [1971], as Defense Minister Denis Healey confirmed in a White Paper last week. A partial U.S. stand-down in Asia is in prospect under Richard Nixon's Guam doctrine, as the President confirmed in his "State of the World" message last week [February, 1970]. The West's withdrawal will make it impossible for Japan to keep its head down much longer. Says Harvard's Historian Edwin O. Reischauer, former Ambassador to Tokyo: "The Japanese choice is either a close special relationship with the U.S. or to become a major force on their own. The concept that they can be an elephant-sized Laos is ridiculous."

While some Asian statesmen would welcome more active Japanese diplomatic participation in the region, few relish the idea of a greater military role for their former conquerors. Says Indonesian Foreign Minister Adam Malik: "An armed Japan which grows into another big military power would certainly make many Asian countries apprehensive and insecure." Asian leaders note that the Japanese today command more firepower than the combined imperial forces did during World War II. They know that the country will soon start building 105 Phantom jets under license from the U.S., and that a submarine fleet is in the talking stage. And they have heard talk that Tokyo may one day send warships to patrol the narrow Strait of Malacca to protect its merchant fleet from Indonesian pirates.

For all that, a sizable Japanese military presence is not likely to materialize overnight. Article 9 of the Peace Constitution imposed by the U.S. restricts Japan to defensive forces. To be sure, "defensive" can be interpreted broadly, as both Washington and Moscow have demonstrated; but so far, Japan's Self-Defense Force numbers only

259,400 men, all volunteers and all entitled to quit any time they want to. The searing memory of Hiroshima and Nagasaki and Japan's signing of the nuclear nonproliferation treaty three weeks ago [February, 1970] seem to rule out a nuclear role for the foreseeable future. Japan is technologically capable of building a nuclear arsenal, but such a move would increase Japan's bargain-rate $1.6 million defense bill, less than 1% of its G.N.P. compared with 9.2% for the U.S.

One U.S. diplomat in Asia suggests that Japan may be the first nation to score a breakthrough—a superpower without superweapons. Almost certainly, however, a nuclear-armed China will eventually persuade Japan to exorcise its post-Hiroshima trauma and begin building its own nukes. Unlike Peking, Tokyo has a head start toward a delivery system; two weeks ago [February, 1970], the Japanese became the fourth member of the exclusive space club (others: the U.S., the Soviet Union and France) by putting a 20-lb. satellite into orbit from a launch pad on Kyushu Island.

A key factor in Japan's postwar success has been its political stability. The last election produced a voter turnout of only 68% —low for Japan. One reason was that the Liberal Democrats, who have ruled almost without a break since the occupation, looked like certain winners (and in fact won an overwhelming 300 of 486 Diet seats). The Socialists once gave promise of becoming an effective opposition, but they are still promoting a shopworn Marxism that does not sound too magnetic to Japan's increasingly affluent workers.

Engulfed in Mist

The only parties to improve in the last Diet election were the Communists (up ten seats, to 14) and the *Komeito* (Clean Government) party, the political arm of the Buddhist *Soka Gakkai* (Value-Creation Society), which went from 25 to 47 seats. *Komeito* is building a growing following among blue-collar urban voters by mixing religion, show business and concern for close-to-home issues such as pollution and prices.

Because Japan is still very much a country of slowly cemented consensus, no swift changes are in prospect. Men who are now in their 60s will rule well into the 1970s, and they are cautious and uncertain. "Today's leaders," says Kyoto University Professor Kei Wakaizuma, "resemble mountain climbers who, finding themselves engulfed in mist, sit down to wait until the fog clears." There are, however, a few details that will not wait. The U.S.-Japan mutual security treaty comes up for reconsideration in June [1970]; Sato intends to keep it in effect, though the negotiations are likely to be punctuated by student demonstrations. Sato's majority in the Diet rules out serious parliamentary opposition, and now that he has secured the return of Okinawa from the U.S., the protests may be muted as well.

Richard Nixon has described U.S.-Japanese cooperation as "the linchpin for peace in the Pacific," and last week [February, 1970] he emphasized that a "cooperative relationship" between Tokyo and Washington is a must for the area. William Bundy, former Assistant Secretary of State for the Far East, agrees. Says Bundy, now attached to M.I.T.: "We consult with the British daily on a broad range of issues. We do the same thing with the Japanese, only more deeply and more intensively."

How long the relationship can endure will depend not on U.S. wishes but Japan's own self-interest. Right now, its interests ally it to the U.S., but they could change as Japan enlarges its role in Asia. In *Alternative in Southeast Asia,* former World Bank President Eugene Black argues that "there is very little prospect that Japan will be willing to become a political, much less a military, partner of the U.S. in Southeast Asia." Nor should the U.S. press too hard for such a partnership, he adds, for "the real danger is that we will, wittingly or unwittingly, force the Japanese to choose rearmament rather than cooperation in the years ahead."

Different Dreams

Economist Keiji Sakamoto puts it another way. "If the U.S. produced a chart of where it wants Japan to go in the coming years," he says, "Japan would accept it. But whether it would follow the chart is another matter. We have an expression: 'Dosho imu'—Same bed, different dreams."

Eisaku Sato's dream, as he expressed it in a speech two weeks ago [February, 1970] is to make the 1970s "an era when Japan's national power will carry unprecedented weight in world affairs." Japan should be a "content but not arrogant" country, he said, whose example would inspire "the whole world to agree that the human race is far richer for Japan's existence." Whether Japan can serve as a model for the rest of the world, or even the rest of Asia, is, however, doubtful. In climate, in resources, but above all, in the will and skill of its people, the country is unique.

That, of course, is Japan's strength. It has also proved to be an endless source of fascination for Western travelers, who are invariably, and rightly, enchanted by the rugged beauty of its mountains and the exquisite manners of its people. For one of Japan's earliest Western advocates, Lafcadio Hearn, the main thing was "the viewless pressure of numberless past generations" at work in the country. These days the focus is on the future generations of Japan. No one knows what pressures they will feel, but one thing is certain: Japan will, as Sato says, carry weight.

Poet, educator, and ambassador to the world, Tagore wrote this poem on the last day of the nineteenth century. The next seventy-odd years were to prove more bloody than the previous one hundred. Already, deaths due to war in the twentieth century are nearly 100 million, compared to less than 30 million in the nineteenth. Will the words of Tagore apply to the sunset of the twentieth century? Perhaps to the sunset of the world?

The Sunset of the Century

Rabīndranāth Tagore

1

The last sun of the century sets amidst the blood-red clouds of the
    West and the whirlwind of hatred.
The naked passion of self-love of Nations, in its drunken delirium of
    greed, is dancing to the clash of steel and the howling verses of
    vengeance.

2

The hungry self of the Nation shall burst in a violence of fury from
    its own shameless feeding.
For it has made the world its food.
And licking it, crunching it, and swallowing it in big morsels,
It swells and swells,
Till in the midst of its unholy feast descends the sudden shaft of
    heaven piercing its heart of grossness.

3

The crimson glow of light on the horizon is not the light of thy dawn
    of peace, my Motherland.
It is the glimmer of the funeral pyre burning to ashes the vast flesh—
    the self-love of the Nation—dead under its own excess.
Thy morning waits behind the patient dark of the East,
Meek and silent.

4

Keep watch, India.
Bring your offerings of worship for that sacred sunrise.
Let the first hymn of its welcome sound in your voice and sing
"Come, Peace, thou daughter of God's own great suffering.
Come with thy treasure of contentment, the sword of fortitude,
And meekness crowning thy forehead."

5

Be not ashamed, my brothers, to stand before the proud and the
  powerful
With your white robe of simpleness.
Let your crown be of humility, your freedom the freedom of the soul.
Build God's throne daily upon the ample bareness of your poverty
And know that what is huge is not great and pride is not everlasting.

Questions

1 Which society offers more to the world in the long run—
  contemporary India, China, or Japan?

2 Many people say that Far Eastern nations must engage
  in programs providing for modernization and progress.
  Is this correct and, if so, why?

3 Southeast and Southwest Asia have been omitted from
  this chapter because of limited space. What influence do
  these areas have on the rest of Asia and the world?

4 The twentieth century may well go down in history as the
  American century. The twenty-first, predictions indicate,
  will be the Japanese. But Mao Tse-tung is sure the
  twenty-first will be the Chinese century. Is this possible?

5 How does the Soviet Union rate presently in the Far East
  and how will it rate in the future?

6 Must the competition for raw materials for use in industry—a competition which is using up the earth's resources—continue?

7 What myths, canons, and hangups of both East and West
  should be eliminated or modified?

9

Characteristics of
the Mid-Twentieth Century

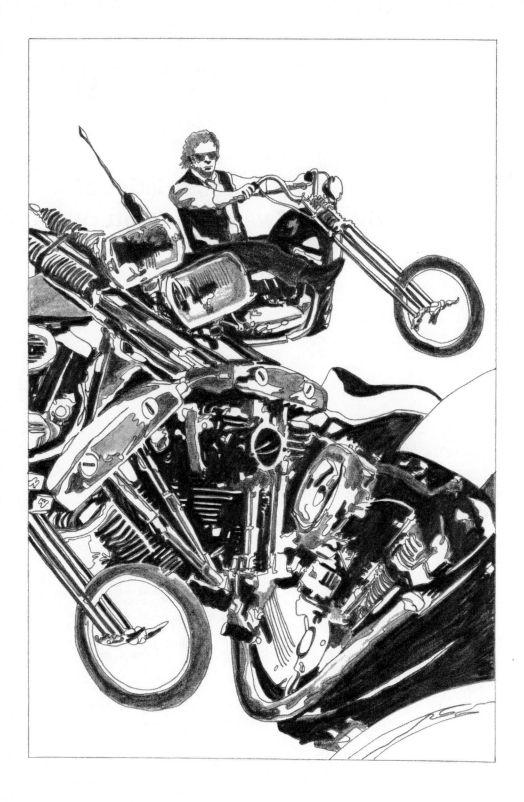

What is the most important event of the period 1945–1970? What age-old problems are now on the verge of being resolved as a result of changes which occurred during those twenty-five years? What new problems have arisen during that time? Has technology helped or hurt man's quest for happiness? These are some of the questions raised in the following descriptive analysis of the years 1945–1970. If you have lived during any portion of that twenty-five year period, you can check the author's statements against your own personal experiences. For, to the extent that you lived through that tumultous time, you are an original historical source.

From Hiroshima to Heart Transplants

Melvin Steinfield

The twenty-five years between 1945 and 1970 constituted the most paradoxical period of man's history on earth. Never before was man so close to the solution of major problems that had long haunted him and long challenged his ingenuity. Yet never before was he so close to total annihilation by his own hands or by forces which he had set into motion and could no longer control.

It was an era of unprecedented change and of incredible, mind-boggling acceleration of the rate of change. Yet some elements of continuity with the past and some hangups persisted stubbornly despite the frenzied atmosphere of hectic change. The polarization of man's potential reached the most disparate extremes imaginable: man could, in 1970, look forward optimistically to a near-Utopia of materialistic affluence and individual self-fulfillment; he could also foresee the possibility of being swallowed up in the maelstrom of nationalistic suicide or environmental pollution or technological revolution. Man was schizoid, and he had every right to be, for the humanistic quality of his life—as well as his very survival—was being threatened significantly.

By 1970, Western man's sense of community was dissipating. How different he was from the ancient Greeks who could identify with their *polis* and feel a warm sense of belonging and of responsibility and of purpose. Modern man, in contrast, had become alienated. Alienated from his impersonal governments, from his mechanical gadgets, from his dehumanizing environment, from his illogical traditions, from his out-of-touch elders, from his irrelevant school systems, and from his confused self.

Tormented by the bewildering pace of change, he tried to make sense out of the recent flow of history. Historians started to concoct their labels as they tried to describe the nature of the post-war world. The period between 1945 and 1970, they wrote, was:

The Atomic Age
The Jet Age
The Space Age
The Computer Age
The Nuclear Age

It was also:

The Age of Anxiety
The Age of American Supremacy
The Age of Technology
The Age of Specialization

In another context, 1945–1970 was the Era of the Cold War. It was also the Era of the Generation Gap. The variety of labels indicates the conflicting trends and dominant features of a frenzied age which defied simplistic labels.

When the period began in 1945, the world recoiled in horror when the full extent of Nazi brutality and bestiality in concentration camps was reported. Yet the Atomic Bomb was exploded twice over dense civilian population centers. As the period drew to a close in 1970, the great powers were conferring about limitations of arms. Yet arms budgets continued to soar to astronomical expenditure levels. It was, in other words, *An Age of Paradoxes.*

In an age of paradoxes, prosperous Western countries paid their farmers to refrain from planting crops because the surpluses were already rotting away in government warehouses. Meanwhile, the bellies of Biafrans and Indians ached for lack of food, and the mouths of many Americans hurled forth the anguished cries of hunger. People were starving, but Senator Eastland of Mississippi got his farmer's allotment check at the same time that the price of wheat was pumped up to artificially high levels.

The United Nations was born in 1945 amid desperate hopes that it had to work for the sake of life on the earth. In 1970, when it was twenty-five years old, most of the causes of the first two world wars persisted and the spectre of thermonuclear warfare—not to mention its superfluous extras such as biological and chemical warfare—haunted men's consciousness. Ministries of Defense continued to wage aggressive wars of expansion, and a country with Peace Corps personnel in Africa dropped napalm on civilians in Asia.

While men were walking on the surface of the moon, newspapers were still printing "Your Daily Horoscope" for millions of ardent readers who retained faith in astrological forecasts. And as the divorce rates of the industrialized countries skyrocketed, troubled partners of dissolving marriages found that if they couldn't bring themselves to communicate with a marriage counselor together, they could at least read "Dear Abby" separately.

The Computer Society, with a number for everyone, created uncertainty about the future of mankind as it projected with increasing accuracy the trends of overpopulation. The more certain we became about population increases, the more uncertain we grew about sources of food supply, or quality of air, or simple living space.

Medical researchers were making outstanding progress in the prevention and cure of such diseases as polio, measles, and mumps; yet more people were dying of cancer than ever before. And, as everyone knows, the common cold resisted successfully the onslaught of vaporizers, atomizers, decongestants, antihistamines, "wonder drugs," and tea with honey.

Automobiles were being built with more safety features than Western man had hangups; yet, despite seatbelts, windshield-defoggers, and shatterproof glass, the number of deaths from automobile accidents in America alone between 1945 and 1970 was greater than the entire population of San Francisco, California!

Perhaps the most pathetic paradox of those twenty-five incredible years came toward the end of the 1960s. The heart of a black man, Clive Haupt, was transplanted into the living body of a white man, Dr. Philip Blaiberg. Dr. Blaiberg lived for nearly two years after the heart transplant. Clive Haupt, the heart donor, was buried in a segregated black cemetery in South Africa. This strange, illogical mixture of scientific progress and social prejudice illustrated a truism of the age: technology had failed to solve the pressing human needs of the mid-twentieth century.

Nevertheless, people were becoming caught up in the opulence of an industrialized world; it was difficult to avoid becoming enmeshed in the network of gadgets and gimmicks which poured forth in amazing array. About the only things that were not invented and marketed during this period were low-calorie chlorophyll beer and electronic fornicators for men. Everything else had been thought of. There were nylon carpets, Banlon T-shirts, Orlon sweaters, Acrilan socks, and rayon underwear. This was the period of push-button telephones, push-button shifts on cars, push-button dishwashers, push-button computers, and push-button warfare. The aerosol can could get rid of bathroom odors, mouth odors, and body odors, plus keep your hair in place, paint your boat, or make heated foam for shaving. There was wrinkle-proof clothing, waterproof paper, fireproof building materials, and frost-free refrigerators. Remote-control dials could change the channel on your television set or open your garage doors. Electricity had a field day: there were electric knives, electric pencil sharpeners, electric toothbrushes, electric typewriters, and electric blankets. Food-processing inventions occurred faster than could be digested, as food was frozen, dehydrated, fortified, enriched, sprayed, and cleansed.

Man was bombarded with technological improvements, but he did not find happiness. An increase in human neuroses and psychoses accompanied the increase in materialistic affluence. Some people felt there was a connection between the two. Dr. Daniel P. Moynihan, special advisor to President Richard Nixon, stated toward the end of the era that most of the ills of modern life can be traced ultimately to technology: "Public officials are particularly aware of this as they struggle daily with the problems of waters polluted by technology, underprivileged populations displaced by technology, drivers and pedestrians maimed by technology, cities choked with technology, and air fouled by technology."[1]

Dr. Moynihan argued that drug use increased during the recent period because people felt they needed drugs due to the onslaught of our environment by technology. His solution:

> It is as simple and complex as that. A society in which people do not need drugs. In which the young are not afraid to grow up. In which the poor are not more interested in death than life. In which the colors of the cityscape and the countryside are so much more beautiful than anything to be attained by hallucinogenic chemicals that the use of them seems counterfeit simply because it will be counterfeit: an experience that does not reward but cheats.[2]

Increased drug dependence was symptomatic of the general ailment of a society saddled with too much leisure time and ambiguous purpose. The upward spiral of consumption did not lead to ultimate contentment because humanistic values were ignored. Sometimes there was a reaction against the superabundant materialism which technology and mass production had made possible. One of the greatest ironies was the utter disbelief of parents (who had lived through the insecurity of the Depression years) that their children (the young people of the sixties) were actually rejecting the world of economic involvement.

Frequently, the reaction against the Era of Prosperity extended beyond the narrow confines of intra-family generation-gaps. The instant awareness by the "have-nots" of Western society's abundance, made possible by rapid communication via television, posed a potential threat to the "haves." How much longer could the have-nots stand to see the accoutrements of affluence flaunted in their face every nine minutes by a television commercial without reaching the boiling point of rage? Weren't the have-nots entitled to a larger share of the gigantic pie of prosperity? The revolution of rising expectations carried with it the irony that the closer a group got to its goal, the more impatient it became and the less tolerant it was of its disadvantaged position. Tensions among rival power-seeking groups heightened as prosperity spread toward all the corners of the world.

Technology, in other words, was assisting in the spread of the democratic ideal of equality, and this meant that it was helping to propel a revolutionary force. Colonial peoples fought to break the yoke of imperial domination; national minorities fought to gain a greater measure of self-determination and equality. Women and students, and other traditionally disenfranchised or disadvantaged groups, took collective action to press vigorously forward in their drive for power, freedom, and equal rights.

The Age of Liberation led to a weakening of many barriers against specific groups. Superficial signs were seen in the liberation of dress styles, hair styles, and life styles. Hippie colonies flourished in the sixties just as beatniks and bohemians flourished in the fifties. These surface signs reflected the awkward adjustment period Western countries were experiencing. Men and women began to reevaluate their respective sex-differentiated roles. People in general were racking their brains, preoccupied with finding their identities.

It was not easy to find one's identity in the technological age of specialization. Nor was it easy to understand what others were doing. Painting had become so specialized that ordinary citizens, including those who passed college art appreciation courses, found it difficult to comprehend, let alone appreciate, the meaning or techniques of abstract art. To Mary Martini as well as to Joe Six-Pack, what the artist said was "Mother and Child, #3" looked more like a drunken monkey regurgitating on a combination pizza.

The academic world furnished the best examples of the degree of specialization of the age. For example, in 1964 a candidate for the degree of Master of Arts at one college had to demonstrate a command of "either Latin or Greek, and of Hebrew or Arabic, plus at least one other Oriental language (such as Akkadian, Ugaritic, or Egyptian)."[3] In addition, there was a "language requirement" of "one modern foreign language (ordinarily French or German)". Plus, of course, English. With his command of these five languages, the candidate for a Master of Arts degree in Mediterranean Studies at Brandeis University was eligible to enroll in the following course: "MEDITERRANEAN STUDIES 109, Akkadian Documents from the Amarna Age." Or he could enroll in "MEDITERRANEAN STUDIES 201, The Cuneiform Records of Anatolia and Adjacent Areas." If he knew how to read "Assyrian cuneiform," he was eligible for "MEDITERRANEAN STUDIES 301, Late Assyrian Civilization." After earning his master's degree, said candidate could pursue his studies for a doctorate. That is, if he showed a command of one other modern European language. With his Ph.D. in Mediterranean Studies, the young man of the 1960s was now equipped . . . to teach Mediterranean Studies.

Increased specialization made possible the pushing back of the frontiers of knowledge to farther outposts, but it also introduced much that was remote from traditional patterns of understanding. A new void was created by the new specialization: the void of synthesis. What did it all mean? How did knowledge in one special field relate to knowledge in another special field? Who would be able to integrate the many diverse and specialized discoveries of increasingly delimited and demarcated fields of inquiry? A new sense of urgency arose toward the end of the period, for people felt that science was compartmentalizing life and that humanity was being engulfed by automation.

Was there any way out of the paradoxical dilemma? Science and technology had made the twenty-five years of the post war world what they were: a mixture of solutions and problems, affluence and anxiety, advances and regressions. These trends were most discernible in the advanced industrialized nations of the Western world, such as Britain, France, Germany, and also in some of the advanced non-Western countries, such as Australia and Japan. But by far the most progressive country, for good and bad, was the United States of America. The world took note of America's rapid rise as a world power during the early part of the century. Now, in the twenty-five years since 1945, its influence had come to exceed that of Rome in the period of the Empire or Britain during the nineteenth century. The world was becoming industrialized and Americanized. In the shadow of the Egyptian pyramids stood Coca Cola stands, and the Cairo Hilton offered Western luxury accommodations. There was, of course, mutual influence: Elvis Presley took Europe by storm, only to be followed by the Beatles' invasion of America. In some ways, humanity did seem to be moving closer to one world, or at least toward a homogeneous culture. Middle-class Americans drove Toyotas or Datsuns from Japan or Volkswagens from Germany, and they admired Fellini and Mastroianni just as much as the Germans admired John Wayne.

Although Americans began to reduce their overseas commitments toward the end of the period, the Yankee influence was destined to linger for a long time. And the rest of the world, now introduced to the American—and therefore the Western—way of life, would never be the same.

In 1945 the period began in horror and hope when those atomic bombs were dropped on people in Japan. In 1970 it was ending in hope and anxiety. Every year produced at least several shooting wars, and there was Korea and Vietnam and the Middle East, but total war did not break out. If technology was fingered as the cause of so much that was new and bad in the world, it was still the best avenue for escape. It might have created many of the current problems, but the more advanced technology of the future would solve them. Technological aids, such as pills, drugs, tranquilizers, and stimulants, had already provided many people the means of escape from the harsh threats of daily existence. And many people still had faith that technology could create plastic bubble-tops over cities with smog problems in order that the whole outdoors could be air-conditioned and pollution-free. This was the Age of Technology, and technology could work wonders.

But even in 1970 there was that back-of-the brain anxiety about the long-term future as men realized that they were nowhere near the Utopia they had imagined a few years ago. As the new decade of the seventies underlined the very real possibility of both Utopia and Holocaust, men and women entered the future with mixed emotions. They wondered about the threshold they sensed they were approaching.

Notes

1 James Cary, "Rising Drug Use Declared Result of Technology," *San Diego Union,* December 7, 1969, p. A-12.

2 *Ibid.*

3 Brandeis University *Bulletin,* 1963–64, Graduate School of Arts and Sciences, pp. 112–115.

The sudden increase in leisure time has created an unprecedented challenge to man's traditional attitudes toward work and careers. The following discussion provides a concise orientation to the wider implications of leisure time in an advanced industrialized nation.

How Do You Have Fun in Heaven?

D. J. R. Bruckner

Recently a national press wire service reported a survey which indicated that Americans are moving towards a three-day weekend, officially through the device of Monday holidays and unofficially as more businesses run half-days on Fridays. In an age when the minds of men are dominated by quickly-communicated images, the fascination of our days robs us of the meaning of our lives; and this little survey is passed over as unimportant, while in fact it might be the big story of our times.

The long weekend is part of a steady development. Within a long lifetime, the working career of men has grown shorter at both ends, and the hours of work in a week have shrunk from 60 or even 72 only 80 years ago, to 40 or 35. At the same time, both population and wealth have grown enormously; increasingly, the great industrial machine of this society runs itself. For most people, the variety of work is also expanding: increasing numbers change not only jobs, but careers, several times in a life.

Most work has always been drudgery, and the end of it is not to be wept over. But the growth of freedom of time requires a profound revolution of life: human life, for the individual an experience never to be repeated. A man who is now old looked forward, when he was young, to spending up to 25% of his total time of life on the job. A young man now may expect to spend less than 10% of his life making a living. But the society continues to plan and schedule work as it did 80 years ago; systematically, we are wasting our lives.

It is wonderful to have so much free time, but the life of freedom often seems to us like the life of a French prisoner described by Genet. It would have been, he says, a simple, easy life if it were being lived by anyone but us.

Most attempts to reschedule life have been frustrating. We retire men at set ages without considering that some work is best done by older men of deep judgment. We lengthen education to prepare for work without testing the real need or value of that education, and without considering the effect on the young of so long a withdrawal from productive work. It would seem that a man might spend his 10% of life at work in large, coherent segments interspersed with times of creativity and education; but we continue to stretch out his life in a long procession of short, tedious days and weeks.

Some ways should be found, it would seem, to open up all the gates of life and profession, to allow a man to pass in and out of the system—industry, education, government, even idleness—with much greater freedom, at times of his own choosing, and with no loss of advantage or honor. One would guess that this is the next great revolution of life in this country; the development of the industrial system itself is demanding it. The two great crimes against the order of life have always been rebellion and futility; our rescheduling of life is producing the futility, and that is giving rise to the rebellion right now.

Much of the bewilderment of the young and of their parents springs from this radical reordering of the times of life and of its priorities. It is a painful period for a young man to enter the world. Necessarily, and increasingly, he is thrown back on himself. It is no longer truthful to teach him skills as though making his living were to be his life or even his life's chief work; it is no longer pertinent to prepare him for a career if we consider a career as one job or a series of jobs.

One senses that we may have misread all the signs of the upheavals of the past decade. Political disorders and social chaos may be only spinoffs from the central processes of change; and if we continue to be occupied with them, in crisis situations, as though they were in fact our biggest problems, we may miss altogether the chance to impose a human orientation on work, on time, on our own goals and satisfactions—which are, after all, the essential operating factors of our lives, those lives which each of us will never live again.

An Associate Justice of the United States Supreme Court, famous as a
world traveler, and no alarmist, stresses the urgent need for a regime of
law. He emphasizes the positive events of the recent past which can provide
the basis for establishing better international arbitration. The tone is
urgent; the outlook is positive. It is the view of a concerned optimist.
Perhaps it is overly optimistic?

The End of the Road

William O. Douglas

Every man, whatever his race or national origin, has a deep-seated
instinct for survival; and the nuclear age underlines for all of us the
increasing risks of turning our cities and factories into nuclear in-
cinerators.

War today is too awful and too expensive to consider. In the old
days a war could be a healthy thing; it could generate a good Chur-
chillian feeling of strong men and proud women. But in the present
the ancient solution of armed force applied to international disputes
will eventually mean the destruction of all our great countries—the
United States, China, Japan, and Russia, and it would spell the end
of civilization as we know it. We have arrived at the end of the road
as far as war is concerned.

The whole sweep of recorded history tells us graphically that preparedness and armaments races ultimately lead to war. There is no
such thing as a deterrent power; there is no such thing as preparing
against an aggressor. The more one nation arms, the more another
follows suit. In the end, an evitable collision will bring us to the ultimate confrontation.

The search for alternatives must begin. The problem is not an
easy one; solutions will not appear overnight. The world needs a new
and wholly different approach, a fresh mood, so that the peoples on
this planet can find in their common bond of humanity a rule for
living to take the place of the rule of destruction and death.

In the nineteen-fifties the United States entered an era of political
bankruptcy. Politicians aped the generals and admirals, and everyone
in America became a military expert. Where should we put the

From "Recipe for Survival: An Untried Approach in an Unprecedented Age"
by William O. Douglas. Reprinted by permission from October 1969 Center
Occasional Paper, *Asian Dilemma: United States, Japan and China,* a publication of The Center for the Study of Democratic Institutions in Santa Barbara,
California.

Seventh Fleet, the Fifth Fleet, or the Sixth Fleet? The troops, the planes, the bases, and the missiles? By now America is spending two and a half billion dollars a month in Vietnam, and the budget for the Pentagon has reached eighty billion dollars this year [1969].

Man is unruly; man is ambitious; man is greedy; man is over-reaching. Nations are made up of men, and accidents happen.

Washington fears Peking; Tokyo is afraid of Moscow; and Russia and China hasten to arm against the West.

When, at the height of his power, Nikita Khrushchev suggested some elementary steps toward a new kind of world security, he was laughed off the front pages of American newspapers. Silly old Mr. Khrushchev! His ridiculous suggestion was that the nations of the world should try to agree upon the amicable settlement of boundary questions and territorial disputes—the beginning of a rule of law in world affairs. Silly old Mr. Khrushchev?

The time has come for Japan and Russia, and eventually China, to sit down with the United States to work out a consensus, to lay down the ground rules for settling international disputes. In America fifty sovereign states submit their conflicts to judicial arbitration without bloodshed. Why not in the world at large?

The countries of the world today need to establish specialized institutions through which many kinds of conflict can be channeled. When we realize that between 1917 and 1968 the United States worked out forty-seven treaties with Soviet Russia, twenty-five of them still in operation, we can understand that legal solutions to our conflicts are not entirely Utopian. How many nations today belong to the Postal Union? *Every one.* These were miniscule treaties aimed at tiny problems, but they contain the ingredients from which a cooperative world regime can one day develop. These little treaties form the first part of a great mosaic that will, if we try, culminate in a world rule of law.

Some machinery exists—the Commission on Human Rights and the International Court of Justice. From the days of John Foster Dulles, the jurisdiction of the International Court has been subject to American approval when the United States is being sued, the so-called Connally Amendment. Eighty-five nations followed the American lead, including the U.S.S.R. The views of John Foster Dulles and the politburo in Moscow are almost identical. When nations will not accept obligatory jurisdiction, they cannot enforce it on others. The International Court has never handled more than six cases in any one year. Last year it had one.

If there is to be a new age in Asia, Japan, China, and the United

States must initially take the lead. Japan is not an American client state. Her achievements in education, science, technology, marketing, diplomacy, and law place her among the great powers. Since I started my Asian journeys twenty years ago, I have felt that of all the Asian nations Japan and India, once freed from American military excitement, could, with China, best produce a regime of law to supplant the present regime of force.

The starting point must be with Japan and the United States. Unilateral action is not the course. Japan and the United States need to reevaluate the entire Asian scene, and each must decide what role to play in developing peaceful resolutions of rivalries and conflicts.

China is, of course, the exponent of a highly competitive ideology. Peking inspires many developing peoples or individuals seeking escape from some form of feudalism that entraps them. Once, the United States was also revolutionary in the sense that it inspired people to revolt. World problems are not soluble if every nation but one must surrender that role and agree not to excite revolution. Coexistence—indeed coevolution—is a necessary tenet of any new world order.

An autopsy of the old order is not helpful. The aim should be building cooperative Asian patterns whereby national boundaries are fixed and guaranteed, where trade and commerce are freely developed, where diplomacy holds sway, and where international tribunals or agencies are created to arbitrate, compromise; or adjudicate conflicting claims among nations.

Asia, dominated by Japan, India, and China, can easily lead the world in showing how a regional regime of the rule of law can flourish.

Do you remember Earth Day in April, 1970? In a similar framework of
concern, the following selection skillfully portrays the many faces of
environmental pollution. It is a frightening picture of the era just beginning.
Is it too late to reverse the destructive elements in these trends?

The Technological Frankenstein

Lord Ritchie-Calder

To hell with posterity! After all, what have the unborn ever done
for us? Nothing. Did they, with sweat and misery, make the Industrial
Revolution possible? Did they go down into the carboniferous forests
of millions of years ago to bring up coal to make wealth and see nine-
tenths of the carbon belched out as chimney soot? Did they drive
the plows that broke the plains to release the dust that the buffalo
had trampled and fertilized for centuries? Did they have to broil in
steel plants to make the machines and see the pickling acids poured
into the sweet waters of rivers and lakes? Did they have to labor to
cut down the tall timbers to make homesteads and provide newsprint
for the Sunday comics and the celluloid for Hollywood spectaculars,
leaving the hills naked to the eroding rains and winds? Did they have
the ingenuity to drill down into the Paleozoic seas to bring up the
oil to feed the internal-combustion engines so that their exhausts
could create smog? Did they have the guts to man rigs out at sea so
that boreholes could probe for oil in the offshore fissures of the San
Andreas Fault? Did they endure the agony and the odium of the
atom bomb and spray the biosphere with radioactive fallout? All that
the people yet unborn have done is to wait and let us make the mistakes. To hell with posterity! That, too, can be arranged. As Shelley
wrote: "Hell is a city much like London, a populous and smoky city."

At a conference held at Princeton, New Jersey, at the end of 1968,
Professor Kingsley Davis, one of the greatest authorities on urban development, took the role of hell's realtor. The prospectus he offered
from his latest survey of world cities was hair-raising. He showed
that thirty-eight per cent of the world's population is already living
in what are defined as "urban places." Over one-fifth of the world's
population is living in cities of a hundred thousand or more. Over
375,000,000 people are living in cities of a million and over. On

From "Polluting the Environment" by Lord Ritchie-Calder, *The Center Magazine,* May, 1969, pp. 7–12. Reprinted by permission from the May 1969 issue
of *The Center Magazine,* a publication of The Center for the Study of Democratic Institutions in Santa Barbara, California.

present trends it will take only fifteen years for half the world's population to be living in cities, and in fifty-five years everyone will be urbanized.

Davis foresaw that within the lifetime of a child born today, on present rates of population increase, there will be fifteen billion people to be fed and housed—over four times as many as now. The whole human species will be living in cities of a million and over and the biggest city will have 1,300,000,000 inhabitants. Yes, 1.3 billion. That is 186 times as many as there are in Greater London today.

In his forebodings of Dystopia (with a "y" as in dyspepsia, but it could just as properly be "Dis," after the ruler of the Underworld), Doxiades has warned about the disorderly growth of cities, oozing into each other like confluent ulcers. He has given us Ecumenopolis— World City. The East Side of Ecumenopolis would have as its Main Street the Eurasian Highway, stretching from Glasgow to Bangkok, with the Channel tunnel as an underpass and a built-up area all the way. West Side, divided not by railroad tracks but by the Atlantic, is already emerging (or, rather, merging) in the United States. There is talk, and evidence, of "Boswash," the urban development of a built-up area from Boston to Washington. On the Pacific Coast, with Los Angeles already sprawling into the desert, the realtor's garden cities, briskly reenforced by industrial estates, are slurring into one another and presently will stretch all the way from San Diego to San Francisco. The Main Street of Sansan will be Route 101. This is insansanity. We do not need a crystal ball to foresee what Davis and Doxiades are predicting—we can see it through smog-colored spectacles; we can smell it seventy years away because it is in our nostrils today; a blind man can see what is coming.

Are these trends inevitable? They are unless we do something about them. I have given up predicting and have taken to prognosis. There is a very important difference. Prediction is based on the projection of trends. Experts plan for the trends and thus confirm them. They regard warnings as instructions. For example, while I was lecturing in that horror city of Calcutta, where three-quarters of the population live in shacks without running water or sewage disposal, and, in the monsoon season, wade through their own floating excrement, I warned that within twenty-five years there would be in India at least five cities, each with populations of over sixty million, ten times bigger than Calcutta. I was warning against the drift into the great conurbations now going on, which has been encouraged by ill-conceived policies of industrialization. I was warning against imitating the German Ruhr, the British Black Country, and America's Pittsburgh. I was arguing for "population dams," for decentralized development based on the villages, which make up the traditional cultural and social pattern of India. These "dams" would prevent the flash floods of population into overpopulated areas. I was *warning,* but they accepted the prediction and ignored the warning. Soon thereafter I learned that an American university had been given a contract to make a feasibility study for a city of sixty million people north of Bombay. When enthusiasts get busy on a feasibility study, they invariably find that it is feasible. When they get to their drawing boards they have a whale of a time. They design skyscrapers above ground and subterranean tenements below ground. They work out minimal requirements of air and hence how much breathing space a family can survive in. They design "living-units," hutches for battery-fed people who are stacked together like kindergarten blocks. They provide water and regulate the sewage on the now well-established cost-efficiency principles of factory-farming. And then they finish up convinced that this is the most economical way of housing people. I thought I had scotched the idea by making representations through influential Indian friends. I asked them, among other things, how many mental hospitals they were planning to take care of the millions who would surely go mad under such conditions. But I have heard rumors that the planners are so slide-rule happy they are planning a city for six hundred million.

Prognosis is something else again. An intelligent doctor, having diagnosed the symptoms and examined the patient's condition, does not say (except in soap operas): "You have six months to live." He says: "Frankly, your condition is serious. Unless you do so-and-so, and unless I do so-and-so, it is bound to deteriorate." The operative phrase is "do so-and-so." One does not have to plan *for* trends; if they are socially undesirable our duty is to plan *away* from them, and treat the symptoms before they become malignant.

A multiplying population multiplies the problems. The prospect of a world of fifteen billion people is intimidating. Three-quarters of the world's present population is inadequately fed—hundreds of millions are not getting the food necessary for well-being. So it is not just a question of quadrupling the present food supply; it means six to eight times that to take care of present deficiencies. It is not a matter of numbers, either; it is the *rate* of increase that mops up any improvements. Nor is it just a question of housing but of clothing and material satisfactions—automobiles, televisions, and the rest. That means greater inroads on natural resources, the steady destruction of amenities, and the conflict of interest between those who want oil and those who want oil-free beaches, or between those who want to get from here to there on wider and wider roads and those whose homes are going to collapse in mud slides because of the making of those roads. Lewis Mumford has suggested that civilization really began with the making of containers—cans, non-returnable bottles, cartons, plastic bags, none of which can be redigested by nature. Every sneeze accounts for a personal tissue. Multiply that by fifteen billion.

Environmental pollution is partly rapacity and partly a conflict of interest between the individual, multimillions of individuals, and the commonweal; but largely, in our generation, it is the exaggerated effects of specialization with no sense of ecology, i.e. the balance of nature. Claude Bernard, the French physiologist, admonished his colleagues over a century ago: "True sciences teaches us to doubt and in ignorance to refrain." Ecologists feel their way with a detector through a minefield of doubts. Specialists, cocksure of their own facts, push ahead, regardless of others.

Behind the sky-high fences of military secrecy, the physicists produced the atomic bomb—just a bigger explosion—without taking into account the biological effects of radiation. Prime Minister Attlee, who consented to the dropping of the bomb on Hiroshima, later said that no one, not Churchill, nor members of the British Cabinet, nor he himself, knew of the possible genetic effects of the blast. "If the scientists knew, they never told us." Twenty years before, Hermann Muller had shown the genetic effects of radiation and had been awarded the Nobel Prize, but he was a biologist and security treated this weapon as a physicist's bomb. In the peacetime bomb-testing, when everyone was alerted to the biological risks, we were told that the fallout of radioactive materials could be localized in the testing grounds. The radioactive dust on The Lucky Dragon, which was fishing well beyond the proscribed area, disproved that. Nevertheless, when it was decided to explode the H-bomb the assurance about localization was blandly repeated. The H-bomb would punch a hole into the stratosphere and the radioactive gases would dissipate. One of those gases is radioactive krypton, which decays into radioactive strontium, a particulate. Somebody must have known that but nobody worried unduly because it would happen above the troposphere, which might be described as the roof of the weather system. What was definitely overlooked was the fact that the troposphere is not continuous. There is the equatorial troposphere and the polar troposphere and they overlap. The radioactive strontium came back through the transom and was spread all over the world by the climatic jet streams to be deposited as rain. The result is that there is radiostrontium (which did not exist in nature) in the bones of every young person who was growing up during the bomb-testing—every young person, everywhere in the world. It may be medically insignificant but it is the brandmark of the Atomic Age generation and a reminder of the mistakes of their elders.

When the mad professor of fiction blows up his laboratory and then himself, that's O.K., but when scientists and decision-makers act out of ignorance and pretend it is knowledge, they are using the biosphere, the living space, as an experimental laboratory. The whole world is put in hazard. And they do it even when they are told not to. During the International Geophysical Year, the Van Allen Belt was discovered. The Van Allen Belt is a region of magnetic phenomena. Immediately the bright boys decided to carry out an experiment and explode a hydrogen bomb in the Belt to see if they could produce an artificial aurora. The colorful draperies, the luminous skirts of the aurora, are caused by drawing cosmic particles magnetically through the rare gases of the upper atmosphere. It is called ionization and is like passing electrons through the vacuum tubes of our familiar neon lighting. It was called the Rainbow Bomb. Every responsible scientist in cosmology, radio-astronomy, and physics of the atmosphere protested against this tampering with a system we did not understand. They exploded their bomb. They got their pyrotechnics. We still do not know the price we may have to pay for this artificial magnetic disturbance.

We could blame the freakish weather on the Rainbow Bomb but, in our ignorance, we could not sustain the indictment. Anyway, there are so many other things happening that could be responsible. We can look with misgiving on the tracks in the sky—the white tails of the jet aircraft and the exhausts of space rockets. These are introducing into the climatic system new factors, the effects of which are immensurable. The triggering of rain clouds depends upon the water vapor having a toehold, a nucleus, on which to form. That is how artificial precipitation, so-called rainmaking, is produced. So the jets, crisscrossing the weather system, playing tic-tac-toe, can produce a man-made change of climate.

On the longer term, we can see even more drastic effects from the many activities of *Homo insapiens,* Unthinking Man. In 1963, at the United Nations Science and Technology Conference, we took stock of the several effects of industrialization on the total environment.

The atmosphere is not only the air which humans, animals, and plants breathe; it is the envelope which protects living things from harmful radiation from the sun and outer space. It is also the medium of climate, the winds and the rain. These are inseparable from the hydrosphere, including the oceans, which cover seven-tenths of the earth's surface with their currents and evaporation; and from the biosphere, with the vegetation and its transpiration and photosynthesis; and from the lithosphere, with its minerals, extracted for man's increasing needs. Millions of years ago the sun encouraged the growth of the primeval forests, which became our coal, and the life-growth in the Paleozoic seas, which became our oil. Those fossil-fuels, locked in the vaults through eons of time, are brought out by modern man and put back into the atmosphere from the chimney stacks and exhaust pipes of modern engineering.

This is an overplus on the natural carbon. About six billion tons of primeval carbon are mixed with the atmosphere every year. During the past century, in the process of industrialization, with its burning of fossil-fuels, more than four hundred billion tons of carbon have been artificially introduced into the atmosphere. The concentration in the air we breathe has been increased by approximately ten per cent; if all the known reserves of coal and oil were burned the concentration would be ten times greater.

This is something more than a public-health problem, more than a question of what goes into the lungs of the individual, more than a question of smog. The carbon cycle in nature is a self-adjusting mechanism. One school of scientific thought stresses that carbon monoxide can reduce solar radiation. Another school points out that an increase in carbon dioxide raises the temperature at the earth's surface. They are both right. Carbon dioxide, of course, is indispensable for plants and hence for the food cycle of creatures, including humans. It is the source of life. But a balance is maintained by excess carbon being absorbed by the seas. The excess is now taxing this absorption, and the effect on the heat balance of the earth can be significant because of what is known as "the greenhouse effect." A greenhouse lets in the sun's rays and retains the heat. Similarly, carbon dioxide, as a transparent diffusion, does likewise; it admits the radiant heat and keeps the convection heat close to the surface. It has been estimated that at the present rate of increase (those six billion tons a year) the mean annual temperature all over the world might increase by 5.8° F. in the next forty to fifty years.

Experts may argue about the time factor or about the effects, but certain things are observable not only in the industrialized Northern Hemisphere but also in the Southern Hemisphere. The ice of the north polar seas is thinning and shrinking. The seas, with their blanket of carbon dioxide, are changing their temperatures with the result that marine life is increasing and transpiring more carbon dioxide. With this combination, fish are migrating, even changing their latitudes. On land, glaciers are melting and the snow line is retreating. In Scandinavia, land which was perennially under snow and ice is thawing. Arrowheads of a thousand years ago, when the black earth was last exposed and when Eric the Red's Greenland was probably still green, have been found there. In the North American sub-Arctic a similar process is observable. Black earth has been exposed and retains the summer heat longer so that each year the effect moves farther north. The melting of the sea ice will not affect the sea level because the volume of floating ice is the same as the water it displaces, but the melting of the land's ice caps and glaciers, in which water is locked up, will introduce additional water to the oceans and raise the sea level. Rivers originating in glaciers and permanent snowfields (in the Himalayas, for instance) will increase their flow, and if the ice dams break the effects could be catastrophic. In this process, the patterns of rainfall will change, with increased precipitation in areas now arid and aridity in places now fertile. I am advising all my friends not to take ninety-nine-year leases on properties at present sea level.

The pollution of sweet-water lakes and rivers has increased so during the past twenty-five years that a Freedom from Thirst campaign is becoming as necessary as a Freedom from Hunger campaign. Again it is a conflict of motives and a conspiracy of ignorance. We can look at the obvious—the unprocessed urban sewage and the influx of industrial effluents. No one could possibly have believed that the Great Lakes in their immensity could ever be overwhelmed, or that Niagara Falls could lose its pristine clearness and fume like brown smoke, or that Lake Erie could become a cesspool. It did its best to oxidize the wastes from the steel plants by giving up its free oxygen until at last it surrendered and the anaerobic microorganisms took over. Of course, one can say that the mortuary smells of Lake Erie are not due to the pickling acids but to the dead fish.

The conflict of interests amounts to a dilemma. To insure that people shall be fed we apply our ingenuity in the form of artificial fertilizers, herbicides, pesticides, and insecticides. The runoff from the lands gets into the streams and rivers and distant oceans. DDT from the rivers of the United States has been found in the fauna of the Antarctic, where no DDT has ever been allowed. The dilemma becomes agonizing in places like India, with its hungry millions. It is now believed that the new strains of Mexican grain and I.R.C. (International Rice Center in the Philippines) rice, with their high yields, will provide enough food for them, belly-filling if not nutritionally balanced. These strains, however, need plenty of water, constant irrigation, plenty of fertilizers to sustain the yields, and tons of pesticides because standardized pedigree plants are highly vulnerable to disease. This means that the production will be concentrated in the river systems, like the Gangeatic Plains, and the chemicals will drain into the rivers.

The glib answer to this sort of thing is "atomic energy." If there is enough energy and it is cheap enough, you can afford to turn rivers into sewers and lakes into cesspools. You can desalinate the seas. But, for the foreseeable future, that energy will come from atomic fission, from the breaking down of the nucleus. The alternative, promised but undelivered, is thermonuclear energy—putting the H-bomb into dungarees by controlling the fusion of hydrogen. Fusion does not produce waste products, fission does. And the more peaceful atomic reactors there are, the more radioactive waste there will be to dispose of. The really dangerous material has to be buried. The biggest disposal area in the world is at Hanford, Washington. It encloses a stretch of the Columbia River and a tract of country covering 650 square miles. There, a twentieth-century Giza, it has cost much more to bury live atoms than it cost to entomb all the mummies of all the Pyramid Kings of Egypt.

At Hanford, the live atoms are kept in tanks constructed of carbon steel, resting in a steel saucer to catch any leakage. These are enclosed in a reenforced concrete structure and the whole construction is buried in the ground with only the vents showing. In the steel sepulchers, each with a million-gallon capacity, the atoms are very much alive. Their radioactivity keeps the acids in the witches' brew boiling. In the bottom of the tanks the temperature is well above the boiling point of water. There has to be a cooling system, therefore, and it must be continuously maintained. In addition, the vapors generated in the tanks have to be condensed and scrubbed, otherwise a radioactive miasma would escape from the vents. Some of the elements in those high-level wastes will remain radioactive for at least 250,000 years. It is most unlikely that the tanks will endure as long as the Egyptian pyramids.

Radioactive wastes from atomic processing stations have to be transported to such burial grounds. By the year 2000, if the present practices continue, the number of six-ton tankers in transit at any given time would be well over three thousand and the amount of radioactive products in them would be 980,000,000 curies—that is a mighty number of curies to be roaming around in a populated country.

There are other ways of disposing of radioactive waste and there are safeguards against the hazards, but those safeguards have to be enforced and constant vigilance maintained. There are already those who say that the safety precautions in the atomic industry are excessive.

Polluting the environment has been sufficiently dramatized by events in recent years to show the price we have to pay for our recklessness. It is not just the destruction of natural beauty or the sacrifice of recreational amenities, which are crimes in themselves, but interference with the whole ecology—with the balance of nature on which persistence of life on this planet depends. We are so fascinated by the gimmicks and gadgetry of science and technology and are in such a hurry to exploit them that we do not count the consequences.

We have plenty of scientific knowledge but knowledge is not wisdom: wisdom is knowledge tempered by judgment. At the moment, the scientists, technologists, and industrialists are the judge and jury in their own assize. Statesmen, politicians, and administrators are ill-equipped to make judgments about the true values of discoveries or developments. On the contrary, they tend to encourage the crash programs to get quick answers—like the Manhattan Project, which turned the laboratory discovery of uranium fission into a cataclysmic bomb in six years; the Computer/Automation Revolution; the Space Program; and now the Bio-engineering Revolution, with its possibilities not only of spare-organ plumbing but of changing the nature of living things by gene manipulation. They blunder into a minefield of undetected ignorance, masquerading as science.

The present younger generation has an unhappy awareness of such matters. They were born into the Atomic Age, programmed into the Computer Age, rocketed into the Space Age, and are poised on the threshold of the Bio-engineering Age. They take all these marvels for granted, but they are also aware that the advances have reduced the world to a neighborhood and that we are all involved one with another in the risks as well as the opportunities. They see the mistakes writ large. They see their elders mucking about with *their* world and *their* future. That accounts for their profound unease, whatever forms their complaints may take. They are the spokesmen for posterity and are justified in their protest. But they do not have the explicit answers, either.

Somehow science and technology must conform to some kind of

social responsibility. Together, they form the social and economic dynamic of our times. They are the pacesetters for politics and it is in the political frame of reference that answers must be found. There can never be any question of restraining or repressing natural curiosity, which is true science, but there is ample justification for evaluating and judging developmental science. The common good requires nothing less.

This description of the new world which biological technology is creating raises the ultimate question of direction: Is Western cultural evolution taking us where we want to go—and taking the rest of humanity where "it" wants to go? The article allows us a forbidding glimpse into a possibly short future.

The Biological Revolution

Paul R. Ehrlich

In the several billion years that life has existed on the earth no event has been as startling as the rise of the species *Homo sapiens* to its present position of prominence. A mere eight thousands years ago mankind—then numbering perhaps five million individuals, far fewer than the number of such a contemporary species as bison—was just one of many kinds of large mammals. But even then man's hunting and food-gathering way of life was causing substantial disturbance in the planetary ecology. There is substantial evidence that Pleistocene man in America brought about the extinction of seventy per cent of the land mammals of large size, such as mammoths, horses, and camels; in Africa, about a third of the megafauna of the land was wiped out. Furthermore, many ecologists attribute the great grasslands of the world to primitive man's use of fire.

About 6000 B.C. the first groups of men, living on the edge of the Fertile Crescent in western Asia, gave up the nomadic life and settled down to agriculture. This change in man's way of life may have been the most important single happening in the history of the earth. It started a trend toward security from hunger for mankind, and initiated an irregular but persistent decline in the death rate in the human population. It also marked the beginning of the potentially lethal disturbance by man of the ecological systems upon which his life depends. When man practices agriculture he arrests the natural processes of ecological change at an unstable midpoint. Much of the planetary environment has already been severely damaged. Now its utter destruction is threatened. In the last century alone the percentage of the earth's land surface classified as desert and wasteland has more than doubled, increasing from less than ten per cent to over twenty-five per cent, largely because of farming and grazing. Now mechanization and the use of pesticides, herbicides, and inor-

From "The Biological Revolution" by Paul R. Ehrlich, *The Center Magazine*, November, 1969, pp. 28–31. Reprinted by permission from the November 1969 issue of *The Center Magazine,* a publication of The Center for the Study of Democratic Institutions in Santa Barbara, California.

ganic nitrogen fertilizers are rapidly accelerating the destruction of the earth's ecosystems. Insecticides alone have the potential of destroying the planet as a habitat for civilized man.

The agricultural revolution has been going on for about eight thousand years now; until a few hundred years ago it was the major cause of decline in the death rate. Population growth is a result of the difference between the birth and death rates, and birth rates have remained relatively high. Agriculture, therefore, has been largely responsible for the spectacular growth of the human population. Virtually alone, it caused the hundred-fold increase from five million to five hundred million between 6000 B.C. and 1650 A.D. Since then other revolutions, industrial and biomedical, have been added to the agricultural revolution. They have all contributed to reducing death rates. The human condition has improved sufficiently since 1650 for a further increase in the population to more than seven hundred times its size at the start of the agricultural revolution. By the nineteen-sixties some 3.5 billion human beings were crowded onto "Spaceship Earth."

While man's population has been growing, his culture has been evolving. He has developed a vast array of techniques for modifying his environment and himself, but he has failed to develop ways of understanding, guiding, and controlling his new-found abilities. Indeed our growing ability to change ourselves and our environments is at the heart of what is being called the biological revolution. For instance:

• Man has been extremely successful at lowering the human death rate, but has made no significant effort to lower the birth rate. As a result the human population is now growing at a rate which will double it in about thirty-five years, and the population growth continues to outstrip mankind's ability to produce and distribute food in proper quantities and of proper quality. We now [1969] have between 1.5 and two billion people living on inadequate diets. That is, there are now more hungry people on earth than the total world population in 1875. Although calories are in short supply, the most serious problem is probably the shortage of high-quality protein.

• Agricultural technology has developed to the point where very high food yields per acre are attained under certain conditions, primarily in the temperate zone. But the ecological consequences of this technology are widely ignored. Furthermore, modern fishing technology and the escalation of pollution threaten to destroy the resources of the sea on which man depends heavily for the all-important protein component of his diet. These resources are not unlimited, contrary to what one often reads in the popular press. We may already have exceeded the annual sustainable yield, and even under the best possible conditions more than a few-fold increase would be difficult to obtain.

• Molecular biologists have uncovered many of the basic chemical mechanisms of life and their work may be put to broad practical use in the near future. It should, for instance, soon be possible to predetermine the sex of a child and to correct certain inborn defects of metabolism. Indeed, the future potential for "genetic engineering" seems incredible. But then so does our lack of consideration of just what kinds of human beings we want to engineer, and to what purpose. The discoveries of molecular biology also pose a direct threat to human survival. Some molecular biologists are at work in chemical and biological warfare laboratories, engineering ever-more-lethal strains of viruses and bacteria which could very well bring the population explosion to an end once and for all.

• Medical scientists in the United States have followed the flow of federal money and, with varying degrees of success, put a great deal of effort into curing the kinds of disease suffered by middle-aged congressmen. Thus we have a spectacle of vast resources poured into programs leading to heart transplants for a very few individuals in a country where many millions are malnourished. The United States, furthermore, ranks only fifteenth in the world in infant mortality. It is, on the other hand, fortunate that the serious ethical problems associated with organ transplants and prostheses are being aired now while they are still a minor sideshow as far as the mass of humanity is concerned. For in the unlikely event that mankind should solve its pressing problems, reduce the size of the human population, and preserve a world in which medical science flourishes, these questions will become more serious than anything contemplated today. The most elemental questions will be: "what is an individual?" and "how long should an individual's life be preserved?" I can see no theoretical barrier standing in the way of our eventually achieving individual life spans of hundreds or even thousands of years, even though we have not yet made any significant progress in this direction. (We have increased the average life span, permitting more people to live out what is probably a genetically determined span. But there is no known reason why we should not discover how greatly to expand that span.) It is quite clear that in the near future the problem of rejection of transplanted foreign tissues will be more or less solved and substantial life extensions by transplants will be possible. But where will the replacements come from, who will pay for them, and who will decide on the allocation of parts in short supply?

• The most revolutionary of all man's prosthetic devices is probably the computer, which may be used as a replacement for, or an extension of, the human mind. Computers, in conjunction with modern communications systems, have already revolutionized the lives of people in the developed countries. They have done much more than facilitate the obvious breakthroughs in science, technology, and social science. Computers have changed the power structures of institutions from universities to governments; to some degree they have taken decision-making away from human beings. Indeed, there is now talk that technological advances in armaments may require such rapid reaction times that computers will have to make the decision about whether we will or will not go to war.

• Man has begun, for the first time, to turn systematically toward the frontiers of the mind. At a strictly empirical level, so-called "brain-washing" has demonstrated the kinds of horrors possible. Holistic [emphasizing the organic or functional relation between parts and wholes] experiments on the mind, using drugs, hypnotism, and electrical and surgical intervention, are being made increasingly in order to "change minds." Computers enter the picture here also. They have, for instance, been used successfully to teach children to read and write. Slowly but surely, biologists are beginning to unravel the secrets of the nervous system and learning the bases of perception and memory. It seems a safe assumption that various kinds of controlled biochemical manipulation of the mind eventually will be possible. Such manipulation could, of course, be used for what almost everyone considers an obvious "good"—for example, the cure of mental illness or retardation. However, the potential for misuse of this power, whether accidental or intentional, needs no elaboration.

From these few examples, we can see that because of biological revolutions we are confronted with a set of extraordinarily difficult social and political problems. Such problems are growing at an incredible rate. At the root of all of them is an increasingly efficacious biological technology, which had its origins in agriculture. (If man had never practiced agriculture it is unlikely that he would ever have practiced molecular biology.)

There is a tendency, in meeting new challenges, to solve the problems accompanying biological technology by encouraging the further growth of biological technology, without any careful consideration of the consequences of such a growth. Thus we see the further development of ecologically naive agriculture technology as a "solution" to the population-food crisis. How do we solve the problem of too many people? Develop a better contraceptive technology, but neglect critical questions of human attitudes toward reproduction. Shortage of organs for transplant? Grow them in tissue culture or develop artificial organs. Information overload? Build bigger and better computers and communications networks.

The questions that need asking are all too rarely raised: What for? What kind of life are those additional people we feed going to live? What will the composite men of the Age of Transplants do with their extra years of life? When we can "improve" our minds genetically or biochemically, what kind of world will we have to think about? What kind of information will flow through our improved communications networks, and be processed by future generations of computers? Is Western cultural evolution taking us where we want to go—and taking the rest of humanity where it wants to go? These are some of the fundamental questions raised by the biological revolutions of the last eight thousand years. As the pace of change accelerates, our chances of answering them satisfactorily and modifying our behavior are diminishing rapidly. It is possible that the rapid growth of technology will lead to that common end of runaway evolutionary trends— extinction. The signs now point that way.

Questions

1 On the whole, has man progressed or regressed between 1945 and 1970?

2 Is it possible for men to achieve a state of general permanent contentment?

3 What is the purpose of your life? Will it be likely to find fulfillment in the remaining three decades of this century?

4 What are some of the major obstacles to man's happiness in today's world?

5 What constructive activities can college students engage in which would help alleviate the problems of society?

6 Is activism futile?

7 Are you optimistic or pessimistic about your own personal future? About the future of the world?

8 Can you actually imagine your own children accusing you of being way out of touch with the changed world of 1990?

9 What kind of life do you expect to be living when the twenty-first century begins? (If it does.)

10 Can you sense the flow of history that is represented in the more or less arbitrary division between Chapter 9 and Chapter 10 of this book?

10

Beyond
the Troublesome Present

Is it possible to predict the future, given so many variables? How much longer can man survive if he retains traditional behavior patterns? What are the obstacles to Utopia?

The Twenty-first Century:
Utopia, Holocaust, or None-of-the-Above?

Melvin Steinfield

Thirty years before the twenty-first century began, what had formerly been considered mere science-fiction fantasies suddenly became realities. From vital organ transplants to men on the moon, all things seemed possible via technology. In the world of the future, men envisioned:

> Desalinization of ocean water, exploration of space, portable video-tape recorders as routine Christmas gifts, guaranteed accuracy in selecting the desired sex of one's unconceived child, computer-communications systems that would make possible daily polling of citizens on every public issue, electronic information-retrieval systems that would make term papers as old-fashioned as the minuet and as useful as a deaf psychiatrist, computer diagnosis of medical ailments, foolproof programmed instruction for all types of learners and all kinds of educational goals, and an infinity of additional gadgets, inventions, and intricate networks all designed to snare elusive dreams of Utopia.

But even as the visions of the benefits of unlocking the final secrets of nature were dangling seductively before men's eyes, there was by 1970 a recognition that technology was starting to backfire: that noise from gigantic supersonic jetliners was contributing to deafness, discomfort, and mental illness; that smog from automobiles and factories was contributing to eye irritation, emphysema, and lung cancer; that radioactive fallout from weapons-testing was contributing to genetic damage, government credibility-gaps, and paranoia; and that food additives like cyclamate, crop sprays like DDT, and fertility pills and birth control pills had harmful side effects. Occasionally, dramatic incidents brought home the mixed blessings of technology to particular regions of the world—England's oil slicks and New England's power failures in the mid-1960's, for instance. And always, the increases in leisure time gave more people more time to nurture neuroses and pamper psychoses.

In the latter part of the twentieth century, society was in flux and the entire pace of evolution had quickened perceptibly. Every institution, no matter how sacrosanct, was undergoing radical transformation. Marriage and divorce, organized religion, nudity and censorship of the arts—all were affected by the attitudinal upheavals. Hedonism was fostered by a lack of absolute purpose as masses of people sought gratification in an aimless, pleasure-seeking world of relativity.

Not everyone was content to suck up the thrills of a sensational society without thinking about where they were headed, however. Many individuals during the last half of the twentieth century wondered aloud: "What will the society of the next century be like?" Besides reading such thought-provoking speculative works as *Brave New World* by Aldous Huxley, *1984* by George Orwell, and *Walden Two*, by B. F. Skinner, plenty of ordinary people tried to imagine what the future would offer for their twenty-first century grandchildren. In so doing, they were not, of course, the first ones to question the nature of the future. Throughout history men had predicted either the Utopia or the Holocaust that was supposed to be just around the corner. Those prophets of doom and oracles of euphoria were always wrong. Neither man's best hopes nor his worst fears had ever been realized in quite the way they were foreseen.

In view of the general inaccuracy of predictions that had been made in the past, it does seem surprising that late twentieth century man would place any value in further predictions. On second thought, perhaps it is not so surprising. After all, people did have some respect for historians, despite the fact that they sometimes engaged in wild speculations about the past. Why shouldn't historians speculate wildly about the future? Was it any less meaningful to guess about the future than to ask such intriguing but impossible questions as: "If Americans had not entered the Second World War, what would have been its outcome?", or "If Napoleon had not lived, how would nineteenth century European history have been altered?", or "If the Atomic Bomb had not been invented, what kind of a world would we now have?"

So man followed the paths of his curiosity and he tried to guess his future. But he used the methods of history, a pseudoscience, and not the methods of chemistry, a science. The chemists of the late twentieth century could quantify their analyses; historians could not. The chemist could say, "This tube of toothpaste with cavity-retarding enzymes, odor-killing agents, toothshining supergloss, and gum-strengthening mumbo-jumbo, contains oxygen, 3.2; hydrogen, 4.7; zinc, 5.3, etc." But the historian attempting to cite the causes of the American Civil War could *not* say, "Slavery, 3.2; tariff, 4.7; abolitionists, 5.3; etc." Despite the progress of the historical craft, the best that historians could offer was: "The major causes of the Civil War were 1, 2, and 3. Secondary causes were 1, 2, and 3. Immediate cause was the firing on Fort Sumter." Nor could historians deal scientifically with the many human elements involved in the forging of history, such as motives of government leaders, how power accrues to a group, or predicting when a charismatic figure would fall from power.

Nevertheless, historians could offer intelligent help to anybody trying to create a composite picture of the coming century. They could cite some major trends that appeared destined to play a large role in the foreseeable future. They could mention some unresolved problems that would have to be tackled sooner or later. They could remind the world of some of its traditional hangups that were being carried forth into the twenty-first century.

Armed with historical insight, thoughtful students of human behavior patterns could note in 1970 that there were at least *five* contingencies upon which the Utopian potential of the twenty-first century needed to be predicated.

1. Would war be avoided?

Perhaps not. Perhaps it was to be just a matter of time before deliberate, conscious government policy or a mad dictator would push the button unleashing the world's massive warmaking capacity. In that case, what sense would it make to bother predicting life styles after the Third World War? Man had moved perilously close to a Third World War on several occasions between 1945 and 1970. Could he be sure that he would be just as successful in avoiding it between 1970 and 1999? How could he be? War was a human institution—and one of man's most persistent hangups.

2. Would man be able to control population growth and pollution?

For man to avoid war, he must eliminate war (if it is going to be a permanent avoidance). But if war were eliminated, man would have to achieve a way to stop or to retard the trends of overpopulation and the corresponding pollution. Or, at least, he would have to figure out how to adjust to crowded cities, dirty air and water, noisy atmosphere, and inadequate waste disposal facilities. Perhaps colonization of the moon to take care of surplus population would be the answer. Perhaps bucket satellites to take care of radioactive waste disposal. For even if man avoids the relatively quick deaths of warfare, what sense would it make to bother predicting life styles in the twenty-first century *if* he will be deafened by the roar of machines, engines, and dynamos; blinded by the smoke of megalopolitan density; immobilized by the congestion of overburdened traffic arteries; stifled by noxious fumes of industrial air; and, in general, poisoned by his own pollutions?

3. *Would wealth be shared more equitably?*

If man somehow managed to overcome the preceding obstacles to Utopia (which have been sketched in broad outline only, and whose full parameters may not come into focus until the twenty-first century), he would still have to determine how gross inequalities could be eliminated. Social, political, and economic disparities have always caused conflict between "haves" and "have-nots." There was no reason to assume in 1970 that these conditions would cease to be matters of friction in the future. Yet man was not very successful in closing the gap between rich and poor, neither among people of the same political entity, nor between nations themselves. A Utopia with gross inequalities would not be much of a Utopia for people who had been reared in democratic traditions.

4. *Would antisocial behavior be curbed effectively?*

One more *if* on the road to Utopia is human greed, one of the most perverse hangups of man's history. This troublesome trait could easily wreck any constructive efforts to establish a society of law, order, and justice. Unless the next century developed adequate safety checks to prevent possible abuses by power-hungry individuals, then Utopia would be, at its best, a one-generation phenomenon. For it is entirely within the realm of probability that the system would be subverted by a tiny minority of noncooperative, antisocial, anti-Utopians. To establish Utopia, in other words, social planners would have to create the first unanimously-monolithic cooperative society in the history of man, as well as the mechanism to prevent its subversion at some later date. The early Christians and the twentieth-century Communists tried it—and failed.

5. *Would individual freedom be sacrificed?*

If all disruptive elements of the potential Utopia were brought under control, would it result in the elimination of individual freedom? Would privacy, of necessity, be destroyed in order to monitor the actions of all? A totalitarian big-brother-is-watching-you syndrome would automatically preclude the kind of freedom situation that Utopia is predicated upon. Yet without highly-centralized governments, how could worldwide massive cooperation be coordinated?

If man survived these five potential time bombs, plus all the other unforeseeable hazards such as the consequences of interplanetary exploration and colonization, then he might discover that his arrival at the threshold of Utopia was just the beginning of his most challenging problem of adjustment. He would have to discover:

What to do with his overdose of leisure time?

How to adjust to a society without jobs or work satisfaction?

How to cope with perpetual superabundance?

How to avoid wallowing in artificially-induced euphoria?

What to do with his new-found total freedom?

As the twenty-first century drew near, humanity was bogged down in its traditional hangups: its propensity for war; its drive for power; its stirrings of greed; its need of recognition, self-esteem, and vain glory; its obsession with materialistic "things"; its reluctance to cooperate; its desire to compete; and its refusal to change.

Whether humanity would arrive at the Utopian potential toward which it was drifting was a matter for future historians to record. In the twenty-first century, they would be able to report whether man conquered his own hangups and assumed a greater measure of intelligent control over his own evolution.

Or, whether he remained his own worst enemy, entangled in a morass of irrational love and hate, thus causing his own extinction.

Or, none-of-the-above.

In addition to pinpointing some unforeseen effects of
recent scientific and technological advances, the author
specifies several foreseeable breakthroughs of enormous
implications for Utopian dreams.

Surprises We'll Never Envision

Jacob Bronowski

Of course, we never know with certainty what the social consequences of any discovery will be. Who would have thought that the
unfortunate character who invented photographic film would have
been responsible for the California film industry? And thus, indirectly,
for contracts that would prevent film stars from having affairs that
might give rise to gossip and scandal? That consequently stars would
lead their love life in public, by repeated divorce and marriage? That
therefore the beautiful pin-ups of films would, in time, become the
models of the divorce business? And the climax, that one-third of all
marriages contracted this year in California are going to end in divorce
—all because somebody invented the process of printing pictures on
a celluloid strip?

On the same lines (which I leave you to trace), who would have
supposed that Henry Ford's devising of the sequential method of as-
sembling a motorcar would finally result in upsetting the whole moral
code of the American middle classes? For it is evident now that the
car provided young people with more privacy than the home, and
that as a result it became usual to begin sexual experience on the
backseat of a motorcar.

Although my examples may seem extravagant, they are not. The
fact is that, in a strange way, the side effects of technical innovation
are more influential than the direct effects, and they spread out in a
civilization to transform its behavior, its outlook, and its moral ethic.
For morality is an organization of life that grows spontaneously from
activities, and not a formula taken ready-made from somebody else.

Of course, we can foresee that certain modern technical developments will have profound social consequences. But we do not know
what these are going to be. Let us take a simple example. I have no
doubt that before my children finish the childbearing age, say roughly
during the next twenty or thirty years [1990–2000], it will become

From "What We Can't Know" by Jacob Bronowski in *The Environment of
Change,* Aaron W. Warner, *et al.,* eds. (New York: Columbia University Press,
1968). Reprinted by permission.

a trivial matter for them to go to the doctor and say, "We've had two girls. We want a boy." The doctor will then be able to guarantee, with 95 per cent assurance, a male child.

We have no idea what the social consequences of this will be. They might be manifold. It might suddenly become modish to have girls. The cover of *Vogue* or *Life* might carry a picture of an alluring-looking woman, and all parents would suddenly decide to have girls. After all, many parents named their daughters "Shirley" not so many years ago.

On the other hand, what might happen is what was tried in Italy and in Germany. There the Fascists tried to encourage people to have boys. It is not out of the question that if the Chinese knew the secret of producing boys and were not producing enough, they would suddenly switch to this practice. (And, you know, what we think about Chinese militarism, the Chinese think about American.)

The birth control pill already has had many social consequences; it will have more profound ones, and some that are unforeseeable. It is already evident that the particular female hormones which produce a good birth control pill also keep the female reproductive cycle going long beyond its present span. As a result, women of fifty and sixty years go on ovulating and, unexpectedly, have the look of younger women—fresher skin, hair, and eyes. Consequently, the whole relation between the old and the young may change. Our society is geared to relations in which women think a man in his fifties still attractive, but men think a woman in her fifties unattractive. Now we may be within a generation of seeing that reversed.

We also now have the unusual situation that men in their thirties and early forties are unexpectedly attractive to many teen-age girls. This is because the American government has chosen astronauts from that age group, and they have ousted the young Italian film star and the young Frenchman as objects of adoration. Who would have thought that the invention of space rocketry would lead to an age shift in the image of the ideal man among many teen-age girls?

I want now to draw your attention to some foreseeable social consequences of modern technology. Whenever people talk about genetic control in biology, they immediately ask such questions as, "Are we all going to be monsters? Or supermen? And what's going to happen to kids like mine?" But, of course, that is *not* where genetics will be important in the near future. Genetics will begin to have its first influence in smaller ways.

For example, the kinds of plants and domestic animals that we breed will be much more nearly tailor-made than they are today. I would like to give two examples. To prepare you for these, let me ask first what is going to be the single greatest technological change in the physical sciences over the next twenty or thirty years. My guess is that desalting of sea water is going to be the most important advance for overall world development. Without this the whole complex problem of bringing underdeveloped countries to an acceptable level of economics, education, and political maturity is insoluble.

If we propose to desalt sea water so as to make it fit for drinking, we are setting a task which is really foolish, because we already have all the drinking water that we need. If we were to keep drinking water now only for drinking, and use the rest of the water for watering plants and other purposes, there would be no shortage of drinking water. So the obvious thing is to have desalinization processes which leave water as brackish as plants can stand it. A great deal of research in desert countries such as Israel is directed to this end.

I guess that the single most important biological contribution to world peace will be to produce plants which grow effectively in quite salty water. This follows from what we know about diminishing return. If we are going to knock out all the salt in sea water, it is going to cost many times more than if we need only knock down 80 per cent of the salt. So if somebody can come along and breed plants which can grow in 20 per cent of the total salt content of sea water, we shall have the means to take a long economic stride. This is the kind of advance that biology in general and genetics in particular will make.

The other example I have in mind concerns the breeding of animals. The potentially most useful animal that we lack at the moment is a sea animal that really harvests the sea efficiently. The countryside is full of animals which do a fairly good job of turning indigestible protein such as grass into digestible protein such as milk, eggs, and meat. But in the sea, although there are such animals, they do it extremely inefficiently. If you take the smallest vegetable algae in the sea and think of the number of steps necessary before they are turned into a sizable fish you can eat—say, a sardine—the answer is discouraging. At present, it takes three tons of algae to feed the small plankton that feed the larger plankton and so on until they make one sardine. This is a ridiculous ratio: three tons of algae to make one sardine. Nobody would breed cows or pigs if that was the required ratio from vegetable to animal. So we are badly in need of sea animals—particularly a scavenging pig of the sea—which have a higher efficiency than this. I have no doubt that we will breed them in the long run. There is no biological reason why we should not.

Familiarity with these modern ideas is the best way of guessing the social consequences. I may know more about biology than many of you, but about social consequences we all start equal. If you know the facts, if you immerse yourself in the facts, you will be more far-sighted than the next man. You may come up with a practical or social gimmick before anybody else. But for this purpose it is necessary to be immersed in the new science, not to run out behind the field and start building computers when everybody else has already gone into biology.

Man cannot continue to live with the relentless pace of change asserts the famous longshoreman-political scientist-philosopher, Eric Hoffer. Therefore, states Hoffer in the following selection, man will of necessity seek to return to older established patterns. As far as he is concerned, there are signs that man has already started this process.

The Utopia We Once Knew

Eric Hoffer

The other day the thought occurred to me that our era of rapid, drastic, ceaseless change is perhaps an interlude that is nearing its end. After all, change such as the world has been experiencing for a century or so is unprecedented in man's stay on this planet, and utterly foreign to any other form of life.

It is indeed questionable whether life can endure and thrive in an environment so lacking in continuity. It is plausible, therefore, that what is waiting for us around the corner is not an utterly novel future but an immemorial past.

Are there portents of such a return to be seen in our midst?

There is no doubt that the totalitarian societies of our time, whether of the right or of the left, are a return to the past, the ancient past of the river-valley civilizations, where everything was planned, predetermined, and minutely supervised by a huge bureaucracy made up of scribes with their papyrus rolls or clay tablets, and overseers with their whips.

It is of interest that almost a century ago the Swiss historian Jacob Burckhardt foresaw this form of a return to the past. In a letter to a friend he predicted the time when life would become "a supervised stint of misery, daily begun and ended to the sound of drums."

The clamor of our scribes (intellectuals) for power should be seen as a reaching out for the distant past. . . . If there is anything certain it is this: wherever the scribes attain power they create a social order that is both hierarchical and regimented. No matter how idealistic, an intelligentsia. They'll probably call such a social order a New Democracy, but it will be a Minocracy.

Another symptom of a return to the past is the recent explosive self-assertion of adolescents. All through the past young adults have acted effectively as members of political parties, creators of business enterprises, advocates of new doctrines and leaders of armies.

The middle-aged came into their own with the advent of the middle class during the 19th century. Even now young men of both the aristocracy and the working class are more in touch with the realities of power than the young of the middle class.

Thus the present revolt of middle class adolescents is an attempt to reestablish a social pattern which had been disrupted by the industrial revolution.

In sharp contrast to the projections of the preceding article, this brief
sketch by a highly respected professor of American civilization envisions a
world never before realized. Is it possible to realize such a society "without
violating too many reality principles"?

The End of Faustian Ruthlessness

Max Lerner

Nyborg, Denmark [1969]—It has been an extraordinary week that
I have spent in this little town near Odense, on one of the Danish
islands. By a happy chance I was asked to bring together a small
group of scholars and writers—American and British—who would
help some film makers make a film about an optimal society by first
designing the society that the film would build on. It is an optimal
society rather than a Utopia because it is the best society we could
invent without violating too many reality principles.

The group included two ecologists, Robert Ardrey and Desmond
Morris; a historian of Utopias, Frank Manuel; a psychoanalyst, Bruno
Bettelheim; an archaeologist, Jacquetta Hawkes; a city planner, Jose
Luis Sert, and a futurist, Herman Kahn. Along with the film's director, Louis Malle, and Commonwealth United's planner and producer, Henry Weinstein, and myself, this made a group of 10, an
ideal number for a symposium.

An optimal society must speak to the human condition today,
especially to the consciousness of the youth, with their disruptions and
rebellion, their revolution against existing life goals and the little
communities they are themselves beginning to found.

We differed on many things, but we also found a remarkable area
of agreement: First, it would be a society without war, since it would
have no neighbors to attack or defend itself against, and no profit or
ownership to aggrandize. Second, it would leave out property, since
a fertile environment and its use for everyone would make property
archaic.

A real discussion revolved around what there is in the whole history of the human track, from the hominoids of 2 million years ago
to the societies of today, which would dictate what must be kept and
built on. Science and technology for one, but not the cancerous industrial production and consumption of today: rather a control of

science and technology which will not keep exploiting nature and changing the landscape with a Faustian ruthlessness.

Competition and leadership must remain, but not in a febrile way: with a minimum of government, mostly by the women, since government will be administration rather than coercion; and with law left also at a minimum, operating not by punishment or prison but by an inner shame at disrupting the community agreements.

Marriage will be not a matter of legal contract, yet the basic pair-bond will be maintained, primarily to rear the children during the crucial years up to 5, after which the community, in kibbutz-fashion, would take over most of their play, instruction and community services. The children will grow up feeling themselves useful and needed, and the sources of disruption and violence will dry up.

It will be a society with tradition, cherishing the past and moving by the phases of the life-cycle into the future, in order to give meaning to the present. Each transition from one age-phase to the next will be cherished by the community and celebrated with ritual. As part of these transitions, there will be a grave and tender education of the child in sexuality, with privacy rather than in some public school system.

The crucial aspects of the society will lie in the emphasis on the confident inner security of the growing-up years, the continuous exploration of mind and feeling all through life in common activities, the understanding that the real golden rule is to help fulfill others through the same acts and relations which fulfill ourselves.

Death will remain, because without that there is no meaning for life. But it will come in the fullness of time that each individual will decide for himself. And when he chooses to end his life, he will hand on his name and his place in the society to a child just born, thereby celebrating a cycle of death and life.

If there were a society in which people neither had to work (because of Utopian affluence) nor had opportunities to work (because of the scarcity of jobs), there would be at least a double problem of adjustment. First, the obvious one of not knowing how to use leisure time enjoyably over a long period. But, writes the author of the following selection elsewhere in his book, "the West believes that a man established his worth in the eyes of his neighbor, and even before God, through industry, and drudgery and savings." Thus, a second challenge to Utopian men would be adjusting to the disappearance of opportunities to live up to the work ethic that is so strongly engrained in Western culture. Americans—with their "Idleness is the enemy of the soul," "Busy people are happy people," and other Puritan ethic hangups—would face the greatest challenge of all: "How to retire at 21 without feeling guilty about it?" That problem would strain Yankee ingenuity as it has never been strained before. And erstwhile Utopia would become living Hell.

The Problem of Leisure Time

Michael Harrington

What, then, would happen if technology rendered work and the work ethic decadent?

Bread and circuses are an obvious, but hardly affirmative, substitute. In a series of Italian films of Antonioni and Fellini, there is a depiction of the empty, orgiastic lives of the leisure and celebrity class. They are tormented by their free time. Significantly, each of these movies contains a scene in which an anguished protagonist looks longingly upon the vitality of working-class or peasant life, admiring its muscularity or simplicity. These particular cases are examples of what Empson defined as the "pastoral" theme in literature and art (the romantic courtier sings of the rustic swain; the middle-class novelist or movie director celebrates the noble proletarian). But they could also be the intimation of a possible nostalgia in the technological future. Will people then turn back to yearn for the working present and the even more hardworking past?

Were it possible to build a society on the principles of bread and circuses, the event would signify the decadence of central Western values. But it is doubtful whether such a society could exist at all. Here, Ortega's inaccurate charge against the twentieth century might apply to the twenty-first. The very existence of technological abundance presupposes a high level of science and skill, at least on the part of the minority. A social order based upon orgy would destroy its own effortless prosperity by failing to reproduce its technological genius. (In terms of myth, Cockaigne,* where there is only consumption, is impossible; utopia, which recognizes some form of work, is still conceivable.)

There is another possible principle of the society that has eliminated work as it is now known: totalitarianism. In the past, hunger has been at least as important for the maintenance of order as for the fomenting of revolution. Out of necessity, millions "voluntarily" chose brutal toil in order to survive. If this indirect discipline were abolished, it might be replaced by the dictatorship of the programmers, of those who decide what decisions the machines will make. Indeed, a society split between the highly educated and sophisticated few on the one side, and the passive, consuming mass on the other, could hardly be democratic, since dialogue between the rulers and ruled would be impossible. Were this to happen, it would confirm the worst fears of sociologists like Weber and Mills that the functional rationalization of life necessarily leads to the loss of substantive rationality for the majority of individuals. . . .

For now, it is clear that the West is already approaching the decadence of the work ethic. Thomas Malthus said, "If our benevolence be indiscriminate . . . we shall raise the worthless above the worthy; we shall encourage indolence and check industry; and in the most marked manner subtract from the sum of human happiness. . . . The laws of nature say with Saint Paul, 'If a man will not work, neither shall he eat.' "

That law of nature, so basic to the recent history of the West, is now being abolished by machines. In 1964, the President of the United States intimated the new era when, in announcing the enactment of a cut in taxes, he urged Americans to spend and consume as a patriotic duty. Paradoxically, this decadence of the Protestant ethic comes at the very moment when it has finally conquered the world. As Sebastian de Grazia has pointed out, the UNESCO Declaration of Human Rights announces, "Everyone has the right to work."

So it is that at that point in history at which the Western work ethic is finally in sight of subverting almost every remnant of tribalism, feudalism, and aristocracy on the globe, it ceases to be a practical guide for the culture that gave it birth.

*Ed. Note—Cockaigne was a legendary country in medieval tales where food and drink and other pleasures were always immediately at hand.

349

Some of the dangers and advantages of comprehensive computer networks
are discussed in the following article.

Calculating the Future

Stanley Penn

It's 1980. A motorist is barreling along an eight-lane freeway.
Traffic is light, so he nudges his car five, ten, then twenty miles an
hour over the speed limit. No police car with flashing light and
screaming siren appears on his tail, and he arrives at his destination
without a care in the world.

The next day he is notified by the police that his car was involved
in a speeding violation and that whoever was driving is due in court.
The infraction had been observed by an electronic device that measured the car's speed, noted the license number and flashed the
information to a police computer. The computer plucked the name
and address of the license-plate holder from its memory and printed
it out, along with details of the offense.

Certainly this is fast, efficient law enforcement—and entirely within the realm of technical feasibility. But the prospect of being nabbed
by an all-knowing assemblage of transistors and circuitry has disturbing aspects for some people. Their doubts about computerized
cops suggest something of a general mood of ambivalence often found
among those who have pondered the role of the computer over the
next few decades.

Without question, computers will bring many benefits. They will
increase factory and office productivity. They will signal new economic trends more quickly. They will store vast amounts of information about law, medicine, science and other fields, with instant access
to any bit of needed data available to thousands of widely scattered
persons via teletypewriter links. They will serve as invaluable educational tools, and they will permit lightning solution of scientific
and technical problems that for all practical purposes would be insoluble otherwise. In all these areas, computers will become easier to
use; in the works are machines that could even follow spoken instructions.

On the negative side is the prospect of an extension of the impersonalization that often seems to accompany the introduction of

computers. The sort of frustrations already encountered by a customer who feels he has been incorrectly billed by a store with computerized bookkeeping could become commonplace in other areas of life. How, for example, do you explain to a police computer that you were speeding because a passenger was suddenly taken ill and needed immediate attention?

Impersonalization caused by computers could also ruin some jobs, a number of observers assert. Dean Champion, a University of Tennessee sociologist, recently went so far as to forecast that many employes of computer-run plants, where a worker frequently will find himself assigned to an isolated station with the task of watching automated machines, will be driven to alcoholism. He reasons that the lone worker will miss the companionship of laboring alongside others on the assembly line and consequently will spend more leisure hours in bars.

Then there is the privacy issue. Already considerable amounts of information on individuals—their incomes, credit ratings, bank balances and tax payments—have accumulated in business and government computer systems. Now moves are afoot to speed this trend. A Federal commission has proposed a nationwide employment service that would use a computer to store information on job openings and on detailed characteristics for job seekers. The Budget Bureau is considering a computerized national data center that would collect information on millions of Americans from the Census Bureau, the Internal Revenue Service and other United States agencies.

Such data storehouses obviously would offer advantages; in particular, the computerized employment service—viewed as a certainty by the 1980s—might cut jobless rolls. But critics fear officials might be tempted to pry too deeply into personal matters or to use information improperly. For such reasons, Representative Cornelius F. Gallagher, a New Jersey Democrat who heads a House subcommittee that has been looking into the question of Federal invasion of privacy, finds the proposal for a national data center "appalling."

"We cannot be certain that such dossiers would always be used by benevolent people for benevolent purposes," warns the Congressman.

Concern about possible harmful effects of computers on society clearly is not going to stop their use from steadily widening. But it could at least lead to some legal curbs on the ways they can be used.

For example, Charles A. Reich, a Yale University professor of Constitutional law, urges several safeguards for individuals if the national data center is established. Among them would be rules prohibiting the Government from asking certain questions, such as a man's religious beliefs; restricting information to the agency that originally obtained it; and giving a person the right to know what information has been supplied about him and its source, plus the opportunity to rebut inaccurate data.

Computers are multiplying at a rapid rate. There were fewer than 1,000 in the United States in 1956. By 1967 over 30,000 were in operation. Radio Corporation of America, which makes computers, predicts the total will reach 85,000 by 1975 and 150,000 by 1985. By the turn of the century, there will be 220,000 computers in the United States, RCA forecasts. . . .

Some computer makers predict that by the late 1970s a new system of credit based on computer networks will have started replacing cash and checks. The heart of the system will be a bank computer hooked up to homes, stores, utilities and employers in a community. One bank's computers will be interconnected with other banks' computers.

The possibilities of such a system are varied. By punching a keyboard in its office, a factory could credit a worker's weekly paycheck to his bank account. When the employe shops, he could pay for purchases by having a store signal his bank's computer to transfer funds from his account to the store's. Eventually, individuals might pay bills for utilities and rent through computer hookups to their homes. The theoretical advantage of all this would be a great saving of time and paper work in conducting financial transactions.

The Bank of Delaware and a chain of four shoe stores in Wilmington have been cooperating since March 1966 in a limited test of "electronic credit." Some 200 account holders at the bank have been given special identification cards. If one of these persons buys a pair of shoes at one of the chain's outlets, he presents his card to the clerk, who inserts it in an automatic dialing device attached to a push-button phone and punches out the charge.

The card causes an identifying signal to be transmitted to the computer, and a recorded voice reports back over the phone whether the shopper has enough funds in his account to cover the purchase. If the funds are sufficient, the computer deducts the price of the shoes from the customer's account and credits it to the chain's account. "It has been very satisfactory so far," says a bank spokesman.

A Federal study group sees a strong likelihood that computer networks for the storage and transmission of medical data will be in operation within a decade or two. The system would be built around computers at regional Government health centers. In these would be stored individual medical histories of all citizens, along with exhaustive general medical information, such as patterns of symptoms for various ailments. The computers would be linked to doctors' offices and hospitals.

The setup would permit physicians to obtain instant medical profiles of patients. It also would aid in diagnosis of unusual cases; the doctor could feed a patient's symptoms into the computer, which would promptly respond with a list of the most likely causes.

"The computer will detect patterns that may not have been apparent to the doctor," says Evon C. Greanias, who is guiding development of a medical information system at International Business Machines Corporation. "It won't make decisions for the doctor. But it will analyze information and save a lot of the doctor's time."

All computer experts agree the use of computers to simulate reality is sure to grow rapidly. This technique involves construction of a mathematical "model" of real behavior or conditions in a computer. It permits researchers to investigate matters that would be impossible or too costly to study in actuality. Already computers have simulated the flights of spacecraft and nuclear attacks.

One important trend for the future is likely to be simulation in the economic field. At the local level, a bank could create an economic model of a marketing area; it would contain information about population, age groups, income levels and buying habits. This could aid businessmen.

"Take a hardware merchant thinking of opening a store in the bank's neighborhood," says an IBM specialist in the use of computers in financial fields. "He'll ask the bank if it thinks he can make a go of it. The computer will help in providing the answer."

The Commerce Department and the Brookings Institution are both developing computer models of the United States economy. It's hoped that within a decade highly detailed models that shed new light on the workings of the economy will be available. Such models would show, among other things, how gross national product, personal income and employment would respond to a cut in Government spending, a rise in business plant and equipment outlays or an income tax reduction. Such foreknowledge would help Government economic officials make sound decisions.

Computers also are likely to find uses in tackling social problems, such as air and water pollution, inadequate mass transit and traffic congestion. The advantage of a computer here is that it can juggle many interrelated variables and evaluate the effect of various courses of action in a fraction of the time it would take human beings. For example, to help plan for road and transit needs, a computer could weigh such factors as present traffic patterns, the impact of future residential and business development on traffic, public preferences for private autos as against mass transit, the deterrent effect of tolls for road use and the effect of fare cuts on transit patronage.

Most of the chores performed by computers in the business world today are routine clerical assignments such as preparation of payrolls or customers' bills. "But, the really significant use of the computer in the coming years will be in giving the head of the company a total picture in graphic form of what his company is doing right now," says Louis Rader, a GE vice president. . . .

Even in some fields where controversy over the introduction of computers would seem unlikely, there are those who doubt the amazing machines will be an unmixed blessing. Some doctors and hospital officials, for example, indicate they might not be willing to hand over patient records to computers to which others would have access; making such information freely available, they fear, might lead to a rise in malpractice suits.

Some observers maintain that computer networks set up by banks or by time-sharing data-processing centers also have their alarming aspects. What would happen, they ask, if a computer linking thousands of users were programmed incorrectly? Most likely, a monumental snarl would ensue. Bills would be deducted from the wrong bank accounts. The boss' paycheck would be credited to the office boy. The solution to a stress problem posed by an engineer would clack out on the doctor's teleprinter.

The final selection of this volume provides a synthesis of much that is relevant to understanding man's future evolutionary possibilities. It discusses problems realistically without resorting to cynicism; it evaluates favorable trends hopefully without resorting to excessive optimism. It is, in effect, a well-tempered survey of the ingredients for a modest Utopia as well as of the obstacles to its actualization. It is the editors' hope that concluding with a relevant question about education in a technological society provides a fitting ending to this inquiry we call a text.

Conquering Civilization's Hangups

Kenneth Boulding

We are living in what I call the second great change in the state of man. The first is the change from pre-civilized to civilized societies. The first five hundred thousand years or so of man's existence on earth were relatively uneventful. Compared with his present condition, he puttered along in an astonishingly stationary state. There may have been changes in language and culture which are not reflected in the artifacts, but if there were, these changes are lost to us. The evidence of the artifacts, however, is conclusive. Whatever changes they were, they were almost unbelievably slow. About ten thousand years ago, we begin to perceive an acceleration in the rate of change. This becomes very noticeable five thousand years ago with the development of the first civilization. The details of this first great change are probably beyond our recovery. However, we do know that it depended on two phenomena: the development of agriculture and the development of exploitation. Agriculture, that is the domestication of crops and livestock and the planting of crops in fields, gave man a secure surplus of food from the food producer. In a hunting and fishing economy it seems to take the food producer all this time to produce enough food for himself and his family. The moment we have agriculture, with its superior productivity of this form of employment of human resources, the food producer can produce more food than he and his family can eat. In some societies in these happy conditions, the food producer has simply relaxed and indulged himself with leisure. As soon, however, as we get politics, that is exploitation, we begin to get cities and civilization. Civilization, it is clear from the origin of the word, is what happens in cities, and the city is dependent (in its early stages, at any rate) on the existence of a food surplus from the food producer and some organization which can take it away from him. With this food surplus, the political organization feeds kings, priests, armies, architects, and builders, and the city comes into being. Political science in its earliest form is the knowledge of how to take the food surplus away from the food producer without giving him very much in return.

Now I argue that we are in the middle of the second great change in the state of man, which is as drastic and as dramatic, and certainly as large as, if not larger than, the change from pre-civilized to civilized society. This I call the change from civilization to post-civilization. It is a strange irony that just at the moment when civilization has almost completed the conquest of pre-civilized societies, post-civilization has been treading heavily upon its heels. The student of civilization may soon find himself in the unfortunate position of the anthropologist who studies pre-civilized societies. Both are like the student of ice on a hot day—the subject matter melts away almost before he can study it.

These great changes can be thought of as a change of gear in the evolutionary process, resulting in progressive acceleration of the rate of evolutionary change. Even before the appearance of man on the earth, we can detect earlier evolutionary gear-shiftings. The formation of life obviously represented one such transition, the movement from the water to the land another, the development of the vertebrates another, and so on. Man himself represents a very large acceleration of the evolutionary process. Whether he evolved from pre-existing forms or landed from a space ship and was not able to get back to where he came from, is immaterial. Once he had arrived on earth, the process of evolution could go on within the confines of the human nervous system at a greatly accelerated rate. The human mind is an enormous mutation-selection process. Instead of the mutation-selection process being confined, as it were, to the flesh, it can take place within the image, and hence, very rapid changes are possible. Man seems to have been pretty slow to exploit this potentiality, but one suspects that even with primitive man, the rate of change in the biosphere was much larger than it had been before, because of the appearance of what Teilhard de Chardin [French paleontologist and explorer] calls the noosphere, or sphere of knowledge.

Civilization represents a further acceleration of the rate of change, mainly because one of the main products of civilization is history. With the food surplus from agriculture it became possible to feed specialized scribes. With the development of writing, man did not have to depend on the uncertain memories of the aged for his records, and a great process of accumulation of social knowledge began. The past could now communicate, at least in one direction, with the present, and this enormously increased the range and possibility of enlargements of the contents of the human mind.

Out of civilization, however, comes science, which is a superior way of organizing the evolution of knowledge. We trace the first beginnings of science, of course, almost as far back as the beginning of civilization itself. Beginning about 1650, however, we begin to see the organization of science into a community of knowledge, and this leads again to an enormous acceleration of the rate of change. The world of 1650 is more remote to us than the world of ancient Egypt or Samaria would have been to the man of 1650. Already in the United States and Western Europe, in a smaller degree in Russia and in some other parts of the world, we see the beginnings of post-civilized society—a state of man as different from civilization as civilization is from savagery. What we really mean, therefore, by the anemic term "economic development" is the second great transition in the state of man. It is the movement from civilized to post-civilized society. It is nothing short of a major revolution in the human condition, and it does not represent a mere continuance and development of the old patterns of civilization.

As a dramatic illustration of the magnitude of the change, we can contemplate Indonesia. This is a country which has about the same extent, population and per capita income as the Roman Empire at its height. For all I know it is producing a literature and an art at least comparable to that of the Augustan age. It is, therefore, a very good example of a country of high civilization. Because of this fact, it is one of the poorest countries in the world. It is desperately anxious to break out of its present condition. Jakarta is a city about the size of ancient Rome, though perhaps a little less splendid. All this points up the fact that the Roman Empire was a desperately poor and underdeveloped society. The Roman cities seem to have been always about three weeks away from starvation, and even at its height it is doubtful whether the Roman Empire ever had less than seventy-five to eighty per cent of its population in agriculture.

Civilization, that is, is a state of society in which techniques are so poor that it takes about eighty per cent of the population to feed the hundred per cent. But we do have about twenty per cent of the people who can be spared from food-producing to build Parthenons and cathedrals, to write literature and poetry, and fight wars. By contrast, in the United States today we are rapidly getting to the point where we can produce all our food with only ten per cent of the population and still have large agricultural surpluses. But for the blessings of agricultural policy, we might soon be able to produce all our food with five per cent of the population. It may even be that agriculture is on its way out altogether and that within another generation or so we will produce our food in a totally different way. Perhaps both fields and cows are merely relics of civilization, the vestiges of a vanishing age. This means, however, that even in our society, which is at a very early stage of post-civilization, we can now spare about ninety per cent of the people to produce bathtubs, automobiles, H-bombs and all the other conveniences of life. Western Europe and Japan are coming along behind the United States very fast. The Russians, likewise, are advancing toward post-civilization, although by a very different road. At the moment their ideology is a handicap to them in some places— especially in agriculture, which still occupies forty-five per cent of the people. And, if the Russians ever discover that super-peasants are a good deal more efficient than collective farms, they may cut away some of the ideology that hangs around their neck and move even more rapidly toward post-civilized society.

I'm not at all sure what post-civilization will look like but it will certainly be a world-wide society. Until very recently, each civilized society was a little island in a sea of barbarism which constantly threatened to overwhelm it. Civilization is haunted by the spectre of decline and fall, though it is noteworthy that in spite of the rise and fall of particular civilizations, civilization itself expanded steadily in geographical coverage, from its very beginnings. We must face the fact, however, that post-civilized society will be world-wide, if only because of its ease of communication and transportation. I flew last year from Idlewild [now John F. Kennedy Airport in New York] to Brussels, and on glimpsing the new Brussels Airport out of the corner of my eye, I thought for a moment that we had come back and landed at Idlewild again.

The characteristic institutions of civilization are, as we have seen, first agriculture, then the city, then war, in the sense of clash of organized armed forces, and finally, inequality, the sharp contrast between the rich and the poor, between the city and the country, between the urbane and the rustic. The state is based very fundamentally on violence and exploitation, and the culture tends to be spiritually monolithic.

In post-civilization all these institutions suffer radical change. Agriculture, as we have seen, diminishes until it is a small proportion of the society; the city, likewise, in the classical sense, disintegrates. Los Angeles is perhaps the first example of the post-civilization, post-urban agglomeration—under no stretch of the imagination could it be called a city. War, likewise, is an institution in process of disintegration. National defense as a social system has quite fundamentally broken down on a world scale. The ICBM and the nuclear warhead have made the nation-state as militarily obsolete as the city-state, for in no country now can the armed forces preserve an area of internal peace by pushing violence to the outskirts. Poverty and inequality, likewise, are tending to disappear, at least on their traditional scale. In civilized societies the king or the emperor could live in a Versailles and the peasant in a hovel. In post-civilized society, it is almost impossible for the rich to consume on a scale which is more, let us say, than ten times that of the poor. There is no sense in having more than ten automobiles!

Another profound change in the passage from civilization to post-civilization is the change in the expectation of life. In civilized society, birth and death rates tend to be about forty per thousand and the expectation of life at birth is twenty-five years. In post-civilized society, the expectation of life at birth rises at least to seventy and perhaps beyond. It may be that we are on the edge of a biological revolution, just as dramatic and far-reaching as the discovery of atomic energy and that we may crack the problem of aging and prolong human life much beyond its present span. Whether or not, however, we go forward to Methuselah, the mere increase of the average age of death to seventy is a startling and far-reaching change. It means, for instance, that in an equilibrium population, the birth and death rate cannot be more than about fourteen per thousand. This unquestionably implies some form of conscious control of births. It means also a much larger proportion of the population in later years.

It is perfectly possible to paint an anti-utopia in which a post-civilized society appears as universally vulgar or dull. On the whole, however, I welcome post-civilization and I have really very little affection for civilization. In most pre-civilized societies the fact that the life of man is for the most part nasty, brutish and short, does not prevent the poets and philosophers from sentimentalizing the noble savage. Similarly, we may expect the same kind of sentimentalizing of the noble Romans and civilized survivals like Winston Churchill. On the whole, though, I will not shed any tears over the grave of civilization any more than I will over pre-civilized society. The credit balance of post-civilization is large. It at least gives us a chance of a modest utopia, in which slavery, poverty, exploitation, gross inequality, war and disease—these prime costs of civilization—will fall to the vanishing point.

What we have at the moment is a chance to make a transition to this modest utopia—a chance which is probably unique in the history of this planet. If we fail, the chance will probably not be repeated in this part of the universe. Whatever experiments may be going on elsewhere, the present moment indeed is unique in the whole four billion years of the history of the planet. In my more pessimistic moments, I think the chance is a slim one, and it may be that man will be written off as an unsuccessful experiment. We must look at the traps which lie along the path of the transition, which might prevent us from making it altogether.

The most urgent trap is, of course, the trap of war. War, as I have suggested, is an institution peculiarly characteristic of civilization. Pre-civilized societies have sporadic feuding and raiding, but they do not generally have permanent organized armed forces, and they do not generally develop conquest and empire; or if they do, they soon pass into a civilized form. An armed force is essentially a mobile city designed to throw things at another mobile or stationary city with presumably evil intent. As far as I know, not more than two or three civilizations have existed without war. The Mayans and the people of Mohenjodaro seem to have lived for fairly long periods without war, but this was an accident of their monopolistic situation and they unquestionably occupied themselves with other kinds of foolishness. If pre-civilized society, however, cannot afford war, post-civilized society can afford far too much of it, and hence will be forced to get rid of the institution because it is simply inappropriate to the technological age. The breakdown in the world social system of national defense really dates from about 1949, when the United States lost its monopoly of nuclear weapons. A system of national defense is only feasible if each nation is stronger at home than its enemies, so that it can preserve a relatively large area of peace within its critical boundaries. Such a system is only possible, however, if the range of the deadly missile is short and if the armed forces of each nation lose power rapidly as they move away from home. The technological developments of the twentieth century have destroyed these foundations of national defense, and have replaced it with another social system altogether, which is "deterrence."

"Deterrence" is a social system with properties very different from that of national defense, which it replaced. Under national defense, for instance, it is possible to use the armed forces; under "deterrence" it is not—that is, if the deterring forces are ever used, the system will have broken down. We live in a society with a positive possibility of irretrievable disaster—a probability which grows every year. Herman Kahn recently said: "All we are doing is buying time, and we are doing nothing with the time that we buy." The armed forces of the world are caught in a technological process which not only destroys their own function, but threatens all of us. Even if a few of us do crawl out of the fallout shelters, it is by no means clear that we can put the world back together again. Even if the human race could survive one nuclear war, it is very doubtful that it could survive a second; and as the purpose of the first nuclear war would be to set up a political system which would produce the second, unless there is a radical change in attitude towards national defense, the prospects of the human race seem to be dim. Fortunately, "there is still time, brother" and evolution can still go on in the minds of men. The critical question is whether it can go on rapidly enough. The abolition of national defense, which is what we must face, is going to be a painful process, as we have come to rely on it to preserve many of the values which we hold dear. If the task can be perceived, however, by a sufficient number of people, there is at least a chance that we may avoid this trap before it is too late.

Even if we avoid the war trap, we may still fall into the population trap. Population control is an unsolved problem even for the developed areas of the world, which have moved the furthest toward post-civilization. An equilibrium of population in a stable post-civilized society may represent a fairly radical interference with ancient human institutions and freedoms. In a stable post-civilized society, as I have suggested, the birth and death rates must be of the order of fourteen per thousand, and the average number of children per family cannot much exceed two. There are many social institutions which might accomplish this end. So far, however, the only really sure-fire method of controlling population is starvation and misery.

In many parts of the world—indeed, for most of the human race for the moment—the impact on certain post-civilized techniques of civilized society has produced a crisis of growth, which may easily be fatal. In the tropics especially, with DDT and a few simple public-health measures, it is easy to reduce the death rate to nine or ten per thousand while the birth rate stays at forty per thousand. This means an annual increase of population of three per cent *per annum,* almost all of it concentrated in the lower age groups. We see dramatic examples of this phenomenon in places like the West Indies, Ceylon, and Formosa; but thanks to the activity of the World Health Organization, it is taking place rapidly all over the tropical world. Perhaps the most important key to the transition to post-civilization is heavy investment in human resources—that is, in education. The conquest of disease and infant mortality, however, before the corresponding adjustment to the birth rate, produces enormous numbers of children in societies which do not have the resources to educate them—especially as those in the middle-age groups, who after all must do all the work of a society, come from the much smaller population of the pre-DDT era.

Even in the developed countries, population control presents a very serious problem. The United States, for instance, at the moment is increasing in population even more rapidly than India. The time when we thought that the mere increase in income would automatically solve the population problem has gone by. In the United States, and certain other societies, in the early stages of post-civilization, the child has become an object of conspicuous domestic consumption. The consumption patterns of the American spending unit seem to follow a certain *"gestalt"* [structure] in which household capital accumulates in a certain order, such as the first car, the first child, the washer and dryer, the second child, the deep freeze, the third child, the second car, the fourth child, and so on. The richer we get, the more children we can afford to have and the more children we do have. We now seem to be able to afford an average of something like four children per family, and as, in a post-civilized society, these four children all survive, the population doubles every generation. A hundred years of this and even the United States is going to find itself uncomfortably crowded. It can be argued, indeed, that from the point of view of the amenities of life we are already well beyond the optimum population.

The third trap on the road to post-civilization is the technological trap. Our present technology is fundamentally suicidal. It is based on the extraction of concentrated deposits of fossil fuels and ores, which in the nature of things are exhaustible. Even at present rates of consumption, they will be exhausted in a time span which is not very long measured against human history and which is infinitesimally small on the geological time scale. If the rest of the world advances to American standards of consumption, these resources will disappear almost overnight. On this view economic development is the process of bringing closer the evil day when everything will be gone—all the oil, the coal, the ores—and we will have to go back to primitive agriculture and scratching in the woods.

There are indications, however, that suicidal technology is not absolutely necessary and that a permanent high-level technology is possible. Beginning in the early part of the twentieth century, it is possible to detect an anti-entropic movement in technology. This begins perhaps with the Haber process for the fixation of nitrogen from the air. A development of similar significance is the Dow process for the extraction of magnesium from the sea. Both these processes take the diffuse and concentrate it, instead of taking the concentrated and diffusing it, as do most processes of mining and economic production. These anti-entropic processes foreshadow a technology in which we shall draw all the materials we need from the virtually inexhaustible reservoirs of the sea and the air and draw our energy from controlled fusion—either artificially produced on the earth or from the sun.

This is why I so much resent spending half the world's income on armaments—because the more we do this, the less chance we have of making the transition to a stable, high-level society. The human race is in a precarious position on its planet and it should act accordingly. It has a chance, never to be repeated, of making its great transition, and if it fails, at least one good experiment in intelligence will have gone to waste. I suppose there are similar experiments of this nature going on in other parts of the universe; but I must confess to a hopelessly anthropocentric prejudice in favor of planet earth. It's a nice planet, and I'm in favor of it and I have no desire to see its principal inhabitant blow it up or starve it out.

When we look at the nature of possible remedies for our immediate problems, it seems clear that we are all engulfed in a profound and appallingly dangerous misallocation of our intellectual resources. The misallocation lies in the fact that although all our major problems are in social systems, we persist in regarding them as if they were essentially problems in physical or biological systems. We persist in regarding agricultural problems, for instance, as one of crops, whereas it is clearly fundamentally a problem of farmers. We persist in regarding the flood-control problem as a problem of the river and we even turn it over to army engineers, who treat the river as an enemy. A flood, however, is no problem at all to a river. It is a perfectly normal part of its way of life. The flood, essentially, is a problem of people and of social institutions, of architecture and zoning. Professor Gilbert White, of the University of Chicago, suggests that after spending over four billion dollars on flood control in this country, we are more in danger of major disasters than we were before. What we really mean by flood control is the substitution of a major disaster every fifty or one hundred years for minor inconveniences every five or ten.

In national defense we have fallen into exactly the same trap. We regard this as a problem in physical systems and in hardware, whereas it is essentially a problem in social systems. Here again, we are building into our societies the eventual certainty of total disaster. In face of the fact that war and peace is the major problem of our age, we are putting practically nothing into peace research; even when we do put money into arms control and disarmament research we spend sixty million dollars for Project Vela, which deals wholly with physical systems, and one hundred and fifty thousand on Project Vulcan, which deals with social systems and with unanswerable questions at that. When we look at biological and medical research, and still more, research into population, the disparity is just as striking. We persist in regarding disease as a biological problem, whereas it is fundamentally a bio-social system. Yet the number of sociologists in our medical schools can be counted almost on the fingers of one hand.

Nevertheless, in spite of the dangers, it is a wonderful age to live in, and I would not wish to be born in any other time. The wonderful and precious thing about the present moment is that there is still time—the Bomb hasn't gone off, the population explosion may be caught, the technological problem can, perhaps, be solved. If the human race is to survive, however, it will have to change more in its ways of thinking in the next twenty-five years than it has done in the last twenty-five thousand. There is hope, however, in the fact that we are very far from having exhausted the capacity of this extraordinary organism that we call man. I once calculated the capacity of the human nervous system in terms of the number of different states it might assume, which is a very rough measure. This comes to two to the ten billionth power, assuming that each of our ten billion neurons is capable of only two states. This is a very large number. It would take you ninety years to write it down at the rate of one digit a second. If you want a standard of comparison, the total number of neutrinos, which are the smallest known particles, which could be packed into the known astronomical universe (this is the largest physical number I could think of) could easily be written down in three minutes. I find it hard to believe, therefore, that the capacity of the human organism has been exhausted.

What we have to do now, however, is to develop almost a new form of learning. We have to learn from rapidly changing systems. Ordinarily we learn from stable systems. It is because the world repeats itself that we catch on to the law of repetition. Learning from changing systems is perhaps another step in the acceleration of evolution that we have to take. I have been haunted by a remark which Norman Meier, the psychologist, made in a seminar a few months ago, when he said that a cat who jumps on a hot stove never jumps on a cold one. This seems precisely to describe the state we may be in today. We have jumped on a lot of hot stoves and now perhaps the cold stove is the only place on which to jump. In the rapidly changing system it is desperately easy to learn things which are no longer true. Perhaps the greatest task of applied social science at the moment is to study the conditions under which we learn from rapidly changing systems. If we can answer this question, there may still be hope for the human race.

Questions

1 Is it possible to maintain individual freedom in a "Utopian" society?

2 Must a Utopian society be organized on a worldwide basis?

3 Does history provide any valuable lessons for Utopian planners?

4 What is your conception of Utopia?

5 How would you propose to implement your answer to question 4?

6 Is Utopia a meaningful concept or is it just another one of man's hangups?